"I often describe pastoral theology as the discipline of pastors seeking convergence between what we say we believe with what we actually do, and between what actually do with the beliefs implicit in these practices. Would anyone infer we believe in the Trinity from what we do? Would what we do point more to pragmatism than providence? Convergence is always a work in progress, requiring continual reexamination of what we believe and do as pastors. In the latest edition of *Pastoral Ethics*, Ross Hastings helps us carry out this kind of pastoral theological examination drawing from his expertise as an ethicist and his experience as a pastor. Grounded in classic Trinitarian theology, yet addressing contemporary challenging ethical issues that pastors face such as transgenderism, *Pastoral Ethics* provides wisdom for greater convergence and congruency. Pastors will especially appreciate, as well as be personally challenged by, specific ethical applications to the pastoral office, such as the absence of any clerical exemption from the fourth commandment to keep the sabbath."

—DAVID A. CURRIE, Dean of the Doctor of Ministry Program, Gordon-Conwell Theological Seminary

"I wished I had read this book as I was beginning my vocational journey as a pastor. Using the Decalogue as his outline, Hastings roots his pastoral theology in the very nature of the Trinity in participation with his people. It's beautiful, doxological, and evangelical . . . pure gospel. I was particularly heartened and equipped as the author provided a robust and timely theological critique of Chris and Richard Hays's new book affirming same sex marriage. As a theologian, Hastings's sexual ethic flows out of his Trinitarian ontology, rooting our relatedness as male and female in the nature of God, three distinct persons-in-relation. As a seasoned pastor, Hastings's approach to our LGBTQ+ family and friends is gracious, compassionate, and humble. Above all, his devotion to Jesus and his bride shines through on every page."

—BRIAN BUHLER, Spiritual Director

"Even for those of us who hold different moral perspectives on the ethical issues discussed in W. Ross Hastings's *Pastoral Ethics*, his book rightly challenges us to engage seriously with what it means to take the qualifier 'theological' into account in our theological ethical discourses, particularly through a commitment to a trinitarian emphasis."

—ROBERT VOSLOO, Professor in Systematic theology, Stellenbosch University

PRAISE FOR THE FIRST EDITION:

"With his finger on the pulse of the ethical challenges pastors face, Hastings offers a winsome and wise work equally full of grace as it is full of biblical convictions. Appreciating the fact that dogma and ethics must never be separated and situating the discussion within a robust trinitarian theology, Hastings makes a case for, and resources, what he rightly terms 'the pastor as ethicist.' May this tribe increase, and may this work strengthen them."

—MYK HABETS, Head of School of Theology, Laidlaw College, Auckland, New Zealand

"Oh, how I wish I had Ross Hasting's book in my hands when I began pastoral ministry fifty years ago now! Ross helps us do 'ethics in the trenches,' ethics deeply informed by God's self-revelation in Scripture, and then worked out in the hard and often painful issues we pastors face day-in and day-out. In his book Ross accomplishes his aim: to prepare pastors (and those they serve) for participation in God's moral and ethical formation, a formation flowing out of and empowered by union with Christ in his relationship with his Father and Spirit. Ross's thorough exposition of the Ten Commandments is a must read for any who seek to expound the life-giving law of the Creator. Oh, how I wish I had this book in hand years ago. I am glad I now have! And so will you be!"

—DARRELL JOHNSON, Teaching Fellow, Regent College

"This fine book did my heart—and mind!—good in many significant ways. For one thing, it presents a powerful and much-needed case for employing the Decalogue as a profound resource for present-day moral formation in ministry. Along the way, though, Ross Hastings teaches many key lessons regarding the theological basis for moral discernment. I hope this book encourages and equips many in facing the complex challenges of contemporary discipleship."
—RICHARD J. MOUW, President Emeritus, Fuller Seminary

"One of the blind spots in pastoral preparation involves deep and reflective thinking about ethics. In our ever-changing world filled with a wild array of ethical claims and alternatives, filling that gap has become more imperative, not less. *Pastoral Ethics* works with core Christian categories like the Trinity and the Ten Commandments to present reflections on moral and ethical formation in a host of specific areas. In doing so, it touches on the challenges of life that a pastor often faces within the congregation. This book opens up a reflective conversation on how to navigate such space beyond rule making so common in Christian spaces. Seeking to root ethics in the character and pursuit of God, it serves its purpose well, to shape ethically rooted church leaders who can minister effectively through the dilemmas life raises in a most challenging time."
—DARRELL BOCK, Executive Director of Cultural Engagement, Dallas Theological Seminary

Pastoral Ethics

SECOND EDITION

Pastoral Ethics

Moral Formation as Life in the Trinity

SECOND EDITION

W. ROSS HASTINGS

CASCADE Books · Eugene, Oregon

PASTORAL ETHICS, SECOND EDITION
Moral Formation as Life in the Trinity

Copyright © 2025 W. Ross Hastings. All rights reserved. Except for brief quotations in critical publications or reviews, no part of this book may be reproduced in any manner without prior written permission from the publisher. Write: Permissions, Wipf and Stock Publishers, 199 W. 8th Ave., Suite 3, Eugene, OR 97401.

Cascade Books
An Imprint of Wipf and Stock Publishers
199 W. 8th Ave., Suite 3
Eugene, OR 97401

www.wipfandstock.com

PAPERBACK ISBN: 979-8-3852-2961-1
HARDCOVER ISBN: 979-8-3852-2962-8
EBOOK ISBN: 979-8-3852-2963-5

Cataloguing-in-Publication data:

Names: Hastings, W. Ross, author.

Title: Pastoral ethics, second edition : moral formation as life in the trinity / W. Ross Hastings.

Description: Eugene, OR : Cascade Books, 2025 | Includes bibliographical references and indexes.

Identifiers: ISBN 979-8-3852-2961-1 (paperback) | ISBN 979-8-3852-2962-8 (hardcover) | ISBN 979-8-3852-2963-5 (ebook)

Subjects: LCSH: Ten commandments. | Christian ethics.

Classification: BJ1251 .H337 2025 (paperback) | BJ1251 (ebook)

08/14/25

Unless otherwise noted, Scripture quotations are from the Holy Bible, NEW INTERNATIONAL VERSION®. Copyright © 1973, 1978, 1984, 2011 by Biblica, Inc. Used by permission. All rights reserved worldwide.
Scripture quotations marked (esv) are from *ESV® Bible (The Holy Bible, English Standard Version®)*, copyright © 2001 by Crossway Bibles, a publishing ministry of Good News Publishers. Used by permission. All rights reserved.
Scripture quotations marked (kjv) are from the King James Version. Public domain.
Scripture quotations marked (nasb) are from the New American Standard Bible®, Copyright 1960, 1962, 1963, 1968, 1971, 1972, 1973, 1975, 1977, 1995 by The Lockman Foundation. Used by permission.
Scripture quotations marked (nkjv) are from the New King James Version. Copyright 1982 by Thomas Nelson. Used by permission. All rights reserved.
Scripture quotations marked (web) are from the World English Bible. Public domain.

To two true friends and outstanding physicians,
Dr. Lourens Perold and
Dr. G. Ivan Stewart

Contents

	Acknowledgments	ix
	Introduction	xi
1	Thinking Theologically about Ethics	1
2	"Trinitarian" as the Most Fitting Category for Ethics	15
3	Trinitarian Ethics as Biblical, Evangelical, and Ecclesial	35
4	The Role of the Word of God	52
5	Moral Formation in the Covenant Love of God (Commandments 1–3)	71
6	Moral Formation through the Sabbath (Commandment 4)	103
7	Authority in Moral Formation and Ethics (Commandment 5)	127
8	Matters of Life and Death (Commandment 6)	151
9	Sexual Ethics (Commandment 7)	187
10	Sexual Ethics (2) Same-Sex Relations (Commandment 7)	209
11	Ethics of Work (Commandment 8)	241
12	Ethics of Speech (Commandment 9)	259
13	Ethics and Ordering Desires (Commandment 10)	272
	Conclusion: Ethics as Freedom	276
	Bibliography	279
	Subject & Author Index	291
	Scripture Index	301

Acknowledgments

I wish to thank the many Regent students who have been in my Pastoral Ethics classes for the past fifteen years. We are blessed to have very bright and engaging students, and I have learned so much from them. In the broader realm of Christian ethics, I have also learned a great deal from my colleagues, professors Iain Provan, Jonathan Wilson, Brittany Melton and Bruce Hindmarsh, and am grateful for their influence. I am grateful also to my research assistants Jacob Raju, Seung Heon Sheen (first edition) and Daniel Choi, Sean Beckett (second edition) for their work in formatting, tracking down references, and proofreading.

Some of the insights reflected in this book have arisen within the context of pastoral ministry. I am grateful for having had the opportunity to serve in these Canadian congregations: St. Johns Vancouver; Peace Portal Alliance Church in White Rock, British Columbia; Westview Bible Church in Montreal, Quebec; Westminster Bible Chapel, Burnaby, British Columbia; and Union Street Gospel Chapel, Kingston, Ontario. The people of God have enriched my life greatly.

I wish also to pay tribute to the formative thought influences of certain theologians/theological ethicists: Karl Barth, John Webster, Klaus Bockmuehl, Oliver O'Donovan, Stanley Hauerwas, Dennis Hollinger, Richard Mouw, Michael Banner, and Alan Torrance. I am also very grateful for the leadership at Regent College of President Jeff Greenman and Academic Dean Paul Spilsbury, especially through the challenging days of the COVID-19 pandemic. The sacrificial work of the volunteer board members of Regent College is also greatly appreciated, as are all the generous gifts of our donors. I do not take for granted the privilege of having sabbaticals to write books such as this one, and I am very thankful.

I am also grateful for the expert and diligent editorial work done by Elliot Ritzema at Lexham Press for the first edition, as well as the fine work of copy editor Claire Brubaker. I am grateful for the work of Charlie Collier, Stephanie Hough, and Savanah N. Landerholm at Wipf & Stock for this second edition.

I was meant to write this book at the University of St. Andrews and St. Edmund's College, Cambridge. This did not materialize as a result of the COVID pandemic, but I am grateful to have been accepted as a visiting scholar at both. Instead, I had the privilege of writing at our cottage on the ocean in Ladysmith, British Columbia, which was no sacrifice! The life-giving personality and sacrificial love of my wife, Tammy, has sustained me all through the writing process of both editions, and I am deeply grateful.

Introduction

One day I was enjoying a cup of afternoon tea while taking a break during sermon preparation at home, and the phone rang. A couple from our church were on the line on their way downtown to a Vancouver medical center that facilitated in vitro fertilization. This couple had journeyed through this process faithfully. True to their own conviction that every fertilized ovum was a human person, the wife had taken on each zygote. They had been able to have two lovely children. Now they were on their way to receive the final zygote. Just around the halfway point of their journey, the medical team had called them to tell them that the zygote was compromised. The doctor told them that they would normally not even give the recipient an option, but because they knew this couple were Christians they would respectfully give them the choice about whether to have the zygote implanted or not. So now, what did they do? They called their pastor! And I had twenty minutes.

If you have been a pastor for any length of time, you have been faced with ethical decisions such as this and many others:

- What are you to do when you discover that an elder in your church is having an affair?
- What are you to do when a teenage girl confides she has had an abortion and doesn't want her parents, who are leaders in the congregation, to know?
- What are you to do when a person wants to have a sex-change operation?
- How is the money in your church managed with integrity that builds the confidence in your congregation to give generously?

- How is the money spent in your congregation, and does this reflect justice and care for the poor?
- When two families get into a conflict related to their businesses, what are the guidelines for conflict resolution?
- What does confidentiality mean for a pastor, and is it different for a registered clinical counselor or a registered psychologist?
- When does confidentiality need to be broken?
- Should pastors counsel with persons of the opposite sex, and in what circumstances and settings?
- What happens when a pastor betrays the trust of a congregation and abuses his power by having an affair with a member of the congregation?[1] Does a pastor who has fallen in this way ever get to be a pastor again?
- What is the role of the pastor with respect to offering ethical guidance through the maze of contemporary issues such as transhumanism and medically assisted dying?
- When should the pastor speak in the public square on ethical issues, and how, in what tone, with what content?

What makes me break out into a sweat most when I think back over twenty years of pastoral ministry is not the moments just before I would step into the pulpit after hours of preparation, sacred and serious though those moments are. Nor is it presenting a vision before the board of elders, though that was stressful at times. Nor was it making a speech at the annual meeting about controversial policy matters. No, what brings back the most anxiety is my memory of handling ethical issues like these. I had zero training in pastoral ethics in my theological degree. I also dreaded hearing about the next victim of moral failure in my denomination and circle of pastoral friends. I suspect I am not alone. Pastors today are often adept at strategic thinking, worship planning, and expository preaching, but weak when it comes to the cultivation of personal holiness and the ability to make just and ethical decisions. Pastors can often pass the preaching test and the pastoral care test, but miserably fail the moral and ethical test in ministry. And this is the most serious, the test that when failed sometimes means the end of ministry.

---

1. It would be wise for anyone reading this book also to read Bell and Grenz, *Betrayal of Trust: Confronting and Preventing Clergy Sexual Misconduct*.

By the sheer grace of God, the scenario above went extremely well, and I will return to it later in the book. My point for now is simply this: it is tough to be an unprepared pastor wrestling with ethical issues.

THE CHALLENGE OF ETHICS

There are many reasons why pastoral ethics is an excruciatingly challenging subject in this era of human history. *First*, the matter of the moral formation of the pastor has not been much spoken of in the pastoral literature, and it has been underemphasized in seminary training. In light of the steady stream of moral failures of pastors in both Protestant and Catholic churches, this can no longer be neglected. Once-revered pastors have weakened the witness of church by their sexual and financial malfeasance, bringing about the mockery and distrust of this generation concerning the church, making an already cynical population even more resistant to the gospel. Pastors with integrity over the long haul, right on to the end of their lives, are a precious commodity.

Second is the difficulty of the ethical issues of our times. In a post-Christian, secular age, ethicists do not agree on what *is* (ontology), and therefore there is precious little grounding for what we can *know* (epistemology) when it comes to ethical inquiry. For pastors, doing ethics in a way that first guides their churches, and then offers guidance to the culture, requires great wisdom and grace. This will involve presenting ethical perspectives that are grounded in an ontology of the being of the triune God, and that require a corresponding epistemology enabled by the revelation of the triune God—an epistemology of "faith seeking understanding." Pastors need to offer ethical counsel in a gospel tenor and tone, but it need not be offered apologetically. Pastors may make the bold assertion in the public square that *all* thought of every political and philosophical stripe is also arrived at in a similar manner.

Beyond the difficulty of establishing a common ground for debate, the complexity and politicized nature of the ethical issues is hugely challenging. The advancement of science has made things possible with respect to beginning- and end-of-life issues that were not anticipated in previous generations. The full gamut of sexual issues—same-sex marriage, homosexuality, transsexual possibilities, gender dysphoria, and in vitro fertilization, to name a few—as well as issues arising within stem cell research, transhumanism, and so on, all require some background scientific knowledge, even if it is only knowing what science does not yet know. Complicating matters further, sometimes the church is so enculturated that it sees ethical issues in exactly the same way its culture does, so that it needs conversion under the influence of biblical narratives and theological teaching.

But *third*, there is the difficulty that has surrounded ethics as a theological discipline in the history of systematic theology. What should be the other half of systematics, that is, the complement to dogmatics, is ethics. Dogmatics and ethics make up the discipline of theology. Theology without ethics becomes Gnosticism; ethics without theology becomes legalism and death. Yet often there is no instruction in seminaries on this issue. There are also theologians such as Karl Barth, who very much believed in ethics but just as staunchly believed it should not be a separate section in dogmatics. This would keep ethics within theology, within the gospel, not separated from it. One could say that the apostle Peter wrote his epistles in a similarly integrated way. Paul may have been less obvious about this, one could say, since he often has two sections in his epistles, one for dogmatics and the other for ethics. But he certainly carried over the inferences of the indicatives of the gospel into the imperatives (and subjunctives!) of the gospel.

In addition, an incipient antinomianism (that is, a disregard of obedience to the law) often characterizes evangelical churches in a way that makes ethical reflection by pastors and the people of God redundant. The emphasis on grace in recent decades of the church's writers and teachers has led to a deemphasis on the moral transformation of character and behavior that grace is intended to bring about. Grace is meant to be opposed to earning, not effort,[2] and that includes effort around our moral formation and effort in our ethical inquiry in pursuit of the holy, shalom-filled life. A belief expressed in the culture, "How can anything be wrong if it is loving?" is uncritically accepted by many in the church who fail to understand that the love of God has moral content.

The awkwardness of ethics is further accentuated by the fact that inside the sphere of the gospel, ethics is *part of the gospel*, whereas when it is attempted outside the gospel and trinitarian participation, *ethics is contrary to the gospel*. In fact, humanity's primal sin in the garden of Eden was to seek the knowledge of good and evil apart from participation

---

2. This is reflective of a statement to this effect by Dallas Willard, in *The Great Omission*, 34.

in God's life, as Dietrich Bonhoeffer reminds us.[3] So the pursuit of the knowledge and practice of the good can be either good news or bad news.

All these challenges and more to the moral and ethical life of the pastor could seem overwhelming, causing us to lose heart and throw in the towel. These other challenges include the power of the secularized culture and popular media, which make it challenging to stand on and proclaim ethical standards that counter the individualistic, consumerist, and populist values of our time. In addition, there are our own personal struggles with holiness and ethics in the Christian life in the "now but not yet" stage of the kingdom of God. It seems that in every pastor's own soul there is an unresolved set of emotions that needs to be healed, a bear that needs to be driven out, a loose cannon that is capable of fatally piercing the hold of our own moral ships. One of the greatest challenges I faced, along with most pastors I have known, was the allure of pandering to people's desires and approval, and the resultant deflection from our true and ancient calling. Pastors face a serious temptation in our culture to become shopkeepers, purveyors of religious goods preoccupied with image and standing, administration, success, and economic viability, rather than prioritizing the three acts that are crucial to pastoral ministry: praying, reading Scripture, and giving spiritual (including moral) direction.[4] Other challenges include the absence of a rulebook, the lack of awareness of phenomena such as transference and countertransference, and the complicated dual-role and sometimes multiple-role relationships that characterize a pastor's life. Pastors often play the role of counselor plus preacher or Bible study leader plus governing elder. Avoidance of dual-role relationships with clients is a clearly stated expectation for professional counselors, whereas pastors almost cannot escape this.

THE SHOCK OF ETHICS

A few years ago I read the story of the American officer Frederick Downs, who had been through officer training for a year and a half at Fort Leonard Wood, Fort Jackson, Fort Benning, and Fort Gordon. Despite all that theoretical training, when he arrived in Vietnam during that war, he required a significant time of immersion in actual combat on the field. Having newly arrived, he wrote: "Now I would find out what it was all

---

3. Bonhoeffer, *Ethics*, 21–22.
4. Peterson, *Working the Angles*.

about. Would I react under fire? Could I stand up to the fear of death, the responsibility of command? Would my men have faith in me and take pride in my leadership? Could I make the right decisions under fire? Would I fail them and myself? All of the training in the world could not answer those questions."[5] His first tough lesson was the loss of one of his men and the serious injuring of two others because he had not realized that electrical storms in that part of the world create static electricity that is enough to detonate claymore mines. He had asked his men to set these up during the buildup to a storm, and the static set off one's blasting cap.

I could not help but see the parallels with seminary graduates who head into the trenches of pastoral ministry and find themselves unsure of what they will do when ethical storms arise with their parishioners, their pastoral staff, and in their personal lives. They have often received inadequate practice in theological, incarnational thinking about moral formation and ethical reflection. They lack a way of responding to ethical crises that is theologically formed. Because of this deficit, they are often shocked in two ways.

The *first shock* is the definiteness with which the pastor may have to respond to moral decisions and dilemmas in ministry. In seminary or graduate theological education, we live in the ivory tower, speculate a fair bit, and are exceedingly careful to be undogmatic about many theological statements we make. We may affirm certain essentials with clarity, but in other, more challenging areas of thought we think dogmatism would be unwise and even uncool. But out in the trenches of ministry, there is pressure to decide, sometimes immediately. With experience, pastors discover that few issues are truly urgent, and they find ways to reflect and consult before responding, if they can. Nevertheless, when some issues come up, it is no good pulling out your theology notes. Concrete action may be required immediately—calling Child Protection Services when child abuse is reported, deciding whether you will marry a couple, figuring out what to do after discovering that two youth leaders are sexually intimate, deciding how money should be allocated, determining how you counsel people of the opposite sex, deciding whether church discipline is required and how it is to be done, or deciding how you will recruit pastors and be recruited from other churches or organizations.

A *second shock* is that there is no rulebook to provide all those answers so that we can anticipate any ethical situation. We often want such

---

5. Downs, *The Killing Zone*, 42.

a rulebook; casuistry is hard to resist. The medieval penance system of the Catholic Church was an example of this approach, in which, for each situation, *that* sin required *this* penance. Desiring these kinds of easy answers can come from a hunger for knowledge of good and evil without relationship with God, without being in communion with Christ, without the leading of the Spirit, without hearing the word of the Lord, without consultation in community. But pastoral ethics is a difficult area of study, with no easy answers.

Given these realities, how can we approach the subject of pastoral ethics? I hope in the following three chapters to offer a hope-filled theological framework for the moral formation and ethical discernment of pastors.

I

Thinking Theologically About Ethics

One way of lessening the shock of considering pastoral ethics is by gaining a theological foundation. Such a foundation will hopefully provide a framework for thought about ethical issues, and also help develop habits for moral and spiritual formation that will enable us to live in the participation with the triune God that is essential for acting justly and righteously in the moment, in the always-new situation. My aim is to prepare *you*, not present a book of rules. I want to prepare you to participate in God's cultivation of your moral formation so that, in the occasion that demands it, you can discern moral issues and give sound judgments for your community that reflect justice and wisdom and bring shalom. We are formed by word and sacrament and community by the Spirit, and this formation prepares us for the moment when we make ethical judgments. The Spirit brings the relevant word to mind from outside ourselves and grants us wisdom to apply that word, especially when conflicting principles apply, as they often do. Psalm 23, when it speaks of "paths of righteousness," depicts circuitous paths in the Judean countryside, not a straight line. This is evocative of ethical life in all aspects of the parish.

This way of speaking of ethics is different from how ethics is usually talked about in a philosophical context. If I were addressing ethics in that way, I would present *metaethics* as the overarching category. Then, under that and guided by it, there would be various branches of *applied ethics*, and then down to *casuistry*, or consideration of individual cases, drawing out rules based on those cases. In a *theological* context, though, we have first *theological ethics* as the overarching category grounded in divine revelation, and then various branches of *applied ethics*, pastoral ethics being one of those. Then we consider individual cases in a way that is consistent with our theological and applied ethics. This last stage might be called *situational ethics*, in the sense that almost every ethical question represents a new situation requiring fresh theological reflection. Pastors are called to function ethically within a theological approach to ethics.

The primary focus in these first few chapters is on the overarching category of theological ethics. In this chapter, I will locate ethics within theology, which will involve developing an understanding of Christian theology as trinitarian theology. On that basis, in the following chapter I will propose a particular trinitarian ethic that is broad enough in scope to contain all pastoral ethical scenarios and that supersedes all deontological, utilitarian, and even virtue-ethical approaches, though each of these may be included under a trinitarian ethic or may be employed within a trinitarian worldview approach.

A way to describe this essentially theological approach to pastoral ethics is that I assume pastors are called to be pastor-theologians, not pastor-therapists or people managers.[1] In *The Pastor as Public Theologian*, Kevin Vanhoozer and Owen Strachan speak of the pastor as evangelist, catechist, liturgist, and apologist. I believe that consideration must also be given to the pastor as ethicist. These authors do reference ethics a few times, but my aim is to expand on what it means for the pastor as theologian to be a pastor as ethicist. The need for the pastor to be a moral guide is urgent in our times, not only for all the reasons that pastors have always been guides for moral formation and ethical inquiry based on the word of God, but also because the complexity of ethical reflection for the people of God in our technical age is so high. In times of crisis, such as a pandemic, this is even more acutely so. For one thing, the subtlety of cultural influence on the church today through social media heightens the need for pastors to expose the cultural hegemony of our times. This need requires rigorous training.

It is significant that when the author of the book of Hebrews defines maturity in chapter 5, it is specifically the ethical implications of theology that are the test of maturity: "But solid food is for the mature, who by constant use have trained themselves to distinguish good from evil" (Heb 5:14). As Søren Kierkegaard would say, it is subjective expressions

---

1. Vanhoozer, *Pastor as Public Theologian*, 183–88.

and not merely assent to doctrinal tenets that defines faith, and the self is formed as a relational person by the loving actions of faith: by *ethic*.[2]

With these expectations in mind, let us consider the first aspect of the training of a pastor: theological-ethical foundations.

ETHICS IS THEOLOGICAL

Any attempt to articulate the good apart from God is in fact to reenact the original sin of Adam. Both Dietrich Bonhoeffer and Jacques Ellul make this point strongly in their discussions of Christian ethics.[3] Ellul, for example, diagnoses the problem with most Christian ethics as the "very desire to know this knowledge" of good and evil. The challenge to articulate the good without reference to God "presupposes that the good is something outside of God, fixed in reality."[4] This is no doubt what Jesus had in mind when he was approached by the rich young ruler in Matt 19:16–17 and asked, "Teacher, what good thing must I do to get eternal life?" Jesus responded by equating the good with God: "'Why do you ask me about what is good?' Jesus replied. 'There is only One who is good. If you want to enter life, keep the commandments.'" Since God had given the commandments with his finger, and since they are prefaced by the gospel of the covenant to be for his people, the rich young ruler's entrance into life was to be marked by obedience, not humanly articulated ethics. For Ellul, "the good can never be an abstract and fixed 'truth,' but it is *only* a reference to the living will of God, known through his revelation in Jesus Christ. Christian ethics, therefore, is not an attempt at articulating the good, but an exercise in obedience."[5]

Pastoral ethics must be grounded in theological ethics, and theological ethics is just that: *theological*. To seek to know what is right or wrong, outside the context of the gospel of the gracious, unconditional covenant of God with humanity, is folly. It is only in the light of God's engagement with humanity in Jesus Christ that ethical obligation can be perceived. In other words, it is only as we know *who* God is and *what* he has done that we can know *who* we are and *how* we ought to be and to act. The being

---

2. Kierkegaard, *Works Of Love*, 19–27.

3. Bonhoeffer, *Ethics*, 17–20; Ellul, *To Will and to Do*. Barth, Kierkegaard, and Bonhoeffer are Ellul's conversation partners in this work.

4. Flynn, *Theological Ethics of Jacques Ellul*, 74.

5. Flynn, *Theological Ethics of Jacques Ellul*, 74. Here Flynn references Ellul, *To Will and to Do*, 6.

and the act of God cannot be separated, including his being-toward-humanity in Christ and by the Spirit.[6] This means that to know God, we must be grounded specifically in trinitarian ethics. It also means that the "ought" of ethical obligation is rooted in the "is" of the self-revelation of God in Jesus Christ as being *for* the world. It is also rooted in our being incorporated into the covenant community, the koinōnia or fellowship that is God's church, which is the body of his Son.

The fallen state of humanity means for Ellul that the good, the will of God, is no longer knowable, and therefore humans create all kinds of moralities, including Christians who seek morality apart from God. These help society to function smoothly, but there is nothing Christian about them. They become something apart from God, fixed and systematic, an example of what Ellul calls technique, the modern tendency toward control. For Ellul, since "morality is of the Fall," it is also of the "order of necessity," and is, as such, opposed to freedom.[7] Both of what Ellul calls moralism and immoralism (rejecting one moral system for another according to personal passions, a moralism in disguise) are, in the end, unfreedom. By contrast, ethics is freedom found in the gospel as grounded in Christ. It is not the freedom to do what you want, however. It is freedom found within relationship with God, a freedom given by God, a freedom that is found within God's own freedom to love. God's freedom also does not mean he is free to be someone other than who he is.

Ellul warns that Christians particularly open themselves up to disaster when seeking ethics apart from life in God:

> When the [Christian] declares himself *autonomous*, when he ascribes to himself the capacity to *judge*, when he *determines the good*, when he *justifies* himself, he is performing four operations which belong exclusively to God: for God alone is autonomous, judge, determiner of the good, justifier. The moralist strips God of his being and claims this for himself. This usurpation is the exact opposite of faith.[8]

Ellul would seem to be saying, therefore, that constructing an autonomous ethics is an impossibility and that if we do attempt to construct one, we must not think we are free in that process. Whatever morality or ethics we can engage in is participatory, for the "Christian life is not a life

---

6. See Torrance, "On Deriving 'Ought' from 'Is,'" 175–76.
7. Ellul, *To Will and to Do*, 39–58.
8. Ellul, *To Will and to Do*, 179 (emphasis original).

conformed to morality, but one conformed to a word revealed, present, and living." For the Christian, faith and not morality is the focus, the center of faith being "not the good, but Jesus Christ."[9]

Ellul's assessment of fallen humanity's inability to discern morality may be a little dark, and indeed there are ways to validate some forms of non-Christian ethics. Within Reformed theology this is possible through concepts such as common grace and the first use of the law, or by asserting that the resurrection of Jesus reaffirms creation and its moral order.[10] But Ellul provides a categoric way of saying that ethics without theology does not exist. It is within relationship with Christ and the community and practices of the church that Christian virtue and action flow. To the extent that Christ fulfills the law of God as summarized in the Great Commandment, it is fulfilled by Christians. Further, to the extent also that the living Word of God is revealed in the written word, Christians receive from outside themselves the Word of God in addition to the work of the Spirit from within.

Another way of saying that ethics is theological is to say that ethics is the neglected half of systematic theology, which should be made up of dogmatics and ethics. We could lament that ethics always seems to be invisible or at best peripheral in most theological texts, as well as that courses in it are largely absent from the curricula of many theological institutions. However, given that ethics cannot exist apart from being ensconced in theology, the failure to separate out or even distinguish ethics from theology may in fact be a good thing. Karl Barth certainly thought so. Ethics is interspersed within theology throughout his *Church Dogmatics*, not as a discrete section, and he even states that "dogmatics itself is ethics."[11] In a similar vein, Alan Torrance affirms that "Christian doctrine is 'ethics-laden' and Christian ethics is 'doctrine-laden,'" since both "articulate the triune grammar of our covenantal participation in Christ. . . . The imperatives of ethical law derive from, repose upon, and witness to, the indicatives of grace. The Christian ethicist *must* derive 'ought' from 'is.'"[12] Ethics does not exist apart from the gospel. Its existence can only be validated once we affirm the theology of the participation of God in humanity in Jesus, as well as the church's participation in God through the Spirit by grace.

9. Ellul, *To Will and to Do*, 85–86, 90.
10. See O'Donovan, *Resurrection and Moral Order*.
11. Barth, *Church Dogmatics I/2*, 793.
12. Torrance, *On Deriving 'Ought' from 'Is,'* 185.

Another author who has expressed these nuances clearly is Stanley Hauerwas (influenced by Karl Barth in this regard). One of Hauerwas's greatest accomplishments has been his lucid critique of Christian theology as it has come under the influence of modernity.[13] With echoes of Ellul, Hauerwas asserts that "at one time Christian ethics did not exist."[14] What he means is that "before the Enlightenment Christian theologians did not distinguish between the ethical and theological dimensions of Christian living."[15] The Enlightenment signaled the drive of modernity to find a basis for action that did not rely on the claims of various religious traditions. An influential example of this was the eighteenth-century German philosopher Immanuel Kant's attempt to identify reason alone as the basis for ethics. This was expressed in his well-known categorical imperative: "Act only according to that maxim by which you can at the same time will that it should be a universal law."[16] Following Kant, modern Protestant liberal theologians considered theology to be optional metaphysics, with some affirming the "ethical dimension" of the kingdom of God and neglecting the atonement of Jesus.[17] Some emulated Kant in "turning to the subject" so that theology might be grounded in the security of the existential, making Christianity simply "disguised humanism."[18]

While post-Enlightenment theologians with more liberal leanings appealed to reason, the more conservative theologians turned to natural theology, seeking also a rational foundation for faith on which special revelation could be built. Religion was to be treated as a natural science, even the greatest of the sciences, but one that discounted "any supposed special exceptional or so-called miraculous revelation."[19] The undergirding concern was that "without a secure epistemological base, beliefs can only be 'arbitrary' and 'dogmatic.'"[20]

---

13. This has been summarized well by Derek Michaud, incorporating material from Josh Reeves, in "Stanley Hauerwas (1940–)."

14. Hauerwas, *Hauerwas Reader*, 37.

15. Michaud and Reeves, "Stanley Hauerwas (1940–)."

16. Hauerwas, *How 'Christian Ethics*, 45.

17. Michaud and Reeves, "Stanley Hauerwas (1940–)," referring to Hauerwas, *How Christian Ethics*, 47.

18. Hauerwas, *With the Grain of the Universe*, 64.

19. Lord Gifford, quoted in Hauerwas, *With the Grain*, 26.

20. Michaud and Reeves, "Stanley Hauerwas (1940–)."

To Hauerwas, both of these responses to modernity are reactive and unsuccessful. On the one hand, promoting Christianity as purely rational is to promote its demise. (Why do Protestant liberals even need Christianity if they do not need theological claims to support their ethics?) On the other hand, reliance on natural theology simply compromises the particularity of Christianity.

Barth earlier rejected both of these alternatives in favor of a distinctively Christian ethic, as Trevor Hart has pointed out:

> For Barth, the distinctively Christian ethic, i.e. the gospel which the church proclaims and the "moral ontology" (borrowed from Charles Taylor) which unfolds from within its logic, provides a quite distinct context and purpose for ethical reflection. This is why for Barth, dogmatics and ethics stand and fall together.[21]

Hauerwas's own conclusion was "that if Christianity is in fact true, it cannot accept the intellectual terms of modernity."[22]

So what is Hauerwas's alternative? As opposed to an approach that looks for universal consent grounded in reason and has the expectation of absolute certainty, Hauerwas suggests that the way Christians know what they know in ethics and in theology is by bearing witness as a community to revealed actions of God—that is, not to what they may know so much as to *whom* they know: God revealed as Father, Son, and Holy Spirit. The church bears witness not so much to "what universally has to be, but what historically has been."[23] Christians thus are *a posteriori* (after-the-fact) witnesses to a story of the revealed God that narrates the particular way God has redemptively intervened into the world. "And stories, precisely because they are about the particular, cannot be universalized to meet modernity's criteria of rational belief."[24] Karl Barth might have added that ethics, which is included in theology, stands within the triune revelation of God. No prefatory remarks or "secure basis" are needed or even possible outside the gracious revelation of the triune God. Revelation of God, his holiness, and the good is not so much a knowledge category as it is a communion category. We can therefore only know ethics in communion with the Father, in the Son, and by the Spirit. Ethics is the ethics of participation, or it does not exist.

21. Hart, *Regarding Karl Barth*, 75.
22. Michaud and Reeves, "Stanley Hauerwas (1940–)."
23. Michaud and Reeves, "Stanley Hauerwas (1940–)."
24. Michaud and Reeves, "Stanley Hauerwas (1940–)."

But to speak of ethics as being theological must mean, if we are referring to Christian theology, that ethics must be trinitarian. The Christian God is not a generic God or the Allah of Islam. He is revealed as the God who is Father, Son, and Holy Spirit, one in essence and communion and three in person.

WHAT IT MEANS FOR ETHICS TO BE TRINITARIAN

I will in the next chapter contend that trinitarian is an appropriate—indeed, the most appropriate—category for Christian ethics. But first we must clarify what the term "trinitarian" means.

Most Christians who are orthodox would say that they believe in the Trinity, given that this is the creedal affirmation of the church. However, they may not have come to see that the Trinity is the core of Christian revelation, indeed, the way of seeing all doctrine and all ethics. It is not just a doctrine; it is a way of seeing the world—the world of theology in all its branches, including moral theology, and even the world of creation.

It was Karl Barth who rescued the doctrine of the Trinity from its Enlightenment obscurity and even from its neglect within Reformed theology in the late twentieth century. In *The Christian Faith in Outline*, Friedrich Schleiermacher, the father of modern liberal theology, had spoken of the Trinity as "not of equal value to other doctrines of the faith."[25] But for Barth, far from being a theological afterthought, the doctrine of the Trinity has both a positive and critical function in Christian theology and in the gospel. He responded to the reduction of theology to ethics, thereby removing God from ethics, and in his *Church Dogmatics* made the Trinity the architectonic of all theology. He maintained that there is no ethics apart from theology, and especially the theology of the Trinity. Robert Jenson, among other theologians (Jürgen Moltmann, Wolfhart Pannenberg, Colin Gunton, T. F. Torrance, Alan Torrance), continued this recovery of the Trinity. He summed its importance up nicely when he said of the Trinity that it is "nothing less than the comprehensive statement of the gospel's most radical claims," and "therefore not a theological puzzle but the framework within which to deal with theological puzzles."[26] Being trinitarian is more than mere adherence to a doctrine. It

---

25. Schleiermacher, *Christian Faith in Outline*, 62.
26. Jenson, "God's Time, Our Time," 33.

is recognition that without the Trinity we have no revelation and no lens for seeing all Christian doctrine as gospel and life-giving truth, which can in turn provide the context and power for all moral thought and action.

Being trinitarian may be summed up in the following ways. First, it grounds our knowledge of who God is in the empirical revelation of the Father by the incarnate Son and through the Spirit. This was ascertained by the church in an *a posteriori* way, rather than in an *a priori* (before-the-fact) manner. It assumes that we move in our way of knowing God from the economic Trinity to the immanent Trinity, not the other way around. Who God is in himself must be true to who he is for us. It means to prioritize revelation rather than to be philosophical in approach (philosophy will be the servant of theology, not the other way around).[27] It implies a "self-consciously comprehensive, unified, and synthetic approach to theology"[28] that is in contrast with approaches that either have an unhealthy emphasis on the Spirit (to the neglect of the Father and the Son) or Christ. This latter is the idea that Jesus, or a "what would Jesus do?" mentality, is the only consideration for theology and ethics, without reference to what new situations and the leading of the Spirit in them might require.[29] It means considering all of the works of each person of the Trinity, that is, patriological, christological, and pneumatological perspectives. It means integrating all the divine works, given that the persons and work of the Trinity are undivided.

Being trinitarian also means to affirm that God is both transcendent and immanent in his relational and personal being. The opposite of these would be to say that God is either deistic (transcendence without immanence) or pantheistic (immanence without transcendence).[30] Furthermore, it means to affirm that this is God's essence, his essential nature. We will not arrive in heaven one day and discover there is a God behind the Father, the Son, and the Holy Spirit. We may discover more than has been revealed, but we will not discover anything contrary to what has been revealed. God has been revealed as Father, Son, and Holy Spirit because that is what he is eternally. There is no shadowy God behind whom Jesus has revealed God to be.

---

27. Witvliet, *Doctrine of the Trinity*, 296.
28. Witvliet, *Doctrine of the Trinity*, 299.
29. Luke Bretherton has dubbed this approach "Jesuology." See Bretherton, *Remembering Our Future*, 37.
30. Witvliet, *Doctrine of the Trinity*, 299.

God is also not just extensively trinitarian, but also *intensively* trinitarian. The triune nature of God is not one attribute among others. It is who he is. That is, he is the one God who *is* Love. He is not a monad of unbridled power or fate, but the triune God of love. To be trinitarian means that God is one God, one in essence and one in communion, but three persons of irreducible identity. Each person is mutually internal to the other, though each is not the other. To be trinitarian is to see this *personal and relational* God, three *persons-in-relation*, as the paradigm for understanding the personal and communal nature of human beings as image bearers and especially the church, which is the icon of the Trinity. This primary characterization of human beings as persons-in-relation means that "person" is the fundamental category in theological anthropology and ethics. Although "character" receives a heavy emphasis in ethics, and especially virtue ethics, it is a property of the larger category of person. More will be said of this later. Persons are not "individuals," as if they were defined by their intellects. Their very being is ensconced in relations—with God, with their parents, with their neighbors, with creation.

To be trinitarian also means to be *gospel oriented*. God has in eternity past chosen as the triune God of love to create out of his fullness and to be *for us*, for the humanity he would create and which would require reconciliation. The incarnation and atonement of the Son was not an afterthought with God, but his first thought. The covenant of grace meant the sending of the Son to be incarnate and to live and die vicariously for humanity. God's orientation was to be in relation with his creation and humanity. The creation of humans to be in his image as the triune God, and their restoration to the fullness of that image in Christ, leads us to understand that theological anthropology must be trinitarian anthropology. That is, human persons are first and foremost "persons in relation." Though that statement cannot be understood in a univocal way, it does describe what we are by way of *analogy*. Human beings are neither individuals, nor an amorphous collective, but persons-in-relation. All human persons reflect this anthropological reality, though the fall has tarnished and twisted it. All human beings are image bearers, persons-in-community, in a *nondegreed* way—that is, irrespective of how much they may be relational or how much cognitive capacity or ability to work they may have. Redeemed human beings begin to recover the fullness of the image of God in a *degreed* way. Being trinitarian in our anthropology means that we do not just *model* the Trinity from a distance, although we do. Christian humans are enabled by grace to pursue becoming like the Trinity, morally speaking, in *participation* with God, as persons-in-relation. Crucially, therefore, participation or union with Christ (what the New Testament means by "in Christ") is the relational context and means of empowerment by which regenerated and ecclesial persons-in-relation pursue moral formation and the ethical life. This is imitation in union. All attempts at the imitation of Christ outside participation in the life of God are futility and folly. All attempts at virtue development outside active participation in the life of Christ by the power of the Spirit are equally futile. This is to be trinitarian at its very core. Moral transformation and ethics must be kept in this context or they will become something in opposition to the gospel.

Protestant theologians, following John Calvin, speak of the "twin graces" of justification and sanctification (and therefore moral formation and ethics) as distinct yet inseparable. Both of these are a product of what was for Calvin the most important soteriological category: *union with Christ*, which automatically results in justification and sanctification. These graces flow logically from that union. Sanctification, including moral formation and ethical behavior, flows from within the believer's practiced communion with Christ, which is possible because of union with Christ.[31] The Reformed heritage has valued the recovery in Calvin and Luther and Barth of the distinct (though inseparable from sanctification) reality that believers are by faith immediately accounted righteous before God, by Christ, by grace and through faith. This sentence has been pronounced over their heads, for it has been accomplished in the history of Jesus Christ, his incarnation, life, death, and resurrection. It is this justification in Christ that makes the pursuit of sanctification, moral formation, and ethics a matter of freedom, and not a performance treadmill. It does not, however, lead to license or easy-believism or passivity in the pursuit of a holy life, because what has made justification possible makes sanctification inevitable in the true believer. The root of both is union with Christ.

Being trinitarian also has everything to do with human response to grace, to justification and all that the triune God has done for us in the

31. Though there has been a fresh appreciation of the importance of union or participation in Reformed and evangelical traditions, it is most often referred to as relational participation or union. In other traditions, such as Eastern Orthodoxy and Roman Catholicism, where union or participation is spoken of as *theosis*, there has often been a conflating of the two graces that result from union with Christ, justification and sanctification, such that justification is achieved through sanctification or assumed to be the same thing.

gospel. Our faith, our worship, our spiritual practices, our pursuit of holy character and just actions all involve divine action with and in us, and are ensconced in grace. It is easy for Christians to believe that God's part in the gospel has been giving us salvation, and now our part is to believe, to worship, to pursue holiness and justice. The reality is that it is not only the history of Jesus Christ that has been given to us by sheer grace. The salvation order, or how we respond in faith, is endowed and ensconced in the action of the Spirit and grace. In other words, all of our human response is engraced and enabled by the risen Christ through the indwelling presence of the Holy Spirit. This is Trinitarianism as the opposite of Pelagianism, the idea that we have innate capacity to be saved or to pray, independent of divine grace. Our worship and our prayer are woefully inadequate in light of who God is in all his majesty and grace. Worship and obedience in the ethical life are impossible apart from the mediating work and grace of Christ, our great High Priest, and the Holy Spirit.

This is not to say that human response and action are not required in the life of union with Christ. The place of divine action and human action is mysterious. In Philippians, after Paul's great description of the story of Jesus in the Christ hymn of Phil 2:5–11, he quickly moves to the subject of human response. From his first words, "continue to work out your own salvation" (2:12), it may seem as though it is all up to us. However, he quickly reveals that our working is only possible because of and in God's working: "for it is God who works in you to will and to act in order to fulfill his good purpose" (2:13). There is an element of mystery in this concurrence of divine and human agency.[32] We simply know and are grateful that even our working out of our salvation is a product of God's prior and contemporaneous working. The key issue here of course is that our action is participatory. We can only worship and grow in holiness in participation with the Son by the Spirit.

Drawing together the earlier point concerning the nature of human persons as persons-in-relation, and this last point regarding human response as engraced through participation, we may conclude that being trinitarian implies "a communitarian approach to ordering human relationships in the church and in society as a mirror or icon of divine life." This is the polar opposite of "individualism."[33] In a Western world where individual autonomy trumps all other values in ethics, the church

---

32. The term "asymmetric concursus" has been used to describe this. I will develop this in the following chapter.

33. Hastings, "Divine and Created Agency," 299.

must reveal another way, the way of community. Regrettably, the church has been enculturated in various ways, including individualism. Within modernity, evangelicalism has moved beyond the legitimately personal nature of (1) human response to the gospel (Gal 2:20, where Paul acknowledges that Christ died for him personally), (2) the study of Scripture (perspicuity is a Reformed tenet), and (3) the role of every priest in the priesthood of all believers, and into the embrace of a "Jesus-and-me" individualism in all three areas.

The myopia of the modern/postmodern church toward history and the community of the saints of the past is one evidence of this, as is the growing population of the dechurched. Speaking the church's worship tendencies, Jason Vickers states that a trinitarian perspective "will help reorient Christian worship itself," since he believes that Protestant worship has devolved into various forms of self-help and therapy with too high a focus on our individual "experience of God." In its place, Vickers speaks of worship as a communal event of communion with the triune God through invocation, word, and sacrament.[34] The most important moral formation of the people of God comes not from individual spiritual practices, important though these are, but from corporate worship, which includes hearing the word and freshly participating in the life of the Son in the Eucharist. It is, in a word, *communal* moral formation. The scattered life of the people of God is then an outflow of its gatherings. Formed people rhythmically move back into their neighborhoods and marketplaces and academies, and by the power of the Holy Spirit they live an ethic and bear witness evangelically, not legally, to the life of shalom. The church is the true home of revealed ethics. From that communal life of the church, ethical perspectives may be offered to the world. The authority of the Scriptures as properly interpreted will be all-important, but part of that interpretation will come from the moral teaching and ethical positions of the saints and doctors of the past, whose words will not be overturned too quickly.

We may sum up all of this reflection on what it means to be trinitarian by saying that the Trinity is conceptually related to all of Christian thought and life, including ethics. The great doctrine of the Trinity "is like a foundation, a grammar, a backbone, a substructure, a linchpin, a capstone, or a cornerstone of Christian theology."[35]

---

34. Vickers, *Invocation and Assent*, 196–97.
35. Witvliet, *Doctrine of the Trinity*, 300.

What does this mean for our approach to ethics in particular? Why is it that trinitarian is the most fitting category for Christian ethics? In the following chapter, I hope to explain why.

2

"Trinitarian" as the Most Fitting Category for Ethics

Given that ethics must be theological, and given that Christian theology must be trinitarian, and having given an exposition of what it means to be trinitarian, we now must answer the question of why "trinitarian" is in fact a fitting category for ethics, and indeed the best overarching category for Christian ethics. Along the way, I hope to show that a trinitarian model of ethics surpasses and at the same time includes other popular models: deontological, utilitarian, and even virtue ethics.

That "trinitarian" is a fitting category for ethics flows from what was affirmed in the previous chapter regarding the being of the Trinity for us as expressed in the gospel, and as lived by participation in Christ by the Spirit. Ethics is illegitimate apart from life in the love of the triune God. In grace, God has not left us alone in the moral quest. The ethos of the trinitarian gospel is the only appropriate grounding for ethics. Authors such as Geoffrey Bromiley and Dennis Hollinger have identified trinitarian ethics as an ethics in which the triune God is its ground, norm, and power.[1]

In his book *Choosing the Good*, Hollinger articulates this most fully as a Christian worldview foundation for ethics. The ground for ethics lies, for Hollinger, first in the *nature* of the triune God. Second, it lies in the *actions* of God, worked out within the biblical narrative in its major events: creation, fall, redemption, and consummation. It is very common to hear ethicists speak of the formative power of narrative. Trinitarian

---

1. Bromiley, "Ethics and Dogmatics," 2:186–90; Hollinger, *Choosing the Good*, 64–68.

ethics includes this emphasis, but insists that the nature and action of God are broader categories that subsume the narrative. It is the nature and action of God that actually inhabits and empowers the stories. The shaping of a worldview does have a narrative component, but it must also have rational and ritual components that relate to knowing and encountering the triune God and his reconciling and redemptive actions in the life of the church.[2] I focus now on this component that sees ethics as grounded in the nature of the triune God.

THE NATURE OF GOD AS THE FOUNDATION OF ETHICS

First, Hollinger asserts that God's nature is the *ground* of ethics. There are two aspects of this. First, the *character* of God—who in his triune being is majestic, moral, and aesthetic holiness—defines the good. Second, the prior and unconditional *covenant love* of the triune God precedes any attempt on our part to fulfill the good. For example, before pronouncing the Ten Commandments (or Decalogue) to Israel, God assures them that he is their God. He is their God before they even attempt to live justly and righteously. For this reason, the Ten Commandments, which form the basis of all ethical material in both the Old and New Testaments, are seen in a gospel light. They are preceded, to use New Testament language, by justification, and are not a means to justification. They are therefore spiritual and moral principles that are a "get to" rather than a "have to." Filling this out more fully in New Testament language, the gospel of the covenant love of the triune God is both what unites and justifies us in Christ, and what commands us (and even in the commanding empowers us by the Spirit) to obey. These realities shape the pattern of the epistles of the New Testaments. We are almost always informed and inspired by the indicatives of the gospel before we are commanded by its imperatives, and even the imperatives are couched in language of participation in Christ by the Spirit.

Second, God's nature is the *norm* for ethics. This teases out in more detail the notion that God is the good and that we are to imitate him. This notion of God as the norm for ethics is justified by texts such as Matt 5:48, where Jesus exhorts his disciples in the Sermon on the Mount to "Be perfect, therefore, as your heavenly Father is perfect," and 1 Thess 2:14,

---

2. Hollinger, *Choosing the Good*, 63.

where Paul exhorts the people of God to be imitators of God. These are high standards. Imitation, as I have noted, is futile apart from participation. This is both the participation of God in our humanity in Jesus and all that was accomplished in him for us, and our participation in Christ by the Spirit, by whom we live into what Christ has accomplished. We cannot reach for God as the norm apart from being in God, in Christ, as our ground.

God as the norm first relates to his attributes. The triune God who is love commands us to love because he has first loved us (Exod 20:1; 1 John 4:10). The God who is perfect holiness calls us to be holy because he is holy (Lev 11:44, 45; 19:2; 1 Pet 1:16), a command that summarizes the moral and ethical call of both Old and New Testaments. Love may be thought of as the most crucial dynamic in biblical ethics. The Ten Commandments are summed up in the New Testament as the Great Commandment, to love God and neighbor. Classical expositions of the Decalogue have expressed the first four commandments under the head of loving God, and the last six as loving one's neighbor. Of course, the attributes cannot be separated, and therefore holiness and love intertwine with each other in the character of God.[3] This fact is actually very relevant to contemporary ethical dialogue, in which it is often assumed that love does not have moral content. As long as two people love each other, whatever they may wish to do sexually is deemed to be fine.

God as the norm also relates to his being as persons-in-communion. In light of the image of God who is revealed in fullness in the New Testament to be the triune God, we are in the image of the Trinity. That means that we are by analogy persons-in-community or persons-in-relation. This simply fleshes out the nature of ethics as both *personal* and communal, or specifically *ecclesial*.

Christian ethics is ecclesial in the sense that the church is the domain for ethics. We must consider the wisdom of the saints and doctors of the church in the past when we make ethical decisions. This also means that the direction of ethical influence must flow from the church to the world, because the church as an icon of the Trinity flows out of its communion in love to the world (*ekstasis in communio*). Just as the

---

3. Augustus H. Strong thought of holiness as the chief attribute of God which subsumed love. See Strong, *Systematic Theology*, 1:199, 2:121. Certainly it is hard to separate these two fundamental attributes of God. Love is presented as that which seems to define the nature of God in 1 John 4:8 ("God *is* love"), and the triune nature of God seems to confirm love as the very essence of God.

triune God overflowed in love to his creation and humanity, as the gospel reveals, so the church must graciously but courageously share its ethics outwards, and the shalom that flows from that ethics, in an evangelical way.

This does not remove the personal dimension of ethics. Humans are persons of irreducible identity just as divine persons are. Whereas individualism has become the dogma of modernity and its ethics, there still remains an appropriate personalism. Human persons are in fact unique in genetic makeup, life history, and relationships. Though no person can make ethical decisions in isolation from community, there is an idiosyncratic nature to persons and to situations that must be respected. Just as persons must come to Christ as persons, so their moral formation and ethics have a personal dimension also. Yet, because humans are persons only as persons-in-relation, they must also be formed in the church and the family, and they must make decisions in community. Nevertheless, persons are a crucial category for Christian ethics, and even more so than the theologically popular category of character. Character is important, to be sure, but it is really a subset of personhood. The person, and not the character, makes decisions. The character is critical to what persons become, and to how persons discern and decide ethics, but it is part of, not the whole of, the person. The character is part of the person's being, but the person is the entity that is the being and does the doing in ethics.

Third, this notion that the triune God is the norm for Christian being and doing has ultimately to do with who *Christ* is as the true human person in communion, the Man for all humanity, the last Adam. If an important criterion in many aspects of Christian ethics is "what it means to be human," then who Jesus was and is provides the ultimate guide. The theology and ethics of vocation for image bearers comes under this rubric also.

God as the *power* for Christian ethics is the third aspect of Hollinger's discussion of ethics as trinitarian. This is a power granted to believers through his presence to them, or what may be termed their union or participation in Christ, which may also be thought of as the regeneration and empowering of the indwelling Spirit. It affects both the being and the doing of persons in Christ and in the church. Our human participation by the Spirit is in turn a participation in the history of Jesus Christ and the Spirit's presence to him in birth, all through life, and even in death (Heb 9:15). The Son became one with us, recapitulated our humanity as the last Adam, put our sinful nature to death, accomplished atonement for all our ethical and moral failures, and rose again from the dead to reaffirm God's purpose for creation and humanity and the moral order of the cosmos. The same Spirit who was at work in Jesus now grafts us into Christ so that we are in Christ, and Christ is in us (Col 1:27). Ethical discernment and life is simply an outflow of the life in us of the one in whom is embodied "all the treasures of wisdom and knowledge" (Col 2:3), and the Spirit of wisdom and revelation (Eph 1:17), and the Father who is the source of all wisdom (Jas 1:5).

ETHICS OF TRINITARIAN PARTICIPATION

To speak of ethics in light of the nature of the triune God is especially to stress that ethics is not possible apart from participation in the life of God. This refers to the relationship of the church and its constituent persons with the triune God. Ethics is only possible because God has become one with humanity in the person of the Son, Jesus Christ, who by his vicarious humanity lived the morally holy and ethically just life for us. He did so in the power of the Holy Spirit. By the power of that same Spirit we are brought into union with that Christ, by grace through faith. As the church fathers asserted, in a variety of ways, God became one with us that we might become one with God. This participation was always understood in a relational way, not in an ontological way. It is as persons in relation with God, who is three persons-in-relation, that we can live toward the ethical life. This emphasis in salvation has informed the church throughout its history, though the fruits of union with Christ (justification and sanctification) are *forensic* in character.

Participation, understood in a Reformation-al way, means that we *can* pursue the ethical life first because we have by the Spirit been regenerated and brought to faith and union with Christ, and are therefore *justified* people. We are able to pursue the moral life with assurance that in all our imperfections, we have assurance that the sentence of righteousness has already been pronounced over our heads in the Christ who stood in our place by his vicarious life, death, and resurrection. We can pursue ethics, second, because in union with Christ we are also being *sanctified* (the second of the twin graces flowing from union with Christ). If justification is associated mostly with Christ, and what he is and has done for us, then sanctification is most often associated with the Spirit, who transforms his people, enabling them in moral formation and the ethical life. There is a rich theology of ethics and sanctification in the Reformed heritage.

Calvin felt so strongly about the second grace of sanctification that he described it first in the *Institutes*, before justification, primarily because he thought Luther had neglected sanctification in favor of justification. Another theologian in the Reformed tradition who spoke overtly about participation in Christ, especially emphasizing that it is brought about by the Spirit, is Jonathan Edwards. Edwards's ethics is profound and couched in the trinitarian language of participation in the Spirit. Employing a modified Augustinian model of the Trinity, Edwards believed that when a person "closed with Christ" (was converted) that person received the Spirit, and since the Spirit is the love of the Father for the Son, the believing person was taken up into the immanent Trinity itself. Love and holiness and ethics flowed from that participation into the life of the believer. Edwards particularly stressed the contemplative nature of participation. By grace the believer shares in the mutual beatific delight with which the Father and the Son view each other, which is the Holy Spirit.[4] Thus the key features of religious affection and moral action become the product of sharing in the very life of God. The believer, having received the Spirit, is caught up in that beatific delight. By this contemplation the believer is transformed from one degree of glory to another (2 Cor 3:18). Through contemplation in communion, the saints are formed and transformed morally into the image of Christ.[5] Edwards was clear that the result of participation in Christ was not human believers becoming God, but human believers becoming like God in character, thereby becoming *more fully human.*

The moral theology of another Reformed theologian, Karl Barth, also flows from union with God in Christ. However, almost as a mirror image of Edwards's thought, Barth's emphasis is on participation *in Christ* rather than by the Spirit, and on justification rather than sanctification. Barth emphasized the participation of the Son in our humanity and his vicarious moral life for us, over our human participation in God. He spoke of justification as ontological in the sense that Christ took on

---

4. See Strobel, *Jonathan Edwards's Theology.*

5. For a more detailed treatment of ethics in Edwards, see Danaher, *Trinitarian Ethics of Jonathan Edwards.* See also Hastings, *Life of God in Jonathan Edwards,* for a critique of participation attempted within the psychological account of the Trinity, and its susceptibility to monism, and a critique of assurance in Edwards and his weighting of sanctification over justification.

sinful humanity and cleansed it as an ontological entity by means of his vicarious humanity and death for us. Justification has therefore been pronounced over our heads in Christ, and we can pursue evangelical repentance, sanctification, and ethics in true freedom in Christ.[6] Perhaps in reaction to Schleiermacher and Kant, Barth is not fond of the inward turn and might in this regard have benefited from Edwards's emphasis on the Spirit and on religious affections as the core source of action. In fact, taking the theological ethics of Edwards and Barth together fills out a fully trinitarian ethic in which the incarnational and the pneumatic, justification and sanctification, contemplation and action, the objective and the subjective, find their proper place. Calvin may have already struck that balance before either of them!

It is important to note that even though the triune God is the ground, norm, and power for ethics, this does not imply that the human agents in participation are passive. God's participation in humanity in Christ, and humanity's participation in God by the Spirit, is the basis for the real agency of human participants. This is evident in the way biblical authors describe sanctification and ethics. Paul, for example, pleads passionately for the Galatian believers that Christ might actually be formed in them: "My dear children, for whom I am again in the pains of childbirth until Christ is formed in you" (Gal 4:19). The Spirit's work of transformation is primary, and yet there is a necessary human agency by which Christ is actually *formed* in us. Paul reflects this same dynamic in Phil 2:12–13, as noted in the previous chapter ("work out . . . for it is God who works"). This may be described as asymmetric concursus,[7] which means that God's work and human work are somehow compatible and complementary, not conflicted. God works and we work, and in his working we work, and in our working he works. This is the very essence of participation.

This exhortational passage actually follows the great christological hymn on the mind of Christ (2:5–11), but the tone for imitating Christ

---

6. For a fuller treatment of Barth's ethics, see Barth, *Ethics*. See also Webster, *Barth's Ethics of Reconciliation* and *Barth's Moral Theology*. Webster insists that a major reason for an inadequate grasp of the *Church Dogmatics* is failure to notice that it is a moral theology, indeed, an ethical dogmatics, in which Barth seeks to overcome the modern dualism of thought and action.

7. This is a concept derived from the work of Karl Barth on divine providence and human action. It describes the reality in divine providence that God is Lord of all, and yet somehow, creaturely agency is permitted such that the creature is free to be the creature. It is asymmetric because he is Lord of all, and our freedom derives from his absolute freedom. For more on this, see Hastings, "Divine and Created Agency," 115–36.

is set by assurances of our participation in him: "Therefore if you have any encouragement from being *united with Christ*, if any comfort from his love, if any *common sharing in the Spirit*" (2:1). This is quintessential trinitarian ethics, in which the persons of the Trinity work together to empower human persons in Christ, including their human actions in character development. The role of the Spirit is especially emphasized in moral and spiritual formation in this era between Pentecost and the second coming of Christ. Evangelical theologian Carl Henry honored the Spirit aptly in this comment in his *Christian Personal Ethics*:

> The Spirit is the dynamic principle of Christian ethics, the personal agency whereby God powerfully enters human life and delivers . . . from enslavement to Satan, sin, death, and law. . . . It was the Holy Spirit alone who had transformed the inescapable and distressing "I ought" which philosophical ethics was compelled to acknowledge and the tormenting "thou shalt" which Hebrew religion adduced as its complement into the "I will" of New Testament ethical dedication and zeal.[8]

THE ACTIONS OF GOD AS THE FOUNDATION OF ETHICS

The actions of God in history (and prehistory) as revealed in the narratives are also an important aspect of the trinitarian ethical paradigm. In this sense, one could speak about ethics as inescapably eschatological. The creation of the cosmos and all inanimate and all living things, including humans as image bearers, is a theological given and therefore has great ethical significance. The goodness of creation speaks volumes ethically, urging the Christian away from all forms of dualism that minimize its goodness. Its goodness implies an inherent created moral order that provides a basis for ethics in the public square, a basis reaffirmed by the resurrection of Jesus in a human body. The creation of human beings in the image of God is the basis for the sacredness and dignity of every human life of every race, every creed, whether unborn or born, whether young or very old. It makes all humans stewards of creation, yet not something other than creatures.

The image of God first and foremost consists of a covenant *relationality* instituted and assigned by God, and then expressed toward the

---

8. Henry, *Christian Personal Ethics*, 437–38.

human other, as male and female in complete equality yet treasured difference (Gen 1:27). Second, it includes *ontological* capacities such as self-reflexive thought, emotions, and will. Yet these must not be stretched to be viewed in a uniquely qualitative way, as if animals do not share some of these qualities.[9] The third aspect of the *imago Dei* is the *functional* aspect. Human beings made in the image of God are called to both represent and to exercise a stewarding rule over creation as servants (Gen 1:26, 28–30). This is a mandate not to abuse the creation, but to care for it. This is the basis for a proper Christian and human ethics of creation care. Under the cultural mandate given to humanity, there are also instructions regarding marriage between a man and a woman (Gen 2) and regarding family (Gen 1),[10] which influence ethics in this area profoundly.

The final picture of what the image of God really means is found in the person of Jesus, the last Adam, who is spoken of in his humanity in the New Testament as the image of God (Col 1:15; 2 Cor 4:4). As a consequence of the fall, the image of God has been defaced and distorted. The capacity for relationship with God has been nullified by sin. All humans are still in *relatedness*, rather than relationship, to their Creator, whether they know it or like it or not. They bear the image in a nondegreed basic way, with some signs of their origin. A regenerating work of the Spirit is required to bring people into relationship with God, and when they are, in a *degreed* rather than *nondegreed* way they begin to recover the fullness of the image of God in Christ. Christ is the recapitulation of the image, and all in him can, from one degree of glory to another, reflect his image (2 Cor 3:18). This concept imagines sanctification in a Christocentric way. This becoming like Christ must include all that the first Adam was mandated to do—that is, Christians should be at the forefront of environmental ethics and of business ethics that affect the creation significantly.

Other implications of the creation concern the notion of embodiment. Moral exhortations in the New Testament uphold the importance of the body already suggested by its createdness. We do not so much have

---

9. G. K. Chesterton says that the capacity for art, the desire to create and notice beauty, is what distinguishes humanity from other species. See Chesterton, *Everlasting Man*, 20–27. This, he said, was new in kind, not just quantitatively superior in humans. I see this as an extension of the self-reflexive capacity. Perhaps some of these traits are gathered up to be expressed fully in humans, and some are distinctive and qualitatively different.

10. Ray S. Anderson has commented that Gen 1 allows for the concept of the "familying" of singles, whereas chapter 2 speaks more directly of marriage. All are meant to live in community.

a body as we *are* a body. The body as created, as redeemed, and in light of its resurrection must not be given over to expressions of sex that transgress the law of God (1 Cor 6). Many of these creational implications will be referenced in discussions of specific ethical issues in later chapters.

The fall introduces a realism about seeking to live the ethical and moral life. Opinions about exact consequences of the fall vary across traditions in ways that mirror the views of Irenaeus (sin is seen as immaturity, though this must not be overplayed) and Augustine (sin is seen as endemic depravity affecting every faculty of human existence). The belief of the Catholic Thomist tradition is that sin has not prevented human beings from being an *analogia entis* (that is, an analogy of the being of God), with capacity for seeking God and for ethical rectitude. That is, all humans, despite being fallen, are already engraced apart from any encounter with Christ. The Reformed tradition, led by Barth and Bonhoeffer, has affirmed rather the *analogia fide* or *relationis* position, which insists that capacity for faith and righteousness is given, not a given. This influences how each tradition speaks of the basis for engagement of the church in the public square. In accordance with the Reformed traditions, the endemic nature of sin in the human person also suggests that governance structures and procedures in society, including the church, must have robust accountability and checks and balances. It also means that the pursuit of sanctification, including ethical behavior, will be characterized by struggle.

The reconciling and redeeming work of Christ by the Spirit gives hope for the forgiveness of sin and failure, and the empowerment to overcome the power of sin in the personal and ecclesial lives of the people of God. All that has been said about participation as the core of trinitarian ethics comes to roost here in the vicarious life, death, resurrection, and ascension of Jesus. The ascension also signals the reality that the kingdom has come, but that it will not fully come until Jesus returns at the parousia. Thus the consummation of all things both inspires hope toward the holy life and fosters realism that in the "now but not yet" realism is needed, not perfectionism. Ethics is often messy in this "in between" period, and much discernment is needed. The whole story is a reflection of the covenant faithfulness of God to his creation and to humanity. The actions of the triune God thus constitute the narrative that shapes our ethical pursuit, along with our rituals and realities concerning the triune nature of the God who is for us. This narrative will be relevant also in many applied ethical pursuits.

HOW TRINITARIAN ETHICS COMPARES TO OTHER ETHICAL CATEGORIES

Having established that "trinitarian" is *an* appropriately fitting category for ethics, we now ask whether it is the *most* fitting category for Christian ethics. Specifically, how does trinitarian ethics compare to the three traditional categories used for ethics: deontological, utilitarian, and virtue ethics?

Deontological ethics is command or rule-based ethics. Its chief proponent was Immanuel Kant. When grounded within a Christian framework, it has also been known as the divine command ethic, which looks to the character and commands of God to discover the "ought" of ethics.[11] An action's status is decided on the basis of whether it is commanded by God, not on the basis of consequences. In the deontological approach, rules are categorized in a hierarchical way (as absolutes or principles). In the Christian tradition, there have been expositions of the Decalogue as the basis for Christian ethics. However, this approach does not automatically imply a deontological or divine command approach. Luther, Calvin, and Barth all expounded these commandments, but they did so in a way that was contextualized by the gospel rather than in a purely deontological manner. That is, the "ought" was grounded in the "is."

Christian ethics may include deontology, but only within the context of trinitarian ethics and virtue ethics.[12] Deontology is evident in some strands of Catholic moralist ethics.[13] It was also notably propounded within evangelicalism in recent times by Norman Geisler, who believed that even when rules conflicted one could use a priority list to resolve the conflict.[14] When Corrie ten Boom offered shelter to Jewish people in her house during the Second World War, Nazi soldiers came to her door asking her whether she had any Jewish people in her house. The deontologist

---

11. Thomas Aquinas is seen, on one account, to be a classic example of this approach with emphasis on natural law. See Clark and Poortenga, *Story of Ethics*. Contemporary proponents are Adams and Quinn. See Adams, *Virtue of Faith*; Adams, *Finite and Infinite Goods*; Quinn, *Divine Commands and Moral Requirements*.

12. Calvin used the principle of synecdoche to suggest that the negative of the commandment included the positive. That is, the Decalogue was not merely provided for the avoidance of vices ("Thou shalt not commit adultery"), but was material for reflection for the cultivation of virtues (the opposite of adultery is the giving of oneself exclusively and fully and self-sacrificially to one's spouse). See John Calvin, *Institutes*, 2.8.9, 169–70.

13. See Salzman, *Deontology and Teleology*.

14. See Geisler, *Christian Ethics*.

would say she should be free to break the ninth commandment (against lying) in order not to break the sixth (against murder). This principle may seem to work in this instance, but in extrapolating to other, more complex situations, it does not always afford an easy solution. The worth of the Ten Commandments is undeniable as the command of God within the Christian theological heritage. However, they must always be interpreted within the broader trinitarian nature and narrative of the actions of God and their gospel context.

The polar opposite of deontology is the *utilitarian* theory of ethics, that is, the invoking of means and ends to decide ethical issues. It is a form of consequentialism, meaning that whether moral actions are right or wrong depends solely on their effects. The results of an action determine whether it is good or bad. The question to be asked is, Does it make the person or a society happier or more prosperous? rather than, Is it right or wrong? There are two main types of utilitarians: *act* utilitarians focus on the effects of individual actions, whereas rule utilitarians focus on the effects of types of action. Rule utilitarianism is a form of proportionalism, which is a middle way between deontological and utilitarian theories. Rule utilitarianism states that a principle may be neglected if there is a proportionate reason that overrides it. This is a "lesser of two evils" approach. Scottish economist Adam Smith (1723–1790), often known as the father of capitalism, employed a concept that undergirds utilitarianism, ethical egoism, to justify his belief that every person pursuing what would make them happy and successful would have the best results for the world. The belief that the world was structured in such a way that in the providence of God the highest good would result from everyone benefiting was tacit in this viewpoint. The action by Hitler to eliminate all "useless mouths" in Nazi Germany was justified in utilitarian manner.

Disillusionment with these approaches has led to the rise of *virtue* or *character* ethics, sometimes also called *narrative* ethics in the sense that the narratives of a community shape the virtues and character of its members. It is derived in large part from Aristotle, and on through the Benedictines, Thomas Aquinas, and more recently Alasdair MacIntyre.[15] The principal concept of virtue ethics is that being determines doing, or that the cultivation of character by narratives and community leads automatically to correct ethical action in the decisive moment. Aristotle states as much when he opines that the person of excellent character

---

15. MacIntyre, *After Virtue*.

does the right thing, at the right time, and in the right way (*Nicomachean Ethics* 2). The telos for Aristotle was living well and *eudaimonia*, a Greek word meaning well-being, happiness, or human flourishing.[16] In addition to cardinal virtues of prudence, temperance, courage, and justice, thoughtful Christian virtue ethicists have prioritized the virtue of love, which is cultivated in participation in the life of God, who is the source of all the virtues.[17]

An Embracive Category

In spite of the positive aspects of these three options, I suggest that they are too narrow and not distinctively Christian. I am in favor rather of a trinitarian ethic that incorporates commandments and principles, allows for the employment of utilitarian and proportionalistic ethics, especially incorporates virtue ethics,[18] and then transcends them all.

Trinitarian ethics surpasses all other ethical theories because it more clearly and fully grounds ethics within the gospel. Ethical life must flow from participation in Christ, who has lived and died vicariously for us and now lives for us and in us by the Spirit. It is cultivated in our life together in the church and its practices of word, sacrament, and discipline, enabling us to live into the narrative that shapes us. It flows from our life in the Spirit, who regenerated and incorporated us into Christ and who enables our formation by imparting love and all the virtues. It flows from and to the Father, who with the Son and the Holy Spirit is the source of love and holiness and justice.

Trinitarian ethics transcends virtue ethics, for example, because the category of "person" is larger and more fundamental than character. Character belongs within personhood and not the other way around. Furthermore, trinitarian ethics removes the possibility that somehow virtue can be present in a human person apart from their ecclesial and personal participation in the life of God, in Christ and by the Spirit.[19]

---

16. Aristotle, *Nichomachean Ethics*, 2.15.

17. See Fergus Kerr, who makes this point with reference to the manner in which Thomas Aquinas borrows but commandeers Aristotle in this regard. Kerr, "Doctrine of God," 77.

18. Wilson, *Gospel Virtues* (2004), illustrates the pursuit of particularly *Christian* virtues, and he does so within a participatory framework.

19. Kerr presents a very compelling case that the exposition of virtue ethics in Thomas Aquinas's *Summa* is grounded in a theology of participation and contemplation

In addition, virtue ethics seems to imply that formed Christians will automatically make good and fair ethical decisions. I think this is only part of the picture. In the moment of being called on to act ethically, it is not enough to rely on virtue, which is only ours by means of our participation in Christ. Well-formed Christians need enlightening and empowering grace in the ethical moment.

We can affirm, then, that trinitarian ethics involves first the formation of the moral subjects, that is, persons-in-relation, in participation with Christ by the Spirit, in the communion of the church. Here they hear the word expounded and encounter the living Word. Here they feed on Christ as he is made really present to them by the Spirit in the Eucharist and are taken up afresh into union with the ascended Christ. Here in the messiness of communal church life they are shaped and formed.[20] These moral subjects are "persons" seen as a whole, not just persons of character. They are formed as persons-in-relation. This means that they are persons whose chief virtue is love, reflecting the triune God of love. The essence of the moral quest, therefore, is to love God and neighbor. In the formation of moral subjects, character is formed. Virtues are cultivated, and vices begin to be overcome. All of the practices that cultivate virtue and mortify vices are enabled and empowered by the Son and the Spirit. Formation is christological in the sense that, as in the epistles, it is accomplished in active and practiced union with Christ in his death (mortification of the vices) and resurrection (vivification of the graces or virtues). The New Testament gives ample testimony to the pneumatological shape or empowerment of participation in Christ (Rom 8:1–8; Gal 5:14–23). In describing the *fruit of the Spirit*, Paul indicates love to be the first virtue, one that includes all the others.

However, trinitarian ethics is not just formation, as if we can *be* and not also *do*, as if we can pursue holiness and justice passively. Trinitarian ethics must also include *ethical decision-making and action*. Grace-ensconced human *persons* in union with Christ and communion with the Holy Spirit are agents who daily encounter ethical situations, often new ones never encountered in exactly the same way. They need to live into the resources God has by grace given them. What will this look like?

---

of the divine beatitude. It is "participation in the divine bliss" for which humans were created, and it is in this that they are able to be formed to be virtuous (Kerr, "Doctrine of God," 82–83).

20. See Jones, *Transformed Judgment*.

The Christian, on encountering a new ethical situation, the answer to which he cannot perceive ahead of time, is first to pray to the Father *above*, for he is the source of all wisdom (Jas 1:5) and discernment, and the originator of the moral order. The second action is surely for the believer to seek to hear the word of Christ as it is properly interpreted, which includes the moral law. This comes from *outside* the believer. Third, though these are not always in sequence, the formed person listens actively for the promptings and guidance of the Holy Spirit *within*. Fourth, the person will, if he is wise, consult, consult, consult, with the church and the community *around* him. This consultation will be with people who have expertise pertinent to the situation he is encountering. Pastors should build up a list of people in their communities that they can consult with on medical, psychiatric, psychological, legal, scientific, and economic matters.

The point is that character is only the beginning. It is not enough. Moral action is executed by human *persons* dependent on divine persons. Character formation is vital to ethical discernment and action, but if this is enabled in participation with Christ by the Spirit, so too there is the need for active participation or communion with God in discernment and action. Human beings, to labor the point, are persons *with* character, but the larger category is required to describe truly trinitarian ethics. Making ethical decisions about complex situations in an imperfect world in this "now but not yet" phase of the kingdom of God desperately calls for deep communion with the triune God of grace and wisdom.

An Epistemological Advantage

Trinitarian ethics also has an epistemological advantage over the other ethical options. As in all branches of theology, we know what we know ethically because of revelation, which has come *from* the Father. The substance of that revelation is *in* Christ, objectively speaking, and it comes to us *by* the Holy Spirit, subjectively speaking, as communicated through the word of God. Our knowing has come to us through apostolic eyewitnesses and the historical testimony of the church.

This way of knowing has been called critical realism, which asserts that our observations of the world correspond to the real world. Though this way of knowing arose first within science, it has been adopted by theologians such as T. F. Torrance, N. T. Wright, and Alister McGrath as applicable to how we know in biblical studies and theology. Wright, for example, calls critical realism "a way of describing the process of 'knowing' that acknowledges the *reality of the thing known, as something other than the knower* (hence 'realism'), while fully acknowledging that the only access we have to this reality lies along the spiralling path of *appropriate dialogue or conversation between the knower and the thing known* (hence 'critical')."[21] In chemistry, our models of the atom gained by evidence correspond to what is really there. In theology and ethics, we assume that the apostolic witness and historical evidence for a doctrine (say, the resurrection of Jesus) correspond to what really happened. The evidence is best explained in this way. We cannot *prove* the resurrection in a hard scientific way, but it makes sense of all the evidence we have.

Even in science, postmodernity has pointed out the impossibility of knowing with certainty by pure reason. This theory of knowledge, known by the name logical positivism, works on the basis that only verifiable statements arrived at by direct observation or hard logical proof have meaning. Postmodernity's contribution to hermeneutics has been to expose the reality that all human reason is skewed by context and presuppositions and bias. Because of the impossibility of eliminating the subjectivity of the thinker, more radical forms of postmodernity have led to nihilism and the acceptance of disjointed human stories that lack ultimate meaning. All attempts to form a metanarrative that makes sense of these stories are considered to be oppressive.

But actually, humans cannot help but hunger for meaning in a big story in which all the little ones may find their place. The trinitarian story offers the contemporary human person a nonoppressive big story, one originating in a triune God who is love in his very essence, not arbitrary power. He is a God who came to be one of us and to be for us by the incarnation, a God who gave himself up for us in Jesus on a cross, a God who by the Spirit woos people to God without coercion and does so often using the imperfect witness of fellow humans. The trinitarian story also includes an incarnational, pneumatological, trinitarian hermeneutic, which helps us find a way through the maze of subjectivity. This hermeneutic makes our subjectivity to be that of God's subjectivity. That is, the presence of the Holy Spirit within us enables us to see and apprehend truth. This is the same Spirit who has indwelled and guided the community of the saints of the past and who continues to do so in the present.

---

21. Wright, *New Testament and the People of God*, 35.

We can find assurance about the validity of doctrinal and ethical truth on this basis. And if this sounds like a faith-seeking-understanding approach, it is. But this is how the church has always done knowledge since Augustine and Anselm. It involves a critically realist, humble posture.[22]

How do the other ways of doing ethics compare with trinitarian ethics with respect to how we know what we know, and in general? Deontological, divine command approaches do acknowledge the reality of divine revelation as expressed in Scripture or in natural law. However, they neglect the hearing of the living Word, Christ, in and for the ethical moment. They also do not provide answers to the question of how the command of God applies, or how it should be interpreted, or what one decides when there are conflicting principles at work, or what about when Scripture is silent, when Scripture has not addressed an issue. The utilitarian approach may very occasionally have a role within trinitarian ethics when all other factors in a case seem equal, but mostly it flounders in a sea of relativity and enculturated subjectivity rather than being informed by any word of God from outside or the Spirit of God from within. Virtue ethics is not devoid of the influence of the word of God, nor does it neglect the work of the Spirit of God in formation. With regard to the moment of ethical discernment and action, however, It does lack an awareness of the need of the transcendent word of God even for those whose character is well-formed. It also does not acknowledge the category of personhood that is broader than character, and one does not always hear participation in Christ as a prominent category.

A major emphasis that drives virtue or character ethics is that being comes before doing, and even that doing in ethics will take care of itself if the being is in order. This would seem to be supported by Scripture texts that champion the heart or character. One such text is: "As water reflects the face, so one's life reflects the heart" (Prov 27:19). Also, Jesus famously said, "What comes out of a person's heart is what defiles them. For it is from within, out of a person's heart, that evil thoughts come—sexual immorality, theft, murder, adultery, greed, malice, deceit, lewdness, envy, slander, arrogance and folly" (Mark 7:20–22) or, stated positively, "Blessed are the pure in heart, for they will see God" (Matt 5:8). This

---

22. Support for a fully trinitarian hermeneutic may be found also in the work of Jens Zimmermann, who in his book *Incarnational Humanism* has argued for an incarnational-trinitarian theory, which proposes a personalist and intersubjectivist ontology, ethics, and hermeneutics, in dialogue with Dietrich Bonhoeffer. See Zimmermann, *Incarnational Humanism*, 2012.

point of view stresses the formation of the character of the Christian in ecclesial community within the narrative of the Christian story of creation, fall, redemption, and the consummation of creation.

All of this can, however, be subsumed by trinitarian ethics. Being is important, but doing and being cannot be separated, and it remains an unavoidable reality that doing, in imitation of Christ and by the power of the Spirit, is needed in ethics. Life involves making ethical decisions, every day. It involves seeking justice, or not bothering. Micah's famous answer to the question of what God requires of us is answered at least in part by a doing or behavioral response: "He has shown you, O mortal, what is good. And what does the Lord require of you? To *act* justly and to love mercy and to walk humbly with your God" (Mic 6:8). To separate being and doing is dualistic, not Christian. Traditional approaches to ethics have typically emphasized either doing (leading to moralism) or being (leading to anthropocentrism and passivity or non-engagement).

Trinitarian ethics seeks to keep being and doing together and subsume both under a higher category still: *being and doing flow from participating relationally in the life and love of the triune God*. Ethics is first about neither doing nor being, but about relating. It is, as Joe Trull and James Carter suggest, through "personal identification with Jesus Christ and full participation in the gospel story" that we gain a "moral vision that synthesizes and harmonizes being, doing and living into a life of moral integrity."[23] In other words, within a trinitarian relational view of reality, there is no being without belonging. It is not so much "Who am I?" but "Whose am I and whom do I serve?" that is in question. Revisiting Mic 6:8 for a moment will lead us to discover these three elements of doing and being in light of the relating. To *act justly* is the doing, to *love mercy* requires a state of being, and both can be a reality that can be approached only in light of the intimate relating conveyed by *walk humbly with your God*.

In sum, therefore, a trinitarian model of ethics is the most comprehensive, most evangelical, most personal, most communal, and most gospel- and participation-based, one that includes virtue ethics but clarifies its source in union with Christ, one that offers the category of personhood as larger than character though inclusive of it. It is a broad enough category to subsume the best in its three rivals, and it is the model that is most in keeping with the tone and content of the covenantal, biblical

---

23. Trull and Carter, *Ministerial Ethics*, 63.

narrative of the gospel. It keeps the categories of human being and human doing together. It acknowledges the category of personhood as the primary way of viewing human beings, and not character, without in any way minimizing the importance of character in persons. It also acknowledges the fundamentally relational nature of human persons who, as persons-in-relation, are an analogy of the three persons-in-relation who are the Godhead. It acknowledges the reality that the *imago Dei* is informed by all of divine revelation to be the image of the Trinity. They are communal and personal, but not a collective, nor atomistic, self-made individuals. These and other trinitarian aspects of personhood and community will be developed in subsequent chapters, and in particular with respect to issues such as the ethics of work and of human sexuality.

And perhaps, to add an important capstone to the argument for the case of trinitarian ethics, it makes two critical aspects of the life of the Trinity central to ethics. The first is *love*, which is the very nature of the eternal God as triune. In what follows I will develop this theme by pointing to the Great Commandment as a central piece in Christian ethics. Our love of God and neighbor will be seen to be pursued in response to the love of God and in participation with his love. The second aspect of trinitarian life that is important for ethics is *beauty*, or aesthetics. The theological ethics of Jonathan Edwards include the trinitarian consideration of beauty as inherent in the God of supreme harmony, and therefore as a characteristic of virtue and ethical life in God. For Edwards, beauty is not something we know as an attribute and then ascribe to God. God *is* beauty. He is three persons in perfect harmony, the supreme harmony of all, a harmony humans can reflect in their well-ordered ethical lives through participation in the Spirit.[24] The ethical life as a reflection of the beauty of the Trinity is a fuller revelation of the Old Testament concept of shalom and of human flourishing. The commands of God are to be obeyed because they are good and because they bring about the good and

---

24. See Edwards, *Religious Affections*, 238, for just one example. As Gerald McDermott claims, Edwards's aesthetic vision "distinguishes him as probably the foremost of Christian theologians who relate God and beauty." See McDermott, review of Wilson H. Kimnach, Kenneth P. Minkema, and Douglas A. Sweeney, eds., *The Sermons of Jonathan Edwards: A Reader*. Robert Jenson sums up his own important study of Edwards in this fashion: "As we have had occasion to note in almost every chapter, the very template of his vision is that God as Triunity is 'the supreme Harmony of all.' . . . Indeed, he did not merely maintain Trinitarianism; he renewed it." See Jenson, *America's Theologian*, 91.

the beautiful. God is not a killjoy but a bringer of beauty to the lives of persons and to their communities.

Thus the approach to ethics in this book is trinitarian and communitarian. It stresses participation in the life of God toward the telos of *being* holy and *acting* justly, within the community of God, but overflowing to influence the world toward the shalomic harmony of the new creation. This will involve the continual receiving of the word of God in community from outside ourselves (which requires knowing and encountering the word of God) and the continual need for discernment by the Spirit from within (encountering the word of God for the situation within the word of God), and consulting the wisdom of the community of expertise from around us, as appropriate.[25]

In spite of the advantages trinitarian ethics has over other traditional ethical models, the question may still be asked, Why can't we just be biblical in our ethics? Or, Why can't we just be evangelical or gospel-based in our approach? And, Isn't it enough that we do ethics together as the church, the community in Christ, the community of the Holy Spirit? The next chapter explains how the category of "trinitarian" includes but is larger than biblical ethics, evangelical ethics, and ecclesial ethics.

---

25. Stanley Grenz flags two other imbalanced approaches within a relational or participatory approach to Christian ethics. The first is an *autonomous* or individualistic approach, which claims to be Spirit-led but neglects the church community and how it is and has been led by the Spirit. This approach emphasizes personhood but fails to recognize that biblical personhood includes the reality that human persons, analogous to divine persons, are persons-in-relation. This ethical discernment comes from within the person, isolated from community, and is prone to neglect or be ignorant of the word of God as it has been taught and reflected on within the church. The second extreme is the *heteronomous* approach. This is the word-only approach, with no regard for how the Spirit leads in the moment and how the Spirit applies the word. In place of these two imbalanced approaches, Grenz advocates for a *theonomic* trinitarian (word and Spirit) approach, which involves responsiveness to Word and Spirit together. See Grenz, *Moral Quest*, 252–53. Grenz would have agreed that this entails a communitarian approach—the word is the word as interpreted by the ecclesial community through the centuries, and the Spirit's leading as affirmed in the community of God.

3

Trinitarian Ethics as Biblical, Evangelical, and Ecclesial

So far, I have argued that ethics is necessarily theological, that Christian ethics must necessarily be trinitarian, and that trinitarian ethics is superior to the other common models of deontological, utilitarian, or virtue ethics. It remains to be clarified, however, how trinitarian ethics relates to the Bible, the gospel, and the church. It is not enough to be "biblical" in our ethics. What do you do as a pastor, for example, when Scripture does not address an ethical issue? Even when Scripture is properly interpreted, this will not resolve all ethical issues. A large number of today's ethical issues were not known in biblical times—for instance, in vitro fertilization, stem cell usage, iPhone usage, Twitter manners, creation and deployment of nuclear weapons, and so on. Even if we are guided by scriptural principles, something more may be needed.

This leads to a deeper question: What is our ultimate authority?

ETHICS AS BIBLICAL

The Bible as properly interpreted is our ultimate authority in ethics insofar as it addresses the issues we deal with. Yet we may still consult the Bible even when it may not address issues directly. What enables us to do this is the personal revelation of the nature of God as the God of triune love and perfect justice, and the tenor of the gospel as it is revealed by the whole content of the Bible. The gospel reveals the God who is for humanity, the God who is trinitarian, intensively (God is love) as well as extensively (Father as lover, Son as loved, Spirit as love). God is described most essentially as love in the Bible (1 John 4:8), and his trinitarian being as coinherent persons in perfect loving relation is evidence of this. God is, as Lesslie Newbigin indicates, the one "Triune God, in whom love is forever given and forever enjoyed in an ever-new exchange."[1] This is who he is for the world, in Christ, and by the Spirit in mercy and in judgment.

What Is Our "First Theology"?

Is our ultimate authority the absolute magisterial authority of God himself, or is it Scripture? This is a question regarding what may be called our "first theology," or the attempt to say which comes first: the doctrine of God or the doctrine of Scripture. We only know the God of our Lord Jesus Christ by reading Scripture, on the one hand; yet, on the other hand, we can only appeal to the Scripture as authoritative because it is the word of God, and the living as well as the written word. We can only perceive the message of the Scriptures because we have already by grace been brought into divine revelation by the triune God who is, as Father, Son, and Spirit, the Revealer, the Revelation, and the Revealedness.[2]

This is not a trivial issue. The doctrine of Scripture finds prominence in many confessions of the Reformers, where there is a concern to emphasize that it trumps the authority of church tradition, though tradition has a place. The clarifying of a doctrine of Scripture and the practice of starting confessions with it was precipitated by the crisis of authority in Reformation and in post-Reformation dogmatics. This made the doctrine of Scripture "the explicit doctrinal locus," whereas it had been implicit in the early church fathers.[3] As Reformed scholar Richard Muller has said, "The logical priority of Scripture over all other means of religious knowing in the church—tradition, present day corporate or official doctrine, and individual insight or illumination—lies at the heart of the teaching of the Reformation and of its great confessional documents."[4] So

---

1 Newbigin, *Foolishness to the Greeks*, 149.

2. This is Karl Barth's way of speaking of the Trinity. See *Church Dogmatics* 1/1, 1. We cannot know God apart from his revelation, and since revelation is a communion category and not merely a cognitive one, there is no prolegomena concerning how we know theology for Barth.

3. Vanhoozer, *Christian Dogmatics*, 30–56, here 37.

4. Muller, *Post-Reformation Reformed Dogmatics*, 151.

the very first article in a number of confessions is the article on Scripture, demonstrating the belief that it is "the cognitive foundation (*principium cognoscendi*) of revealed theology."[5] Such confessions include the Ten Conclusions of Bern (1528), the Geneva Confession (1536), the First (1536) and Second (1566) Helvetic Confessions, the Irish Articles of Religion (1615), and the Westminster Confession of Faith (1647).

The question may be asked, however, whether this tendency to begin with Scripture was a result in part of the influence of dawning modernity and its obsession with epistemology (and its relative neglect of ontology). There are definite dangers with this view. As William Abraham has noted, these include seeing Scripture as a "cognitive foundation of theology" that serves as "an independent epistemic criterion, something like a slide rule to see if a doctrinal formulation measures up," or viewing Scripture "as the solution to an epistemological problem rather than as a solution to a soteriological problem, that is, sin and its effects."[6] Similarly, Kevin Vanhoozer affirms,

> Holy Scripture is not a textbook of divinely revealed data on which scientific theologians set to work developing doctrine. It is rather God's life- and light-giving loving overture to humans stumbling in the darkness of sin and death: it is God's presentation of Jesus Christ. Scripture is not merely the source and norm of other doctrines (a formal principle in the economy of revelation) but also an ingredient in the economy of redemption.[7]

However, other Reformation-era confessions of faith begin with the doctrine of God, such as the French Confession (1559), the Scots Confession (1561), and the Thirty-Nine Articles of the Church of England (1571). One solution to this dilemma is to suggest that we begin with both together, that is, with a first theology that is the Bible as a communicative act of God, as may be demonstrated in a number of the Reformed confessions.[8] This is because the Reformed faith is a religion not merely of the book, the canonical Scriptures, but of the word of God, in that it concerns the living Word as subject and as the one who speaks through the written word by the Holy Spirit. God and his word cannot be separated, whether it be his living or his written word. The close association of the

5. Vanhoozer, *Holy Scripture*, 37.
6. These are the sentiments of Abraham, *Bible*, 64, made more precise by Vanhoozer, *Holy Scripture*, 37.
7. Vanhoozer, "Holy Scripture," 39.
8. Vanhoozer, *First Theology*, 15–41, has argued in this way.

living Word with the written word removes the dichotomy. For example, in the Scots Confession, Scripture is affirmed as being "of God" and "sufficient to instruct and make the man of God perfect."[9] Conversely, the Westminster Confession, which begins with the authority of Holy Scripture, describes itself as depending "not upon the testimony of any man or Church, but wholly upon God (who is truth itself), the author thereof."[10] There is not really a dichotomy between God and his word. Scripture as God's word, notes Vanhoozer, "serves his authorial purposes," which include as a high priority, "to serve as means for gathering, governing, and putting the finishing touches on those who will be his treasured possession.... In this respect, the church figures in 'first theology' too, namely as the addressee of God's Word."[11] Seeing our first theology in this way does not eliminate the role of the church in interpreting the word of God, even if the Scriptures are the final authority.

My own tendency is to lean ever so slightly with the Scots Confession toward the triune God as first theology, largely because we do not worship the Bible, but the God of the Bible. This has influenced my choice of the term "trinitarian" to describe Christian ethics over against the term "biblical ethics." However, in light of what has just been said about a resolution between the doctrine of Scripture and the doctrine of God, the whole question may be moot.

Nevertheless, there are some important issues at stake here for ethics. The *first* is that a purely prescriptive approach to the Bible that ignores the nature and character of God and his salvific work in the world cannot be in keeping with the revelatory purposes and intent of God. Thus, to simply say that ethics is "biblical" is not enough. This is not to deny that some passages of Scripture function prescriptively. Those who affirm the verbal and plenary inspiration of Scripture take every passage of it seriously. However, we should also recognize that all passages must be interpreted grammatically, historically, rhetorically, and especially canonically. It must be asked what they reveal of the whole story and the whole character of God and the whole of "the faith that was once for all entrusted to God's holy people" (Jude 1:3).

Another way to say this is that our interpretations of Scripture take into account the creedal theology that has been discerned by the church

---

9. Scots Confession (1560), article 19, in Cochrane, *Reformed Confessions of the Sixteenth Century*, 178.

10. Westminster Confession of Faith, 1.4.

11. Vanhoozer, *Holy Scripture*, 37–38.

since the time of the apostles (including the "rule of faith" and the Niceno-Constantinopolitan Creed). Theological interpretation is part of the proper interpretation of Scripture, alongside the grammatical-historical approach. The two seem to me to be best considered as vital parts of an iterative process that still allows for the Scripture as the ultimate authority. Acknowledging Scripture as *norma normans* (the norming norm) does not preclude seeing the essentials of the faith expressed in the historic creeds as the *norma normata* (the normed norm). The Reformation axiom *sola Scriptura* was not *nuda Scriptura*; the Reformers valued tradition, creedal theology, and the contribution of the church in the process of interpreting Scripture, even if the Bible was still the ultimate authority. "Theological," and thus specifically "trinitarian," is a wider and more suitable term than "biblical" ethics precisely because it is more inclusive and because it is more incisive. It is more inclusive because it includes what Scripture affirms and gives it meaning, and is the basis for wise ethical deliberation when Scripture is silent. It is more incisive because it assumes that the Bible must be interpreted by the nature of the God who is self-revealed in the Bible, and by the gospel-filled and covenantal approach to ethics in the Bible. I will consider shortly how this works out in a prescriptive approach to ethics.

The *second* issue is that when there are seeming paradoxes in biblical revelation, or when Scripture does not speak directly to ethical issues, we must go to the higher court of appeal in the theology of who God is in his incarnate and pneumatic self-revelation, and of his revealed purposes, in our ethical deliberations. This too points to the inadequacy of "biblical" and the validity of "trinitarian" as the appropriate title for Christian ethics. Even when Scripture does speak ethically with clarity, it will still be important to ask *why* and to look for meaning behind the ethical command. This will be illustrated when we come to consider sexual ethical issues. It is one thing to hear from the Old Testament and the New Testament that certain sexual relations are forbidden, but it will be insufficient in our culture to say that something is wrong because the Bible says so. People are entitled to know why, and this has everything to do with the nature and character of the triune God and his good, shalom-filled purposes for humanity made in his image and in society.

The Nature and Character of the God of the Bible

Pertinent to the question of who God is, is the debate as to which is the most fundamental attribute of God: his love (Barth) or his holiness (Augustus Strong). God's most essential *natural* attribute is that he is triune, three persons in one essence and one communion of love. Love defined by the perichoretic (the mutual internality and involution of the persons) divine persons is therefore considered to be primary in a metaphysical sense. This would seem to be a logical conclusion flowing from the fact that God is spoken of in a predicate sense as love in a unique way in the Scriptures (1 John 4:8). Yet one cannot escape the reality that for the divine intratrinitarian relations to be perfectly loving means that they must also be just and righteous and holy. Thus, the chief moral attribute of holiness cannot be separated from the metaphysical. The modern and postmodern tendency to separate love from any moral content is misguided, to say the least. Love has moral content. Love is holy or it is not love. Holiness is also moral. It is a richly complex and beautiful attribute, conveying the ideas of majestic otherness and aesthetic holiness, both of which point the finger toward the triunity of God. It includes the perfect justice of God in his discernment and judgment of the world, and the perfect righteousness of his actions in the world. God's call for a holy life is grounded in his own holiness, which is in turn grounded in his love. Similarly, all moral formation and all ethics, that is, all holiness of being and action in humans, is evangelical. It is the result of God's love to us expressed in the giving and life of Jesus Christ, and our participation by the Spirit in the divine love and holiness.

Thus, when we say ethics is biblical we mean that the *foundation* of ethics, the theological foundation or meta-ethic of the Bible, is the love of God, which is the very essence of the Trinity and is revealed in the economy of redemption. We also mean, however, that the *form* of Christian ethics (normative and applied ethics) is also love. But just as God's love is characterized by holiness, so also his love is expressed such that it has moral content as expressed in the love commandment, which is the core of Christian ethics and which in turn summarizes the Decalogue. As we come soon to consider the Decalogue and its place in Christian ethics, it will be important to consider its location within the wider narrative of Scripture and the wider covenantal purposes of God.

Thus, being biblical in our ethics, in addition to paying attention to the details of prescriptive passages of Scripture, involves paying attention to the broad undergirding of ethics by the narrative, redemptive, and covenantal themes of the Bible. This means paying attention to the grounding of all ethics in the prior acceptance by God that the gospel assures us of. This is so that our ethics is evangelical and not legal. It also means that in our ethical deliberations, we will pay attention to the spirit, tone, and sweep of divine revelation.

In sum, why is it not sufficient to say that ethics is biblical? When neither the details nor the narrative arc of Scripture seems sufficient to deal with an ethical issue, or when there seems to be a tension between biblical principles, one needs to be able to appeal to the leading of the Holy Spirit, as this is sought by a person or, even better, by a community or a person in a community. These kinds of circumstances may be called situational. The situational ethics we have in mind here involve situations that are new, that the Bible does not directly address, and the solution to which cannot be decided in advance. Orthodox scholars of this persuasion will of course insist that ethical decisions made in this way, by directly looking to God for guidance, will not and cannot contradict what Scripture clearly prescribes or the tone and tenor of the biblical story from creation to consummation.

Three Ethical Motifs

Edward L. Long has suggested three motifs to summarize the way in which moral theologians in the tradition have approached ethics.[12] These, with some modifications, can serve to summarize what I have said thus far about ethics as biblical.

Deliberative. In this motif, which has been associated with Thomas Aquinas, Adolf von Harnack, James Gustafson, and C. S. Lewis, reason is seen as synonymous with revelation or as a supplement to reason in making ethical decisions. Ethics is thus subsumed under philosophy, or philosophical reflection is used to serve theology. Thus, moral philosophy is the tool of Christian ethics. The theo-anthropological assumption of this motif is that human reason is reliable since natural law has been implanted within human consciousness. This motif is grounded in the *analogia entis* ("analogy of being"), the idea that human beings have the capacity to know God innately, apart from the revelation of Jesus Christ.

---

12. Long, *Survey of Christian Ethics* (1967); Long, *Survey of Recent Christian Ethics* (1982). These are summarized nicely in Hollinger, *Choosing the Good*, 135–48.

A gain that has been ascribed to it is that it speaks to all human beings, not just Christians. It thus can be a rationale for enabling Christians to speak in the public square. The Bible and Jesus did not say everything there is to be said on every issue, and thus we need reason. Undergirding this viewpoint is the belief that there is a moral order in the creation and that there is a natural telos to the created world such that ethics works according to the grain of the universe.

However, this motif overestimates the capacity for reason of fallen people who, though they are image bearers, are tarnished and blinded by sin. More importantly, it isolates ethics from the gospel and robs the church of its revelatory right to be the home of ethics, and its responsibility to share ethical perspective outward to the world in evangelical or shalom-based ways. This motif, at its worst, also makes ethics autonomous. Biblical ethics, above all, is evangelical ethics, and that requires that people doing ethics have come under the influence of the good news. Ethics is always a response to grace and the grace-filled biblical story of creation, fall, redemption, and consummation. There is also a lack of clear agreement on what natural law is and what it contains. Even theologians who are very critical of the natural-law approach have to admit that there is some form of natural law at work in society, as passages such as Rom 1:20; 2:14–15; 13:1–7; and 1 Tim 2:8–11 make clear.

Having been critical of the deliberative motif, I want to suggest that it can be appropriately co-opted to describe a *theological* deliberative approach that observes the broad undergirding of ethics precisely by trinitarian theology and all that it entails. That is the tenor and tone of the gospel as revealed by the sweeping narrative of the redemptive and covenantal themes of the Bible, as it has been received and processed by the church. Another way to say this is to say that the theological deliberative approach is one that employs a theological interpretation of Scripture. Once we put philosophy under theology, once we say that reason comes under revelation, once we insist that reason must be graced[13] by the encounter with the *euangelion*, the good news, then the deliberative approach has value. Once an *analogia relationis* ("analogy of relations," meaning the gift given by grace for human persons to enter relationship with the God who is three persons-in-relation, through Christ) has replaced the *analogia entis*, the belief can be entertained that when ethics is spoken evangelically by the church to the public square, it may be

13. I am aware that Thomistic theologians will say it is always already graced as it is a product of creation.

expected by faith that the Spirit of God may awaken the perception of the hearers. I wish to argue for the primacy of this approach, for prescriptive and situational ethics that are not first guided by the narrative and theological interpretation of the good-news story of the Bible can be subject to atomistic interpretation of ethical texts and legalism on the one hand, and to frightening subjectivity on the other.

Prescriptive. This motif looks to explicit principles and rules and moral actions derived from Scripture as the way to do ethics. There are two major types of this motif: one that shows adherence to broad principles (love your neighbor), and another that speaks of adherence to moral codes. The English Puritan Richard Baxter is well known for his moral code and casuistry for every aspect of Christian life. One must not assume this was legally motivated, for Baxter was simply working out the sentiments of the Westminster Shorter Confession that the chief end of humanity is "to glorify God and enjoy him forever." John Calvin, however, resisted moral codes, opting instead for a life of obedience to principles drawn from the moral law or the Decalogue. For Calvin, the chief consideration in ethics is pleasing the God who is sovereign and responding in grace to the gospel, but he saw God's law as extant for the New Testament believer and relevant to both moral formation and ethical deliberation in every age. The Decalogue is thus the basis for Christian ethics, since it had been revealed by God to humanity. Other theologians who have followed this motif in its various forms have been Klaus Bockmuehl, Carl Henry, Richard Mouw, and John Howard Yoder. It has the feel of a deontological approach. Its greatest value is that it gives appropriate weight to the authority of the Bible. Forms of it, however, can tend toward legalism. It can also never cover all the bases in ethics and requires the deliberative context and the situational approach when Scripture is silent.

Relational/situational. This motif sees ethics as a response to the leading of God in a spontaneous fashion by direct encounter with God. This is to appeal directly for encounter with the divine source of moral guidance. It seems to me that there are two subtypes within this motif. The *first* is what might be termed a charismatic relational motif. This is practiced within charismatic settings and involves seeking moral guidance based on impressions, works of knowledge, words of wisdom, and prophetic words. The best in this tradition sit under the ultimate authority of Scripture and its teaching, and would not permit ethical stances or decisions gained from spiritual gifts that contradict biblical or theological orthodoxy. They are well aware of the dangers of subjectivity and the loss of connectedness to the principles of the word. Yet when the Bible does not speak clearly in ethical situations, these gifts of the Holy Spirit are and should be valued.

The *second* subtype within this motif, the one intended by Long, is not necessarily within the charismatic tradition. This we might call the dynamic word tradition. Since we cannot know in advance of an ethical situation what the answer might be, we need to hear the word of God for the situation, but not in a static way. Adherents of the situational/relational motif expect God to speak through the word of God and his community in a living and relational way. They believe precisely in the need for the fresh encounter with the living Word within the written word. They "find agreement in a common rejection of prescriptive ethics and natural law formulations," as Hollinger states, and he explains that ethics understood this way "is conceived to be relational in the sense that even the content and direction of moral decisions flow from an immediate relationship with God and relationships with others." It is not so much about "norms to which humans must aspire,"[14] but understanding "the ethos in which they live."[15] Rather than seeing the Scriptures, including its ethical sections such as the Decalogue, the Sermon on the Mount, and Paul's paraenetic sections, as a *"fixed moral deposit,"* Long indicates that the communities that follow this motif tend to see the Scriptures as *"precious community records"* of how Israel and then the church tried to be the people of God. The Bible thus shapes identity rather than offering specific moral and ethical direction.

Long insists that this way of doing ethics has a long tradition and that evidences of its practice may be seen in theologians such as Augustine, Luther, Edwards, and Barth, for whom he believes there is the commonality that their ethics was relational. He substantiates this impression by citing Augustine's emphasis on the will and the loves of the moral agent, Luther's emphasis on morality as the product of justifying faith, Edwards's emphasis on the heart and his dispositional approach to ethics, and Barth's emphasis on the command of God. Hollinger quite correctly challenges this reductionistic sweep. Edwards and Luther would certainly have consulted the Scriptures in a prescriptive way where there was clarity of divine revelation on ethical issues.

---

14. Hollinger, *Choosing the Good*, 141. Hollinger points to Birch and Rasmussen, *Bible and Ethics in the Christian*, for a clear articulation of the relational motif.

15. Long, *Survey of Christian Ethics*, 119.

Barth, on the one hand, as Hollinger points out, seems to be in opposition to "all forms of ethics that seek to formulate moral decisions on the basis of natural law (the deliberative motif) or moral rules and principles (the prescriptive motif)." This was simply autonomous human ethics isolated from the grace and redemption in Christ. The great danger was that the command of God discovered as a universal rule would take the place of God himself. Barth's first theology is God as revealed, not the revelation itself as Scripture. Prescriptiveness as an approach was to deny the majesty and freedom of God, for Barth. Yet, on the other hand, it is not as if Barth did not take seriously what Scripture did say on any ethical issue. His engagement is always first with the Decalogue and all the ethical passages of the Scriptures. It was just that when all the exegesis had been done, this was for him still only a preparation for hearing the word of God speak. This was related to Barth's view of the nature of Scripture as a *witness* to revelation, rather than revelation itself, a viewpoint most evangelicals reject. It was also related to the fact that for Barth theological ethics *is* theology and should be carried out not as an independent discipline but, as with theology, by hearing God speak, the living Word encountered through the written word. In a nutshell, the command of God was not to be heard as prescribed in a text; rather, it was "an event in which God speaks and commands at the moment of decision."[16] Response to the Word and the command of God was something that included the right interpretation of the text, but it was more than that: it was about being predisposed to hearing God speak, actually speak, through the text. The texts "prepare the way for that openness of heart which . . . has to be demonstrated and realized in a specific obedience which is always new."[17]

So, in fact, the categories or motifs do in fact overlap in many theologians. What Barth was unsure of (the verbal inspiration of Scripture) did not prevent him from seeking to hear God speak. It seems to me that evangelicals who deeply reverence the text itself, and rightly so, should even more so expect the encounter with God that comes from an open heart and sensitivity to the voice of the Holy Spirit. Given that even Barth himself does not neglect the prescriptive approach, yet moves beyond it, it would seem to me that a combination of the prescriptive and the relational/situational motifs must be employed.

---

16. Hollinger, *Choosing the Good*, 143.
17. Karl Barth, *Church Dogmatics II/2*, 700.

In sum, the greatest value of the relational or situational approach is that it encourages the living encounter with God through the Word, in community, in a way that forms the character, and in a manner that prepares us as persons to be led by the Spirit and to hear his voice.

With the above qualification that the deliberative form be modified, all three approaches are necessary: a theological deliberative approach that is trinitarian in its essence, and prescriptive and situational approaches guided by the deliberative approach and that are themselves discovered within the life of the Trinity. We must be conscious of the wide view of the biblical narrative and its theological inferences, *and* we look for guidance from the Bible's ethical passages and affirm the principles that can be drawn from them, but this does not address every scenario, and it cannot. Ultimately, we are *persons* making decisions all the time in new scenarios, for us and for the world. Scripture is not just a *moral deposit* but a text and a story inviting us to be persons in communion with God. It keeps us connected to the gospel and the God of the gospel. It leads to dynamic encounter with God, which forms our character and guides our ethical decision making. "Biblical" ethics is not sufficiently broad and adequately nuanced.

ETHICS AS EVANGELICAL

Trinitarian ethics, empowered in this way, invokes another category, that of ethics as *evangelical*, that is, of the gospel and not legal. The category of evangelical ethics has been considered by some ethicists to be the preferred title for Christian ethics.[18] I think it is preferable to think of evangelical ethics as a necessary consequence of ethics as trinitarian, as a subset of trinitarian ethics. It describes an important necessary qualitative aspect and outcome of ethics as trinitarian, yet the scope of trinitarian ethics is larger because it points to the source and ethos of ethics in the triune God of love. That said, it is important to explore what is meant by the term "evangelical ethics."

Ethics as evangelical are not to be confused with "evangelistic," though evangelical ethics (ethics of and according to the gospel) will by their practice and proclamation hopefully become evangelistic. Ethics as evangelical conveys the idea that ethics can only be done appropriately

---

18. See for example, O'Donovan, *Resurrection and Moral Order*. This is the burden also of the essay by Torrance, "On Deriving 'Ought' from 'Is.'"

when it is a response to divine grace, and enabled and enacted within relationship or participation in Christ. Ethics must always be idolatrous outside the gospel. The right decision, the right character, is not god. Only the triune God of grace is God. The ethical life can only be a product of divine reconciliation in the Son and redemption by the Spirit. And any particular ethical judgment is never itself the lord. Only the God who speaks to us to declare his ethical judgment is the Lord. Positively, ethics understood within participation in the life of God becomes not a burden, but a gift, indeed a delight.

To say that ethics is evangelical means, first, that though ethics outside of the gospel is legal and idolatrous, ethics understood and pursued with the gospel is in fact part of the gospel. Second, evangelical ethics, though it is preceded by justification and enabled by participation with Christ, still includes human effort and action (Phil 2:12–13; see chapter 1), including especially spiritual practices that are both ecclesial and personal.

Third, in this "now but not yet" or "in-between" time of the kingdom of God, evangelical ethics includes realism. This includes the tension between the twin realities that we are justified before God and therefore accepted by him, and yet we are in ourselves sinful. Our journey toward holiness is incomplete. There is therefore a realism about failure and imperfection in evangelical ethical pursuit. This pursuit thus involves the need for frequent confession, not in order that we may be justified again, but so that our communion with the Father might be restored. It also includes realism about what degree of change might occur within the believer who is being sanctified but not quite glorified, and therefore what degree of ethical discernment can be achieved. The notion that perfection is possible this side of the eschaton does not correlate with New Testament expectations, nor does the mere suppression of our sinful tendencies. If John Wesley and Barth might in some sense align with these two positions, Augustine and Calvin seem to have caught the drift of the New Testament by depicting a journey of realistic optimism alongside realistic activism. What seems possible and properly realistic according to the New Testament is "*growth* in grace" (see Rom 6:11–14, for example). This was reflected in both Augustine's realism and his activism, rather than passivity, concerning sanctification. Growth is only possible for Christians who are dependent on the Spirit but who are also *active* in fighting sin and putting on graces (called asymmetric concursus in the previous chapter). This they do by pursuing practices that facilitate participation with Christ in his death (mortification, disciplines of abstinence) and resurrection (disciplines of engagement).[19]

Fourth, to say that ethics is evangelical determines the tone and content of how the church and Christians can speak in the public square. It is vital that whenever the church does speak on ethical issues it does so in a gospel way. This means offering an alternative to societal views that points to what the good God had in mind behind moral commands, and to the flourishing that accompanies the ways of God. It also means speaking in a way that offers the forgiveness and redemptiveness of the love of God and the gospel. The church must not speak from above, as if aloof from human sin and its detrimental effects. I have noted that to seek ethical judgments (the "ought") apart from relationship with God (the "is") reproduces the primal sin made by our ancestors. They desired idolatrously to know good and evil apart from communion with God. Contemporary human dialogue on popular media is often characterized by an ironic dogmatism about ethical issues—ironic because of the relativistic nature of post-Christian secular society. In truth, any opinion that might run contrary to the individual autonomy and "freedom" of any person to be who they *feel* they are or do what they want to do is not permitted. So, there is a selectivity to this individualistic philosophy. The idolatry of these ethical opinions demands to be challenged by the evangelical ethicist, especially on issues of justice and issues of human sexuality.

There is a variety of ways in which Christian ethicists have responded to the challenge to speak in the public square in this relativistic ethical milieu. The first is to appeal to reason on the assumption that the moral conscience of all humans gives everyone universal access to the divine will or law, a kind of innate conscience, or intuition based on natural law. A second approach is to invoke revelation and speak in condemnation. Both of these illustrate what it is to appeal to moral reason or even revelation or torah, teaching, outside the context of the gospel. This is to answer modernity in a modern way. Ethical approaches that are not bolstered by a gospel context and a community where the gospel and its ethics are lived visibly are likewise unfruitful. How, then, can the church speak evangelically in the public arena?

19. Classifying disciplines or practices into disciplines of abstinence (fasting, silence, solitude, chastity, secrecy, etc.) and disciplines of engagement (worship, hearing the word, participating in the Lord's Supper, community, prayer, confession, fellowship, service, etc.) is Dallas Willard's helpful way of making sure spiritual disciplines or practices are practiced in the crucible of grace and in participation with Christ and his saving history. See Willard, *Spirit of the Disciplines*, 156–92.

ETHICS AS ECCLESIALLY CENTERED BUT PUBLICLY ORIENTED

The conclusion of what we have said so far about ethics being trinitarian and therefore evangelical seems to raise the question of who can actually do ethics. Can it only really be done by the church? And should it be shared and heard in the public square? Proponents of virtue ethics have proposed that the church is the ethical community formed in virtue by gospel narratives in a way that does not obviously lead to influence in the secular world. What, after all, is the point of ethical engagement of the church with the world? To make it just a little less adulterous, a little less greedy, a little less racist, and so on?

In response, we could say that Jesus did in fact suggest that the people of God should be salt and light (Matt 5:13–16), and that does suggest a purifying effect. The missional mandate of the church necessitates a social influence of the church. It involves evangelism, to be sure, but this must be pursued within the wider contexts of the Great Commandment, which includes love of neighbor, and the cultural mandate. It has justice and rehumanization as its goal. Thus, engaging ethics in the public square in an evangelical way is part of our mandate. Of course, this means that there can be no way in which ethical engagement on any issue could be done without explaining the gospel reasons and gospel empowerment and gospel shalom associated with the Christian ethical position on it. The approach is, "God loves the good and wants the good for us because it is good for us!" An evangelical rather than a legal approach ensures that the church does not go about this in ways that are oppressive and invoke earthly power. People are to be wooed by the ways of the gospel, not browbeaten or politicked into submission. Tolerance of other viewpoints, secular or religious (and in fact the secular position is religious, for the assumptions of a neutral saeculum are religious), within pluralistic, liberal democracies is a Christian value, a gospel value.

It is true that the church as the community of revelation and redemption is the true home of ethical deliberation. However, since the church is the image of the Trinity, it cannot keep its shalomic truth to itself but in love shares it with the world. Alan Torrance speaks of the body of Christ imaging the nature of the persons of the Trinity, and as such, having "its *hypostasis* in a radically inclusive *ekstasis* towards the secular world."[20] The church as a community, a deep community, a hos-

---

20. Torrance, "On Deriving 'Ought' from 'Is,'" 184.

pitable community, takes its character from the communion of the Holy Trinity, and therefore it must inevitably engage the world around it. If it truly does reflect the Trinity, the church will be a community whose influence spills over into the society around it, just as the triune God, who lacked nothing in all eternity, created the cosmos as an outflow of his infinite divine love, and has now redeemed that creation by that same love. Another way to express this is to say that the eternal communion within the Trinity has overflowed "into an involvement with history that aims at drawing humanity and creation in general into this communion with God's (His) very life."[21] The love, power, and holiness within that communion spilled over in the *ekstasis* of God in the act of creation and in his covenant to reconcile it, drawing humanity to himself in Christ by the Spirit.

The church cannot be a morally formed and deeply spiritual community and *not* be engaged and expressive concerning moral matters concerning humanity and creation. For the church to fail to be aware of and vocal concerning ethics is to reflect an inward orientation and a remnant theology. It is not enough for the church to model loving community as the sign of the new humanity and kingdom of God. That is basic, but it is simply *not enough*. The missing piece in such a construal of the church is its missional identity. Or, to use a Petrine metaphor, it has a *royal* priesthood toward the world and in regency with Christ over creation, not just a *holy* priesthood of worship within itself. Even its prayers as a holy priesthood will be representative of all humanity.

When the church gets ethics right, its potential for influence on the world is unlimited. Conversely, when the church gets ethics wrong, despite its revelatory privilege, the results are disastrous. One scenario in which the church has frequently failed the modern world is with respect to the ethics of race. "The struggle for racial equality and societal diversity is," as Martin Luther King Jr. suggested, "a church problem."[22] The role of the Dutch Reformed Church in justifying the apartheid system of South Africa was another case in point. How can church communities not understand in light of the gospel that all human persons are made in the image of the triune God and that in Christ Jesus there is neither Jew nor Greek, and neither black nor white? The only little bit of good news from the South African situation is that the Reformed church under the

---

21. Bevans and Schroeder, *Constants in Context*, 288–89.
22. Dates, *Why We Can't Wait for Christ-Exalting Diversity*, 171.

influence of theologians such as David Bosch, James Torrance, and Ray S. Anderson repented of its faulty theology and began to have a significant influence in the state toward recognizing the equality of people of all races in the rainbow nation.[23]

Thus, if ethics is indeed trinitarian and evangelical and biblical, this means that it is also ecclesial in its reception and therefore missional in its transmission. This is because God is the sent and sending God who loves all of humanity and seeks to draw it to himself. Stanley Grenz sums this up aptly:

> Christians declare that the touchstone of community is the eternal triune life and God's gracious inclusion of humans in Christ by the Spirit, constituting them as participants in the perichoretic Trinitarian life. This theological-ecclesiological perspective leads Christians to view every social reality in accordance with its potential for being a contribution to, prolepsis of, or signpost on the way toward the participation in the divine life that God desires humans enjoy.[24]

There is in Christian ethics a need for the church to engage seriously with Scripture within a trinitarian framework, and therefore in a way that is evangelical and ecclesial. This is a necessary step in preparing our hearts to encounter God himself to hear his command for particular situations that are often new and not addressed directly by the text. The next chapter develops this approach to Scripture with particular attention to the most central and critical ethical material of the Bible: the Ten Commandments. It will serve to answer the question, What is the role of the Bible and the Decalogue within this overarching trinitarian ethic?

---

23. Livingstone, *Missiology of the Road*, 350.
24. Grenz, *Renewing the Center*, 324.

4

The Role of the Word of God

If it is not enough just to say that ethics should be biblical, what function does the Bible have in Christian ethics? Specifically, what role do the Ten Commandments have, given that they seem to be the nerve center of canonical ethics? In terms of the previous chapter's discussion of the motifs of doing ethics, there is a validity to the prescriptive approach within a trinitarian framework. After all, the word of God is our final authority in all matters of faith and practice. However, treatment of prescriptive texts must be hermeneutically appropriate; they should be understood within the wider frame of the *theological deliberative* approach. This undergirds both the prescriptive and the situational/relational motifs. *Theological* considerations and *theological* interpretation of the word of God is crucial to how we use the Bible in our ethical considerations. We must take into account the whole canon and the broad sweep of its redemptive, covenantal themes to guide and illumine our use of prescriptive passages. Both the deliberative and the properly and canonically prescriptive approaches will also inform the situational/relational approach and form a boundary around it.

The three motifs might be envisaged as three interlocking circles (see fig. 4.1). The prescriptive motif without the deliberative motif can become atomistic and legalistic; the prescriptive motif without the situational/relational motif can be sterile and casuistic; the deliberative motif without the biblical input of the prescriptive motif can become distanced from exegesis and theoretical; the deliberative motif without the situational/relational motif can lack concrete applicability; and the situational/relational motif apart from the deliberative and prescriptive could lean toward relativism.

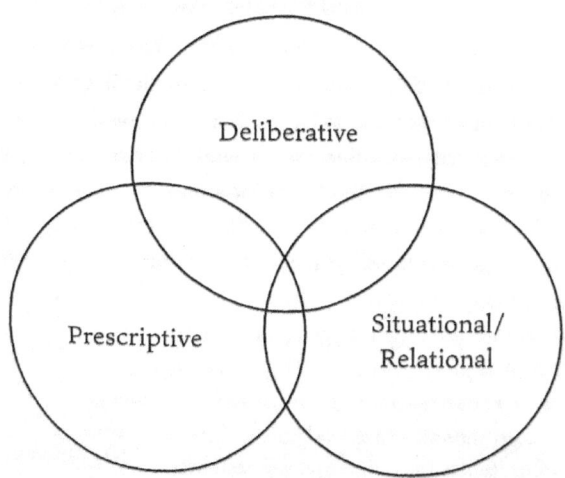

The gospel that empowers and forms us as persons also undergirds and guides our use of Holy Scripture, and specifically the Ten Commandments as these are repeated and expounded throughout the canon. The gospel also makes possible our needed encounters with the living God in the unavoidably situational ethical life. The written word of God must lead us to encounter the living Word of God in every situational ethical challenge.

Given that the Decalogue is the central and pervasive ethical prescription of the Bible, we must then ask, how are we to view the Decalogue in Christian ethics?

THE DECALOGUE AS COVENANTAL AND EVANGELICAL

From the moment of the revelation of the Ten Commandments in Exod 20:1–2 ("And God spoke all these words: 'I am the Lord your God, who brought you out of Egypt, out of the land of slavery'"), the intent was that they would be covenantal and evangelical, grounded in a freedom that contrasted to the Israelites' previous slavery. They were to be obeyed not in order to obtain a covenant with God, but because God's covenantal grace and promise already existed. This is the theological deliberative motif in which the exposition of the Decalogue as prescriptive is grounded. These commandments were to be a matter of freedom, not bondage (Gal 5:1, 13). They would engender a freedom *from* sin and a freedom *for* the good. They define what shalom means, what the life of human flourishing entails, and what is forfeited when they are not obeyed.

In the New Testament, the law is spoken of in at least three ways. First, it makes it clear that the ceremonial law has been fulfilled in Christ's life, death, and resurrection. Second, it is clear that the law is not to be considered as a way of salvation or as the primary way of conceiving of the Christian life. However, the New Testament does speak of the law in a third sense, as being applicable to Christians. This is in keeping with the law's original intent. Paul speaks of the law as "holy, and the commandment is holy, righteous and good" (Rom 7:12). He even calls it "spiritual" (7:14) and makes it clear that Christians *will* keep the law because people who are in Christ and filled with the Holy Spirit end up keeping the law almost without trying. In Romans 8 Paul speaks of the sending of the Son to take up our sinful nature vicariously and to put sin to death "in order that the righteous requirement of the law might be fully met in us, who do not live according to the flesh but according to the Spirit" (8:3–4). Thus, the primary ethos of the Christian life is union with Christ in his death and resurrection and life in the empowering Spirit, but this issues freely in obedience to the Decalogue and human flourishing.

There is, therefore, still an important place for the Decalogue in New Testament ethical reflection. In Galatians 5, Paul makes it clear that "if you are led by the Spirit, you are not under the law" (5:18), but not being under the law for Paul did not mean lawlessness. In fact, a few verses later he indicates that life in the Spirit inevitably means obedience to the moral law of God: "But the fruit of the Spirit is love, joy, peace, forbearance, kindness, goodness, faithfulness, gentleness and self-control. Against such things there is no law" (5:22–23). At the beginning of this paragraph, Paul had clarified two important ethical themes: "You, my brothers and sisters, were called to be free. But do not use your freedom to indulge the flesh; rather, serve one another humbly in love. For the entire law is fulfilled in keeping this one command: 'Love your neighbor as yourself'" (5:13–14). First, he proclaims the freedom of the Christian in ethical matters, which in the context of Galatians is defined from a filial perspective as union with Christ (2:20), adoption into sonship (4:5–7), and life in the Spirit (3:14). Forensically, this freedom is defined as justification (3:24). But second, Paul preserves the Decalogue as the subject matter of Christian moral living in freedom: "Do not use your freedom to indulge the flesh; rather, serve one another humbly in love. For the entire law is fulfilled in keeping this one command: 'Love your neighbor as yourself.'"

Christians are people who, because they are in union with Christ, justified by faith, and indwelled and filled by the Holy Spirit, keep this one commandment, which is in fact the sum of the last six commandments. We obey the law not to gain salvation but to reflect what salvation means in all aspects of social life. This is in keeping with what Jesus did in Matthew 22, when he summed up the commandments as "love God," reflecting the first four commandments, and "love neighbor," the last six commandments. The commandments express what loving really is, both toward God (our spirituality) and toward our fellow humans (our ethics). Such love is not possible, according to John, unless we have entered into being loved. "We love because he first loved us" (1 John 4:19)! This is the evangelical, that is, the gospel nature of Christian spirituality and ethics. For these reasons, Karl Barth spoke of law as gospel and gospel as law.[1]

The unity of law and gospel also has grounding in the resurrection of Jesus. The resurrection is the reaffirmation of the creation, and with it the created moral order. This is the contention especially of the eminent ethicist Oliver O'Donovan, who maintains that part of God's creation included a moral order. Though it is not salvific, it informs all humanity.

That moral order is inferred by Paul's reference in Rom 1:20, "For since the creation of the world God's invisible qualities—his eternal power and divine nature—have been clearly seen, being understood from what has been made, so that people are without excuse." That creation order has the form of the moral law, according to 2:15, "They show that the requirements of the law are written on their hearts." In addition to the many other realities Jesus's resurrection secured—our justification (Rom 4:25), our regeneration (Eph 2:5), our bodily resurrection (1 Cor 15)—it also enacted the reaffirmation of the creation and its moral order. It was God's way of expressing his ongoing commitment to his creation. This leads O'Donovan to bring together the renewal of creation with the dawning of the kingdom and to reject the notion that there is an "ethics of creation" and a separate "ethics of the kingdom":

> The very act of God which ushers in the kingdom is the resurrection from the dead which is the reaffirmation of the creation.

---

1 Barth, *Church Dogmatics II/2*, 1–7.

> If we maintain the dichotomy we end up with a kingdom ethics of dualism, in which a kingdom is set up in opposition to creation, and in which progress in history to its completion is denies its beginnings. Or we end up with a creation ethics which cannot be evangelical, since it would fail to take into account the good news that God has acted to bring all that He has made to fulfillment.[2]

On the basis that the resurrection has reaffirmed creation and human nature, O'Donovan renounces the idea that Christian ethics is only for the few who choose it. Instead, "prohibitions of adultery and murder are for all humanity, not just the church, and the church must speak in a way that recognizes creation and the divinely-given order of things in which humanity itself is located." He acknowledges that because of the fall, human nature is flawed and rebels against that creation order, yet "this order still stands over against us and makes its claims upon us."[3] The ongoing use of the moral law of God centered on the Decalogue in this era of salvation history is thus vindicated by the resurrection.

In sum, we may say that *the ethos of the Decalogue is salvific reality*. The call to obedience to the moral law of God flows from evangelical reality. It is not a case of, "if you do this, I will be your God," but rather, "I am the Lord, Yahweh, the covenant God of relationship. You get to do this and you can do it!" The exodus, which is such an important motif in the redemptive Christian story, is prior to the call for obedience—it is evangelical obedience.

THE DECALOGUE AS PERVASIVE

Since the moral law is present within creation and reaffirmed by the resurrection of Jesus, it is not surprising that the Decalogue is pervasive in the New Testament. All of the Ten Commandments are repeated there, and they form the foundation of New Testament ethics. The Swiss theologian Klaus Bockmuehl said there is no new ethical material in the New Testament and no new law, but only new motivation and new power.[4] The New Testament generally refers to the commandments in clusters, though all ten are not present in any one place. Thus, for example, Jesus

---

2. O'Donovan, *Resurrection and Moral Order*, 15.
3. O'Donovan, *Resurrection and Moral Order*, 16–17.
4. Bockmuehl, *Christian Way of Living*, 18.

makes several references in the Sermon on the Mount (Matt 5–7). The phrase Jesus uses repeatedly is "You have heard it said . . . but I say to you." Jesus is not negating the commandments against murder, adultery, and swearing oaths (the sixth, seventh, and third). Rather, he is, as Bockmuehl says, "radicalizing them": he is restoring their original meaning and intent, interiorizing the commands by exposing the root of behavior in the affections and motivations.[5] Jesus is speaking as Yahweh speaks to indicate their true authorial intent.

Other clusters include Matt 15:4–6, where Jesus contrasts the commandments as the true word of God with human traditions that nullified them; Matt 15:19, in which Jesus speaks of five of the commandments by way of prophetic conviction; and Matthew 19, where Jesus refers to the sixth, seventh, eighth, ninth, and fifth commandments along with the summing-up commandment, "love your neighbor" (Lev 19:18). Romans 13:9, where Paul cites the seventh, sixth, eighth, and tenth commandments, assumes the rest with the phrase "and whatever other command there may be," and then sums up these commandments with "love your neighbor as yourself." By doing this, Bockmuehl writes, Paul indicates that "love is not the reduction of the Ten Commandments, their lowest common denominator," but is their "rubric and touchstone"; and conversely, "the Ten Commandments are the exposition of the central commandment to love."[6] Paul also quotes the sixth, seventh, eighth, and ninth commandments in 1 Tim 1:8–10, again as part of an open-ended list, and asserts that they need to be interpreted properly.

Whereas Paul speaks of the commandments as good, and of the goal of the commandments for the believer as love, he also speaks of two other uses of the law: to convict unbelieving persons and to be the basis of civil government and the penal code. This thus reflects three uses of the law in the Old Testament—legislation, accusation, and catechism—and anticipates the Reformer Philip Melanchthon's three uses of the law. These were the civil use, which refers to the incorporation of the Decalogue into the law of the land; the convicting or accusing use, designed to convict sinners and bring them to Christ; and the teaching or catechetical use, which treats the Decalogue as that which guides the Christian life of sanctification.[7] This final use Bockmuehl sums up with these words: "The

---

5. Bockmuehl, *Christian Way of Living*, 9.
6. Bockmuehl, *Christian Way of Living*, 10.
7. Melancthon, *Melancthon on Christian Doctrine*, 122–28, cited in Bockmuehl, *Christian Way of Living*, 22.

Ten Commandments, shorn of their curse and condemnation, return to the regenerate believer as ethical instruction, lights by which to steer the life of sanctification."[8]

Since the Ten Commandments are ubiquitous throughout the Scriptures, in both Old and New Testaments, it seems obvious that they should have a prominent place in Christian ethics. The matter of Christian moral formation cannot neglect the catechesis and internalization of the Ten Commandments in a way that is anticipated in the new covenant (Heb 8). The matter of Christian ethical reflection also cannot evade the careful evaluation of all ethical issues in light of the Decalogue as a bare minimum. As mentioned above, relational and deliberative theological interpretation of Scripture must measure, empower, and qualify our prescriptive ethical reflection, but prescription cannot be avoided.

THE DECALOGUE AS PROPERLY INTERPRETED

To use the Ten Commandments prescriptively, we must interpret them properly. As already illustrated, they must be interpreted canonically and distinguished from ceremonial law and laws associated with the reign of God over Israel centered in the tabernacle and the temple. In seeking to interpret the commandments rightly, John Calvin stressed that a negative commandment implies its opposite positive commandment. If the Lord forbids something, he desires its opposite. For example, if the sixth commandment proscribes murder, it also prescribes the giving of life, or being a life-giving person. If the seventh commandment rules against adultery (in all its forms, as described in the exposition of the Decalogue in the books of the Pentateuch), it also commands it opposite, which may be described as faithful and self-sacrificing love of one spouse to the other. This opens up many "hidden dimensions, rich and vast," especially as each commandment in both negative and positive form is expounded in the Old and New Testaments. Many great Reformed expositions of the Decalogue follow this pattern.[9] This approach can, however, lead to "massive casuistry," and indeed did so.[10] Casuistic approaches to ethics are attractive for some people and traditions. A textbook that reveals the

---

8. Melancthon, *Melancthon on Christian Doctrine*, 122–28, cited in Bockmuehl, *Christian Way of Living*, 22.

9. See Johannes Wollebius's *Compendium Theologiae Christianae* (1626), for example.

10. Bockmuehl, *Christian Way of Living*, 21, where he describes how in Puritan England sleeping in church became a violation of the third commandment.

answers to every ethical situation a pastor may encounter would be a wonderful thing, but it does not exist, nor should it. There is no equivalent to the Talmud for Christian ethics. Rather, there is Torah and its exposition in all of Scripture. Our approach to prescriptive ethics is not casuistic but requires the leading of the Spirit, the cultivation of character, and listening to the word of God again and again.

In addition to Calvin's method, another appropriate use of the commandments is to see each of them as an area of ethics within which to consider all ethical issues. Placing ethical issues under the area of a commandment keeps ethical reflection grounded. Here Bockmuehl uses the analogy of area codes.[11] The first four commandments have to do with our relationship to God. The first three are stated in the negative, and their opposites have profound formative value, along with the Sabbath commandment. Then the life of worship and the discovery of the rest of God flows into the life of neighbor love, the experience of the shalom of the covenant people of God.

I am not quite committed to going as far as Bockmuehl in his assertion that "the Ten Commandments sufficiently describe and subsume the whole of Christian ethics,"[12] given my commitments to a trinitarian deliberative and relational superstructure for ethics. I will, however, say that there can be no ethics that neglects the Decalogue. In the rest of this book, therefore, we will consider ethical issues as they come under each commandment in turn. So, for example, under the seventh commandment we will consider all of the sexually related issues of our time, including the meaning of "gender," same-sex relations, and transgenderism. Under the Sabbath command, we will consider the issue of what it means to be human and therefore speak of transhumanism. Under the sixth commandment, we will consider matters such as medical assistance in dying, or more generally, euthanasia. In no way am I assuming that all can be known in assessing these issues just from the commandment. We will, however, put ourselves in the right posture of acknowledging the role of the word that comes from outside ourselves, looking to the sovereign Spirit within us, surrounded by and consulting the community around us.

---

11. Bockmuehl, *Christian Way of Living*, 132.
12. Bockmuehl, *Christian Way of Living*, 20.

A SUMMARY OF KEY MOTTOS IN TRINITARIAN THEOLOGICAL ETHICS

As we move from considering theological ethics more broadly in the first part of this book to applied pastoral ethics in the remaining chapters, the following key mottos sum up what has been said and become guidelines for ethical consideration.

- Trinitarian participation is the space in which moral formation and ethical decision-making occur. Moral formation is the development of virtue in union with Christ by the Spirit in the community of the church through the means of spiritual practices. Ethical reflection, action, and speaking require a doxological and dependent posture toward the Father above us, the hearing of the word of God from outside ourselves, the empowerment by the Holy Spirit who is within us, and the consultation of the community of wisdom past and present around ourselves.

- The telos of Christian living is restoration to the image of God, that is, likeness to Christ, by the Spirit's transformation, to personhood-in-community, to image-bearing in church and creation, to being fully human. It is the cradle of ethical behavior.

- Likeness to Christ is a "being-for-the other." We are not individuals but persons-in-relation called to realize this by the love of God and love of neighbor as described in the first and second tables of the Decalogue.

- "Ought is determined by is"—that is, trinitarian ethics is evangelical. The imperative must be preceded by and ensconced within the indicative—the "is" of the nature of the triune God and his gospel, the "is" of the covenant love of God in which we have found justification, the "is" of identity in Christ.

- Ethics is a listening to being (as being is grounded in Christ by the Spirit), *and* it is doing. Being without doing is gnostic; doing without being is behaviorism.

- "Hearing and doing" (epistemology) is grounded in and inseparable from "being" (ontology). Both sacrament (the Catholic way, which emphasizes being) and word (the Protestant way, which emphasizes hearing) are needed in the moral formation of persons.

- Torah is grace, which means that obedience to the moral law is evangelical obedience empowered by the Spirit. New-covenant reality is the interiorizing and enfleshing of the Torah. The Decalogue is not to be considered in a deontological way but rather as the word of God given in both covenants as material for ethical reflection in the larger context of life in the triune God and the gospel. Its individual commands may be treated as area codes for classification of ethical issues.

- That Torah is grace also means that there can be no Christian Talmud that tells us what to do in a casuistic way. We need to hear the word of God afresh for situations that are never completely alike.

Pastors who want to grow in moral formation and seek courageously to engage in ethical reflection and action and public speech must rely on trinitarian and participational ethics to guide them. This means they must seek to discern ethics, as they encounter always-new ethical dilemmas as *persons-in-relation* with God, living with a doxological and dependent orientation to the Father *above themselves*, as persons ensconced in Christ and empowered by the Spirit. The moral character *inside themselves* will prepare them for moral action, but there will always be the need for in-the-moment communion with Christ by the Spirit. They must seek to hear a biblical word from *outside themselves* (the ethical material of the Old and New Testaments of which the Decalogue, properly interpreted, is the core), consult the community of wisdom *around themselves*, and make a decision to the best of their ability, recognizing with realism that in the "now-but-not-yet" reality of this era of human history they may not always get it right. They will always have a posture of confession and humility, and a contemplative looking away to the Christ who can redeem any situation.

AN APOSTOLIC EXAMPLE

All of this may seem daunting for young pastors entering ministry, perhaps tempting them to lose heart. Thus, before we apply theological ethics to pastoral ethics, it may be helpful to look at how the apostle Paul did it. In a vulnerable yet defiantly hopeful way, Paul describes in 2 Cor 3:1—4:18 the realities that sustained him spiritually and morally in ministry. What was it that enabled him to be able to say emphatically, "We do not lose heart" (4:1, 16)? How can Paul's reflections, which bring together and embody the themes of theological ethics we have been considering, embolden the pastor who wants to live in an evangelical, trinitarian, and biblical way?

Confidence

First, in this passage, Paul expresses a persistent, even defiant *confidence* with regard to whether his life has made the integrity grade. The source of that confidence seems to have been a combination of things that are instructive for every pastor. The first is that the God of the new covenant had clearly been at work in and through him. God had written a letter of recommendation on his heart, a metaphorical letter that represented the evidence of God being at work in the lives of his converts in Corinth, a letter inscribed by none other than the "Spirit of the living God." This is a valid source of confidence for all ministers of the gospel today. There are people in our churches whose lives have been transformed by new covenant, gospel grace, as we have preached it and pastored them. Their lives are a letter that reassures us that God is at work. There have been people like that in each of my own church ministries. People I have led to Christ and to whom I have become bonded for life. People who have listened with rapt attention during the preaching of the word and brought words of encouragement that God had been at work in them through the preaching moment. People who came up to me after a sermon to say that three sermons ago they had trusted Christ for salvation and were only now sharing it.

But this is not the only, or even the main, source of Paul's confidence. People can be fickle, congregants can leave for another church down the road, or they can ask *you* to leave. Paul's primary source of confidence is expressed in the words "through Christ before God" (2 Cor 3:4). It is certainly not in himself ("believe in yourself" is not Paul's mantra), but rather in God: "Not that we are competent in ourselves to claim anything for ourselves, but our competence comes from God. He has made us competent as ministers of a new covenant—not of the letter but of the Spirit; for the letter kills, but the Spirit gives life" (2 Cor 3:5–6). The triune God, and not any human, is the bedrock source of his confidence. Our confidence as ministers that we can live with integrity for a lifetime, and finish well, lies in understanding and practicing life and ministry through the agency of the Son and before the audience of the Father. In context, here, that means in communion with and through the enabling of the "Spirit of the living God" (2 Cor 3:3, 6).

We can have confidence as we are caught up in the triune life of God. We are competent as we participate in the high priesthood of Christ the one who ministered with an ultimate competence for us. This competence the Son derived from his perfect communion with the Father and from his "without limit" (John 3:34) fullness and empowerment of the Holy Spirit. We are competent as we are led by the Spirit, we pray in the Spirit, we are filled with the Spirit, and we are anointed by the Spirit for every sermon and every pastoral interview and every board meeting. We are competent as we orient our whole lives toward the face of the Father who delights in us. Our ministry is not *our* ministry. It is *God's* ministry. Our ministry needs to be crucified, as Andrew Purves has reminded us.[13] True freedom in ministry, including moral and ethical freedom, is found in discovering ministry *in* the ministry of the triune God. It is found in the Christ in whose ministry we participate, the one who takes up our worship, our prayer, our preaching, our counsel, and our imperfect ethical decision-making and presents it to the Father as a fragrance for his delight.

This is not to say there is no human agency or responsibility in this. Trinitarian participation has *two* aspects: *On the one hand* is the divine participation of the Son, by which he became human and stood in our place as the sin bearer and as the one who was God's covenant partner for us—who died, rose again, and ascended for us, and who ministered and still ministers for us. *On the other hand* is our human participation by the Spirit in the life and ministry of the Son, one that involves death and resurrection as it did for Jesus. Trinitarian participation, as the key to Christian life and holiness and justice and ministry, is not our ungraced response to what Christ has done. It is not as if justification is by grace through faith, but ministry is by works. Even in our ministry, *we* minister as *Christ* ministers, and in *our* ministry *Christ* ministers. He is Lord in all ministry, and yet he permits us to be ministers with real agency, precisely in his ministry.

In practical terms, Christian ministry as a participation in Christ's ministry requires a posture of dependence toward God, and it involves making space for communion with Christ and contemplating the glory of God through spiritual practices: "And we all, who with unveiled faces

---

13. Purves, *Crucifixion of Ministry*.

contemplate the Lord's glory, are being transformed into his image with ever-increasing glory, which comes from the Lord, who is the Spirit" (2 Cor 3:18). Many pastors flounder at just this point. We become too busy to sit at the feet of Jesus, and so our ministry becomes duty, jaded by exhaustion and dampened in its power by distance from Jesus. Our competence as ministers of the gospel, which includes moral transformation and ethical discernment, is diminished. I have never forgotten the words of the late Howard Hendricks, who at a Moody pastors' conference in the mid-1980s made this comment: "Just because you are a pastor does not excuse you from being a Christian." Making space for communion with Christ as the ultimate priority in pastoral life is the primary equipping for the pastor as ethicist. Hendricks also commented that Peter's defection when he denied his Lord was not a blowout but a slow leak produced by pride and loss of communion with his Lord in his path toward the cross.[14]

In this passage, Paul asserts that competence is not "in ourselves to claim anything of ourselves." Rather, competence "comes from God" (2 Cor 3:5). However, Paul was a real agent who speaks even in this chapter about operating in a "freedom" ("Now the Lord is the Spirit, and where the Spirit of the Lord is, there is freedom," 3:17) that ironically comes from his being bound to God and his word. It is a freedom *from* the law as the primary ethos or gestalt of Christian life, from the law as a means for salvation, from the dominance of sin and self-ism, in the crucified Christ. In union with the risen Christ, it is a freedom *for* contemplation of Christ, for transformation by the Spirit ("beholding, are changed," 2 Cor 3:18 KJV), for obedience to the moral law of God imparted into the human heart under the new covenant. Freedom *from* and freedom *for* is a participation in his freedom. Yet freedom from the law does not make the people of God lawless. Paul's description of the "letter of the law" in verse 5 suggests a freedom from its condemnation, from its ceremonial aspects that certain Judaizers insisted gentile converts should keep, and from an approach to the law that is legalistic and picky and Pharisaical.

But the fact that the competence and freedom Paul is referring to is that of the new covenant and of the Spirit ("He has made us competent as ministers of a new covenant—not of the letter but of the Spirit; for the letter kills, but the Spirit gives life," 2 Cor 3:6) does not imply that there is now no use for the law in the lives of the people of God. When the prophets speak of the new covenant, they not only speak of it as grounded in

---

14. Hendricks, *Process of Failure*.

the union between God and his people ("I will be their God and they shall be my people"), and not only of the forgiveness that God gives to his people ("their sins and iniquities will I remember no more"). In Jeremiah's statement of Yahweh's new-covenant words, a radical planting of the moral law in regenerated human hearts comes even before mention of the union and the forgiveness: "I will put my law in their minds and write it on their hearts" (Jer 31:33). This is even more explicit in Ezekiel's version of the new covenant: "I will give you a new heart and put a new spirit in you; I will remove from you your heart of stone and give you a heart of flesh. And I will put my Spirit in you and move you to follow my decrees and be careful to keep my laws" (Ezek 36:26–27). The work of the Spirit is not to annul the moral law of God, which Paul asserts is "holy, righteous and good" (Rom 7:12). It is to move us toward obeying it in freedom, as those already forgiven and already in covenantal union with Christ in God. Thus, we may be assured that the moral law, upheld by Christ, indeed recovered in its original intent by him in the Sermon on the Mount, continues as a guide for the people of God today for the life of moral formation and ethical discernment.

These realities of participation in the life and freedom of Christ have a central bearing on how the pastor goes about moral formation, ethical discernment, and the tone and content of communication from the church to the culture around it. Competence in all these areas is impossible apart from personal and ecclesial communion with Christ and the empowerment of the Holy Spirit. Moral formation, a minimized aspect in teaching about spiritual formation in the contemporary church, is therefore underemphasized in the lives of many pastors, often with disastrous consequences. The failure of the character to bear the charism is evident in the lives of both great theologians and even, maybe especially, exceptionally gifted pastors.

Moral formation of pastors is vital to the cultivation of virtue. The pastor of character is prepared well for the many moments of ethical response. Precedent may play a role, but every ethical dilemma is a new situation in which the pastor needs to encounter the grace and leading of the Spirit as a person, even if the pastor is a person of character and virtue. This participational approach is the heart of this book. It gives us humble confidence that we can do this!

Hope

Second, Paul speaks of a *hope* that sustains his confidence to the point even of "boldness," that great word (Greek parrēsia) that characterizes the witness of the church and the apostles in the book of Acts. In its antecedent context, the hope Paul is referring to is grounded in the ministry of the Holy Spirit under the new covenant. It has a life-giving power, a surpassing glory, and a permanence that surpasses that of the old covenant. This is hugely comforting for the people of God and its pastors in our day, in which we face the challenges of moral malformation, the ethical confusion and the uncertain ethical sound that emanates from the church to the world.

This confirms the participational nature of the ethical life. As pastors are awakened by the Spirit and walk in the fullness and power of the Spirit, ethical renewal becomes possible. We can be bold about that. In the context that follows this statement of hope, the key idea is that the Spirit transforms the people of God permanently as they contemplate the glory of the Lord Jesus. If the *objective* focus of a contemplative life is on the Lord who is the Son, the *subjective* transformation is effected by the Lord who is the Spirit. Each divine person has a distinct role in our transformation and in our moral integrity and ethical judgment.

This working together of the Son and the Spirit, who each have their roles and yet work in and with each other, is in harmony with two classical trinitarian axioms. The first is the doctrine of appropriations of roles, which states that economic roles are assigned to each person in the Trinity, and the second asserts the indivisibility of the divine persons and their works. This is true because in the Trinity, each person is in the other by coinherence. The specific divine work referred to here is to accomplish our real transformation into the moral glory of the Lord, "from one degree of glory to another" (2 Cor 3:18 KJV). This is real moral formation, leading to the just and shalom-filled life, the life of true freedom ("where the Spirit of the Lord is, there is freedom," 3:17). But notice: it is a progressive product of life lived in participation in the Lord who is the Son, by the Lord who is the Spirit. We are transformed successively by degree "into [the Son's] image with ever-increasing glory, which comes from the Lord, who is the Spirit" (3:18). This participational path is a strong hope for pastoral ethics, the only hope. If it seems like the road less traveled, that is not because it has been tried and found wanting, but because it has not much been tried.

It is on the ground of this strong hope for the Christian life that Paul then expresses twice in chapter 4 that "he does not lose heart."

Resilience

Third, Paul speaks about *resilience* (4:1, 16). On the first occasion when Paul states, *"we do not lose heart"* (4:1), he expresses this courage as a consequence of the glorious ministry of the Spirit, which he has just expounded in unforgettable ways. He does not lose heart because of the ministry of transformation through contemplation. In light of the power of the Spirit who is Lord, change to recover the image of Christ who is Lord can really happen—in Paul, and even in the people of God at promiscuous, culture-bound Corinth. A resilience can be ours in the face of the great challenges of our time too, by virtue of our union and communion with the same faithful, triune God. It is made possible under the new covenant, grounded in a righteousness given in Christ, who is the one true covenant partner for us. This is a covenant far more glorious than the first, expressed by the lasting glory of the Christ, not the fading glory of Moses. We need not lose heart. We can be resilient.

But what does a resilient ministry look like? What has Paul been faithful in? What does not losing heart look like? Paul answers in the verses following his assurance of steadfastness in verse 1 with a description of ministry in verse 2 that has everything to do with moral integrity and discernment: "Rather, we have renounced secret and shameful ways; we do not use deception, nor do we distort the word of God. On the contrary, by setting forth the truth plainly we commend ourselves to everyone's conscience in the sight of God." I will consider the ethics of preaching later, but suffice it to say now that the following are all moral and ethical issues: the *moral character* of the preacher, the *authenticity* of the way the person preaches, the *focus* of the preaching (Christ, not the preacher), the *tone* of the preaching (evangelical, not legal), the *power* of the preaching (of the Spirit, not manipulation), the *veracity* of the content of what is preached (expository, not text-as-diving board for what the pastor wants to say), and the *originality* of the material (the product of exegetical study, not plagiarism). For Paul, resilience means paying attention to all this in his life and preaching.

Paul further develops his theology of preaching in 2 Corinthians 4 in ways that both challenge the inner life and shape the idea that preaching is a participation in the life of God. Here I touch on just a few aspects of this life. In verses 3–6, Paul shows that he has enough internal fortitude and purity of motive to be able to preach even when his message is rejected. This is because he is conscious of the blinding of the minds of unbelievers. He can only have this fortitude because he is conscious that they were rejecting the glory of Christ, so it wasn't really about him. And he is confident that his preaching has been about Christ, not himself, so they were rejecting him, and he was happy to be rejected with Christ. He is also conscious that when the lights do come on it is the work of God. I remember well the feedback a trusted friend, Ivan Stewart, gave me once after he had heard me preach as a young man. "Ross," he said, "You are trying too hard." Whatever motivations were present in my heart needed to be unraveled and purified. Paul's view of the sovereignty of God meant that he did not have to try too hard.

In verses 7–11, Paul expresses a dynamic that kept his sense of self in perspective. He affirms the "treasure" of the gospel of the glory of God radiating from the face of Jesus Christ to transform sinful people, and then expresses the sheer wonder of the fact that this treasure is given away though "jars of clay" to make sure that the source of the power of the gospel preached is "from God and not from us" (v. 7). Jars of clay assumes imperfections, cracks, persecutions, brokenness. This is fellowshiping with the sufferings of Christ. Paul speaks of carrying around in his "body the death of Jesus" (v. 10). The power was not in him, but rather in a body that shows all the marks of identification with Jesus. It is a body that is used by God—for preaching is embodied, not disembodied—but a body that lets the rays of the glory of Christ be seen through its cracks, its vulnerability, its brokenness, and the grace of Christ at work in that brokenness.

For Paul, there was no place for pastoral leaders of the kind that were threatening to influence the church in Corinth. These were leaders without any blemishes, who emphasized their own power, their own sophistry, their own rhetoric. Paul led with brokenness, with speech that flowed from dependence on the Spirit and focused on the glory of Christ. With unimpressive physical presence. With scars from persecution and some just from life. With openness about that fact that he even despaired of his life at one point. He was open about this, yet not obsessed with it. Being properly vulnerable as a pastor and preacher does not mean that every Sunday there is a self-focused, tell-it-all approach trying to show off our brokenness. It may involve some vulnerable sharing, but rather, what speaks most loudly is an unpretentious consciousness that is evident to the discerning people of God. In the economy of God, our greatest wounds do become our greatest ministry. But let us not let our wounds be the constant focus, but rather the wounds of Christ.

But Paul does not speak of the death of Christ without also speaking of the resurrection in verses 13–15. His faith is grounded in the resurrection of Jesus (v. 14), that when he speaks the good news, God will do his work "so that the grace that is reaching more and more people may cause thanksgiving to overflow to the glory of God" (v. 15). Jesus's resurrection meant that resurrection power would be at work in his preaching and in the regeneration of those who were given grace to respond. It is the resurrection of Jesus that authorizes and empowers our preaching by the Spirit, and that therefore keeps us from trying too hard and from manipulating people. It is the resurrection of Jesus that, because it has reaffirmed God's creation, has also reaffirmed God's created moral order. God's created moral order is what gives us assurance to speak the gospel, including its ethical content, in our public squares, and know that God will by his Spirit bring about the influence that salt and light are meant to bring.

For all these reasons, Paul concludes in verse 16, "Therefore we do not lose heart."

The challenge of resilience and the patterns of life in God that are required for it have been well documented in *Resilient Ministry: What Pastors Told Us about Surviving and Thriving*.[15] The authors of this helpful book spent five years in significant relationship with pastors. Five key themes emerged within resilient pastors. Notably, the first was spiritual formation. Further areas were appropriate self-care, good emotional and cultural intelligence, prioritizing of marriage and family, and skills in leadership and management. I am convinced that the *moral* nature of spiritual formation is particularly neglected in consideration of formation. Emotional and cultural intelligence is vital for ethical discernment and for the holy life. Affections, not just cognition, are crucial in a life with God.

I am convinced also that pastoral care and soul care must be grounded in word and sacrament. Its basis is not in scientifically grounded personality theories and inventories (though these have their value) or schools of psychotherapeutic modalities. Its grounding is in Scripture and

---

15. Burns et al., *Resilient Ministry*.

the tradition, in the life of prayer, in public and private proclamation, and in care of the soul, keeping the community attentive to God. Until this is recovered, pastor by pastor, and church by church, we cannot hope to win the battle for moral integrity, for the pursuit of other models is without integrity. So how do we begin, or get back, to the life of moral formation? The next section will be expositions of the first four commandments with an orientation toward moral formation in the life of God.

5

Moral Formation in the Covenant Love of God (Commandments 1–3)

The battle for resilience and moral integrity begins with who we are. It begins on the inside. That is, it begins with the moral formation of the pastor. Our focal point, biblically speaking, will be the first three commandments in this chapter, and the fourth commandment in the next chapter. Before considering each of these commandments in turn, we need to ask why we should look to the Decalogue for the motivation and substance of moral formation.

THE DECALOGUE WITHIN THE TRINITARIAN LOVE ETHIC

To answer this question, we need to be reminded of the wider context in which to consider the Decalogue in moral formation. All that I have said about trinitarian ethics applies as we pursue specifically the matter of character formation in the first table of the Decalogue. The pursuit is impossible apart from the covenantal context of God's love, union with Christ, dependence on the Spirit, and a doxological orientation toward the Father. For example, this means we speak of character with the awareness that it comes under the broader trinitarian category of "person." This does not diminish the importance of character and virtue, but it keeps the discussion always within a personal, participatory context. Character formation is not self-determined obedience to the commandments.

Rather, character formation is an outflow of our life in God, and our life in God is in turn further shaped by character formation. The indicatives of life lived as persons in God empower the imperatives of obedience; spiritual practices for receiving this life and obedience then shape a lifestyle in which character grows.

This is in keeping with how the New Testament envisions the mutual relationship between life in God and obedience to the commandments that builds virtue. The apostle Peter, for example, makes this clear when he provides a list of the Christian virtues we are to pursue: "For this very reason, make every effort to add to your faith goodness; and to goodness, knowledge; and to knowledge, self-control; and to self-control, perseverance; and to perseverance, godliness; and to godliness, mutual affection; and to mutual affection, love" (2 Pet 1:5–7). We are to "make every effort" (the imperative), but the pursuit of virtue is only possible because of the prior indicatives of the gospel to which Peter refers: "His divine power has given us everything we need for a godly *life through our knowledge of him*" (v. 3) and because we "*participate in the divine nature*" (v. 4). Peter reiterates this after the list of virtues using similar words. Virtue is a by-product of "knowledge of our Lord Jesus Christ" (v. 8). So, there is a definite place for human obedience in moral formation ("make every effort," v. 5) and the pursuit of character ("add to your faith," v. 5), but it is ensconced in the power and life of God ("His power," "participate in the divine nature," vv. 3–4). This is the shape of life in God: obedience to commands and practices empowered by that life that forms virtue. And love is the capstone of the virtues (v. 7), which is a concept relevant to the commandments, as we will see.

John the apostle emphasized even more clearly the connection between life in union with Christ and love motivated by obedience to the commands of God. For example, in John 14, in the context of his speaking of the coming of the Spirit to indwell the people of God, Jesus references three unions: "On that day you will realize that I am in my Father, and you are in me, and I am in you" (John 14:20). "I am in my Father" refers to the union of the holy Trinity. "You are in me" refers to the fact that by the incarnation God the Son had become one with humanity. This we may refer to as the incarnational union, the participation of God in humanity. And third, "I am in you" refers to the coming of the Holy Spirit into the apostles, the topic Jesus was addressing with them. It is remarkable that Jesus links these three unions together. Every believer in Jesus Christ participates in the life and love of the Trinity because of the incarnation of Christ and the Spirit's indwelling. But notice that Jesus moves immediately from this deeply theological discussion of trinitarian realities into an ethical one.[1] "Whoever has my commands and obeys them is the one who loves me. The one who loves me will be loved by my Father, and I too will love them and show myself to them" (John 14:21).

What "commands" did Jesus have in mind here? Most likely they included the Ten Commandments, which he upheld in the Sermon on the Mount (Matt 5) as applicable in all their probing depth for his kingdom. His "new commandment" given in John 13 has to do with disciples loving each other, and this is certainly in keeping with the spirit and content of the Decalogue. The crucial point is that obedience to the commands of God (ethics) flows from a life of character built in deep communion with God. Both moral character and ethical actions have been made possible by the vicarious obedience of Jesus and by the present power of the Spirit. As God's covenant partner, Jesus became one with us and has by his vicarious life, death, and resurrection provided justification and enabled sanctification. The Spirit applies the work of Christ but also in his own right regenerates and transforms us. He is the gracious Giving Gift to us, the Lord and Giver of life, who transforms us from the inside out in progressive degrees of glory (2 Cor 3:16–18).[2] Inner transformation in accordance with the presence of the moral law in the hearts of the believer and outward obedience to the moral law are a real expectation of the gospel. Thus, we must not lose sight of the fact that formation in character and virtue is engraced and empowered from start to finish in the Son and by the Spirit.

In John 15, Jesus says: "As the Father has loved me, so have I loved you. Now remain in my love. If you obey my commands, you will remain

---

1. Although the word "Trinity" was not yet articulated by the church, the concepts that led to the church's affirmation of it are here in John and elsewhere.

2. Tom Smail uses "Giving Gift" for the Holy Spirit, who is the precious *Gift* given to the church commensurate with the price paid by Jesus in his atoning death for us, and not merely the person of the Trinity who applies the atonement to human hearts. He is also the *Giving* Gift, that is, as God he gives regeneration, sanctification, the charismata (spiritual gifts) for ministry, and so on. See Smail, *Giving Gift*. John Milbank expresses concern that if in the workings of the economic Trinity we only speak of the Spirit as the one that applies the benefits of Christ's work, we reduce the Spirit "to the power of Christ's person." He goes so far as to suggest that the Holy Spirit is involved directly in atonement as "another atoner," not just mediately in communion with the Son as he offers himself up to God (Heb 9:15). See Milbank, "Second Difference: For A Trinitarianism without Reserve." If this shows a Hegelian influence in Milbank, it paradoxically elevates the personhood and deity of the Spirit.

in my love, just as I have obeyed my Father's commands and remain in his love.... This is my command: Love each other" (John 15:9–10, 17). Jesus emphasizes the love connection in ethics: moral formation flows from abiding in the love between the Father and the Son, through the Holy Spirit. This is then shown by obedience to the commands he gives to love our brother and sister or neighbor. Enabled by the Spirit's power, the virtue of reflexive love forms in us as it is lived out in active obedience that is also enabled by the Spirit's power. True formation must involve both the contemplative practice of loving communion with God *and* loving action toward my neighbor.

This New Testament approach is reflected faithfully in the Reformational treatments of the Ten Commandments that consistently acknowledge that their "formative power" lies precisely in their centeredness in Christ and the gospel.[3] This employs the theological deliberative trinitarian approach to ethics and ethical texts. The sections in Calvin's *Institutes of the Christian Religion* on the Decalogue (book 2) and the Christian life (book 3) are closely interwoven.[4] The law and Christ are complementary, not contradictory. For Calvin, Christ's way of self-denial, and the resurrection life in him, are in fact described by the negations and positive assumptions of the commandments. We enter "more fully into the life of God" by them.[5]

This christocentricity remains in the tradition following Calvin, as seen, for example, in both the Geneva and the Westminster confessions, which communicate that the moral law of God teaches us "how much they are bound to Christ." That Christ has perfectly fulfilled the law for them moves the believing community to thankfulness, which is expressed in devotion to obeying the law.[6] This is consonant with a view of theological ethics that permits the prescriptive yet endorses the theologically deliberative gospel approach.

What does pursuing character transformation look like, then? It looks like abiding in the love of the Trinity, which means obeying the commands that simply summarize love and describe virtuous loving character.

---

3. Burgess, "Reformed Explication," 88.
4. Calvin, *Institutes of the Christian Religion*, 684.
5. Burgess, "Reformed Explication," 88.
6. See the Westminster Larger Catechism, *Book of Confessions*, 97.

THE DECALOGUE WITHIN EVANGELICAL ETHICS

The commandments are not something we "have to" do to live in the life of God. They are the "get to" aspect of life in God designed for human flourishing. In a nutshell, then, the ethical approach of the Scriptures and of Reformational ethics is this: that the pursuit of obedience to the commandments understood within a trinitarian framework is *evangelical* in its nature. It has gospel origin and a gospel tone. It is grounded and motivated in the good news of God's love for us, and its shape is love. The ethical pursuit is only made possible by the prior covenantal commitment of the God of love to be the God of his people (Exod 20:1). It is only feasible because the God of love even enables our response to him in love. Love is the foundation of ethics, and our human response in love for God and neighbor means that love is also the form of ethics. Jesus captures the essence of the Ten Commandments when he speaks of the Greatest Commandments as love for God and love for neighbor (see Matt 22:34–35), which is a summing up of the first four commandments and the last six (see also Gal 5:13–14; Rom 13:8–10).[7] In short, the foundation or evangelical character of Christian morality is grounded in triune participation in Christ by the Spirit, and the form of Christian ethics is love for God and human.

The connection between the inner life of formation and the outward life of obedience is therefore established in the relationship between the two greatest commandments, which sum up the Decalogue. They are a single commandment of love. Oliver O'Donovan states, "Love is the principle which confers unifying order both upon the moral field and upon the character of the moral subject. It is the fulfillment of the moral law on the one hand, and the form of the virtues on the other." The relationship between the love-God and love-neighbor commands is, according to O'Donovan, a *duality-in-unity*.[8]

---

7. John Calvin is seen to reflect "the wider tradition" when he "associates the first table with the first half of the great love commandments (to love God with heart, soul, and mind) and the second table with the second half (to love our neighbor as ourselves; see Matt 22:37–39). Calvin argues that the first table is the foundation for the second table—only if we learnt to love God rightly will we also love our neighbor rightly. But conversely we will have learned to love God rightly if we also demonstrate love for our neighbor. Right worship leads to a right concern for social justice; social justice must be rooted in orthodoxy ('right praise')." See Burgess, "Reformed Explication," 82.

8. O'Donovan, *Resurrection and Moral Order,* 226, 228.

The *unity* is grounded in the unity of God himself and in his creation of and good purpose for humanity. The love that flowed ecstatically out of the triune Godhead in creation is the same love he has imparted to his human creatures made in his image. The unity of the loves arises because love-of-neighbor originates in and has its end in love-of-God, which in turn can only be a reality because he has first loved us, as John reminds us (1 John 4:10–12). Love of neighbor has no meaning apart from God and his love for my neighbor as well as for me. The common origin of myself and my neighbor is in God by creation and as reaffirmed in the incarnation. The common telos of myself and my neighbor according to the gospel is the high calling and destiny of fellowship with God. Were these assertions not true, love of neighbor would not have any ontological grounding. It would, as O'Donovan asserts, collapse into one of two possible corruptions: the tyrannizing of our fellow people, or the enslavement of the self to fellow people: "Take away love for God, and the ontological parity which makes true neighbor-love possible is upset; one human being takes the place of God and confers value or significance upon the other."[9]

The *duality* arises because the second command is toward persons that are created and therefore are not God. God's act of creating the creation flowed from the will of God, not out of his being. That is, creation was not the product of the "self-differentiation of God," as in the generation of the persons within the Trinity. Creation is thus ontologically distinct from God (contra pantheism). Love of neighbor is a love of something that is not God, and so is to be kept in distinction from love of God. The secondary object (neighbor) is nevertheless given by and depends on the primary object (God), hence the unity in the duality. Thus the love-of-neighbor stream of the one command, although distinct, is inseparable from the first command. Later John makes our love of neighbor the test of our professed love for God: "Whoever claims to love God yet hates a brother or sister is a liar. For whoever does not love their brother and sister, whom they have seen, cannot love God, whom they have not seen" (1 John 4:20).

As O'Donovan points out, Saint Augustine's statement that our first duty to our neighbor is to "seize him for God" sheds light on the meaning that the first aspect of the love command gives to the second. Augustine did not mean that all acts of love should be manipulative. He meant that

---

9. O'Donovan, *Resurrection and Moral Order*, 229.

we should love our neighbor recognizing "their calling and destiny to fellowship with God" and with a view to furthering that destiny. O'Donovan goes on to say, "We must be wary on the one hand, of evangelistic zeal that ignores all aspects of the neighbor's being, and on the other hand, give consideration to the possibility that repudiation of evangelism which is fashionable in some ecclesiastical circles may in fact reveal a refusal to take the neighbor's vocation seriously."[10]

There is thus in the duality-in-unity of the Great Commandment, or the two tables of the Decalogue, two pursuits: the quest for a contemplative solitariness in the cultivation of the worship and love of God, on the one hand, *and* the pursuit of an activeness that is a consequence of the communitarian nature of the human person, on the other. It seems to me that pastors lean in one of two directions. The *contemplative* pastors spend their lives alone, always seeking to be with God. These pastors may need to work at connecting with the needs of their neighbor, doing practical things that may prevent them from being too much into themselves. These are the pastors who seem to drop down out of heaven five minutes before their sermon and fly back up to heaven immediately after shaking a few hands. Then there are the very *active* pastors who lose a sense of the presence and love of God in their endless activity for others. The formation of pastors morally and in every way must involve both contemplation and action. As Teresa of Ávila said, "Mary and Martha never fail, as it were, to work together" in the mature soul.[11]

That the Ten Commandments have a gospel tone is evident from the fact that they are given only after Exod 20:1–2, where God says, "I am your God, no matter what." The covenant of God with his Old Testament people, which the Decalogue embodies, involves the expectation and possibility of obedience. But this covenant is a reflection of the covenant of grace made within the triune Godhead, with humanity, before human history began. Ephesians 1 describes God as "the God and Father of our Lord Jesus Christ" (1:3). The God of Abraham, Isaac, and Jacob is now revealed as the God and Father of our Lord Jesus Christ, the God of covenant. That covenant involved the election of God to be *for* humanity. It was at its core the decision to elect the Son to become human for us,

---

10. O'Donovan, *Resurrection and Moral Order*, 229.

11. Teresa of Ávila, *Complete Works*, 396. Amy Plantinga Pauw speaks of Carmelite mystics Teresa of Ávila and St. John of the Cross as well, known for their advocacy of the notion of "a transforming union of the soul with Christ leading to incorporation into the life of the Trinity." See Pauw, *Supreme Harmony of All*, 142.

to be God's covenant partner for us, to live and die vicariously for us. In the embodied Christ, God declared the first half of the covenant, which is echoed in the words of the new covenant: "I will be their God." By the coming of the Son to be human for us, and by his vicarious life and death and resurrection for us, God elected to justify humanity and indeed all of creation. It was only on this evangelical basis that God uttered the second aspect of the covenant—"they will be my people." The command of God to us is holiness: "Be holy, for I am holy." It involves obedience to the law of God. But it is grounded in and empowered by the first half of the covenant. Obedience to the law of God is evangelical, for God has already accomplished his reconciling work in Christ. We are responsive to that work of grace, and in our obedience we are engraced by the power of the Holy Spirit and the high-priestly ministry of Christ. The new covenant people have internalized the law and are empowered by the Spirit for obedience. The law is thus undoubtedly part of the gospel.

The commandments function within the gospel in more than one way. First, they have a convicting purpose that is a part of our being drawn to Christ in repentance and faith. Though we are saved by faith alone, our union with Christ means that faith is never alone—it shows in love to God and neighbor, which is in fact our conversion or sanctification, viewed as both initial and lifelong. In fact, given that the Great Commandment and its component commandments are all repeated in the New Testament for the believer, we may say that the Decalogue is the norm for loving Christian living, probing and shaping our motivation and behavior at their very core. This is justified in at least two ways by scholars in their treatment of the Decalogue. First, the "commandments themselves set forth divine grace" in light of their transcovenantal nature and their association with divine love.[12]

Second, in light of their exposition in the New Testament, they have a "christological determinacy" in both law and gospel that are not in opposition to one another.[13] As John P. Burgess insists, "The first Reformed angle on the formative power of the Ten Commandments relates to their christological center. For Calvin, each of the commandments finds its fulfillment in Christ." People who are in union with Christ are able to

---

12. Burgess, "Reformed Explication," 79.
13. Welker, *Travail and Mission: Theology Reformed*, 143. It is acknowledged that there are differences between law and gospel in Calvin's theology, as Michael Horton has indicated, but there is significant overlap, not total opposition, in both Testaments. See Horton, "Calvin and the Law-Gospel Hermeneutic," 27–42.

live out that union as expressed by their baptism through mortification of the vices suggested in the negative statements of the commandments. By sharing in his life, they put on the graces of Christ that are the positive statements of the commandments. This integration of the commandments with the way of Christ leads to the formation of "one's true self."[14] This is the Christian way of living.

The commandments are also, third, the means for engaging our culture's standards and ethics. In Calvin's magisterial exposition of the Ten Commandments in three different locations of his corpus,[15] he indicates three dimensions of this civil use of the law (which is generally referred to as the "first" use of the law in Reformed ethics). The commandments used in the civil context are first *personal*. They are not only prescriptive but descriptive in that they direct us to Christ, who is the fulfilment of the law in a complete way, and help us to know who we are in Christ. Second, they are very much a *social* imaginary depicting life in the kingdom of God, enabling the "transformation of human relationships" in both the church and in society.[16] Third, they summarize but are not intended to be exhaustive of the law of God. They present trajectories for the development of ethical deliberation in a manner that is governed by the gospel. These three descriptions of the civil use of the Decalogue will be helpful in discussions of how the pastor and the church should function in the public square. Hearing the word of God in the commandments as they are expounded in the Old and New Testaments is not to capitulate to a merely prescriptive way of doing ethics. Rather, is to take account of the word of God in the deliberative broader context of the triune nature and holy, loving character of God and his good gospel intentions for people and the world.

These sentiments reflect the three uses of the law outlined in the previous chapter: the civil, the convicting, and the teaching or "normative for Christian living" use. All three have a vital role as we consider the commandments in moral formation, for they give shape to a lifestyle of repentance and sanctification lived out in social relationships.

---

14. Burgess, "Reformed Explication," 89.

15. In Calvin's *Institutes*, his *Sermons on Deuteronomy*, and *Commentaries on the Last Four Books of Moses*. Burgess, "Reformed Explication," 79.

16. Burgess, "Reformed Explication," 87.

A TRINITARIAN HEURISTIC?

The three uses of the law have sometimes led to Christian ethics being classified into three layers, though not with exact correspondence.[17] First is creation ethics for all humanity, including Christians (called *ethics of the Father*), which includes the cultural mandate of Genesis 2 and the natural law (Decalogue) within the human heart. The second is salvation or kingdom ethics (*ethics of the Son*), which include commands like "turn the other cheek" in the Sermon on the Mount that are intended for Christian disciples undergoing persecution, as well as the "put off/put on" directives in the epistles that are intended for regenerate people. Finally, individual ethics (*ethics of the Spirit*), such as in Romans 14, speaks of issues of conscience (called in ethics *adiaphora*) where Christians can validly land on different sides of an ethical issue. Issues in this third category would include whether Christians should eat meat offered to idols or abstain from alcohol. The clear mandate from the moral law is that drunkenness is wrong, whereas moderate use of alcohol is another matter left to individual conscience, circumstances, and the conviction of the Spirit. Issues of personal or vocational direction come under this heading also. As noted earlier, Heb 5:13–14 goes so far as to say that our obedience to what is right and good for us as individuals is a test of our spiritual maturity.

There is at first glance some validity to this approach, and it helps in the pursuit of moral formation and the classification of ethical issues. However, I fear that if viewed uncritically this classification violates truly evangelical, trinitarian Christian ethics and the role of the Decalogue within it. For one thing, it reflects a degree of individuation of the persons of the Trinity that is too great. It is an important axiom of the doctrine of the Trinity that each divine person is for the others and vitally involved in all of the works of the others, including in ethics. Second, the distinction between creation and kingdom ethics is questionable, as indicated in the previous chapter. The content of kingdom ethics is not other than creational. This would be gnostic and not Christian. The whole created order is taken up representatively in the person of Christ. All humanity has been affected in an *ontological* way, though not yet in a *noetic* way, by the incarnation, death, and resurrection of Christ, which reaffirms the creation order, and the moral law, which is part of that order. Thus, what God calls humanity to as a whole is still the moral law that

---

17. For more on this approach, see Bockmuehl, *Christian Way of Living*, 25–27.

is in their hearts because he implanted it there (Rom 2:15). Thus, third, the *content* of ethics as the Decalogue is common for all humans. Jesus radicalizes and applies the law to the heart, but even this does not move beyond the original intent of the law. It would appear that there are many non-Christians who live better ethically than many professed Christians I have known. They are by "common grace" more refined that many who are recipients of "saving grace."

What then is distinct about the believer, including the pastor, who seeks moral formation? Three things differentiate the Christian and the non-Christian with respect to ethics. First, only believers enter into the knowledge and experience of what Christ has done and of their "being-in-Christ" by faith, as the Spirit regenerates and works in them. Second, the *power* to live ethics as love for God (spiritual formation, the moral subject) enabled by the Spirit shows in evangelical repentance and obedience. Mortification in Christ (participation in his death; Rom 6; Col 3), by the Spirit (Rom 8:13), and vivification in Christ (participation in his resurrection) are the key themes of spiritual and moral formation in the New Testament epistles, and the Decalogue serves as a guide in this process. But third, the Christian has a recovered *sense of authority* as a son or daughter of God that restores the creation mandate—Christ in his humanity is the subject of Psalm 8 and Hebrews 2 in a way that anticipates the kingdom to come (a fully renewed creation). In the *now* aspect of the kingdom, we as Christians are bold to engage in ethical issues in situations that humanity has never encountered before. We can enter into situations that confront us confidently and dependently, though not arrogantly, in any field in which the moral law can be applied with new wisdom. We have this authority as children of God, albeit still and always in transformation.

THE FIRST COMMANDMENT

And God spoke all these words: "I am the Lord your God, who brought you out of Egypt, out of the land of slavery. You shall have no other gods before me."

Exodus 20:1–3

Speaking to the role of the Ten Commandments in Reformed theology, Burgess has commented that they are "dynamic expressions of God's gracious will that call the church to a continuing process of conversion." By them "Christians come to a deeper understanding of God's grace, are invited to respond to it, and are enabled to grow in it."[18] F. D. Maurice, a nineteenth-century theologian, wrote in a similar vein that "if [the Commandments] are *kept*, if they are watched over and thought about and cherished . . . they will give us an acquaintance with Him which we can obtain in no other way."[19] They are, above all, an encounter with Christ and formation in the way of Christ. The first commandment is especially relevant in this regard.

It is very brief, yet it packs unparalleled spiritual power. By employing Calvin's method spoken of in the previous chapter, it is clear that the power of this commandment lies both in its exposure of the propensity of the human heart toward idolatry, through its negative version, and in its encouragement of the application of the heart toward sole devotion to God, through its positive restatement. Those positive statements are implicit from the negative statement, but are made explicit in various ways in both Testaments. Detailed expositions of this commandment in its negative and positive statements in both Testaments can be found in Calvin, and more recently in Klaus Bockmuehl. My purpose here is to draw on their summary conclusions and apply them to the immediate situations of pastors in formation.

Pastoral Applications of the Negative Commandment

Why does Yahweh lead with the negative statements most often in the commandments? The negative is most searching and grants the deepest exposure of the heart. It is easy to affirm my love for God with bold claims, but until the rivals of God are exposed, I cannot really know the quality of my love. The negative statement of this first commandment is repeated often in both Testaments. God commands that nothing—no god, whether spiritual or physical or material—can be allowed to rival him in our heart's devotion. He is unique as the one God and in his exclusive sovereignty as the Lord of all. God is jealous with a jealousy that can only be morally appropriate for the one who is the self-existent God, who

---

18. Burgess, "Reformed Explication," 80.
19. Maurice, *Reconstructing Christian Ethics*, 74.

created everything in the cosmos. There is a continuity of the Testaments in this regard, illustrated in Deut 4:24 and Heb 12:19, both of which refer to God as a consuming fire. Turning from false gods is consistently marked by vehemence. Idols are typically torn down.

What are the false gods of pastoral ministry that the *negative statement* of this commandment speaks to? This is a question that most pastors would, I think, find easy to answer. Success, measured in the ways of modernity, easily becomes the god of pastors and boards who assess them by criteria such as filled seats and money in the offering. This reductionism leads to what Eugene Peterson called the great defection of pastors who drift to becoming "shopkeepers":

> The pastors of America have metamorphosed into a company of shopkeepers, and the shops they keep are churches. They are preoccupied with shopkeeper's concerns—how to keep the customers happy, how to lure customers away from competitors down the street, how to package the goods so that the customers will lay out more money.[20]

It is so easy to be distracted from the primary calling of pastors to study the word, pray, and give spiritual counsel publicly and privately. For David Hansen, a pastor who has modeled the contemplative way, his temptation to see success as a god was counseling.

> I could fill up many hours every day with counseling. People believe counseling is a great panacea. Yet many are loath to go to a professional counselor. That costs money, and real counselors ask hard questions. . . . For me, trying to be a counselor is a shortcut. It is pandering to my people's desires to have me do something to them rather than admonish them to live through the thick forests of their lives by following Christ in discipleship.[21]

It is not, of course, that pastoral counseling is not needed. Some associate pastors in larger churches may have this as their primary focus, if they are appropriately trained. It is just that often there are others more gifted to do this than the pastor who preaches and offers spiritual counsel out of the pastor's life with God. For those pastors, the cost of engaging in counseling is too high. It involves dual roles, and they may not be equipped to deal with clinical depression and serious anxiety disorders.

20. Peterson, *Working the Angles*, 2.
21. Hansen, *Art of Pastoring*, 71–74.

Word, sacrament, and wise spiritual counsel that directs attentiveness toward God is what pastors are called to do. The failure to do so makes burnout and moral failure imminent.

For others, the success god is wrapped up in their vision, sometimes closely aligned with a desire for fame. Pastors who move from church to church seeking to find one that gets their "vision," and who often leave in anger because after six months the congregation did not "get it," need to hear the stern warning of Dietrich Bonhoeffer. He called the process in which one person inflicts a vision on a congregation something "God hates":

> It makes the dreamer proud and pretentious. The man who fashions a visionary ideal of community demands that it be realized by God, by others, and by himself. He enters the community of Christians with his demands, sets up his own law, and judges the brethren and God himself accordingly. He stands adamant, a living reproach to all others in the circle of brethren. He acts as if he is the creator of the Christian community, as if his dream binds men together. When things do not go his way, he calls the effort a failure. When his ideal picture is destroyed, he sees the community going to smash. So he becomes, first an accuser of his brethren, then an accuser of God, and finally the despairing accuser of himself.[22]

It is not that a particular vision for how the missional life of God is to be manifest in a particular church is not important. The contemplative approach to pastoring sometimes neglects the missional character of God and the missional identity of the church and each member of the church. A true contemplative is also a true "active." Missional identity makes the church both deep *and* wide. I do expect healthy churches to grow. The challenge for pastors who have traded the true calling for a mess of pottage is that they do not first see that "God has already laid the only foundation of our fellowship," and thus they do not see themselves as "thankful recipients" of the community and the resident vision already there.[23] Deep within their souls, the god replacing God is someone they need to prove themselves to, or receive affection of approval from. Their souls have yet to be formed with a robustness that can come only from God, and that persists whether their church is "successful" or not.

---

22. Bonhoeffer, *Life Together*, 27–28.
23. Bonhoeffer, *Life Together*, 27.

Underlying these preoccupations, then, are idols of a more subtle kind: people and their approval. The popularly cited temptations of the pastorate—money, sex, and power—all have their allure, and pastors have a particular vulnerability to all three. However, the deeper issue is the displacement of God by people who must be pleased, and the consequences when this desire becomes insatiable. I can attest to the presence of this temptation in my ministry life. As well as the vague sense that I must please the people who were paying my salary, there was in each church I served a particular person who featured in my conscious and unconscious thought far too much. God was not big in my soul because these people were big in my psyche. They could be politically powerful people who opposed the visionary direction of the church, or just attractive people of the opposite sex.

I will never forget what one of my favorite seminary professors, church historian John Hannah, said about ambition. He shared that his greatest ambition was to raise children who would have a strong enough sense of worth that they could be called to work as missionaries in a remote village somewhere and not ever be known. That kind of robust formation is what paying attention to the first commandment does.

The temptations that immediately preceded Jesus's public ministry were largely to do with this first commandment. Its negative assertions are implicit, and then its positive statement is explicit in Jesus's final rebuttal of Satan. "Command these stones" was an invitation to the abuse of power for his own ends. It was above all an invitation to distrust the God who by his word would preserve and strengthen him in his intense season of intimate prayer through fasting. Divided hearts look for a shortcut to appearing spiritual without making the sacrifices involved in really being spiritual people. "Throw yourself down" was an invitation to the spectacular, from the "pinnacle of the temple," a place Jesus did not aspire to, but one that none too subtly depicts the dangers of pastoral leadership when idols or "glittering images" prevail.[24] This is the way of pandering to popularity grounded on gimmicks, a shortcutting of the cross and the cost of discipleship, promises of prosperity grounded in faulty misinterpretations of Scripture. "Fall down and worship me" is the devil's last resort, the call for Jesus to break the first commandment in the plainest terms. It is the shocking place in which pastors may find themselves after

---

24. This is a reference to Susan Howatch, *Glittering Images*, a novel that describes the spiritual hubris and seductions of power in the life of the bishop of the fictional Starbridge Cathedral. It is a must read for all pastors.

repeated compromise. It is the result of years of professing a spirituality they did not truly own, of having a sphere of influence that was larger than their character. It is the stunning realization that their self-worship has in fact become a form of enslavement to the deceiver himself. Jesus rebukes this with the positive form of the first commandment, which we now consider.

Pastoral Applications of the Positive Commandment

The *positive statements* of this commandment make it clear that a mere profession of monotheism is not what is in mind. If the turning from idols is to be made with passion, so much more is the zeal and single-mindedness of the turning to one true God. This positive version may be expressed as *to love God alone with one's whole being, and to do so not just by profession, but by obeying his commandments*. Bockmuehl comments that there "is a remarkable affinity between the Old Testament and the writings of John (cf. Jn. 14:15; 15:10)," the common theme being that loving God means keeping his commandments. However, nowhere is this first commandment in its positive "love God" aspect more powerfully illustrated and fulfilled than in Jesus's quotation of it in his temptation by Satan: "Worship the Lord your God, and serve him only" (Matt 4:10).

What then does this commandment mean for pastors? First, pastors must live in the posture of receptivity to the love of God in order to be able to love God in a maturing way. They must live into grace-filled practices that facilitate this. Our human love for God is a response to prior divine love, love that births love in us and that nurtures love in us so that we may minister out of love rather than the many other possible motivations that may drive a pastor into and in the ministry. To love God, we must live in constant awareness of his love, in a posture of receptivity to his love, in communion with the one who is love. Living the life of receptiveness to the love of God leads to love of God and love of neighbor. By this cycle, John tells us that "God lives in us and his love is made complete in us" (1 John 4:12). As I have stressed already, the commandments are not given so that Yahweh might be the God of his people. They are given because he is already their Creator, their covenant-keeping and redeeming God. The commandments are in response to acceptance, not for gaining acceptance.

This is without doubt the most crucial soul issue for pastors (and Christians). Congregations know whether they are loved by their pastors or are just a guinea pig for their unbridled ambition, the root of which is often an inability to receive and believe they are loved by God. The pastorate can function so easily as a place to work out broken relationships. This is why many spouses in a marriage to a pastor feel as if the church is the mistress in the relationship, a third person that makes for, as Princess Diana once quipped, a "crowded" marriage.

This may reflect in the pastor a hunger to attain the approval of a father, for example. If the church becomes a father substitute, it will demand his every waking second and yet never deliver the approval and love the pastor longs for. Ultimately, the only person who can deliver this kind of love is the Father in heaven. He has done so in Jesus, who, when he received the approbation of his Father at his baptism, received our approval vicariously for us. Jesus received the Father's love and was grounded deeply into his identity, named as the "beloved Son." We too at our baptisms were named in the name of the Father and of the Son and of the Holy Spirit (Matt 28), and find our identity in the Beloved One, in whom we also are the beloved of God. The possibility of finding the acceptance and approval of an earthly father or mother through asking for it, or through a counseling process, is always a good thing. However, the ultimate solution is to saturate oneself with the love of the Father in heaven, in his Son, and though the gracious work of the Holy Spirit. Many people who have been abused by their fathers will ultimately heal their broken images as they encounter the real Father.

This saturation and healing happens, on the one hand, through faithfulness in reading and hearing the word of God as the *first* priority of the day, in keeping with this commandment, which is about priority. I am not speaking of reading to create sermons. I am not speaking even of a Bible-reading program. I believe in disciplined Bible reading, and I do not discourage such reading in a day when it seems that there are very few Bible readers in the church. I began a Bible-reading habit at the age of fourteen at my father's prompting and read the Bible through each year until my mid-thirties. I cannot estimate how important this was in preparing me as a pastor and theologian. However, there is another kind of Bible reading in which one reads to encounter and receive the presence and love of God. It begins with the invitation for God to speak. It is a reading and rereading with attentiveness to what God may be saying through a phrase or sentence. It is accompanied by meditating on what

God has spoken, leading into contemplation, where all of a sudden the presence and love of God are sensed. This prayer, reading and rereading attentively, meditation, and contemplation is called *lectio divina*, which is an ancient tradition. I practiced this before I knew it had a name.

In addition to faithfulness in reading and in other spiritual practices, formation and healing in the love of the Father may come in undeserved and surprising ways. As an illustration, my family had for thirteen years a bright little border collie. We estimate she knew over a hundred human words. I often went on bike rides with her in suburbia without any fear even though she was unleashed. But she would nuzzle up with her cold nose time and again, and she would also come back repeatedly on a walk looking for an approving pat. My wife, seeing that I would often just push her away, would say, "Honey, she just wants to love you." She just wanted to be by me and with me, but her unconditional faithfulness was difficult for me to receive. She was for me in a small way an echo of the Father's love. It wasn't until she died that I realized how much I loved that dog, and I wept sorely when she was put down. We have difficulty receiving love, it seems.

My own story uncovers a good deal of drivenness. I have loving parents who went to Angola as missionaries from Scotland at the age of twenty-two and twenty-three. They are my heroes. They made sacrifices in the cause of the gospel. When I was six, they sent me to boarding school in Zambia, as missionaries did, and for eight months of the year I was separated from them by five hundred miles. I do not remember a great deal of the life there, but I do remember harsh discipline being handed out from a volatile headmaster. It seems that the bonding with my parents was fractured, and I suppose the child in me vowed never to get close to them again for fear I would be separated again. After two years of this, we went home to Scotland on furlough, and I was for the rest of my schooling in Scotland and Zimbabwe (then Rhodesia) always at day schools.

It was not until my early thirties that this caught up with me. I had completed one year of seminary and then a PhD in chemistry, and then entered pastoral ministry. The drive to succeed was fueled first by a fear that, having given up a career in chemistry, I would look rather silly if I failed at ministry. It was fueled, second, by my unresolved relationship with my dad. A great dad in many ways, he was typically Scottish and stoic. I had never heard the words "I love you" from him. I had often heard him say if I got 95 percent on a test, "Where was the other 5 percent?" I probably craved his approval but was actually doing something he disapproved—he wanted me to be a chemistry professor and minister as a lay preacher in his denomination, but I wanted to be a preaching pastor. I was so driven by the approval of the people in the church and the desire for success defined by church growth that after two years I experienced a significant clinical depression. My wife had grown tired of trying to prop me up and withdrew emotionally from me. This loss plunged me deep into depression. I was cared for by a great psychiatrist, who suggested that this loss was in fact the trigger for entering into the losses of my childhood, which I had up to that point not explored or even thought of as relevant. I went through two years of intensive therapy and good medication. Having worked through a great deal of the loss and pain and anger, I began to be more in touch, more emotionally intelligent, more in tune with the brokenness of others, more receptive to love, more holistic in worship.

One incident serves to illustrate one of the mysterious and undeserved experiences of the love of God. My wife had become ill and was bedridden. We had two young children. All day I had battled the "Monday blues" that often assail preachers, on top of the more generalized depression. There had been no Bible reading and prayers that morning, as I was too busy getting the kids to school. I had done the housework, made dinner, got the washing on, put the kids to bed, and went off to get some groceries. I was in a very angry space. Every traffic light on the way seemed to turn at the wrong moment. The line for the grocery clerk was very long, and she was slow. Swear words filled my consciousness, even if I did not say them out loud. Finally, I got the groceries bagged and plonked them in my trunk. I jumped into the car and noticed as I drove away that there was a tape of worship songs and hymns on the passenger seat. I thought, *The last thing I want to do right now is listen to worship music*, but something made me put it in. The words I heard were those of a hymn: "Loved with everlasting love, led by grace that love to know. Spirit breathing from above, Thou hast taught me it is so. Oh what full and perfect peace, Oh what rapture all divine, In a love which cannot cease, I am his and he is mine. His forever, only His, who the Lord and me shall part."[25]

As I listened, I began to weep. I was feeling the love of God in a way I never had before. Sure, I knew the theology of love, but this was

---

25. "Loved with Everlasting Love," lyrics by George Wade Robinson.

something visceral and emotional and deep. I cried all the way home—this was the first time I had ever cried as an adult—and when my wife saw me she asked what was wrong. I said, "Nothing is wrong. Nothing has ever felt so right." I was overwhelmed by a gracious outpouring of the Father's love, and I had a profound sense of his voice, saying, "Through all you went through as a child, I was always there with you. My outpoured love in Jesus is always going to carry you through all that may be ahead." When I shared this event with the psychiatrist, she commented, "And do you see that you received this experience of God's love on the day you least deserved it?"

We cannot predict or even expect these experiences, and especially we cannot merit them. The faithful practices by which we participate in the love of the triune God and receive his love may or may not yield profound experiences of the love of God. They do restore our souls in ways we may not even discern, but seeking them too much becomes banal and self-centered. At the same time, when we are unexpectedly moved by the felt presence of God, we must treasure these moments and express gratitude for deep things God does to help us really believe and more fully receive his love. This is the core of ministry for the pastor. If we cannot receive the love of God, we cannot express it. If you have "left your first love," as the church at Ephesus had (Rev 2:4 NASB), the remedy is to draw near to God, to commune within his triune communion, and so to minister with love to your congregation and to your near and distant neighbors.

This means pastors should regularly engage in practices to express the passionate turning toward God, for receiving the love of God and expressing it back to him. Religious affections require to be ordered in the hearts of pastors by the love and holiness of God encountered in the life of communion with him. They are ordered through ecclesial practices—the life of worship, regularly feeding on Christ in the Lord's Supper, and the hearing of the word of God. Pastors who never hear the preaching of others run the great risk of spiritual starvation, of running on empty, of dampened affections for Christ and his people. Pastors who do not find ways to be in the church like a normal Christian already signal the hubris that they are different from other people. They are ordered also through personal practices, the reading of the word systematically and through *lectio divina*, prayer, friendships, silence, solitude, and Sabbath. At the core of these disciplines must be the receiving of divine love by the Spirit. Love is the core for the development of all the virtues, as noted in 2 Pet 1;

John 14; Rom 5; and Gal 5:22–23. These practices are not for achieving, but for receiving. They are spaces for grace.

THE SECOND COMMANDMENT

You shall not make for yourself an idol in the form of anything in heaven above or on the earth beneath or in the waters below. You shall not bow down to them or worship them; for I, the Lord your God, am a jealous God, punishing the children for the sin of the fathers to the third and fourth generation of those who hate me, but showing love to a thousand [generations] of those who love me and keep my commandments.

EXODUS 20:4–6

This commandment is not so much about rivals to the supremacy of God as it is about *incorrectly representing the one true God*. It is about not worshiping the one true God in the same way that the heathen nations did by making representations of their gods. Deuteronomy 12 is devoted to the exposition of this theme: "You must not worship the Lord your God in their way" (12:4). He will not be represented by spatially limited and aesthetically inadequate objects crafted by humans. This preserves and protects the invisible character and incomparability and transcendence of God. It is a commandment against the materialization of God and earthly localization of God. It is a protection of the transcendence of God.

The context here is clearly one of idol worship, and this commandment should not be inappropriately used to condemn art forms that depict Jesus. The commandment is referring to idols, things crafted for the purpose of representing God and in order to worship God, not icons that are to be looked *through* in order to see God and evoke worship. The primary applications to the Christian life and that of the pastor have to do with people's projections of God that are often projections of their own psyche.

This theme forms one of the central messages of the book of Malachi. A key revelation of that prophecy is the unchanging nature of God, and in particular of his love: "I the Lord do not change" (Mal 3:6). The returned exiles engage in disputations with God throughout this prophecy that reveal a number of false projections of what Yahweh was really like, and that lead them to seek to worship God in their own way. For example, after the Lord declares his love for them in 1:2 they ask, "*How have you loved us?*" In Mal 1:6—2:9, the disputation of the priests in particular conveys doubt about the fatherhood of God, and they demonstrate their distortion of the character of the Father in their offering of damaged sacrifices. As a result, they receive the discipline of the curses associated with the covenant of God. He always keeps his end of the covenant, and when his people do not, they are still in covenant but must endure the curses of the covenant. They despised his name by offering polluted sacrifices, and they paid the price.

After stating categorically that he does not change (3:6), Yahweh pleads for the people of God to return to him, and they cynically say, "How are we to return?" This leads to exposure of their robbing of God by withholding tithes and offerings. God's heart was set toward blessing them, but they misread his heart. In 3:10–12 readers reach one of the high points of the book: "'Bring the whole tithe into the storehouse, that there may be food in my house. Test me in this,' says the Lord Almighty, 'and see if I will not throw open the floodgates of heaven and pour out so much blessing that there will not be room enough to store it.'" This reflects the true disposition of God, which is that he is for his people, that he longs to bless us.

Doubt about the unchanging nature of the love of God is a common issue for the Christian, including pastors who compare their church, their "success," and their lot in life to others and feel resentful. It is easy to project that God has forgotten us or failed to notice our sacrifices. This is what happened with the person who was given one talent in Jesus's parable in Matt 25:24–25: "'Master,' he said, 'I knew that you are a hard man, harvesting where you have not sown and gathering where you have not scattered seed. So I was afraid and went out and hid your gold in the ground. See, here is what belongs to you.'" The servants who were truly fruitful in this story were those with an accurate understanding of the heart of the Father. There are pastors who believe in and practice an economy of plenty in their personal ministry and their view of the ministry of the church, and there are those who function on the basis of an economy of scarcity that is largely determined by their perception of the character of their Father in heaven.

We should not imagine from this that there are direct correlations between earthly prosperity and the pleasure of God. The point is that in this life and in the new creation, God will superabundantly reward his people who give faithfully and serve him sacrificially. When he hears

Jesus's kingdom reversal of values about the rich and the poor in Mark 10, Peter expresses concern over whether all his sacrifices as a disciple might be noticed and acknowledged: "We have left everything to follow you!" (v. 28). Jesus's response is unequivocal: "Truly I tell you . . . no one who has left home or brothers or sisters or mother or father or children or fields for me and the gospel will fail to receive a hundred times as much in this present age: homes, brothers, sisters, mothers, children and fields—along with persecutions—and in the age to come eternal life. But many who are first will be last, and the last first."

How does this change in our hearts? How are we formed and transformed to have an accurate perception of the fatherhood of God, especially when that perception may have been formed by the experience of earthly fathers and mothers who were less than generous and maybe downright abusive?

The same practices mentioned already for receiving the love of God apply here again. Reading Scripture under the guidance of the Holy Spirit reveals what the Father is truly like. We encounter the Father's love by means of the indwelling Holy Spirit, as Rom 8 indicates: "The Spirit you received brought about your adoption to sonship. And by him we cry, '*Abba*, Father.' The Spirit himself testifies with our spirit that we are God's children" (8:15–16). Most of us need healing for our false projections of the Father by means of the deep work of the Spirit within us that will cause us to cry out, "Daddy." This is a sovereign work of the Spirit, yet it does not eliminate our agency or the need for practices that prepare the way for a fresh work of the Spirit. Liturgical and musical worship can be instruments for these revelations that correct our minds and warm our hearts. This is crucial to the formation of a pastor. Keeping in step with the Spirit implies being in tune with what the Spirit of the Father and the Son communes to our spirits.

For pastors, living in the consciousness of the presence of God who sees us, knows our work, and will surely reward it with superabundant generosity forms us to be joyful in ministry. Laboring on a performance treadmill to please a God who is always looking to find fault is crippling. There is something deeply incongruous about a pastor with a legal spirit purporting to preach good news. If our whole message is evangelical, we must live and serve and preach evangelically. The tone of that gospel is one of "an inexpressible and glorious joy" (1 Pet 1:9), even when circumstances may be very difficult (1:6–7).

How does one become formed to see God as he really has revealed himself to be, a God of infinite gospel generosity, and therefore to have an irrepressible and defiant joy? In one of the churches I served there was a very perceptive elder. If I was running myself ragged in ministry leadership concerns and neglecting renewal time in the presence of God, he would somehow see it in my face. And he would come to me and ask, "Have you been in the tent lately?" He was of course referring to Joshua and Moses in Exodus 33–34. Moses would spend time in the tent until his face shone, and he would go out to meet and minister to the people with a face that shone so much he had to cover it. Then he would return to the tent for renewal in the place of communion with Yahweh. Joshua, the leader in formation, "did not leave the tent" (33:11).

The practice of contemplative prayer in communion with God is crucial for replenishing the sense of who God really is, who he is for us, and the joy that comes from this. Discovering prayer as a participation in the prayers of our great high priest by the enabling of the Holy Spirit to a loving Father makes prayer joyful, not legal. Prayer is not my ungraced response to God's goodness, but a graced entry into the communion already and always going on in the Trinity. One cannot help but be formed joyfully by such praying. The message of the second commandment is that the invisible, ineffable God requires spiritual worship in spirit and in truth (John 4:24), and freedom or bondage depends on our response to it. Blessedness or true happiness flows from true worship of the one true God.

The practice of joyful tithing is also crucial in the life of the pastor. I spent too many years as a pastor believing I was immune from tithing and giving offerings on top of my service in ministry. The joy of making the first expenditure of the month my tithe brought great joy, and it had an effect on our whole budgeting process. God provided in so many ways, because he is faithful. "God loves a cheerful [hilarious, joyful] giver" (2 Cor 9:7), and that includes pastors. Being a pastor does not exclude you from being a Christian, as Howard Hendricks used to say.

THE THIRD COMMANDMENT

You shall not misuse the name of the Lord your God, for the Lord will not hold anyone guiltless who misuses his name.

Exodus 20:7

Applying the method of Calvin to the third commandment (that is, considering the positive implied in the negative as this is expounded in the Old and New Testaments), the meaning of the third commandment may be summarized as: God commands us to revere and to honor and to worship his Name. Significantly, in the first phrase of the Lord's Prayer, the Lord Jesus expressed the third commandment: "Our Father in heaven, *hallowed* be your name" (Matt 6:9). To *hallow* is to revere, to be in awe of. It is to pray, to praise God, to worship him as he really is. Like the first two commandments, the positive comes under the broad heading of loving God.

The negative form in the Old Testament, "You shall not misuse the Name of the Lord [Yahweh] your God [Elohim]," was principally a prohibition of using the name of God to curse or blaspheme, which meant not merely using the name to curse, but using it casually or irreverently (Lev 24:10–16). It was also a prohibition of taking oaths falsely, of pretending to tell the truth when an oath in God's name has been taken (Lev 19:12). It also included empty prayers, invoking God carelessly, "where we reel off pious words while our minds are elsewhere."[26] Within Judaism, fear of misusing the name of God led to an ethics of avoidance that went well beyond the intent of the Old Testament understanding of this commandment. At a certain point, the Lord's name (YHWH with vowels supplied, translated as "Lord" in the NIV) was discouraged from being vocalized. "Adonai" (translated as "Lord" in the NIV) was to be used instead. There are evidences of this in the ancient Greek translation of the Hebrew Old Testament, the Septuagint (LXX), which translates Lev 24:10–16 as though the crime is speaking the name "Yahweh." This was overscrupulous and robbed Israelites of the opportunity of the positive fulfillment of the commandment, which is to extol, honor, and worship the name of the Lord!

In the New Testament, Jesus was accused of breaking this commandment in John 5:18 when he called God his Father and thereby made himself equal with God. This commandment was also in the background when Jesus spoke about the seriousness of the blasphemy of the person of the Holy Spirit (Matt 12:31–32). This passage gives clear evidence of the deity of the Spirit, which adds weight to the fact that the Spirit is called the "Spirit of Yahweh" many times in the Old Testament, and the "Lord who is the Spirit" in the New (2 Cor 3:17–18). The particular severity of

---

26. Bockmuehl, *Christian Way of Living*, 65.

blasphemy of the Spirit must be understood perhaps first in light of the fact that he is the underemphasized person of the Trinity, who delights to reveal Christ rather than speak of himself. Therefore, Jesus demands special honor. Second, blasphemy of the Spirit characterizes a heart that has been habitually hardened beyond redemption. A person of sensitive disposition who fears this sin need not worry that they may be guilty of it.

Why was God so concerned about his name? A name represents the identity of the person and their character in Hebrew and biblical culture and revelation. God's name represents who God is. He is holy, he is sovereign, and his name rightly and only ever deserves reverence and awe. The names or titles given to God in the Bible reveal much about his character—who he is, what he is like, and what he does. When the Bible uses the phrase the "name of God" or "in the name of the Lord," it refers to his total person—all that he is. And God's name is excellent and majestic (Ps 8:1).

Pastoral Applications of the Negative Commandment

Here are two applications for Christians and pastors of this negative aspect of the commandment. First, even within church culture, it is common to hear Christians treating the name of God or Jesus casually when they say, "Oh my God" or "OMG," or when they use mutilations or euphemisms of God's name such as "Jeez" or "gosh." These are unwitting but nevertheless real manifestations of our proneness to disobey this commandment, and our need of repentance. I have often wondered when I hear people blaspheming why they do so at a deep psychological or unconscious level. Is it an expression of our innate defiance and rebellion against the God that, according to Paul in Romans 1:20, all humans are conscious of? Is it an emotional and verbal instinctive expression of the "suppression" of the truth about the reality of the existence of God that we are all unconsciously aware of? In our culture, people tend not to blaspheme using the names of the gods of other religions. Is this perhaps because only the one true God is in our deep human consciousness? As pastors being formed and seeking to form others, we want to make sure that instead of the stench of what God hears emanating from the mouth of millions every day, he will hear honoring words from us about him and the fragrant aroma of his praise instead. The positive meaning of this commandment is to be characterized as those who "call on his name" in prayer and who worship his name in praise.

Second, it is easy in the pastoral life to develop a grumbling, ungrateful, and angry spirit when surrounded by pervasive cultural ingratitude and blasphemy. Cultivating the habit of gratitude to the name above all names is very important in the Christian life. My colleague at Regent College Darrell Johnson has a habit of writing down twenty things he is grateful for every morning. Adopting a similar habit will change our brain chemistry (to put it scientifically) or (to put it theologically) transform our dispositions. Ephesians speaks of the Spirit-filled life in precisely these habitual terms: "always giving thanks to God the Father for everything, in the *name* of our Lord Jesus Christ" (Eph 5:20).

Pastoral Applications of the Positive Commandment

Positively speaking, obeying the third commandment means to honor, praise, and reverently invoke the name of God, the God of Abraham, Isaac, and Jacob, who is revealed in the New Testament as the God and Father of our Lord Jesus Christ. It is the reverent and abject adoration of created human persons for a personal God who is fundamentally relational and essentially loving in his triune being. It is the reverence and adoration of failing, fickle, and sinful human beings who have been brought by grace into covenant relationship with a God who is unchanging in nature and abidingly faithful to his covenant. It is the reverence and loving adoration of children for a loving Father. Its positive version has the same outcome as the first two commandments, which is to love the Lord with our whole being. It is to honor and invoke specifically the name of the Lord Jesus for salvation (Joel 2:32; Rom 10:13; John 1:12; Acts 4:12; 1 Cor 6:11).

There is something particularly profound with respect to naming that grounds our identity as believers and pastors in God's identity. This is expressed in our baptism *into the name* of the Father, the Son, and the Holy Spirit (Matt 28:18–20) and our confession of that name. There is a profound linking of our baptisms and that of Jesus. The humanity of Jesus, God made man for us, was vicarious, and that includes his baptism. His baptism was that moment in the beginning of his ministry when the Father pronounced his identity. This is the only occasion in all of divine revelation when all three persons of the Trinity are visibly or audibly present: "As soon as Jesus was baptized, he went up out of the water. At that moment heaven was opened, and he saw the Spirit of God descending like a dove and alighting on him. And a voice from heaven said, 'This is my Son, whom I love; with him I am well pleased'" (Matt 3:16–17). When we are baptized into the name of the Trinity, we are participating in the baptism of Jesus. When we are baptized and live the baptized life, we enter into our core identity as sons and daughters in the Son, children in the Elder Brother (Heb 2:11–13), joint heirs with Christ the beloved Son (Eph 1:5). We have received the Father's affirmation in Christ's affirmation vicariously.

Issues of identity can plague us as pastors. The third commandment is about knowing who God really is and who we really are in Christ. How we were parented, how many moves we made as a child, where we are in the family birth order—all these and many other factors can affect our sense of self. Congregations, elders, deacons, and politically powerful people may subtly influence us to be what they want us to be. I am not against accountability of pastors to leaders in the church; in fact, it is vital. However, it is crucial to know who you are and not to allow yourself to be the victim of the winds and waves of public opinion. I have seen pastors who were empty shells, who somehow lost themselves trying to please people. Know the name, and know your name in his name.

A major application of the third commandment is prayer in the name of the Lord Jesus that honors the name of God. The way Jesus prayed as described in the Gospels is intended to be the pattern for our praying. He is, after all, our great high priest, and we are his holy and royal priesthood. There is a great emphasis in Jesus's praying on the fatherhood of God. He addresses God as "Abba" (Mark 14:36; John 17). He is constantly refreshed as a man in his identity as the Son in relation to the Father by his prayers. And when we pray, it is not surprising that we also cry out "Abba" (Rom 8:15; Gal 4:6). The life of prayer is where the pastor ultimately restores a fractured identity and solidifies it in relation to the Father. It may well be that pastors, like other people, need counseling to recover from childhood wounds that fractured a sense of identity. However, the efficacy of that experience depends ultimately not on the counselor, but on the gracious work of the Spirit, who can use this intimate form of community (what counseling really is) to restore a sense of Abba in the soul. We reap the benefit of wise counsel most on our knees in the presence of the Father.

An aspect of the soul of the pastor that is linked to identity in the name is self-hatred. There has been a tendency sometimes within warped versions of Christian spirituality to assume self-hatred is a good thing. Self-hatred is *not* a Christian virtue. It is a blasphemy of the name of the God who created you and every human being with absolutely unique DNA. It is a dishonoring of the name of the Son, who thought you were worth enough that he died for you. It is a dishonoring of the Holy Spirit, who has watched over your journey from preconception all the way until now, who has regenerated you, who has gifted you with precious charisms, who is guiding your story and crafting your character. Traditions that emphasize our sinfulness and depravity are prone to confusing hatred of our sin and practices that seek to mortify it with hatred of the self. God gave you a name, and with it a personality and character, and so love what God has given humbly but with assurance. Robust character and identity gives you the power to give your self away in a healthy way. People who are secure in their identity, who know their name, do not think less of themselves; they think of themselves less.[27] Darlene Fozard Weaver gets to the heart of the matter when she affirms that "the right self-love designates a morally proper form of self-relation characterized by the moral norms of love for God and neighbor."[28]

In John 13, Jesus was about to wash his disciples' feet and then go on to the ordeal of the cross. Strikingly, none of the disciples were able to give themselves to the other. Another Gospel suggests they were arguing on the way to this supper about who was the greatest of them. They had too much to prove and so were not free to serve. Fragile identities led to standing on dignities. Only Jesus washed feet that day. Why? Because he knew who he was. He had nothing to prove, so he was free to serve. Notice his orientation toward the Father as he faces the cross: "Jesus knew that the hour had come for him to leave this world and *go to the Father*" (John 13:1a). And notice his selfless concern for his disciples: "Having loved his own who were in the world, he loved them to the end" (John 13:1b). And notice Jesus's firm understanding of his identity: "Jesus knew that the Father had put all things under his power, and that he had come from God and was returning to God; so he got up" (13:3–4).

---

27. C. S. Lewis stated, "The real test of being in the presence of God is, that you either forget about yourself altogether or see yourself as a small, dirty object." See Lewis, *Mere Christianity*, 125.

28. Weaver, *Self-Love and Christian Ethics*, 91.

The concepts of identity and proper self-love can be difficult for Western evangelicals, some of whom may have been taught to be wary of any introspection. It can also be confusing because of the Western trinitarian doctrine of God that has emphasized God's unity and neglected God as persons-in-relation. It is made even more difficult by our contemporary pop-psychological cultural obsession with loving oneself, which is idolatrous. C. S. Lewis speaks to the heart of this confusion. It is not that Christians are being encouraged to love the self only to a certain degree. Rather, Lewis said, "There are two kinds of self-hatred that look rather alike at the early stages, but of which one is wrong from the beginning, and the other right to the end." The first un-Christian self-hatred leads to a poor view of all people. "When Shelley speaks of self-contempt as the source of cruelty, or when a later poet says that he has no stomach for the man 'who loathes his neighbor as himself,' they are referring to a very unreal and very un-Christian hatred of the self." The second, appropriate "Christian self-hatred" is a hatred of the preference for independence, or of the "flesh" or sin, which taints every aspect of the person. "The Christian," writes Lewis, "must wage endless war against the clamour of the *ego* as *ego*." Yet this is compatible with a concurrent love and acceptance of the self as God's good creation. In summary, Lewis says that "the wrong asceticism torments the self: the right kind kills the self-ness."[29]

The Catholic theologian John Powell speaks incisively to the importance of this proper sense of self, which arises from a proper knowledge of God. This double knowledge is also spoken of by Calvin.[30] Powell observes that "fully 'human people' are 'their own persons.' . . . They do not bend to every wind which blows, that they are not at the mercy of all the pettiness, the meanness, the impatience and anger of others." He described a conversation between a man who responded very kindly to a rude newspaper man, and his friend, who asked, "Why are you so nice to him when he is so unfriendly to you?" The first man responded, "Because I don't want *him* to decide how I'm going to act."[31] These are timely words for pastors, who are often a scapegoat and convenient sinkhole for negative emotions.

Perhaps it was partly in response to this confusion between loving and renouncing the self that David Benner wrote a book titled *The Gift of Being Yourself*, where in the preface he begins, "It is a profound irony

29. Lewis, "Two Ways with the Self," 210–11.
30. Calvin, *Institutes*, 1.1.1.
31. Powell, *Why Am I Afraid to Tell You Who I Am*, 36.

to write a book promoting self-discovery to people who are seeking to follow a self-sacrificing Christ. It may well be that you fear that I have forgotten—or worse, failed to take seriously—Jesus's paradoxical teaching that it is losing our self that we truly find it (Matthew 10:39)."[32] Benner goes on to say that if Christians were to mistakenly reject their selves, they would also be inadvertently rejecting the fullness of the possibility of personally knowing God. All that would be left is a detached cognitive knowing of the structure of God and self—a very "thin" existence, indeed.

Having struggled most of my life with a broken sense of self, I have found healing in these affirmations, which I have tried to appropriate through prayer:

I am a child of God, and that is *relationship* with the Father;

I am a child of God, and that means I am a person-in-relation in union with and ensconced in the life of the triune God;

I am a child of God, and that is *identity*;

I am a child of God, and that means *affection*, for I am in the Son of his love;

I am a child of God, and that means *affirmation* in the Son in whom the Father delights, for he was affirmed vicariously for me;

I am a son of God (with all my sisters and brothers), and that means *heirship* of every spiritual blessing now and of the whole creation then;

I am a son of God, and that means I am an *image bearer* in the one who is the image of the invisible God, becoming more fully human every day.

Paradoxically, restoration and perspective on the self comes from the fulfillment of the third commandment, that is, through hallowing the name of the Father. Saturating oneself with the prayer of Jesus to his Father may be hugely helpful in forming us. It is a model of what it means to honor the Name. It does not begin with confession of sin, for that would attract attention right away to the self, even if in repentance. Instead, the prayer begins with God and the expression of the honor of his name. The Son expresses his consuming passion at the outset of that prayer. Through the cross and the redemption of the people who are his, his passion was first and foremost for the glorification of the Father: "Father, the hour has come. Glorify your Son, that Your Son may glorify You" (John

---

32. Benner, *Gift of Being Yourself*, 25.

17:1). The identity of the Son and the revelation of his glory is, in a trinitarian, coinherent way, wrapped up in the identity of the Father and his glorification by the Son. As we pray, honoring the name of the Father in the Son and by the Spirit, we enter into the trinitarian life even as we ask *in his name*: "I will do whatever you ask in my name, so that the Father may be glorified in the Son" (14:13). This is the trinitarian culmination of the third commandment.

The first three commandments, when considered in light of the gospel, are deeply searching and yet profoundly promising with respect to pastoral formation and the formation of the whole people of God. They inspire us toward loving God deeply through ecclesial and personal practices. They move us toward gratitude. They help us recover a sense of who we are in light of who God is. This will help us as we move into consideration of the fourth commandment, the Sabbath command, which tests us regarding whether we really trust God to be God and to be at work when we are not working. This formation around the identity and character of God in the first three commandments, and around finding rest in God in the fourth, will then prepare us for formation in the realm of family relations, with the ethics of life and death and of sexuality.

6

Moral Formation through the Sabbath (Commandment 4)

Remember the Sabbath day by keeping it holy. Six days you shall labor and do all your work, but the seventh day is a sabbath to the Lord your God. On it you shall not do any work, neither you, nor your son or daughter, nor your male servant or female servant, nor your animals, nor any foreigner residing in your towns. For in six days the Lord made the heavens and the earth, the sea, and all that is in them, but he rested on the seventh day. Therefore the Lord blessed the Sabbath day and made it holy.

Exodus 20:8–11

I do not know of an issue that affects the integrity of a pastor more than the issue of the Sabbath. Pastors are intended to equip the people of God for mission and ministry by modeling life patterns of rest and work, of depth and width with God and neighbor. They are meant to equip others to be holy priests to live deeply into the life of God through prayer and Sabbath, so that they can as royal priests mediate the presence of God and his rest to their worlds. Yet pastors' proneness to burnout, depression, and workaholism suggests a deep underlying problem. The statistics are concerning:

- 72 percent of pastors report working between fifty-five and seventy-five hours per week.
- 84 percent of pastors feel they are on call 24/7.
- 65 percent of pastors feel they have not taken enough vacation time with their family over the last five years.
- 80 percent believe pastoral ministry has negatively affected their families. Many pastors' children do not attend church now because of what the church has done to their parents.
- 70 percent of pastors report they have a lower self-image now than when they first started.
- 35 percent of pastors battle depression or fear of inadequacy.[1]
- 50 percent of pastors starting out will not last five years.
- 50 percent of pastors feel so discouraged that they would leave the ministry if they could, but have no other way of making a living.
- 71 percent of churches have no plan for a pastor to receive a periodic sabbatical.[2]

So, what is the solution to these challenges for today's church leaders? It must at minimum include one word: Sabbath, life-giving rhythms of work and rest around Sabbath. The regular practice of Sabbath enables us to live ethically in relation to God and to neighbor, for this commandment is a bridge between the love of God and the love of neighbor. Keeping Sabbath is not possible apart from loving and trusting *God* enough to cease working so as to rest in him, and people who live in the rest of God relate to their *neighbors* lovingly out of that rest. They rest and renew shalom so as not to project their unresolved inner conflicts onto their relationships. Rather, they are a source of shalom to their neighbor in all the aspects of life suggested by commandments five to ten.

---

1. It is unclear whether this means serious clinical depression and over what time period. If this does refer to clinical depression of various sorts, then the incidence of depression in pastors is significantly above the national average in the US, which is reported to be 7.1 percent for persons over eighteen in one year (2017). The average is higher for the age range eighteen to twenty-five, at 13.1 percent. See National Institute of Mental Health, "Major Depression."

2. Pastoral Care, "Statistics in the Ministry." Statistics are provided by the Fuller Institute, George Barna, Lifeway, Schaeffer Institute of Leadership Development, and Pastoral Care Inc. If, as suggested by Pastoral Care, thirty-five hundred people per day leave the church in the US, this might be one factor accounting for ministerial depression. There are multiple factors in this regard. One is failure to keep Sabbath.

Since burnout has been linked to erosion in pastoral ethics, Sabbath is a central ethical issue. And beyond the pastorate, Sabbath affects the whole work world, because the fourth commandment is as much about work as it is about rest. Imagine you could find a secret strategy that could enhance the creativity and productivity of employees, reduce the occurrence of burnout and depression, enhance job satisfaction, and increase the probability of longevity in the workplace. Such a strategy exists, and it is called the sabbath principle. The surprise is that it is a "do nothing" strategy, a "give me a break" strategy, or a "royal waste of time" strategy, as Marva Dawn has described it.[3]

A note about teaching on the Sabbath in the New Testament. Some might say that, according to Hebrews 3–4, the fourth commandment has been spiritualized. Others might say, "Doesn't Paul clinch the issue in Rom 14:5, where he makes the issue of observing religious days an issue of personal conscience?" In other words, practicing Sabbath seems to be in the *adiaphora* or nonessentials category. Against these, I suggest that entering into the rest of God does not happen in a gnostic, spiritual way apart from embodied practice of the Sabbath. And, although how and when one practices the Sabbath may be a matter of personal choice, obedience to the fourth commandment as *principle* is not optional, for reasons that will emerge in this chapter.

So let us look at the first phrase of the commandment (Exod 20:8): "Remember the Sabbath day."

A CALL TO KEEP SABBATH ... IN LIGHT OF ITS CLARIFIED ESSENCE

It is a call ... but to what? Strict rules about what I, and even animals, can and cannot do on Saturday—or is it Sunday now? I remember when my Aunt Sophia in Scotland bought us kids ice cream on a Sunday and told us to crouch down in the backseat of the car in case any elders of the church might see us eating it! You might have your own memories of legalistic adherence to Sabbatarian legalism. Or perhaps the movie *Chariots of Fire* (dir. Hugh Hudson) comes to mind, in which the runner Eric Liddell would not compete on Sunday. He said, "God made me fast, and I run for his pleasure," but also, we might wonder, "If that's true, why would God not take pleasure in that running if it happens on a Sunday?"

---

3. Dawn, *Royal "Waste" of Time*.

I want to make a case for preserving Sabbath keeping as a principle and not rules and casuistry. It is the call to be a nonsabbatarian Sabbatarian. It is adopting the creational practice of protecting and taking a day off a week, while also heading off a legalistic observance of a day of rest that has caused wrangling in some sectors of the church over which day is meant for the Christian and what people may or may not do on that day. We should avoid this kind of legalism while pointing to the creational, transcovenantal, renewing, life-giving, grace-filled practice of Sabbath, irrespective of the day of the week. In this chapter, I will offer guidelines for what such a day may look like.

At first glance, this commandment may look like a piece of ceremonial law that strayed into the moral law category.[4] Singling out a day for worship and service seems ritualistic. It can seem like confining God temporally in a way we would not think of doing spatially. Jesus's saying in Mark 2:27 that "the Sabbath was made for man, not man for the Sabbath" has led both moral relativists and antinomians to minimize all commandments of the Decalogue, protesting that there is no record of Sabbath keeping for the New Testament church.

Let me point out a number of facts in response to this question about the *importance* of this commandment. The first is that this commandment is long, just like the second. The second is that it is the only positively stated one of the Ten Commandments. The third is that in fact it is two commandments in one. It represents a theology and ethic of work as well as of rest or leisure. Verse 9 says, "Six days you shall *labor* and do all your *work*," and only then, "but the seventh day is a sabbath." This commandment is the right place for the discussion of an ethic of work because talk of rest has no meaning if there is not first talk of work. And the obverse is also true; it is reflection and rest on Sabbath that gives meaning to work. In fact, in the creation account of Gen 1–2, the cause-effect connection between work and rest is clear in the work of God: "By the seventh day God had finished the work he had been doing; so on the seventh day he rested from his work" (Gen 2:2). Sabbath is therefore part of a doctrine of creation. It is a creational principle grounded in the work-rest action of God himself. God rested because he had first worked, and worked to completion.

These factors indicate something of the importance of this commandment. However, above all it is the lexical meaning of the term

---

4. Bockmuehl, *Christian Way of Living*, 69.

"Sabbath" that establishes its relevance in all time, its transcendence of the covenantal eras. The meaning of the word is not Saturday or Sunday. It comes from the Hebrew verb "to rest." It means to "stop doing what one up to that point has been doing."[5] The inference is that if you give yourself a break you will be refreshed and renewed again for more work, whereas if you do not you are built such that you are likely to break down. As God rested, so must humans rest.

The word for Sabbath is related to the Hebrew term nephesh, "to breathe," which is also the root word for "soul." The Sabbath is a time to catch your breath, to take a breather. As God initially breathed into man the breath of life to make him a living soul, so Sabbath re-creates us as we take a breath again. With this re-creation comes refreshment. In Exod 23:12, where the Sabbath commandment is expounded in the book of the covenant, its purpose is defined in this way: "so that your ox and your donkey may rest, and so that the slave born in your household and the foreigner living among you may be refreshed." This is directly connected with the treatment of laborers and the economically disadvantaged. It thus becomes an "ethics of work" commandment. The meaning of Sabbath as rest suggests that it is a principle that transcends the era of the old covenant. Rest is needed in all seasons, and humans have been created in a cyclical fashion for all time. It is part of what it means to be human, to work and create and then to rest and recreate in order to be able to re-create. This is creational in its origin, not merely covenantal. It is not just being Jewish or even Christian.

Abraham Joshua Heschel, one of the most competent recent interpreters of the Jewish Sabbath, has suggested that Judaism has always been oriented more to time than to space. He describes Sabbath as the creation of hallowed time, "a palace in time." He affirms that "'the day of the Lord' is more important to the prophets than 'the house of the Lord.'" His interpretation of the Sabbath command is that it is grounded in the nature of humanity as created, and that as a wise respite it is the gift of a Creator who knows our limitations better than we know them ourselves.[6]

That God did not need to rest, in that he has inexhaustible resources of strength, adds further meaning to "Sabbath." It is not just the mere cessation of labor that is mandated for humans, because they are built to need restoration of strength. It is reflection and enjoyment of the work

---

5. Bockmuehl, *Christian Way of Living*, 70.
6. Heschel, *Sabbath*, 15, 20–21, 79.

that has been accomplished, what has been created. So Sabbath is rest for re-creation and, second, reflection. God certainly looked over all he made on each creation day, but at the end of six days he reflected for a day. He took delight in all that he had created. For the Old Testament people of God, Sabbath was anything but a day of dark dirges and rules. From its inception and as properly practiced, it was a day of refreshment and reflection, of community and joy! It was intended to be "a delight," according to Isa 58:13. It was gift. There is an apocryphal reference to Judith, who broke her widowhood fasting for the joy of the Sabbath (Jdt 8:6). A Jewish folksong says, "On the Sabbath, every Jew is a king and he feels like a new man."[7] The Jewish Sabbath began with a "joyful fellowship meal."[8] Of course, when Sabbath appears to change from Saturday to Sunday as resurrection day, then the joy theme is even more prominent.

This is something we twenty-first-century human beings do too little of: keeping Sabbath by reflecting on and celebrating what we have accomplished. In modernity, very few of us actually make things that we can look at and enjoy. We are often forced to reflect on and celebrate intangible things. We may create computer programs, and we should enjoy that as we reflect. We may achieve the selling of car or the winning of a contract, and we should reflect on that in rest in order to become re-created again. This is the meaning of Sabbath—and this is for all creation and for all time. We tend rather to want to press on to the next task.

This has great significance for pastors. Our work is intangible also. How can you measure the effects of a sermon or a discipleship conversation or a counseling session? This intangibility of pastoral work can create a sense of a lack of accomplishment and can justify our rationalizations for avoiding taking a Sabbath. The effects of our work will be revealed in a day to come, and in the meantime we must observe the law of our being, the creational principle of taking a day off.

I remember all too well the challenging nature of being a preacher. Sunday after Sunday I tried to do my best exegetical work and produce the best sermons possible. The sermon was barely delivered each week, and the brief euphoria of the postservice high was barely relished, when next week's sermon was already pressing. Even if I worked months ahead, there was still a worship-planning meeting on Tuesday, the review and then the planning. I took Mondays off, even if they could often be blue

---

7. Cited in Bockmuehl, *Christian Way of Living*, 72.
8. Bockmuehl, *Christian Way of Living*, 72.

Mondays.[9] I was barely functional when I got up, but after a morning of catching up with my wife and a game of squash in the early afternoon, I would feel somewhat human by dinnertime. I took time to reflect in prayer on what God had done, as far as I could discern it. I presented it back to God and tried to leave behind the darker feelings I was capable of. Even affirmations I had heard from people after the service could be twisted. If somebody said, "That was the best sermon I have ever heard you preach," I would wonder about all the other sermons prior to that! If somebody said I had knocked the ball out of the park, I would internalize that as pressure to knock the ball out of the park even further the next week. But with the rest and reflection and re-creation in God's presence, I would be recharged for another week of ministry.

A CALL TO KEEP SABBATH . . . IN LIGHT OF A COMPELLING RATIONALE

Note the orientation of the Sabbath suggested in Exod 20:10: "but the seventh day is a sabbath *to the Lord your God.*" And note the rationale expressed in verse 11: "For in six days the Lord made the heavens and the earth, the sea, and all that is in them."

The first rationale for Sabbath that is evident when it is introduced in the Old Testament is related to its meaning in a *creational* context. It arises from the creating history of God, in whose image we are made. Our work is part of the divine-human analogy from above. It has a motivation of reflecting the Creator. We are called to reflect not just on our own work, therefore, but on God's work, recognizing that we are vice-regents. It points us to God, who himself worked and then rested, and who also fashioned us in his image and calls us to be image bearers in both our work and our rest. Sabbath, therefore, has a contemplative worship orientation that transcends any merely legal motivation. It is a resting in the presence and rest of God. It is a re-creation and reflection with more than a purely human horizon; it is worship. This Godward orientation is critical to Sabbath keeping, in that taking Sabbath requires faith. We must believe that leaving our work for a day will not cause our work and our profits to suffer.

---

9. A common phenomenon for preaching pastors. Adrenalin buildup in anticipation of the sermon on Sunday is followed by a massive shutdown of adrenalin after the sermon, leading to a temporary sense of depression.

The second rationale that compels us toward Sabbath keeping is reflection on and participation in the divine *redemptive* work. This comes from the passage in Deuteronomy commanding the Sabbath: "Remember that you were slaves in Egypt and that the Lord your God brought you out of there with a mighty hand and an outstretched arm. Therefore the Lord your God has commanded you to observe the Sabbath day" (Deut 5:12–15). Sabbath is not just rest for physical and emotional refreshment. It also for reflection on the creative and redeeming activity of God. It has a *liberation* motif, linked to the liberation of Israel from Egyptian bondage, and anticipates the New Testament fulfillment of redemption (1 Cor 5:7). Sabbath is a rejoicing in the liberation of the Redeemer or "Re-Creator" God, the God of new creation, whose work in new creation was one of incarnational living and cross bearing. And the new moment of divine pleasure and cessation of work is resurrection Sunday. This is the new Sabbath. Sabbath is the symbol of and a means for the returning of humanity into the freedom and dignity of paradise, what was lost and has now been recovered in Christ. Sabbath is therefore spiritual; it is a call for humans to participate in God's rest. And it is missional, because those who are brought into redemption and re-creation are called on, in participation with Christ, to be agents of redemption for others in every aspect of life.

This is the key to understanding how Jesus interacted with the Sabbath. Jesus in his teaching and healing ministry was all about recovering the original intent of the Sabbath in light of the severe legalism and formalism that had developed around it. He did not trespass it. When his disciples picked grain in Mark 2 (cf. Matt 12), they did it because they were hungry, not because they were harvesting. That was in line with the refreshment purpose of the Sabbath. This helps us understand Jesus's comment: "The Sabbath was made for man, not man for the Sabbath" (Mark 2:27). When Jesus healed on the Sabbath, as he did on several occasions (Matt 3:1–6; Luke 13:10–17), he was fulfilling the restoration and liberation aspect of the Sabbath, which had been lost. He understood feeding and healing to be acts of sustaining and restoring creation. If they could untie animals on the Sabbath, he could liberate people from their diseases (Luke 13:15–16).

For this reason, Karl Barth called this commandment the entrance door to all the other commandments that have to do with the human neighbor, and the other six days, the days of work.[10] Sabbath has a ser-

---

10. "The Holy Day," in Barth, *Church Dogmatics III*, 47–72, here 71–72.

vice orientation. It is not just rest and reflection; it is worship of God, and it is service to neighbor. It is not just that by the Sabbath we recover and are once again useful to people after it. Rather, it is that we recover the sense of positive mission to people that Jesus anticipated: to do good, to save, to heal.

The importance of the order of the commandments becomes clear again in this context. Sabbath is preceded by the "God" commandments, which give it its Godward orientation, and is followed by the love-neighbor commandments, which are more likely to be obeyed and to be characterized by shalom if the rest, reflection, refreshment, contemplative worship, and active service dimensions of Sabbath are observed.

A further New Testament fulfillment of the Sabbath lies in the salvation history of Jesus. Redemption and creation must be kept together, for Christ's work is the redemption *of* creation. In a sense these two works are one. In Jesus's ministry and the book of Hebrews we get a sense that God in Christ had worked his redemptive work, that once again he rested as he had in the initial creation. Indeed, that rest after the initial creation may be considered in the mind of God to have been constituted by the rest that he could anticipate in the work of Christ.

Jesus is himself the Sabbath in Matt 11:28. Prefacing and determining the discussion of Sabbath that follows it, Jesus says, "Come to me, all you who are weary and burdened, and I will give you rest." This is unfolded in the New Testament in his person and work in the history is salvation. One could argue that his incarnation, life, and death is the work of the new creation, without which creation is not complete. Somehow the creation depicted as complete in Gen 2 is only retroactively complete through Christ (Heb 4:4). His work when finished brings in the true Sabbath rest of the people of God. It is enjoyed in the present to a measure, but only fully in the kingdom to come.

Hebrews 4 can only be understood within the whole argument of the book of Hebrews, and specifically within a christological perspective that creation and redemption are one act. Christ is the representative human who brings us into the rest of God spoken of in Gen 2. As divine Son (Heb 1) he became our fully human (Heb 2) great High Priest. By his vicarious obedience in life and his sacrificial death, he saves our lives and re-creates us as sons and daughters destined for glory (2:10). He carries our humanity to the throne, where he "sits" at rest (1:3; 8:1; 10:12; 12:2), having accomplished the atoning work his Father had given him to do. And he calls us in him as last Adam to enter the rest of God in an imitative way that reflects the identity of humans as image bearers: "There remains, then, a Sabbath-rest for the people of God; for anyone who enters God's rest also rests from their works, just as God did from his" (Heb 4:9–10). Our access to the presence of God (4:14–16; 10:19–21) enables us to enter his rest, which is not restricted to one day of the week.

But there is work to be done in entering into the rest of God. In Heb 4:11 the author exhorts, "Let us, therefore, *make every effort* to enter that rest." The means of entering into God's rest is devotion to the living and active Word of God, which penetrates the heart and searches for its sources of rest (vv. 12–13), and to prayer: "Let us then approach God's throne of grace with confidence, so that we may receive mercy and find grace to help us in our time of need" (v. 16). However, given the close connection between redemption and creation, it would seem feasible that this exhortation assumes the creational structure of observing Sabbath. Sabbath is a day for recovering experientially through the Word and prayer the rest that is always ours by virtue of Christ's sacrifice and session at the right hand of the Father. Certainly, John Calvin insisted that a distinction between the moral aspect of this commandment and the ceremonial aspect of it was not valid even in the New Testament era.[11] We need the creational, embodied practice of Sabbath to renew our experience of the rest of God each week.

The early church's apparent assumption of Sabbath as Sunday (Acts 17:2: "Sabbath"; Acts 20:7; 1 Cor 16:2) probably reflects its understanding of the salvation history of Jesus. He rose again on Sunday, and the Spirit came on Sunday. The church understood Christ's history as determinative. The church's pattern of Sunday Sabbath keeping according to the history of Jesus Christ enables us to recapture and reappropriate the rest he has accomplished for us, in our hearts, week by week. We do this especially as we participate in the word and feed on the Lord's Supper. The *ordo historia* (the order of the saving history) of Jesus becomes the *ordo salutis* (order of salvation) of his people. The resurrection dynamic is critical in this. Having completed the work of atonement on the cross, Jesus rises again and is exalted. His resurrection is critical to the re-creation process. He rises in a created body, and in him we are thereby representatively re-created. The resurrection of Christ reaffirms, vindicates, and fulfills the creation, and with it God's mandate that his image bearers should work and steward his good creation as well as rest.

---

11. Calvin, *Institutes of the Christian Religion*, 2.8.34..

They work with a sense of the resurrection life of God on them, and with the awareness that they are participating in the new creation.

A CALL TO KEEP SABBATH ... IN LIGHT OF ITS PROFOUND INTERIORITY

The negative statement of the commandment and its emphasis throughout the history of Israel tell us that there is more to this commandment than meets the eye: "On it you shall not do any work, neither you, nor your son or daughter, nor your male servant or female servant, nor your animals, nor any foreigner residing in your towns." Failure to observe the Sabbath was treated very seriously. In fact, the death penalty was invoked (Exod 31:14–15; 35:2–3; Num 15:32–36). Therefore, the Sabbath was not just gift. It was also test. It was a matter of life and death. This signals the seriousness of when humans attempt to be more than human. What is at stake here is the matter of whether one belongs to the covenant community or not. It is a faith issue that marks out those in covenant relationship with God, the redeemed from those who are not. Sabbath keeping and circumcision were the two primary signs of the covenant people of God in the Old Testament. Baptism has replaced the first in the new covenant, but practicing the rest of God is transcovenantal.

A primary burden of the major and minor prophets is the business of Sabbath. Its spiritual depth becomes apparent there (Isa 1:13–14; Jer 17:21–23; Amos 8:5). The failure to give the land Sabbath ultimately led God to give it an enforced Sabbath in the Babylonian exile. On the other hand, the highest eschatological promises are related to keeping the Sabbath. In fact, Isa 58 makes the full observance of Sabbath (rest, reflection, worship, service) the criterion for the spiritual renewal and revival of the nation: "If you call the Sabbath a delight and the Lord's holy day honorable, and if you honor it by not going your own way and not doing as you please or speaking idle words, *then* you will find your joy in the Lord, and I will cause you to ride on the heights of the land and to feast on the inheritance of your father Jacob" (Isa 58:13–14).

This explains the belief within later Judaism that "if Israel would only keep Sabbath once, the kingdom of God would come instantaneously."[12] But this also anticipates the primary gospel criterion of faith. The primary sign of the new-covenant people of God is whether they have entered

---

12. Cited in Bockmuehl, *Christian Way of Living*, 73.

into the rest of God by faith, and whether they demonstrate that authentically by living that by entering rest of God spiritually and through the embodied practice of practicing Sabbath. A life characterized by Sabbath discipline is a life that reflects interior Sabbath rest. Whether we enter into Sabbath is a defining test of how we view God. Do we take seriously our analogous relationality with him? Do we trust his work enough that we can rest in it? Will we then carry that rest into the other six days of our work lives? This commandment is certainly a critique of our spiritual state and of the way we live our lives. It is a reflection for pastors on whose work our work really is.

Let us keep Sabbath, therefore: as principle, not rule, but as principle nevertheless. This means entering into God's rest in our souls as a spiritual pursuit. It also means taking a Sabbath day to recover our enjoyment of that rest because of the creational rootedness of this command. What we do with that day should reflect re-creation through reflection and worship. Recreational activities for the body should also be included: service to the poor outside churchly duties; eating good meals we actually taste; taking walks to reconnect with creation; reading the word for nurture, not ministry; prayer as enjoyment of God's presence; listening to worshipful psalms, hymns, and spiritual songs; making love to our spouses.[13]

Matthew 11:29–30, which speaks of finding rest for our souls, teaches us that life in Christ should reflect the "easy yoke" of practicing Sabbath and all other spiritual disciplines in union and communion with Christ, who is our rest. If all Christians must live this easy yoke of practicing Sabbath, so too must pastors. In light of their work on Sunday, this means that pastors should take a Sabbath day other than Sunday. Pastors should also develop a larger sabbatical pattern, being renewed by substantial sabbaticals every seventh year. Above all, pastors and leaders in both the church and the marketplace can learn to live in the rest of God by means of these practices.[14]

In sum, Sabbath is gift, Sabbath is test, and Sabbath is task. We demonstrate the reality of faith and spiritual rest by practicing Sabbath in all its aspects: rest, recreation, reflection, worship, and service to fellow humans as we bring rest and recreation and liberation to them.

---

13. According to Mishnah Torah, Shabbat 30.14, "Sexual relations are considered a dimension of Sabbath pleasure."

14. A website that is helpful in this regard is run by Sandy and Brita Colero. See www.restedleaders.com, which provides an online community forum for pastors and their work-life balance.

The communal practice of Sabbath by the early church was recorded by Pliny, governor of Pontus and Bithynia, who wrote to the Emperor Trajan about early Christian observance of "Sunday Sabbath": "The Christians rose early to worship, held a holy meal, and promised each other to lead holy lives."[15] Sunday was a festive, purifying, and liberating experience for the early church. Its horizon is eschatological, and it therefore inspires hope. It anticipates the day when recovery and replenishment and healing will no longer be needed, and when the celebrations of worship will give way to an unending celebration "which our best Sunday services are but a taste of."[16]

A CALL TO KEEP SABBATH . . . IN LIGHT OF THE MEANING IT GIVES TO WORK

As mentioned above, this commandment is not just about rest; it is a seminal text for a theology and ethics of work. It looks *back* on a theology of work and rest suggested in the creation account in Genesis, as Exod 20:11 indicates: "For in six days the Lord made the heavens and the earth, the sea, and all that is in them, but he rested on the seventh day. Therefore the Lord blessed the Sabbath day and made it holy." God's pattern of work and rest is the paradigm for human work and rest. But the Sabbath commandment also flows *forward* in the biblical narrative into a fully trinitarian theology of work. This involves the purposes of work as personal, communal, and divine.

First, work imparts personal individuating significance for each of us according to our vocation. Work is one of the functional components of the image of God in each person, as is evident from the fact that when the first humans are pronounced as image bearers, they receive the command to act in ways that reflect God: "Then God said, 'Let us make mankind in our image, in our likeness, so that they may rule over the fish in the sea and the birds in the sky, over the livestock and all the wild animals, and over all the creatures that move along the ground'" (Gen 1:26). Work is part of the givenness of creation for each person. Human persons work just as God worked (the human is *homo faber*, the person as doer or maker) to steward the earth and to live in families reflecting a social God. Paul speaks of the personal and idiosyncratic nature of work

---

15. Bockmuehl, *Christian Way of Living*, 77.
16. Bockmuehl, *Christian Way of Living*, 78.

when he tells the Thessalonians "to make it your ambition to lead a quiet life: You should mind your own business and work with your hands, just as we told you, so that your daily life may win the respect of outsiders and so that you will not be dependent on anybody" (1 Thess 4:11–12). Paul acknowledges the appropriate goal of the dignity and independence of the worker while also speaking of a missional orientation toward others.

Second, then, work has an orientation toward the human "other" and the creation. Work is a communal experience with a community orientation. Work provides for the needs of the community and especially the poor. This is reflected in Eph 4:28, where Paul emphasizes the communal purpose of personal work: "Anyone who has been stealing must steal no longer, but must work, doing something useful with their own hands, that they may have something to share with those in need." Work is to be done also in a way that is conducive to the care, continuation, and consummation of creation, not its destruction, as is evident from the context of Gen 1–2, as well as passages such as Rom 8:19–21.

Third, work is done for and even with the divine other. It is done with a worshipful orientation toward the Lord, with a view to reflecting his glory (Col 3:23), and is carried out in participation with him.[17] Work continues God's creation toward its completion, though the *creatio continua* (continuing creative activity) is not of the same order as God's *creatio ex nihilo* (creation from nothing). God is not just the example or paradigm for work and rest; he works as we work, in and through our work, to accomplish his own ends, for his own glory. This trinitarian theology of work echoes the irreducible identity of divine persons in human persons and their work, and the coinherence of the divine persons in the communal nature of human persons. It also envisages human work as participation in the work of the whole triune God, who is both Creator and Redeemer of creation. Human work, in Christ, moves toward the praise of his glory.

A theology of work shapes ethics at work. Since work was first modeled by God, then commanded by him, and then enabled by him, meaningful work is therefore very important for human beings, even core to our identity, a clear responsibility and even a human right. This explains the pain that unemployment brings to human persons. It means societies and governments should do all they can to provide meaningful work for their people. It also explains why failure to work when a person can work

---

17. This threefold purpose of work was suggested first in Stott, *Issues Facing Christians Today*, 185–209.

is so strongly condemned in Scripture. Paul sternly expresses this to the Thessalonians:

> In the name of the Lord Jesus Christ, we command you, brothers and sisters, to keep away from every believer who is idle and disruptive and does not live according to the teaching you received from us. For you yourselves know how you ought to follow our example. We were not idle when we were with you, nor did we eat anyone's food without paying for it. On the contrary, we worked night and day, laboring and toiling so that we would not be a burden to any of you. We did this, not because we do not have the right to such help, but in order to offer ourselves as a model for you to imitate. For even when we were with you, we gave you this rule: "The one who is unwilling to work shall not eat." (2 Thess 3:6–10)

For pastors, evaluating the needs of people when they ask for money from the church's benevolence fund must begin by asking, "Can this person work? Are there opportunities for work? Can we provide work for them, or help them find just work?" Paul's instructions about how to evaluate the needs of widows in 1 Tim 5 can serve the church today. I have visited some communities in Africa where everybody seems to want to be a pastor and where many even call themselves apostle or pastor. This thinking is coupled with a dualistic understanding of work—pastoral work matters, working in fields as a farmer does not—and results in great hardship for the families of these persons (often men) who refuse to work and want the church to recognize them as pastors (without qualification). Paul's example in the passage above needs to be heard. Even though he could as an apostle insist on being paid by the church, in this context where work ethics were poor he chose to work hard with his hands.

In light of this brief overview of a theology of work, we may now ask, How does this theology of work shape the ethics of pastoral work? And how does it shape the ethics of other work for which the pastor seeks to equip and inspire a congregation?

Ethics of the Pastor's Work

The value and dignity of human work heads off all dualisms related to work that are prominent in evangelical subculture. The idea that the vocation and the work the pastor does is of a higher worth than what a lawyer or plumber does is one of these. Martin Luther, in the Reformation, recovered the dignity of work and vocation for the whole people of God.[18] The Protestant Reformers as a whole strongly emphasized the doctrine of vocation, which stressed first that all persons, not just pastors, are called. R. Paul Stevens speaks of a sense of calling that overcomes aimless consumerism and "gives our lives direction and purpose because our Creator summons us into a personal relationship with God and into a wonderful purpose that will outlast the world."[19] Still, pastoral work is of value, and in what follows I will lay out a theology of pastoral work, followed by some thoughts on the ethics of pastoral work.

First, work as one source of legitimate personal significance is reflected in Paul's discussion of spiritual gifts in Romans 12. Pastoral leaders should, by means of personal sober evaluation and feedback from others, gain a secure but not proud sense of their giftedness and value to the people of God.

Second, Paul affirms the communal nature and purpose of leadership in ministry in passages such as Eph 4:11–16 and 1 Cor 12–14. Note that the leadership ethos of Ephesians 4 is one of plurality, of five types of leaders who lead together in community. Note also that the purpose of leadership is to equip the whole church for the work of the ministry, so that the body "builds itself up in love" (4:16). The mature unity of a church is dependent not just on the ministry of the leaders but on the ministry of each member who is equipped by that leadership. Every child of God in the church is a charismatic center of ministry, including the pastor, whose role is leadership among (not over) the people of God, and whose leadership gifts are for the equipping of every other Christian in the church.

It seems to me that two reformations are still needed in the church in the West. The first is the recovery of the priesthood and giftedness and mission of all believers.[20] This becomes an ethical issue when the people of God are robbed of their ministry by controlling, power-hungry pastors. The second is acknowledgment of all five of the leadership gifts in a community of leadership. Not every church is able to employ all five

---

18. "Temporal Authority: To What Extent It Should Be Obeyed," in Luther, *Luther's Works*, 45:96. Luther's encouragement toward engagement did not mean an indiscriminate endorsement of temporal authority, including endorsements of war. See Hinlicky Wilson, "Martin Luther, Pacifist?"

19. Stevens, *Doing God's Business*, 20.

20. Ogden, *New Reformation*.

kinds of leaders, but it is likely that these gifts exist in most churches. It is their synchronous operation that makes for effective leadership teams.[21]

Regarding the gift of apostleship, while it is true that there were only twelve apostles, there is another use of the word "apostle" in the New Testament that extends beyond the Twelve to people such as Barnabas (Acts 14:14) and Andronicus and Junia (Rom 16:7). The word "apostle" literally means "sent one." Apostles in the church then and now have a large view of the mission (sentness) of the church, and they exhort and equip the people of God to understand and live out their identity as missional in the missional God. One person I considered to have an apostolic gifting in my last ministry was the chairperson of the elders, Len Hordyk. He had an enormous vision, an enormous desire for the church to be its missional self, and an enormous capacity for work—he was a husband and father of six kids, was a CEO of a large company, and still served effectively as an elder. He knew every pastor on our team (fifteen of us) and their ministry well. He was a huge encouragement to me as the lead pastor-teacher—and a corrector when needed! His capacity to hear criticism toward the board or pastors well was also remarkable. Our church was at its healthiest and grew rapidly during his time as our board chair.

The ministry of "prophets" may also be challenging for some church contexts, and given the abuses of this gift, this is understandable. However, Paul must have thought of them as necessary for a healthy church life given that he expresses their value as being for the "strengthening, encouraging and comfort" of the people of God (1 Cor 14:3). Paul provides a crucial key to the operation of this gift that has often been neglected in charismatic settings: the rule of community evaluation, or quality control (1 Cor 14:29–33). When prophets (or any other kind of leader, for that matter) start to control and manipulate a congregation, people get damaged. On the other hand, failure to permit properly managed prophetic ministry shortchanges the people of God of being strengthened, encouraged, and comforted. Perhaps burnout in pastors might be lessened if there were a greater awareness of the need for these five kinds of leaders, even if some members of the team were not paid employees of the church.

Third, both Paul and Peter stress the divine orientation of pastors in their work and their participation in God's ministry. The former depends on the latter. In 1 Peter 5, after speaking of his ministry as a "fellow elder," Peter concludes with a statement about where our eyes are to be fixed and

---

21. See Peter Wagner on this apostolic reformation in *New Apostolic Leadership*. Though this book has some questionable elements, I believe the basic thesis to be sound.

whose approval and glory is to be sought: "And when the Chief Shepherd appears, you will receive the crown of glory that will never fade away" (1 Pet 5:4). In the previous chapter, although he is speaking to the wider church, Peter makes a statement that is true for pastors also: "But rejoice inasmuch as you participate in the sufferings of Christ, so that you may be overjoyed when his glory is revealed" (4:13). Work as a pastor has a primary orientation toward God, not to the community (though pastors are accountable to communities) or the self.

On this matter of participation, Paul speaks of himself as one of "God's fellow workers" (Greek synergoi; 1 Cor 3:9 NASB). The tendency for pastors to speak of "my ministry" betrays the nature of ministry as participation in God's ministry, and in particular in the cross and resurrection of Jesus.[22] Ministry is not done so much "for" the Lord as "with" the Lord, though that is never a relationship between two equals. Christ is the Lord, and our participation in his work is one of asymmetry. Within his freedom we have freedom and agency. But it is always toward him and his greater glory. Pastors are surely included in this Pauline exhortation: "Whatever you do, work at it with all your heart, as working for the Lord, not for human masters" (Col 3:23). Being a pastor is an incredible privilege and a high calling, and Paul can hardly believe it is his to do: "Surely you have heard about the administration of God's grace that was given to me for you. . . . Although I am less than the least of all the Lord's people, this grace was given me: to preach to the Gentiles the boundless riches of Christ" (Eph 3:2, 8).

What does this personal, communal, and divine understanding of ministry have to say to the ethics surrounding a pastor's work? First, Paul insists that pastors are worthy of their wage (1 Tim 5:17–21, "worthy of double honor"). Yet Paul is clear that pastors must be sensitive to the needs and culture of the church and the community they are serving, as noted in 2 Thessalonians 3. There Paul says that, although he had the apostolic right to ask to be paid by the church, the need for him to stay independent in that young church and to model a good work ethic kept him from asking for a wage.

What ethical principles should govern a pastor's wages? One of the greatest hurts pastors have relates to the poor manner in which their work is viewed, and how it is sometimes compensated poorly in ways that

---

22. The works of Andrew Purves are profoundly helpful in emphasizing the participational Godward orientation of ministry. See *Reconstructing Pastoral Theology*; *Crucifixion of Ministry*; and *Resurrection Of Ministry*.

compromise healthy family living and a sense of significance. Equally, it has been my experience that congregations are rightly angered if pastors have a poor work ethic and are disorganized or lazy. John Stott once joked that, from the perspective of the unknowing congregation member, the pastor is "six days invisible and one day incomprehensible."[23]

Pastors live in a tension between the renunciation of material wealth encouraged by Jesus (Luke 10:4) and modeled by Paul (Acts 20:34–35; Phil 4:11–13), including refusal to insist on their rights (1 Cor 9:12a), and the need to encourage churches to rise to their responsibility to pay their ministers (Phil 4:10; 1 Cor 9:1–12a; 1 Tim 5:17–18). The need to care for their spouses and families is also clear; this may sometimes require a pastor to work bivocationally, as Paul did on many occasions. One solution I have heard is for a pastor to earn an average salary for the congregation. A higher salary than that would insult the poorer members of the congregation, while a lower salary would make it impossible for pastors and their families to live in that community. A pastoral family below the poverty line is not a credible witness in the community. Other churches give a salary that is the average of the salaries of the board members, arguing that these are the pastor's peers. This would satisfy the criteria of personal significance and communal integrity, and still keeps the pastor looking to God as ultimate provider.

My first church ministry illustrates the pitfall of giving a salary a pastor cannot live on. After months of going into debt just so we could pay rent and eat, I mustered up the courage to approach the board. Just how humiliating that was may be measured by the fact that I had barely begun when I broke down and wept in front of them. They corrected the error, which was founded on the idea that the pastor should look to God in faith to make up the difference. But when pastors are asked to have faith to live, this must also apply to congregations. Faith is not just the responsibility of the pastor.

Especially in multiple-staff churches, there is a need for fairness and justice in administering salaries to all the pastors. A grid that is shaped by criteria such as years served, academic qualifications, role, cost of living, and so on is important for maintaining justice and healthy relationships between pastors. Health benefits and investment in retirement preparation are just as important for pastors as the whole people of God.

---

23. Stott, *Issues Facing Christians Today*, 185.

Second, in the area of the hiring and dismissal of pastors, it is vital to keep in mind that we honor the pastor, the community, and God above all. The following should be clear: salary and benefits, working hours, Sundays away, holidays, Sabbaths and sabbaticals, annual evaluation procedures, and terms and processes for dismissal. Sometimes churches act naively, believing they can dismiss pastors on a whim. Justice and fairness must not only be done, but must be done with as much transparency to the congregation as possible. Regrettably, legal proceedings can be levied against a church for wrongful dismissal. Churches should make sure all of the appropriate documentation is there, just as for any employer in any corporation. Repeated warnings should be given to pastors in writing when they are failing to carry out their duties. Pastors should be treated in ways that honor the dignity of their personhood and work, so that the gospel is advanced and the glory of God magnified.

Third, the New Testament makes clear that when a Christian leader falls morally, church discipline must be invoked in a public way. Their work must be terminated, perhaps for a while, perhaps forever: "Do not entertain an accusation against an elder unless it is brought by two or three witnesses. But those elders who are sinning you are to reprove before everyone, so that the others may take warning. I charge you, in the sight of God and Christ Jesus and the elect angels, to keep these instructions without partiality, and to do nothing out of favoritism" (1 Tim 5:19–21). This passage instructs us about proper procedure and justice, and also indicates the public nature of a reproof if guilt is indeed established. This may seem strange, since elsewhere the New Testament informs us that, upon confession of our sins, God forgives us immediately (1 John 1:9). But church discipline seems to be administered only for those who are not repentant of their sin, and even their excommunication is intended to lead to restoration (1 Cor 5:11). Trust within the community, and the reputation of the church community, is damaged when failure of a sexual, financial, or other relational kind is hidden. Discipline, when enacted, should always be with a view to restoration, always with tears, always with love, but unapologetically in light of the holiness of God and his church.

Should a pastor who is disciplined be restored when they repent? Yes, though we must be "quick to restore, and slow to reinstate."[24] They are restored to fellowship with the Father whenever they confess, and

---

24. I first heard this from Stuart Briscoe, long-term pastor at Elmbrook Church in Milwaukee, when he shared it with me at a conference at Willingdon Church, Burnaby, BC, Canada.

they will probably not feel forgiven until they confess to their fellow leaders (Jas 5:16, "confess your sins to each other"). But they should not be reinstated in the community until they have demonstrated real change and the trust of the community has been restored. A final word on this matter is that church leaders should take legal advice whenever these disciplinary events are enacted. In lecturing for years at Regent College on pastoral ethics, I have always invited a Christian lawyer to come to the class for a lecture on when a pastor or a church should call a lawyer. This is one occasion, and there will be others as we proceed.

I have chosen not to go into detail here regarding the sexual malfeasance of pastors. This will be discussed in some detail under the seventh commandment. Suffice it to say that this is always a betrayal of trust and always an abuse of power. A pastor is not on the same plane as the congregant; it is never a fifty-fifty equal-blame situation. All parties—the victim and their spouse and family, the spouse and family of the pastor, the pastor, and the whole church community—are going to need expert help following such a tragic event. Pastors who do this must be removed. Some would say that they can never again work in the church as a pastor, and others that they can, after a long period of counseling and accountability, be reinstated. It is hard to make a blanket statement about this. As we shall see in chapter 9, whether a pastor may be restored depends on a number of factors.[25]

Ethics of All Work

The dynamics of personal significance, communal benefit, and divine participation and orientation are no different for the pastor than for those in every other vocation. A creational, biblically shaped understanding of work overcomes the dualism that sees what we do in the church as more valuable than what we do in the work world. The popular movement that states that in the second period of our work lives we can move from "success to significance" is flawed in this regard. The work done in the first half in a business setting, or in a school, or fighting fires is no less valuable than work done with a so-called parachurch organization or a church in the second half. They have equal significance.

The mission of God for humans must begin with the first command, the cultural mandate, which involves the command to work, to create, to

---

25. For a fuller discussion, see Grenz and Bell, *Betrayal of Trust*.

care for creation, and to be families. It was renewed in the resurrected Jesus, who is the last Adam, the new head of the human race. As believers conjoined to the last Adam, we are called to fulfill that mandate in the new creation. The second command of God was summarized by Jesus as loving God and loving neighbor. The gospel includes and empowers both of these. It is not appropriate to speak of "the gospel and justice," for justice is part of the gospel just as much as justification is. It is not appropriate to speak of "the gospel and creation care," but rather of creation care within the gospel. The third great command of God is the Great Commission, which is our participation as redeemed people in the mission of God to reconcile people and the whole creation. The great commission is housed within the other two commands, and in turn it leads to obedience of the other two.

Thus, when we go about work in communion with the Creator, our work matters to God. When we act justly as employers toward our employees, it matters to God. When we take measures to make sure our manufacturing does not harm but rather benefits the environment, this matters to God. When we do what we can about the trauma of unemployment, this matters to God. When we apply the biblical principle of the dignity and worth of persons and the biblical principle of mutuality to industrial relations, when we abolish racial or gender discrimination, when we increase the participation and ownership of employees, when we emphasize cooperation, when we in tangible ways take care of the poor and marginalized in our communities, in all these ways we live out the gospel.[26]

The evangelical movement as a whole has not in recent decades done very much to equip people well for the thing they spend most of their life doing—work. Too many Christians go to work feeling that their work does not matter nearly as much as their verbal witness to the gospel or the work those in church ministry do. But there is no clergy-laity dualism in the Bible—the laity (laos) are the clergy (kleros), every Christian a called one. Too many Christians go to work assuming it is just something they have to do, rather than something they get to do, and something that is actually a participation in the work of the divine triune Worker in his new creation. They may not realize that their work itself is missional, even if they never open their mouths to share about Jesus.

---

26. These are all categories discussed in detail by Stott in *Issues Facing Christians Today*, 210–33, 260–84.

One further dualism that affects the way Christians sometimes view work is the contemplative-active dualism. An important conclusion one may draw from the functional aspect of the image of God is that human doing is important for human beings, that doing cannot be separated from being, and that being is not sufficient on its own. Undue emphasis on being that neglects doing is actually a modern form of Gnosticism. There are Christians who emphasize contemplation, and there are those who emphasize action. There is a wide spectrum that is determined by personality, denominational tradition, and so on. What it takes for one person to stay in balance or in a state of shalom may be different for another person. But to deny the importance of the need for action altogether, including work, is to be mistaken about the mixed life to which we are all called, Mary and Martha together, by turn.

THE NEED FOR A THEOLOGY OF VOCATION

The fourth commandment points to the need for a theology of vocation that affirms that every Christian is called by God. We are called, first, to be human in accordance with the cultural mandate—to be in community and to work in accordance with our abilities. We are called, second, to be Christian—to conversion, to worship, to Christlikeness of character, and to be obedient to all of the commands of God in the Scriptures. Third, we are uniquely gifted and called into particular vocations in the church and in the world. This view of vocation can be likened to a wedding cake, where each layer narrows toward the top. Klaus Bockmuehl associated the three persons of the Trinity with each level of calling: the Father with the human mandate, the Son with the Christian vocation, and the Holy Spirit with the equipping and guiding that takes us into our personal vocations.[27] The Western obsession with particular individual calling is overcome by living faithfully and obediently into the larger layers of the wedding cake.

To be properly trinitarian, one must consider also the overlap of each of these layers grounded in the indivisible nature of the works of the Trinity. Too great an emphasis on God as Creator and Father of all can issue in a secularized notion of vocation, in which work is a "comfortable

---

27. This has been referred to and employed also by R. Paul Stevens in his excellent work on calling, *Other Six Days*, 73–74.

chaplaincy to secular, pluralistic societies and workplaces."[28] An obsession with the Spirit without reference to the christological layer can lead to antinomianism, to a deep frustration about work as if it is a waste of time, or to seeing work as a means to an evangelistic end. Neglect of the Spirit robs the worker of a sense of "the Spirit's intimate and intrusive involvement in our life and work in creation,"[29] and so on. The coinherence of the three levels, reflective of the coinherence of the persons of the Trinity, along with a good doctrine of creation, will go a long way toward ridding the church of dualisms with respect to work. These dualisms include between faith and reason, between Sunday and Monday, between clergy and laity, between the Great Commission, the Great Commandment, and the cultural mandate, between evangelism and justice and creation care. A theology of vocation rooted in creation and its reaffirmation in the incarnation spells death to all such dualisms.

---

28. Theology of Work, "Vocation in Historical-Theological Perspective."
29. Theology of Work, "Vocation in Historical-Theological Perspective."

7

Authority in Moral Formation and Ethics (Commandment 5)

Honor your father and your mother, so that you may live long in the land the Lord your God is giving you.

Exodus 20:12

This fifth commandment is relevant to both the personal moral formation of pastors and the broader ethics of authority and submission. Considering it will help us answer questions such as, How important is it for pastors to deal with issues with their parents? How do pastors function well as parents of their own children while caring for the family of God? How should pastors view the authority God has given them as leaders in the church? How do pastors provide leadership on how the people in their church should view elected government officials? And, How do pastors view political parties in a liberal democracy, and should they influence how the people should vote?

In other words, this commandment can be treated as an area code for discussing all relationships that involve authority and submission—including between leaders and the people of the church, and between the church and the state. I have chosen the word "submission" over against "subordination." The first implies leadership among equals, among fellow human beings, whereas the latter implies an ontological difference. A commonality between parenting, church leadership, and leadership of the nation is that neither parents, nor pastors, nor presidents (and especially not political parties) ever have absolute authority. Leaders require our respect, but they are all mere humans. They are always under the authority of God and are to be held accountable to the second half of the Decalogue. A brief consideration of the commandment using Calvin's method will lay the groundwork for this challenging subject area.

THE PATTERN OF THE COMMANDMENT IN SCRIPTURE

The Old Testament: Positive and Negative Versions

Since this is one of only two commandments that are expressed positively, it seems appropriate to begin with the positive version. In this commandment, the word "honor" (KBD) means "to make heavy," to take seriously, or give serious weighting in determining priorities. This command is reiterated in Lev 19:3 using the word "respect" (yr'), part of a chapter that is all about the practice of holiness. Honoring parents is a significant aspect of holiness. In Josh 4:14, this term is used to describe the attitude that is appropriate for a revered servant of God, in Exod 14:31 the attitude the people should have toward the temple, and in Prov 3:7 toward Yahweh himself. There is a great deal of material in the book of Proverbs that works out the meaning of this commandment, including the exhortation that fathers and mothers are to be honored and cared for even after they are old (23:22).

The negative version of this commandment emphasizes its gravity by the severity of the penalties that were to be meted out within a theocratic society. This even includes the death penalty if parents were cursed (Exod 21:15, 17; Lev 20:9; Deut 12:18–21; Prov 20:20). The repetition of this commandment in Prov 19 reveals the situation of a son who dishonors his parents by driving them out of the home when things get too tough economically to continue looking after them: "Whoever robs their father and drives out their mother is a child who brings shame and disgrace" (Prov 19:26). This highlights the situation where a mother is driven out of the home because she has become an economic liability. Men in Old Testament times were most tempted not to look after their parents in the middle season of their lives, when the most was required of them economically. This was to violate the fifth commandment as an adult child.

There is also a relativization of the commandment in the Old Testament that is developed further in an eschatological way in the New. Allegiance to God should supplant allegiance to parents if the demands of parents are contrary to the will of God. The psalmist is conscious that even if his parents neglected or disowned him, God would be his Father: "Though my father and mother forsake me, the Lord will receive me" (Ps 27:10).

The New Testament: Negative and Positive Versions

The negative version of this commandment is present in the New Testament in lists of sins (1 Tim 1:9; 2 Tim 3:2; Rom 1:30). An important discussion between Jesus and the Pharisees clarifies that one cannot invoke the higher authority of God to duck out of the responsibility that adult children have to look after their parents (Matt 15:4; Mark 7:10; cf. Eph 6:2). Paul makes it clear that adult children are to take care of their parents and grandparents if the latter are unable to do so. The church is directed not to help widows financially if they have family that could look after them. In 2 Cor 12:14, he indicates that "children should not have to save up for their parents, but parents for their children," yet sometimes parents cannot look after themselves financially, perhaps though widowhood or in other circumstances of poverty. Adult children then have an "honoring" responsibility. If they ignore this, they are, says Paul, "worse than an unbeliever" (1 Tim 5:8). One principle that seems to arise out of Paul's candid discussion of how the church should care for its poor is that family, the "smallest social unit,"[1] is the first court of appeal.

Regarding the positive nature of this commandment, we must first note that it is reciprocal. The most significant quotation in this regard is Eph 6:1-4, where, common to the mutuality structure of the whole passage, Paul views the respective responsibilities of parents and children in a reciprocal manner.

Second, although the commandment is addressed to adult children, it also includes young children. This explains why Paul uses the term "obey" in Eph 6, even though this commandment stated "honor" originally. Adult children who are married and not under the authority of parents any longer are still called on to honor their parents, though not to obey them. In Matt 15:3-9, where people were nullifying the true intent

---

1. Bockmuehl, *Christian Way of Living*, 81.

of the moral law by avoiding caring for their parents, it is clear that Jesus is speaking of adult children.

This means the commandment is for all children at whatever age, though its fulfillment means different things at different ages. As adults, our responsibility is not one of obedience and servility. In the transition from young child to adult child, a good parent will make sure that children not only have been given good spiritual, emotional, and behavioral roots, but also good wings to fly. When they become adults or leave to be married, they really are freed from parental domination and inappropriate interference and control. To fail to do so affects the maturity of children and their ability to unite in covenant relationship with their spouse in marriage (Gen 2:24). But the honoring still continues: this means being respectful, and it means caring for parents if they do not have the means themselves. It may also mean confronting parents where they have relational patterns that do not permit wings to be formed, or where emotional or other abuses have been inflicted. It is not honoring to let such things be unconfronted, although timing and age need to be considered, and always with healing and restoration in mind.

Third, in Eph 6 Paul changes the promissory aspect of the commandment from "so that you may live long in *the land* the Lord your God is giving you" to "that it may go well with you and that you may enjoy long life on *the earth*" (Eph 6:3). Paul not only provides convincing evidence of the validity of the Decalogue for Christians, but he draws attention to the fact that it has a promise associated with it for people beyond the Jewish nation. He extrapolates it to all believing people everywhere. How are we to understand the promise of longevity for those in mutually honoring parent-child relationships, and why does Paul extrapolate this to include all people irrespective of ethnicity and geography?

The promised longevity of this commandment was not just because people who cursed their parents received the death penalty in the Old Testament theocracy (Lev 20:9; Prov 20:20). Some scholars suggest that in Exod 20 this meant that the nation would have a long spell in the promised land if this commandment were obeyed. Disobedience to it would be symptomatic of unfaithfulness to God, with its consequences in terms of exile. They also suggest that Eph 6 is merely a quotation of Exod 20, not meant to indicate fulfillment.[2] However, I think a fairer interpretation involves two truths. It is clear, first, that there is a trans-covenantal

---

2. Keil and Delitzsch, *Exodus*, 420–21.

continuity with regard to the nature of the promise between Exod 20 and Eph 6. This is the promise of longevity. There is however, second, a covenantal progression with respect to who this applies to and where. It is true in the new covenant for all people everywhere. The land in old-covenant times is replaced with the whole earth as that which the people of God inherit, and "long life" might conceivably mean eternal life in the kingdom of God. Those who honor their parents are simply those who obey the commandments in general. By their conformity to the moral law in general and the honoring of parents in particular, they give evidence that they are people of grace and faith. They do not do this in order to be the people of God; they are the people of God in Christ so they honor their parents. This commandment is therefore a diagnostic of true Christian profession.

Returning for a moment to the common assumption that there is a connection between obedience to this commandment and longevity, it is often the case with moral axioms and their consequences (as in Proverbs) that they are generalizations and not intended always to be true. Those who honor their parents as children and then as adults will enjoy shalom, or soul health. The peace in their soul and in their relationships will make it more likely that they will live long. This is related to the Sabbath commandment in the sense that that shalom in the soul (Sabbath) leads to shalom in relationships (parent-child commandment). Stress kills, and there is no greater stress inducer than brokenness and tension in relationships, particularly those with our parents. Stress affects our physical beings and our longevity. While there are exceptions, shalom in our relationships generally leads to health and longevity. This is true for both parents and children: the effect on children of having healthy and respectful relationships with parents is self-evident, but the effect on parents is also reflected in Prov 10:1 ("A wise son brings joy to his father, but a foolish son brings grief to his mother") and 19:13 ("A foolish child is his father's ruin").

Healthy relationships between adult children and their parents also have beneficial effects on their children. A study by a Finnish researcher of family life in Finland and Canada showed that "when granny is around, more children live to adulthood," and that when she assists with childrearing, "the parents live longer and healthier lives." This extension of the human lifespan "appears to be due to grandmother's contribution to childcare, and more specifically, to feeding children."[3]

A further aspect of this commandment as Paul adapts it for the new covenant is what it says about what good parenting means in practical terms: "Fathers, do not exasperate your children; instead, bring them up in the training and instruction of the Lord" (Eph 6:4). This suggests one thing to avoid and three ways to engage. What to avoid in parenting is exasperation of children—more literally, provoking them to anger (NASB). Paul does not say how, but biblical precedent and contemporary experience might lead us to the following possibilities: favoritism of one child over another; discipline with "unreasonable severity";[4] all forms of emotional, physical, and spiritual abuse; guilting and manipulating children rather than motivating them through the gospel and the goodness of God; and not being physically present, or being emotionally absent even when physically present.

Paul then moves from what to avoid to providing insight into how to positively engage for the formation of healthy and holy children. First, the word for "bring them up" has connotations of gentleness, which John Calvin comments on: "But Paul goes on to say, 'let them be fondly cherished'; for the Greek word (ektrephete) which is translated 'bring up,' unquestionably conveys the idea of gentleness and forbearance."[5] He speaks of the "mild and considerate" manner in which children should be raised. This insight into the impressionable nature of little hearts is remarkable for a Reformer sometimes considered to be severe. He is quick to add that this does not mean "excessive indulgence," for he comments that Paul "again draws the rein which he had slackened, and adds, 'in the instruction and reproof of the Lord.'" The Greek word behind "instruction" is the idea of the passing on of the content of the faith, which is done by word of mouth or in writing. "Reproof" is the idea of the formation in a moral and spiritual sense of children by means of loving and appropriate discipline. The first is mental discipline that brings about the good; the second is correction that averts what is bad.

But how is this possible? How can you parent in way that maintains the balance between indulgence and rebuke, staying gentle all the time?

---

3. Picard, "Role of Grandmothers Crucial for Tree of Life." Picard reports on the work of Lahdenperä et al., "Fitness Benefits of Prolonged Post-reproductive Lifespan in Women."

4. Calvin, *Commentary on Ephesians*.

5. Calvin, *Commentary on Ephesians*.

How do you encourage children to follow the Lord and yet give them the freedom to rebel, the freedom to come back when they want to follow the Lord? Pastors who are parents feel the weight of these things intensely at times, given that one of the qualifications of pastors/elders is that their homes must be well-managed and their children must be believers and well-disciplined and not wild (1 Tim 3:4; Titus 1:6–7).

Given this daunting task, Paul writes a hugely comforting phrase: "of the Lord." This reminds us that we can only parent, we can only instruct and train children, in union and communion with the Lord. This is a genitive construction that may either be objective or subjective. The objective genitive would make Christ the object, but the subjective makes Christ the one who teaches our children though our teaching. Both are probably true, but the second is probably more fitting here. As with all of the commandments, the power to fulfill them lies in participation in the life of God. This makes the life of prayer an important priority in the way that we parent and in the way we respond as children to our parents and their parenting. Paul makes a deliberate connection between life in God, which he speaks of as being "filled with the Holy Spirit," and the life of parenting and being parented. The ethics of marriage, family, and workplace spelled out throughout Eph 5:19—6:9 are empowered by the spiritual dynamic expressed in the primary command of the section to be "filled with the Spirit" in 5:18. And the whole section on relationships comes under the heading of mutual submission.

Submission is impossible apart from the example of Christ, the power of the Spirit, and an orientation toward the Father. It is a difficult concept and a difficult term, whether we are referring to submission to God, to parents, or to children. Perhaps in our culture it may not even be the best term to use. However, if we extricate it from its abusive connotation, there are reasons for retaining it. It is central in the life of a Christian disciple. It assumes a letting go that is important in the life of the soul. Most important is the depth of its challenge and its paradoxical relationship to freedom. Richard Foster has written extensively on the freedom of submission:

> Do you know the liberation that comes from giving up your rights? It means you are set free from the seething anger and bitterness.... It means you are free to obey Jesus' command, "Love your enemies and pray for those who persecute you" (*Matt. 5:44*) It means that for the first time you understand how it is

possible to surrender the right to retaliate: "If any one strikes you on the right cheek, turn to him the other also" (*Matt. 5:39*).[6]

He speaks of kingdom liberation found through committing our cause to God, who sees and will act justly. He speaks of healthy self-denial, which is not self-hatred. As noted already, appropriate self-identity and self-love is required for healthy self-denial (Jesus in John 13), and healthy further self-identity comes through giving ourselves away and relinquishing the right to always be right. The notion of submission is endemic to being a Christian, and being a Christian means you become a member of the order of the basin and the towel. This commandment calls us to live the life of the cross in a way that is rooted in the cross life of Christ. The self-emptying of the Son in Phil 2 is a pattern for all who claim to be in Christ. That is what makes submission to imperfect people possible.

In sum, this commandment really matters. Our spiritual state and our physical well-being are affected by this. Just how important it is may be measured by its positioning with respect to the commandments before and after it.

THE UNDERGIRDING PROTOTYPE: ECHOES OF THE TRINITY AND THE GOSPEL

It should not be a surprise that this parenting commandment comes immediately after the commands that make us aware of who God is. It is empowered and qualified by the first four. The existence of parents and children as the basic unit of humanity is not by accident. Humanity looks like this because it is image bearing. It echoes aspects of the very nature of the Godhead. For example, in Eph 3, Paul speaks of the heavenly Father "from whom every family [fatherhood] . . . derives its name" (Eph 3:15). That earthly fathers are an echo of God as Father is, according to Paul's theology, an echo from above.[7] We have fathers and mothers, commissioned to raise and care for children, not by some random accident but because there is an ontological resonance between parents and God. The "ultimate foundation for human relationships resides," as Stanley Grenz

---

6. Foster, *Celebration of Discipline*, 111–12.

7. Mothers also reflect the character of God, as a number of biblical passages indicate. Fathers and mothers, as male and female together, constitute the image of God (Gen 1:26–27). However, God is not named as "Mother" in Scripture. God chose to reveal himself as "Father," not because he is male, for he transcends gender, but because it was his will to do so.

notes, "in the eternal dynamic of the triune God."[8] God reveals his very being to us in familial terms as Father and Son.

We learn the heart of parenting as we watch the Father and the Son interacting as recorded by the gospel writers. We are given evidence that this is a reflection of what they are eternally. The Trinity is three equal persons-in-relation, *submitting* gladly to one another, not *subordinated* to one another,[9] in perichoretic relations, each for the other, each animating the other. The Spirit is a person who shares in the mutual love of the Father and the Son. Theological ethicist Gilbert Meilaender sums up the proper trinitarian nature of ethics in a way that is appropriate to this command: "Our task is nothing less than this: to achieve within human life the love that is a dim reflection of the life of God. In the triune God—Father as initiating ground, Son as co-equal respondent, and Spirit as mutual bond which springs from their giving and receiving—we have a picture of love."[10]

The authority-submission relation is also evident in this paradigmatic relationship. The Son submitted to the command of the Father to create the cosmos, and then to become human and to reconcile it. This is not a relationship of two unequal persons, but of two persons equal in essence and one in communion. The Father sending the Son may sound like an unequal relationship, but the Father was always in the Son as he was sent. On earth the Son constantly submits with joy to his Father's will: "I do always what pleases him" (John 8:29). Hebrews 10:5–10 sums up the advent of Jesus from incarnation to the cross using the words of Ps 40:8: "I desire to do your will, my God." In turn, the Father expresses his affirmation, approval, and delight in the Son on a number of occasions, ultimately exalting him to his own right hand. This is the paradigm for all parenting. It is also the source of all healing when our earthly relationships are less than ideal. We may assume that, being in the Son, we too have received the approval of the Father expressed at his baptism. This needs to be internalized. None of us have perfect earthly fathers and mothers, and all of us need healing in a way that Malachi predicted for the eschaton: "He will turn the hearts of the parents to their children, and the hearts of the children to their parents" (Mal 4:6). Even persons

---

8. Grenz, *Social God and the Relational Self*, 320.

9. "Subordinationism" is an ontological term (i.e., related to being) and is heresy if used of the divine persons.

10. Meilaender, *Faith and Faithfulness*, 48.

who had excellent fathers are called on to find ultimate approval from the heavenly Father.

I once shared my own journey of seeking healing with my father with a friend who walked very closely with God, Bob Birch. I have never forgotten his words: "It is a painful journey from our earthly fathers to our heavenly Father." For me, this journey involved in-depth counseling, consistency in reading and hearing the word of God to be assured of who the heavenly Father is, and immersing myself in the Lord's Supper. There I learned how great is the Father's love expressed in the giving of the Son, and I was caught up with the ascended Christ in the presence of the Father. It involved confronting without dishonoring my father. It involved claiming the love and affirmation he did not know how to give. It involved the compassionate realization that he, too, was the product of imperfect parenting, taking him down off a pedestal and seeing him as merely human.

It should not surprise us that this parenting commandment is the first of the humanward commandments and may in fact be the overarching head of the love-neighbor commands. Entering into the reality of this relationship with the Father in the Son by the work of the Holy Spirit is to enter into the proper place for evangelical obedience to the neighbor commands. The ethos for joyful obedience to parents or to the state is shaped by the nature of God as Father, by the triune love of the three persons, and his gospel of grace toward us.

John Calvin recognized that within the life of union with Christ, obedience to the law involves not cravenly obeying a master but pleasing a father with respect to the whole law. John Kelsay, reflecting on Calvin's "Treatise on Christian Liberty," comments that "one who 'receives the grace of his Redeemer' is called on to obey the Law, but understands it is as the guidance of a loving parent. The mood of obedience thus shifts from that of the slave who obeys a powerful and fearsome master to that of a child who revels in pleasing a parent." The new mood of obedience is that of a heart set free (Ps 119:32). Rather than grudging obedience, Christian freedom involves "a liberation *from* the difficulty of unwilling service, an a liberation *for* the performance of deeds that will glorify God."[11]

Parenting needs to be of the gospel—it is evangelical, not legal. As pastors, our parenting of our churches needs to be the same. Pastors who do not parent evangelically in the home, or who are not aware that

---

11. Kelsay, "Prayer and Ethics: Reflections on Calvin and Barth," 170, commenting on Calvin, *Institutes of the Christian Religion* 3.19.4–5.

they are to at least some extent in recovery from parenting that was not evangelical, are not likely to parent evangelically in the church. When the "is" of the gospel is drowned out by the "ought" of the law, pastors have slipped away from their calling. Giving people the imperatives of the gospel without the indicatives of the gospel will attract those who like black-and-white clarity beyond what Scripture offers, but their allegiance will not last long because their life will be sapped.

THE WIDER IMPLICATIONS OF THE COMMANDMENT IN CONTEXT

For Personal Moral Formation

This commandment is crucial in moral formation in that it deals with the most significant of human relationships, that between parents and children. It is true that in the books of Kings, for example, sometimes good kings produced bad children, and bad kings ended up with good children. However, it is still true in general terms that parents are the primary influence in the spiritual, emotional, and moral development of children. Even if by grace children transcend their upbringings, their self-understanding is enhanced by their awareness of how their parents affected them. Pastors who have little or no awareness of how their parents affected them are pastors with little maturity. Pastors who have not resolved issues in their soul that relate to their parents are not yet ready to pastor others. Pastors who have not sought and gained, if possible, their father's affirmation are likely to use the church as a surrogate father for those purposes. Pastors who honor their parents even when they have seen them for who they are, and seen themselves for who they are in light of the parents they had, are pastors who are likely to honor the people in their church and care for them with patience and insight.

For Relationships with the Other in the Love-Neighbor Commandments

Our childhood relationship with our parents is the cradle out of which we will perform as adults with respect to all the other love-neighbor commandments. How we are formed in that core relationship has a significant impact on how we relate in all other relationships. If the Sabbath commandment is the door inviting God into all human relationships, it opens first into the commandment to honor parents. How we do in that arena is, in turn, the door into all the remaining human-sphere commandments. It has a profound influence on them, though it is not ultimate. Redemption and healing can occur. That redemption occurs ultimately in relationship with the God of the first three commandments.

The influence that wholeness of the parent-child relationship has on all areas of morality is self-evident. While it is true that sometimes immoral and broken people come from good homes, it is generally true that good parenting leads to less challenge in the areas indicated by the rest of the commandments. Take the sixth, the murder commandment, and its positive correlate of being a life-giving person in relationships. Rage gives rise to murder, according to Jesus in Matthew 5. A primary place where rage is built, according to Ephesians 6, is in the relationship with fathers, who are exhorted not to provoke their children to anger (Eph 6:4). A loving home gives life, and that love is usually passed on.

In the case of the adultery commandment and its opposite, loving well to build strong relationships and marriage, it seems self-evident that the development of the following all have a direct relationship to parenting in one way or another: normal, healthy sexuality; covenant faithfulness in marriage; other-orientation or mutuality in marital sexuality (1 Cor 7:3–4; 1 Pet 3:7); the avoiding of premarital sex; and compulsiveness with respect to autosexuality or homosexuality. In the case of the eighth, the theft commandment, and positively, the work commandment—although there can certainly be exceptions, and results that are influenced by personality types—habits of work are very much learned in a home context. In the case of the lying commandment, integrity in the home is critical to the development of the same in children. Kids pick up lack of integrity and honesty and consistency with ease. With respect to the tenth, the covetousness commandment, the issue of contentment is largely modeled and caught in the home.

For Limitations of the Commandment

I noted above that this commandment has limitations within its development in Scripture. Submission to parents does not mean submission to abuse or neglect. Furthermore, it is clear in both Testaments that if obedience to parents means disobeying the command of God, God must take precedence. This is already apparent in how this commandment was considered in the context of the Ten Commandments as a whole. There is an implied order in the commandments related to their order as written. Our first allegiance is to God in a way that not even our parents can usurp. If an earthly father commands a child to put their hand in a fire or to commit murder, they are not to do so. There is a higher authority than that of parents to which parents must submit. In Acts 5:29, Peter and the other apostles state this: "We must obey God rather than human beings!"

Jesus, who quoted and applied the fifth commandment, also made a lot of its limitations. Creational loyalties are placed in second place to covenant loyalties, and creational family loyalties behind loyalty to God. Jesus, despite being the Son of God, submitted as a fully human child to his own parents (Luke 2:51), and loved and cared for his mother even on the cross (John 19:26–27). However, at the same time he was, to use a term from modern psychology, properly differentiated, with a higher allegiance to his Father in heaven. Thus, even at twelve years old, when his parents find him dialoguing with the theologians, he asks, "Why were you searching for me? . . . Didn't you know I had to be in my Father's house?" (Luke 2:49). Similarly, he differentiates himself from his mother at the wedding in Cana (John 2:3–4). When there is a conflict of agendas between his Father and his earthly mother and brothers, Jesus makes clear who his companions will be and where his allegiance is placed: "Here are my mother and my brothers. For whoever does the will of my Father in heaven is my brother and sister and mother" (Matt 12:48–50).

Jesus spells out this question of preferred allegiance with a clarity that rattles our modern sensibilities: "If anyone comes to me and does not hate father and mother, wife and children, brothers and sisters—yes, even their own life—such a person cannot be my disciple. And whoever does not carry their cross and follow me cannot be my disciple" (Luke 14:26–27). The word "hate" reflects a Hebrew idiom for preference or allegiance.[12] Matthew seems to offer a slightly more comfortable rendering: "Anyone who loves his father or mother *more than me* is not worthy of me; anyone who loves his son or daughter more than me is not worthy of me" (Matt 10:37). Leaving family behind in order to follow Jesus was like

---

12. Jeannine K. Brown notes also, "The use of 'hate' in Luke might reflect an idiom that comes from Hebrew. In Genesis 29:30–31, we hear that Jacob loved Rachel more than Leah and that Leah was 'hated' by Jacob. A similar use of the Hebrew word for 'hate' occurs in Deuteronomy 21:15–17 where it is also clear that the issue is one of preference or allegiance." See Brown, "Commentary on Luke 14:25–33."

dying to them. It was to count one's relatives as dead, because they would never want to see one again. This would be interpreted by family as "hating" them. At any rate, choosing God over family when this is necessary, either because family is insisting on a moral path contrary to the word of God or because family is standing in the way of a clear vocational or geographical calling, is exactly what carrying the cross means. Our first and exclusive loyalty is to God. This tension is most keenly felt when people who do not belong to Christian families are converted, when they are baptized, and when they are discerning a call to ministry. The consolation is that the new disciple will receive new family, the family of God (Mark 10:29–30).

What are the implications of this ordering of allegiances? First, these sentiments work against any idolatry of the creational family, an idolatry all too common in contemporary culture. They also provide comfort for people whose experience of creational family has been anything but positive. The possibility of acceptance and healing within the family of God, his church, is a significant hope for the beginning of redemption in this life and the fullness of healing in the age to come. This relativization of family is also the context in which confronting and dealing with abusive parenting should be discussed. It is not in the kingdom purposes of God to brush aside issues of either emotional or relational ill health in parents who have become toxic and who have abused their children emotionally or physically. So many people in our culture suffer the ill effects of absentee or abusive parenting. These people need to find healing, and the church needs to be a safe place for that healing. So many people have crumbling marriages because they have never confronted their own emotional and relational patterns and brokenness, which is most often a product of the parental relationship. Any person who says they had perfect parents and that they have no issues to confront is much like the Pharisees, who said they had no need of a physician. Emotional pharisaism is a blind spot of Christians who use this fifth commandment to live unhealthy lives and have toxic relationships with their children.

On the other hand, if this commandment is to be obeyed, all confrontations must be done in a way that honors the parent, with a view toward forgiveness and restoration. Healing in this relationship is critical to all of life. Godly parents need to have hearts open to their own shortcomings and to this healing in their children, which will also lead to their own healing. If we believe in the doctrine of depravity, we must believe that it affects this primary relationship and that there must therefore be kingdom openness to healing. This is not about blame; it is about emotional honesty and living in truth. It is about seeking redemption. In cases where parents will not take ownership of abuse or toxic imperfections, we must seek forgiveness and continue to honor them but also keep from putting ourselves back under their abuse.[13] Ultimately, all healing comes from our heavenly Father. Even the best and godliest parents must seek to direct the ultimate dependency of their child away from themselves to the unchanging God and Father of our Lord Jesus Christ.

The authority-submission pattern for parents and children, including the limitations of submission, serves well as a rubric for considering other relationships. This includes the relationship between leaders and people in the church, at work, and between the church and the state.

For Authority and Submission in the Church

The paradigm of authority and submission arising from the parenting command is a fitting one for leadership in the church in terms of what leadership looks like as expounded in the New Testament, how people are to respond to it, their mutuality, and especially with regard to the limitations of submission to leadership.

First, the character of leadership is what makes submission to leadership possible. The qualifications of an elder given in 1 Timothy 3 and Titus 1 do include a few gifts the leader must have, and they do validate that a desire born of right motive is a sign of a leader, but the qualifications are really about character, character, character. Related to this, leaders must have a clear sense of identity and know who they are and what they are not. Jesus made it clear that the disciples were not to call any one leader by the name "Father" (Matt 23:9). This suggests that the leaders of his church were not to usurp the place of God or Jesus as the Head of his church. Leaders in the New Testament were not in a different ontological category from the people but were rather leaders among the people. Peter is called one of the pillars of the church (1 Cor 16:15), not the first pope. He calls himself an elder among elders, a "fellow elder," in 1 Pet 5:1, and in that same spirit calls on all elders not to lord it over the people of God (1 Pet 5:3). A clear vision of who a pastor or leader is—merely human, merely a redeemed child of God—is the first key to good leadership that makes submission easy.

---

13. Allender and Longman, *Bold Love*, is helpful in this regard.

Peter hints at a few reasons why a leader may *not* function well in this passage: "not because you must, but because you are willing" implies issues in the souls of pastors that make them driven, serving out of compulsion, not the freedom of grace (5:2). "Not pursuing dishonest gain, but eager to serve" implies a monetary motivation, which may be surprising in our time given that pastors' salaries are not usually that competitive, yet there may be some who place their security in salary and have doubts about being able to do any other job (5:2). "Not lording it over those entrusted to you" suggests that for some the power of the ministry position is alluring, which they are certain to abuse (5:3). In place of these false motivations and understandings of what leadership means, Peter gives three positive statements that give insight into the kind of affect and attitude that characterize true leadership: pastors are to "be shepherds" who truly feed and care for the flock (5:2); they are to be "eager to serve," the very hallmark of Jesus himself (5:2); and they are to be "examples to the flock," leading through *influence* rather than control (5:3). The incentive Peter ends with, "And when the Chief Shepherd appears, you will receive the crown of glory that will never fade away" (5:4), suggests that although the pastor deeply cares for a nourishes and woos the people of God toward Christ and the life of the gospel, a true Christian leader has an orientation ultimately toward the Lord and is responsible to God and not humans.

The call for submission of the people of God to leaders (Heb 13:17; 1 Pet 5:5), while real, must be qualified by the presence of these traits in a leader. Paul seems to suggest that some leaders are more worthy of following than others when in 1 Tim 5:17 he states, "The elders who direct the affairs of the church well are worthy of double honor, especially those whose work is preaching and teaching." He seems to imply the same in 1 Thess 5:12–13: "Now we ask you, brothers and sisters, to acknowledge those who work hard among you, who care for you in the Lord and who admonish you. Hold them in the highest regard in love because of their work." This is not to justify a critical spirit toward pastors because they are not perfect. But it does motivate pastors to be what Christian leaders are intended to be, and it motivates the people of God to hold high standards for church leaders and to pray for their pastors. The idea that the people of God should submit to their fellow human leaders seems to me to be contingent on whether in doing so they are submitting to Christ, as is implied in Eph 5:24 ("Now as the church submits to Christ. . ."). Submission to leaders is qualified by their submission to Christ and the word of God. The final authority of the word of God as that is expressed in the historic creeds of the church is a higher authority than that of a pastor or elder.

Paul gives a further development of what it means to be a servant leader in Ephesians 4. There he makes it clear that the primary purpose of the giftings of the church leader is to *equip* the people of God for ministry. The fivefold charisms of leadership are not given to leaders so that they can *do* the ministry, but so that the people of God are equipped to minister in an every-member community of the priesthood of all believers. One of the most significant challenges in the authority-submission paradigm in churches is pastors who cannot delegate, who cannot trust others to do the same quality of work that they do, who see ministry as their unique domain. It takes humility to serve as an equipper. I was privileged to work with a pastor who took seriously this understanding of pastor as equipper, Jim Postlewaite. As a lead pastor, I often had to defend his ministry to the elders because he was barely visible in the life of the church. He worked under the radar, equipping all kinds of ministers and leaders in our church, and was content to be unseen. It was so countercultural that the elders were not always quite sure what to do with it.

While preaching the word is itself equipping, the way in which it is taught and preached can work against the spirit of equipping. Preachers must study and exegete and expound the text in the power of the Spirit as the spokespersons of the risen Jesus, as expository preachers. But what if all the preacher does is dazzle the congregation with their brilliant exegesis? Would it not be better to preach more transparently about what the preacher has done to get where they have arrived? Another significant challenge is when the people do not want to minister because they have become accustomed to passivity by the services of the church. This is a great challenge in churches where people sit in rows, watch a worship band, listen to a preacher, and go home and imagine that this was church! Somewhere in the life of the church there need to be house churches in which people can be equipped and discover and develop their gifts and their ministries.

This understanding of who leaders and the people of God are is an important foundation for a raft of ethical issues that arise in the life of the church. It defines expectations for the ministry of a pastor. It guides the proper remuneration of a pastor. Acknowledging that there is such a thing as a leader, even if among the people, makes it important for pastors to know that they are ethically speaking in a position of power. They need to be conscious of the power and hold it humbly and lightly. They need to know, however, that potential for abuse of power is always present, including in the manipulation of decisions surrounding finances, buildings, and so on. Pastors who take advantage of a person sexually need to know that this is not just a terrible violation of moral standards, but that ethically it is an abuse of power and liable to litigation. Pastors may not be at an ontological remove from the people of God, but they are functionally in a role that demands the highest standards, and the respect and the proper submission of the people of God.

For Leaders and Employees in the Workplace

The authority and submission principles of the parent-child commandment also have a natural application in the marketplace or work environment. What is most noticeable in the New Testament as it addresses the master-slave relationship is the mutuality and the reciprocal instructions given to both parties. This fact, and the Onesimus incident recorded in Philemon, suggests that social reform was part of the Christian gospel. The tenor of the gospel, as recorded in passages such as Gal 3:28, ultimately brought down the institution of slavery. In the meantime, Peter (1 Pet 2:18–26) and Paul (Eph 6:5–9; Col 3:22–25) gave instructions for slaves to respect and submit to their masters and even to serve well when they had bad masters. The model of the sufferings of Christ and participation in his sufferings act as Paul's motivating influences.

Application of these exhortations in modern-day labor relations cannot be direct, given that slavery has mercifully gone from most nations of the world. Christian leaders, with their churches, should be active in protesting and facilitating deliverance from all forms of slavery and sex trafficking. However, there are certainly principles that can be drawn from what the apostles had to say to masters and slaves. Some applicable ones are the reciprocity of respect, the sharing of power, the mutuality of relationship between employers and employees, and the restrictions that qualify obedience to employers when they ask employees to participate in something that is unbiblical or unethical. The foundation for all of this will be the rights of all human persons as people made in the image of God.

For Authority and Submission in the State

The principles relevant to authority-submission relationships in the state can also be included within the area code of this commandment.[14] This includes respect and prayer for government at all levels, as well as submission to its laws, within the limits of the law of God. Christians should not dismiss the state, nor should they deify it. Christians may engage in peaceful protest and even civil disobedience when governments overstep their limits, or when they legislate or act in violation of the higher authority of God as revealed in his moral law. In Romans 13, Paul upholds both ends of the spectrum of how the Christian is to act toward government. On the one hand, he exhorts submission to even a cruel and dictatorial government like that of Rome. In fact, he speaks better of Rome than some Christians do of elected governments today. Government is God's "instrument for justice," an evidence of natural law. It is a gift to humanity, Bockmuehl insists, for, "were it not for government, we would be at war with each other at all levels."[15] However, while acknowledging its legitimacy, the Christian knows that it also has limits under the reign of God, as Peter signaled in the conflict with the authorities of his day: "We must obey God rather than human beings!" (Acts 5:29). Christians only position themselves under the government "knowing that it is under God."[16]

One way of speaking of this is to say that the "state is not under the church, but it is under God."[17] It is under creational, as opposed to covenantal, ordinances. The task of the state, therefore, is not to enact the standards of the Sermon on the Mount but to hold people accountable to laws that are at least approximately related to the second table of the ten commandments. In the time of the Reformation, Martin Luther developed the doctrine of two kingdoms, in which the kingdom of this world is under the law, and the kingdom—which is often closely equated with the church—is under the gospel. Calvin's version of the two-kingdom theology is slightly different from that of Luther, though even interpreting Luther properly is somewhat difficult. The viewpoint of both Luther and Calvin was expressed against the Roman Catholic perspective, in

---

14. The Lutheran Magdeburg Confession does precisely this. See Whitford, *Tyranny and Resistance*, 68.

15. Bockmuehl, *Christian Way of Living*, 88.

16. Bockmuehl, *Christian Way of Living*, 88.

17. Bockmuehl, *Christian Way of Living*, 88.

which church and state were intertwined, and against the Anabaptist withdrawal of the church from the state.

Luther distinguished between the church and the state on the basis of gospel and law, and therefore seemingly encouraged the *passivity* of the church with respect to any influence on the state. This quietist interpretation of Luther's view makes it barely distinguishable from the Anabaptist view, but it is not the only interpretation. His mature view of "the duties of citizens and of Christian magistrates in the face of tyranny" argues against it.[18]

Calvin also used two-kingdoms language, but his aims were not merely to distinguish between the state and the church, but also to allow for and encourage *activism* on the part of the church toward the state. The temporal realm was not independent from the church; they were in limited interdependence. The way Calvin functioned in Geneva showed that Christian virtues and moral concerns had an important influence in the public square.[19] This has typically led the Reformed tradition toward social and political activism.

Calvin's interpretation of the two kingdoms is related to the fact that he viewed law and its functions differently from Luther. The latter dichotomized law and gospel more radically due to a primary emphasis on the condemning function of the law. Calvin and Reformed theology after him considered law to be conditioned by the doctrine of the covenant, and understood gospel to bring about freedom from both the condemnation and the power of sin. Thus, as mentioned in a previous chapter, the Reformed uses of the law involved both the first (or civil) use and the third (or normative) use, in which the law returned as gift once its condemnation was removed. This is reflected in the Westminster Confession of Faith, which speaks of law under the covenant of works, and then of law as a "rule of life" that does "sweetly comply" with "the grace of the Gospel."[20] Law and gospel are thus less distinguishable in Calvin than in Luther. Luther is somewhat unimpressed with the potential of the church to have any influence on the state other than through evangelism, whereas the Reformed tradition has typically sought to be influential, speaking to the public square in appropriate ways in the spirit of being salt and light, rather than in the hope of taking over the state's functions. The hope of the church being transformational in the culture

---

18. MacPherson, "Magdeburg Interpretation of Romans 13."
19. John Calvin, *Institutes* 4.19.15; 4.20.1–32.
20. Westminster Confession of Faith 19.6–7.

has been a cherished one within North American evangelicalism. It has roots in the Puritans, was developed in the neo-Calvinist movement led by Abraham Kuyper, and then further through the influence of Cornelius Van Til and Francis Schaeffer, among others. Theocracy was not the goal of these influencers, but rather that the church would have a voice in the culture and influence on the state.

However, two opposite-leaning movements within Reformed and evangelical circles have stretched the direction of the church's influence. Some have attempted to move the church in a more theocratic direction, in which the church is aligned with a political party and intent on returning to Christendom. This has been the case with the Religious Right and the smaller Christian reconstructionist or theonomist movement, and it is a grave mistake. The church should not ever form allegiance with political parties in a democracy, for this is to blur the boundaries of church and state and to confuse the modes of operation of the church (peaceful protest, forgiveness) and the state (law making, use of force).

During the rise of Nazism and German nationalism, Karl Barth and Dietrich Bonhoeffer led a movement called the Confessing Church that demonstrated the need for the church to speak in the public square in the way that Calvin championed and yet to retain the clear distinction between church and state. These theologians reaffirmed Calvin's view of church and state as separate, with both under God. Barth led the Confessing Church in its opposition to government-sponsored efforts to unify all Protestant churches into a single pro-Nazi Protestant Reich Church. The Theological Declaration of Barmen, written largely by Barth (but modified in its two-kingdom section by Lutheran theologians), affirmed that the Word of Christ alone is the Lord of the church, and no political leader. At the same time it reflected an awareness that the church did not exist for itself but for the world. Thus, the declaration states, "We may not keep silent, since we believe that we have been given a common message to utter in a time of common need and temptation."[21] Barth urged churches and Christians to speak up as they could.

In the opposite direction, an influential group of mainly Reformed theologians has appealed to Martin Luther and his two-kingdom theology to form the 2K (Two Kingdoms) or R2K (Reformed Two Kingdoms) or NL2K (Natural Law Two Kingdoms) movement, which rejects the possibility that the church might influence the world or transform

---

21. Theological Declaration of Barmen 8.08, in *Constitution of the Presbyterian Church (USA)*, 282, cited in Cochrane, *Church's Confessions Under Hitler*, 237–42.

society. Christians should rather view themselves as citizens of two distinct kingdoms (the church and the world) and function independently within each realm.[22] If Luther is used to defend the 2K view, then it makes Luther's view indistinguishable from a separatistic Anabaptist view. This movement, by its abandonment of the world, continues to foster the tenets of modernity and the continued creation of a secular age.

Neither the two-kingdom view of Luther nor that of Calvin should be confused with Augustine's kingdom of heaven and kingdom of this world. In the Reformed view, both of these kingdoms were ruled by God, the state being responsible for preserving the creation order, and the church the redemption order. Force was permissible for the state, but not for the church, which exerted the reign of God through grace and forgiveness. As Bockmuehl states, "The church should not be conducting police investigations; the state should not be forgiving seventy times seven."[23] Christians operating as citizens of a country are subject to the laws of the state, whereas when operating as citizens of heaven and members of the church, they operate according to the Sermon on the Mount, turning the other cheek.

An example that may clarify this is that if, as a citizen of Vancouver and Canada, I am assaulted by someone for no reason, I should call the police and I should hold my assailant accountable to the law. The motivation for this is love of my neighbor, my fellow citizen who could be attacked by the same person if they are not charged with their crime. I may in my spirit forgive this attacker, but that does not mean I will not participate in his accountability process so that he is no longer a threat to my neighbor. On the other hand, if I am on a Vancouver street and I am respectfully and graciously sharing the gospel with someone, and that person lashes out at me and punches me in the face, I must turn the other cheek and not prosecute. If there is police intervention and the police decide to prosecute, it may be out of my hands. I will certainly not press charges, however.

---

22. This movement has been closely associated with present and former faculty members at Westminster Seminary in Escondido, California—ethicist David VanDrunen, theologian Michael Horton, historian Darryl Hart, and their students. See VanDrunen, *Living in God's Two Kingdoms*; VanDrunen, *Natural Law and the Two Kingdoms*; and Hart, *Secular Faith*. It has been described by John Frame as the "Escondido theology." See Frame, *Escondido Theology*. Other critiques include McIlhenny, *Kingdoms Apart*; Dennison, "Review of VanDrunen's Natural Law"; and Strange, "Not Ashamed!"

23. Bockmuehl, *Christian Way of Living*, 89.

When the state moves to legislate in ways that clearly contravene the laws of God or when it moves toward persecution of the church, the church may respond in one or more of the following directions:

1. The church and its members can speak in protest through writing and through wise speaking and preaching, using the weapon of language, not arms, in a prophetic and evangelical way. They should speak in the tone of the gospel, pointing to the good that God intends when his commands are obeyed, offering alternatives to the way of the world. The mode will never be coercion but persuasion—persuasion, not the making of laws.

2. They can exert civil disobedience in these areas in which the state has violated the laws of God and endure the persecution that will result from this.

3. They can emigrate from their city or country to a place where they will not be persecuted, in the spirit of Jesus's advice to his disciples ("When you are persecuted in one place, flee to another," Matt 10:23). If the church's realm is not that of the state, its pastors may speak to the state prophetically in all the ways that they can without blurring the boundaries of church and state.

But what about the individual Christian? Can Christians be politicians? This is a different question from that of the church as an organization being in the state's business. Even Martin Luther had no doubt that the wise Christian person who was called to be involved in government could surely do that.[24]

This distinguishing of the church and the state has many important ramifications in pastoral ethics. For example, when child abuse is uncovered in the life of the church, this cannot be resolved in-house. It must be reported to Child Services. Crimes that are uncovered by or confessed to a pastor must also be disclosed to civil authorities. Confidentiality cannot be held in these instances. They may lead to church discipline, but the state and not the church solves and sentences crime. Pastors, depending on which country they may live in, have a duty to report certain crimes they become aware of before they become complicit with the crime. Churches in traditions that are characterized by withdrawal from the state are more likely to blur these boundaries. Neither anarchy nor antinomianism is a Christian virtue. A pastor in Vancouver that I

---

24. See Estes, "Role of Godly Magistrates in the Church," 463–83.

know once received a confession of murder at the communion table on a Sunday. At the board meeting Monday night, one of the board members, a lawyer, informed him that he should have reported it to a lawyer or the police within twenty-four hours. Fortunately, the lawyer was able to help both the confessor and the pastor process this to completion without any recrimination.

Another situation related to church and state and their distinction is affiliation with political parties. I strongly discouraged this from a theological point of view above, but this is reinforced in many countries from a political perspective. In Canada, where I live, it is illegal for a church to host a meeting of any political party, even if it is in a side hall or gymnasium. The church can lose its charitable status if it insists on doing this. At one church I served, a candidate for a political party that was favored by many in my church approached me about using our gymnasium for a rally. I consulted with our denominational headquarters and was informed about this legislation. The candidate also asked for a copy of our church address and telephone book, and I refused him on the grounds of privacy laws.

Presence and Speech of the Church in the Public Square

The relationship between the church and state that has been described here does permit the presence and the speech of the church in the public square without commandeering the state's role. In democracies, it is very much in keeping with the church's wider mission of evangelism and justice and creation care to be visible as communities of shalom in fulfillment of the law of God, and also to speak with wisdom and truth in any way possible regarding issues where the state acts in disobedience to the law. How and when the pastor or the church should speak will be considered in more detail under the ninth commandment.

In sum, a fascinating range of applications all the way from the home to the workplace and on to national politics and the relationship between church and state has emerged from this commandment. The actual applications to each situation must be determined with care, but there is a consonance in all aspects of human life that makes this commandment always relevant. Establishing the legitimacy and limits of the state will have a great bearing on consideration of the ethics of life and death as we consider the sixth commandment.

8

Matters of Life and Death (Commandment 6)

You shall not murder.
EXODUS 20:13

This commandment provides a framework for thinking ethically about issues of life and death. In synecdoche fashion, as Calvin practiced it (see the discussion in chapter 4), this commandment is a prohibition of the taking of the life of one person by another person, *and* its opposite is an encouragement to be a life-giving person. The applications of this commandment extend to an area code of ethical issues that include how to think Christianly about capital punishment, war, abortion, euthanasia or MAID (medical assistance in dying), and suicide. In this chapter, I will consider the correct reading of this commandment, the rationale behind God's statement regarding the value of human life, and then its ramifications for these ethical areas.

THE RIGHT READING OF THIS COMMANDMENT IN SCRIPTURE

I will clarify what this commandment says in order that we may discover what it means. It is accurately translated "You shall not commit homicide," not "You shall not kill." The Hebrew verb form in Exod 20:13

is apparently rare, communicating that what is prohibited is the killing of one person by another. This includes murder with intentionality, or as a premeditated act, but also unintentional killing.[1] The commandment is elaborated in other laws (Exod 21:12–14; Num 25:15–28; Deut 19:4–13) to describe two types of killing, which are differentiated by way of intentionality, premeditated or accidental, and severity of judgment. The death penalty for intentional murder was never negotiable (Num 35:31–33; cf. Lev 24:17, 21), whereas the brazen altar of sacrifice (Exod 21:13–14) or cities of refuge (Num 35:6–15; Deut 19:1–13; Josh 20) were provided for accidental or unpremeditated murder. Significantly, this Hebrew verb is not used of capital punishment or killings in war. This verb would also not apply to types of killing such as abortion or in euthanasia. However, as Old Testament scholar David L. Baker has said, the "commandment implies the sanctity of human life, and may influence our views on these matters."[2] It is singular, and so is addressed to individual persons, not to the state.

Therefore, this commandment prohibits the taking of a human life by another human, but it does not prohibit capital punishment by the state (which is taught in the Pentateuch), though there may be more to be said on this subject in light of all of divine revelation. The point of capital punishment is that the value of a human life taken cannot be ignored in the moral universe God has created, and it must be compensated in "eye for an eye, tooth for a tooth" fashion. Even in the New Testament, Paul grants that the state has the right to wield the "sword" to punish the evildoer (Rom 13:4).

Therefore, second, this commandment prohibits an individual from taking another human life by taking justice into their own hands, but it does not preclude war. The issue of just and unjust wars is an important one to think through, but there is no prohibition on war and on soldiering in the Old or New Testaments, and issues of international justice and the protection of nations from tyrants are very much a part of justice in the moral universe God has made. The right of a nation to defend itself against aggression seems essential to good justice.

---

1. Baker, *Decalogue*, 103.
2. Baker, *Decalogue*, 103.

THE RATIONALE FOR THIS COMMANDMENT IN SCRIPTURE

The rationale behind this commandment is given well before the giving of the Ten Commandments, in Genesis 9. God as the giver of life asserts his authority over it:

> And for your lifeblood I will surely demand an accounting. I will demand an accounting from every animal. And from each human being, too, I will demand an accounting for the life of another human being.
> "Whoever sheds human blood,
> by humans shall their blood be shed;
> for in the image of God
> has God made mankind.
> As for you, be fruitful and increase in number; multiply on the earth and increase upon it." (Gen 9:5–7)

Note the hint of a positive equivalent for this commandment in the last phrase, which is the proliferation of life through procreation, though not only in that way. Fecundity in general is the opposite of killing.

This was said by God the Creator of human life, significantly, *after* the fall. The invasion of sin into human life did not reduce the value of each human being, for we are still creatures made in the image of God. The value of every human life is based on the reality that human beings, one with and yet distinct from every other creature, are made in the image of God and have breath that originates in the breath of God himself (Gen 2:7). Rabbi Akiva (ad 50–135), a Jewish scholar, explains, "Whoever sheds blood, scripture accounts it as if he had diminished the image of [God], for 'God made people in his image.'"[3] Speaking of the occasion when Jewish boys are circumcised (the *brith*), a modern Jewish theologian comments that everyone at the ceremony "stands up, everyone rises, the old and the young cry out '*Baruch haba*—blessed be the one who comes.'" "Why do we rise?" he asks. "We rise because this infant is born with the imprint of divine image, what we call *tzelem Elohim*, which the philosophers call 'Imago Dei.' This *tzelem* is a cardinal conception that lies at the root of Jewish belief, ethics, theology, psychology and social

---

3. Rabbi Akiva, Tosefta Yevamot 8.4, cited in Avioz, "On the Religious Significance of Shedding Blood."

action."[4] It is on this foundation that the condemnation of the taking of human lives is viewed.

Paul confirms in Acts 17:25–28 that, whether Christian or otherwise, people's life breath is the result of God's sustaining activity, and God watches over the beginning and the middle and the end of that life breathing. Psalm 104 gets even more specific: "When you take away their breath, they die and return to the dust" (Ps 104:29). The sanctity of human life and the sovereign right of God provide the rationale for this commandment: no individual has the right to take the life of another, not even a mother when a new human being is conceived within her body. That new human being is not her body over which she has rights; it is a new person made in the image of the triune God. Our mandate as God's vice-regents in managing the earth does not extend to the taking of other human lives—that is God's prerogative. His sovereignty limits ours in this area.

THE RAMIFICATIONS OF THIS COMMANDMENT IN SCRIPTURE AND SOCIETY

The Negative and Positive Statements

There is a *negative* restatement of this commandment in the New Testament by Jesus, in which he does not negate it but internalizes the commandment. In Matthew 5, Jesus reveals that it is not just murderers who violate this commandment. Anyone who is angry with his or her brother or sister will be subject to judgment, Jesus says. And when in anger we call our brother a "fool," gentle Jesus informs us we are in danger of hellfire. We need to understand this in the context of the whole New Testament and the reality that anger itself is not sin. God himself expresses anger against sin and those who remain unrepentant despite his offer of grace. For God, this expression of anger is never a mood or a loss of temper, but his settled and righteous reaction to sin, to injustice, as a holy God. Paul indicates in Ephesians 4 that to be angry is not to sin, but that in our anger, unlike God, we are prone to sin. The impulse of anger easily becomes hatred and intent to bring about self-justification and vengeance. Our selfish perspective on things often makes our anger lead to murderous

---

4. Schulweis, "Uniqueness of Judaism, Lecture 1, The Image of God."

impulses that are often unconscious but lead to depression, self-hatred, or passive-aggressive behaviors.

Jesus was showing the extent to which sin has twisted human nature and revealing our hopelessness and guilt without his righteousness. He was pointing us to the righteousness that exceeded that of the Pharisees—his righteousness that has become our righteousness by his becoming human for us and dying for us, and by our participation in it through repentance and faith. But he was also pointing us toward transformation in this area, as Paul confirms in Ephesians 4. As a concrete example of the putting off of the old self and the putting on of the new self in Christ, in union with Christ in his death and resurrection, Paul acknowledges the legitimacy of anger, the healthy experiencing of anger ("in your anger do not sin," v. 26), and the appropriate processing of anger: "Do not let the sun go down while you are still angry" (v. 26b). However, he warns of the distortions and Satanic manipulations of anger that are to be "put off": "do not give the devil a foothold" (v. 27), "get rid of all bitterness, rage and anger, brawling" (the aggressive expression of anger) "and slander, along with every form of malice" (v. 31, the passive-aggressive expressions of anger). Here is the antidote, the putting on of the new self: "Be kind and compassionate to one another, forgiving each other, just as in Christ God forgave you" (v. 32). The palliation for our anger and personal feelings of vengeance is the cross. There we have seen and been forgiven of our own faults and failings, and in light of that forgiveness we are able to forgive others so that our anger dissipates. Those who cannot forgive are those have not yet experienced forgiveness. Irrespective of what justice may or may not be done, personal feelings of anger and vengeance will need to be processed.

The positive statement of this commandment is evident not only from its transposition in Exod 20 but also from its foundation in Gen 9. There it is clear that we fulfill the opposite of this commandment in a creational sense through procreation in marriage. The opposite of murder is expressed in these terms: "As for you, be fruitful and increase in number; multiply on the earth and increase upon it" (Gen 9:7). This was one of the reasons why the Jewish nation did not practice abortion, though the nations surrounding it did. They understood the creation mandate to include being fruitful and multiplying. But procreation is not the only way we fulfill this command, since not all are married and not all have children. When Jesus worked his miracles, he equated "doing good" with "saving lives" (Mark 3:4). This commandment, therefore, is an encouragement for the medical profession, which is devoted to the saving of lives. The picture of the good Samaritan is an inspiration for those in all healing professions that are devoted to sustaining and saving life. This has an application for many vocations, including psychologists and counselors or anyone who counsels people toward the recovery of more joyful and whole relationships. Providers of food for humanity also do the work of this commandment. Furthermore, Christians who point people to Christ for salvation so that they may be saved eternally in resurrection life, rather than being condemned to eternal separation from God, are doing good by saving lives in a truly holistic sense.

Beyond the negative and positive statements of the commandment, it has many more specific ramifications for church and state, which we will now consider.

Capital Punishment

The negative statement of this commandment is a prohibition of the intentional taking of human life, no matter what form that human life may have. Homicide is the obvious case. As noted above, the Old Testament distinguishes between intentional and unintentional killing in a way that is reflected in legal systems to this day.

Where does personal forgiveness and mercy come into play on this issue? And how does this relate to social ethics? On the basis of the distinction drawn in the previous chapter between church and state, the state does not extend forgiveness but justice. It must act for the protection of the victim's neighbor to ensure the neighbor does not become the next victim. Indeed, the church must, in light of the first table of the Decalogue, hold the state accountable for justice. On a personal level, on the basis of Jesus's teaching in the Sermon on the Mount, we are discouraged from taking revenge and are encouraged to move on from anger to find a place of forgiveness. Jesus, as noted, does not negate the murder commandment but moves the discussion to the internal roots of murder, implicating every human being. This means that pastors need real sensitivity when walking alongside relatives who have lost a loved one to homicide or any other violent crime. One does not tell them in the initial stages of their journey that they need to forgive and move on. Walking with them will involve hearing and feeling their anger with them, and the pain that inevitably undergirds the anger. It may involve guiding them to an appropriate counselor. But there will come a time when they can be encouraged to forgive and let go, irrespective of what the state has meted out by way of a sentence. The Christian and the church, concerned about the vicious cycles of abuse and homicide in their community, can also participate in transformational initiatives and societal healing, while at the same time justice is being pursued in the state courts.

But what of capital punishment as administered by the state? Should the church support or oppose this? Arguments about this have sometimes focused on the effects of capital punishment, but the effects are hard to compute, and studies have shown conflicting results. Some studies seem to show that capital punishment is a deterrent.[5] Others state that the statistics are unconvincing.[6] Studying these ends is typical of utilitarian arguments. There is also a deontological approach. The utilitarian idea that one person's death is for the well-being of a society is refuted in the deontological approach of Immanuel Kant, who insisted that a person is always to be treated as an end and not as a means to an end. The matter of capital punishment was to be decided on the basis of rules or principles, not consequences.[7] So where else might we turn in deciding this issue, one that transcends both of these approaches?

Biblical texts seem at first take to favor capital punishment, for it is mandated in the law. However, the biblical witness thereafter is anything but clear. Even in the Old Testament era, there is a move away from the practice of the death penalty toward its abolition. The death penalty is commanded in the Pentateuch for a number of offenses, not just homicide—Sabbath breaking (Exod 31:14), homosexual behavior (Lev 20:13), bestiality (Lev 22:19), adultery (Lev 20:10), witchcraft and sorcery (Lev 20:27)—but these commands do not actually function in a way that leads to the killing of the offenders in Israel's history. Rather, the point seems to be that these offenses are grave and are to be taken with the greatest of

---

5. Liptak, "Does Death Penalty Save Lives? A New Debate." Liptak writes, "According to roughly a dozen recent studies, executions save lives. For each inmate put to death, the studies say, 3 to 18 murders are prevented."

6. An article titled "Revenge Begins to Seem Less Sweet: Capital Punishment in America," *The Economist*, August 30, 2007, questions the deterrent statistics. For example, the author states: "A crude way of trying to settle which camp is correct is to compare murder rates in jurisdictions with and without capital punishment. This offers no support for the notion of deterrence. In 2005 there were 46% more murders per head in states with the death penalty than in those without it, and that gap has widened since 1990. The murder rate in the United States as a whole, moreover, is far higher than in western Europe, where capital punishment is a thing of the past." There are too many variables at play to make conclusions about deterrence.

7. Yoder, "Noah's Covenant and the Purpose of Punishment," 2:480.

seriousness. In fact, God himself does not inflict the penalty in the case of the following people in the Old Testament who commit murder: Cain, Moses, David, Tamar, and Gomer. There also is not one single example of capital punishment for adultery in the Old Testament. Furthermore, there are no affirmations or discussions of capital punishment in the Prophets or later writings such as the Psalms or the Proverbs, Ecclesiastes, or Job.

Genesis 9:6 has been an important text in considering this issue: "Whoever sheds human blood, by humans shall their blood be shed; for in the image of God has God made mankind." This text has been used to justify capital punishment as universally applicable since it is given pre-law and not limited to Israel. Scholars in favor of the death penalty point to the fact that Jesus said nothing about the issue, that natural moral law continues to guide government, and that Jesus was interested only in personal responses and attitudes.[8] Counter to this is the possibility that Jesus is echoing Gen 9:6 when Peter cut off the ear of Malchus in Gethsemane: "'Put your sword back in its place,' Jesus said to him, 'for all who draw the sword will die by the sword'" (Matt 26:52). This is, according to New Testament scholar Claus Westermann, a chiastic proverb that could be rendered "all who draw the sword by the sword will die" (A-B-B-A pattern) and means "relying on the sword in your life will end up getting you killed," or "if you kill someone you will end up getting killed." This has led to the conclusion that Gen 9:6 is also a chiastic proverb that teaches proverbial wisdom rather than a command to enact capital punishment. John Howard Yoder sees the Genesis passage in this way, adding that since Christ has once for all expiated sin we do not need to expiate the cosmic moral order by means of capital punishment.[9]

It should be noted also that the Mishnah, which is the record of the authoritative oral interpretation of the Torah by Jewish theologians from 200 BC–AD 200, renders the death sentence almost impossible to carry out. Death-penalty trials required twenty-three judges, the testimony of near relatives was not admissible, and false witnesses ran the risk of the death penalty themselves.[10] By contrast, biblical law required two eyewitnesses (Deut 9:15). The Mishnah expresses an opinion about a court that executed as many as one man in seven years as "ruinous" or "destructive." Rabbi Eliezar ben Azariah adds, "Or one in even seventy years." Rabbi Tarfon and Rabbi Akiba assert that "Had we been in the Sanhedrin none

---

8. House and Yoder, "Noah's Covenant and the Purpose of Punishment," 2:461.

9. Yoder, "Noah's Covenant," 477–80.

10. Moore, *Judaism in the First Centuries of the Christian Era*, 2:184–87.

would ever have been put to death." Rabbi Simeon ben Gamaliel in a similar vein says, "[for the Sanhedrin to put someone to death] would have multiplied the shedders of blood in Israel."[11] While not authoritative, these rabbinic commentaries do seem to reflect the work of the most competent legal scholars in the centuries around the New Testament era.[12] These interpreters wrestle with a tension between the command of God given in the early history of the people of God and the reality of the dignity and value of every human life as made in the image of God.

The conflict over the centuries is between legal texts and community practice. It is important to note that the practice of capital punishment is not removed, but just becomes exceedingly rare. We can also not neglect the theocratic context in which the command was originally given. The command was given during the era of the direct rule of God over a covenantal community that was expected through its prophetic leaders, such as Moses and Joshua, to discern justice in communion with God. In most of Israel's history after this, the nation was under kings and was prone to spiritual declension.

What does church tradition have to teach us? A full consideration of the various views and their development is beyond our scope here.[13] There is piquant irony in the fact that the early church suffered capital punishment at the hands of Rome and then in Constantinian times found itself embroiled in inflicting it on others. The syncretistic combination of Roman law and biblical law became lethal. There are varieties of opinions in the church fathers and onward, but it is possible to discern a broad consensus in the Catholic and the Reformed traditions of the church, arising from the influence of Augustine and then Aquinas, that granted permission in rare circumstances and with the strictest of judicial processes. The

---

11. Danby, *The Mishnah*, 403. Makkoth 1.10.

12. See also "Christians and Capital Punishment." On page 48 these authors conclude that their work "strongly argues that in the final analysis, biblical teaching does not support capital punishment as it is practiced in contemporary society. Well-intentioned people of faith have and will continue to underwrite capital punishment with scriptural authority. . . . It is tragic that the church became intractably enmeshed in a nexus of violence which was foreign to the high calling of Christian discipleship. . . . The practice of capital punishment in our nation and state is an affront to biblical justice, both in terms of its impact on the marginalized in society and in terms of simple fairness. How can we perpetuate a system which is clearly so unfair and so broken?"

13. Two useful treatments of the historical development of this doctrine and its qualifications in the church's history and its differing traditions may be found in Owens et al., *Religion and the Death Penalty*; and "Christians and Capital Punishment."

Eastern Orthodox church does not offer a definitive statement on capital punishment, though some jurisdictions have denounced it.[14]

On this basis, it is possible to say that legitimate grounds exist both biblically and in the theological tradition for carefully administered capital punishment. The majority opinion has been that the state does have the right to effect capital punishment. However, along with cautious approval, there has been a similarly pervasive caution about carrying it out. The trend throughout the history of Israel to make it an extremely rare event has been repeated in the history of the church. Pope John Paul II, seen as the apostle of Vatican II and responding to the horrors of the world wars and concentration camps of the twentieth century, considered capital punishment to be the only major ethical issue needing reform in the tradition. He did not go as far as to say that it was immoral, but he treats it in a "purely negative light as a sentence only to be executed when unavoidable."[15] His position is grounded in a self-defense argument, prioritizing the safety of the victim and society, and he believed that "the conditions that necessitate capital punishment are largely a thing of the past."[16]

One factor influencing this trend of "legitimacy with lessening of use" has been consideration of the life-giving half of the commandment. John Paul II, for example, titled his encyclical "Evangelium Vitae," "The Gospel of Life," with this in mind. Capital punishment has, on the one hand, been rationalized on the basis of the protection of the neighbors of the victim. This is a self-defense argument that can be extended to include the protection of society at large. However, it has been countered that it may not in modern society with its prison system be necessary to put the perpetrator to death for the protection of society. Another argument against frequent use has been the reality that capital punishment removes the possibility of seeking a redemptive process in the life of the murderer—though it must be said that a number of years usually pass between sentencing and death that allow for such reformation. Theologians

---

14. The Orthodox Church in America issued a "Resolution on the Death Penalty" in 1989, which denounced it, but it has been neither fully accepted nor denounced by the church as a whole.

15. "Evangelium Vitae," para. 56. supra note 5, in John Paul II, *Encyclicals of Pope John Paul II*.

16. Bromberg, "Pope John Paul II, Vatican II, and Capital Punishment," here reflecting "Evangelium Vitae," supra note 5, para. 56 ("Today however, as a result of steady improvements in the organization of the penal system, [cases of absolute necessity to capital punishment] are very rare, if not practically non-existent").

have also expressed concern about the fairness of trials. There has been a particular concern for the fairness of trials for the marginalized or the poor, who may not have expert legal assistance and representation.

A most significant challenge has been presented to the "approval with qualifications" approach offered by "Evangelium Vitae."[17] Oliver O'Donovan has suggested that it justifies capital punishment on the grounds of classical retributive justice while seeking qualifications for the lessening of its practice based on remedial considerations that are by no means verifiable (they are utilitarian arguments) and tend to confuse the boundaries between church and state. While the boundary between church and state is permeable in terms of the church's influence as salt and light on the state and its practices, the state is still responsible for justice, which seems to be the main point of capital punishment. It is the loss of a life that is required to be compensated on the grounds of mere justice (O'Donovan) or at least as a way of putting limits around vengeance (Yoder).[18]

But is this position that permits capital punishment in keeping with a *trinitarian or gospel approach*? Yes, because justice is an attribute of the triune God that is intended to be present in the societies of his image bearers. O'Donovan's justification of capital punishment as justice is compelling. Retribution, he insists, cannot be ignored by civil authorities. Proper punishment by public courts "must pronounce judgement on the offense, describing it, disowning it, and refounding the moral basis for the common life which the offense has challenged."[19] O'Donovan speaks of the function of punishment as that which "gives back" the offense, in a way that transcends vengeance, which he describes as being purely "private." The end goal of punishment is just retribution in much the same way that truth is the reason why we make a statement. Punishment is therefore not a "means to some other end," even that of "making the offender good. Justice is inherent to the punishment itself."[20]

---

17. "Evangelium Vitae," para. 56, in John Paul II, *Encyclicals of Pope John Paul II*. For a more recent update on Catholic theology in this regard, see Brugger, *Capital Punishment and Roman Catholic Moral Tradition*. He argues that Pope John Paul II's position marked a watershed and that Pope Benedict XVI maintained the status quo on the teaching of his predecessor that capital punishment is societal self-defense.

18. O'Donovan, "Death Penalty in *Evangelium Vitae*," 220–23; Yoder, *Christian and Capital Punishment*, 7.

19. O'Donovan, "Death Penalty In *Evangelium Vitae*," 224.

20. As summarized in Hauerwas, *Religion and the Death Penalty*, "Punishing Christians: A Pacifist Approach to the Issue of Capital Punishment," in Owens et al., *Religion and the Death Penalty*, 64..

Capital punishment can be in keeping with trinitarian or evangelical ethics in the sense that it is the just requirement of the state, governed ultimately by the Son who is King of the state as well as Head of the church—entities that are distinct yet interdependent. It is in keeping with the teaching of the word of God in both its permission and the implicit carefulness in its practice. It still permits the church to be the church in the power of the Spirit, influencing the state, holding the state accountable with regard to the justice of legal proceedings through nonviolent protest and winsome influence on political and legal leaders within a democratic system. The church in the power of the Spirit can also help to bring redemption to convicted murderers on death row before their death through the Christian witness of guards or ministers who can access them before they die. Even if the witness of the Bible and tradition is that capital punishment is permissible for the state yet should be used extremely sparingly, there is a circumstantial nature to this issue. One cannot know in advance what should be done in any case. Wisdom is required. Even if it is not the church or even Christians who are deliberating on capital cases, the contingent nature of the decision-making at least echoes the trinitarian and evangelical nature of Christian deliberation on ethical matters.

One major objection to the death penalty that is gospel related has been expressed by Yoder in "Against the Death Penalty." There he states that the very culmination of the gospel story "is that the Cross of Christ puts an end to sacrifice for sin. . . . The Epistle to the Hebrews takes as its central theme the way the death of Christ is the end of all sacrifice."[21] This he believes to have implications for the death penalty, and therefore for the justice argument:

> Christians begin to deny their Lord when they admit that there are certain realms of life in which it would be inappropriate to bring Christ's rule to bear. Of course, non-Christians will insist that we should keep our *religion* out of the way of their *politics*. But the reason for that is not that Jesus has nothing to do with the public realm; it is that they want nothing to do with Jesus as Lord. . . . What we believe about Christ must apply to all our behaviour, no matter how many of our neighbors remain unconvinced.[22]

---

21. House and Yoder, *Death Penalty Debate*, 159, 176; Yoder, "Noah's Covenant," 474.

22. House and Yoder, *Death Penalty Debate*, 144; see also Hauerwas, *Punishing Christians*, 57–72.

Compelling as the notion that Christ's rule does extend everywhere is, Yoder's assertion here is somewhat triumphalistic and confuses church and state. The Son is waiting until the cosmic nature of his redemption will be fully realized. The book of Hebrews celebrates in the "now" the reality that "by one sacrifice he has made perfect forever those who are being made holy" (Heb 10:14) while recognizing that the perfected (justification) are still "being made holy" (sanctification). In the build-up to this great gospel text, the "now" or *finished* dimension of the offering of our King Priest is reflected in his seated posture: "When this priest had offered for all time one sacrifice for sins, he sat down at the right hand of God." But there is also an *unfinished* dimension to the atoning work of Christ, for "since that time he waits for his enemies to be made his footstool" (Heb 10:12-13).

It is true that in this era the implications and power of the suffering Christ and his atoning work must be lived and proclaimed by the church toward the state by way of influence, not coercion or legislation. But even if there is a permeable boundary of dialogue between the church and the state, the state remains the state until Christ returns to reign in the full and final sense. The state is responsible for administering justice, not forgiveness. Thus Yoder confuses church and state, or personal and social ethics. The state's administration of justice in capital punishment can, in the "now but not yet," be a provisional witness to the justice of God that will one day be fully revealed. The underlying issue is the created moral order in the universe. This is affirmed in Old Testament texts such as Num 35:33-34, where the land is polluted by unredressed murder, reaffirmed in the resurrection of Jesus from the dead, and ultimately made right in the atonement of Jesus.

Just War

There are three main positions in the Christian tradition regarding war enacted by the state: the pacificist position (Peace Churches, Quakers, Mennonites, United Brethren, some Plymouth Brethren, a minority within the Reformed tradition), which disavows war in all its forms; the relative pacifist position, which may allow war but never nuclear war; and the just-war tradition (most mainline and Reformed churches), which allows for war in the "now but not yet" era of the church's history, under given circumstances that are considered to be just.[23] One thing these positions have in common is that all responsible adherents to each must be committed to just peacemaking as a priority. War, for the just war theorist, is only just once all attempts at peacemaking have been exhausted. A good summary of each position can be found in *Kingdom Ethics* by David Gushee and Glen Stassen.[24] All three positions have strengths and weaknesses, but the one that has the greatest strength and the least weaknesses, and is supported best by Scripture and the tradition, is the just-war position.

O'Donovan's defense of this position is persuasive and convincing.[25] According to him, the background for considering just war involves three propositions:

1. that "God's peace is the original *ontological* truth of creation," and so creation was not made with inherent conflict in a dualist manner;

2. that "God's peace is the goal of *history*," and therefore there is no cultural value in war and there should be no heroic glorification of war as if it is "an advancement in civilization," for "war serves the end of history only as evil serves good, and the power to bring good out of evil belongs to God alone"; and

3. that "God's peace is a *practical demand* laid upon us"—meaning that we are to be peacemakers, not peacekeepers, that there is no such thing as a "right" to pursue war, that we must renounce all goods that can only be attained by war in which we sacrifice "our neighbors' good."[26]

O'Donovan could have with consistency added a description of "Jesus' way of peace-making" as described by Gushee and Stassen.[27] They quote Richard Hays, who notes "how impressively univocal is the testimony of the New Testament" in reinforcing the Sermon on the Mount's teaching on nonviolence.[28] They also affirm that the way of the kingdom of God is one of righteousness and peace, saying that "any legitimate use

---

23. Gushee and Stassen prefer to speak of three positions—just war theory, nonviolence or pacifism theory, and just peacemaking theory—but I have preferred to make the latter the foundation of all responsible adherence to the first two. See Gushee and Stassen, *Kingdom Ethics*, 149–75.

24. Gushee and Stassen, *Kingdom Ethics*, 149–75.

25. O'Donovan, *Just War Revisited*.

26. O'Donovan, *Just War Revisited*, 2.

27. Gushee and Stassen, *Kingdom Ethics*, 149–58.

28. Hays, *Moral Vision of the New Testament*, 332–33.

of just war theory must be based on non-violence and justice, as taught by Jesus . . . as the most effective way to minimize violence and injustice, not merely to rationalize making war."[29]

The point remains, however, that this teaching on nonviolence was for the kingdom and people of God in order that they might influence nations toward peace and justice. Yes, Jesus communicated to his own Jewish nation that they should not engage in war with the Romans, and their failure to pursue nonviolence led to the destruction of the temple in AD 70. However, he was addressing them as the people of God in his day. It is also true that the victory of God has already been won by the nonviolent submission of Jesus to suffering and death, which in turn invites his people to participate in the victory of God by bearing witness and martyrdom. It is also true that Christ's church ultimately had a significant influence on Rome through nonviolent proclamation of the word of God. However, it still seems to me that to expect nation-states in a fallen world to respond always in nonviolent ways is to confuse church or kingdom with state, to minimize justice as the basis for peace, and to forget where we are in history.

On this point, O'Donovan affirms that in our world that is not yet fully reconciled, crimes against peace happen. This is a reality in a world in which the kingdom has come but has not yet fully come, that has been redeemed yet not fully so. In such a world caught in the radical middle, a form of natural law persists, a created moral order that has been reaffirmed by the resurrection of Jesus. The upshot of this is that there is no peace without justice. The core of this law is the Great Commandment, the love and protection of the neighbor. Thus, to permit a dictator to plunder a neighbor's country is neither loving nor honoring of justice. In such a world, "secular" forms of judgment exist, having been sanctioned by God according to Rom 13, to the extent that these parties uphold justice. These principles may be extrapolated to international law.

This viewpoint relies on a distinction between church and state, and therefore between personal ethics gleaned from the Sermon on the Mount and social or international ethics grounded knowingly or unknowingly in the Decalogue. On the basis of the personal ethics of the believer and the corporate ethics of the kingdom community, the dynamics of personal forgiveness are to be pursued in the interests of peace and justice, and transformative initiatives are to be sought within society. However, this

---

29. Gushee and Stassen, *Kingdom Ethics*, 164.

dynamic does not pertain to the realm of international relations. Political and international ethics involve retribution, not forgiveness, in the restoration of justice for a nation that has been the victim of aggression. This sometimes involves war when all other forms of negotiation break down.

When this occurs, O'Donovan points out that the praxis of mortal combat is not destructive to human sociality and that there are codes of ethics even among soldiers. He also notices that "war" killings are always "separated off" in Old Testament history, meaning that they are not considered to violate the sixth commandment. That Jesus seems to validate the vocation of soldiers in the Gospels speaks also to this. O'Donovan points out that one cannot wage peace against violence in the service of international reconciliation: "Christians believe that violence in the radical ontological sense, 'is not'; and to oppose violence with peace is to agree that violence 'is.'" Therefore, he concludes, the praxis "which corresponds to the ontology of peace is not a practice *of peace* simply and as such, but a practice of winning peace out of opposition. 'Not the simple *being* of peace' as Bernd Wannenwetsch declares, but the *service* of reconciliation."[30]

However, he also insists that evangelical rejection of antagonistic praxis can be consistent with evangelical acceptance of just war. It is within the scope of the teachings of the Scriptures and the tradition, therefore, to suggest, as O'Donovan does, that evangelical counterpraxis to war involves armed conflict "reconceived as an extraordinary extension of ordinary acts of judgement." This must be subject to the limits and the discipline of ordinary acts of judgment. He states, "In the face of criminal warmaking, judgement may take effect through armed conflict but only as armed conflict is conformed to the law-governed and law-generating shape of judgement."[31] A war waged justly may therefore be a provisional witness to the unity of God's rule in the face of antagonistic practice of "*duellum*."[32] In the Anabaptist pacifist tradition, the state is

---

30. O'Donovan, *Just War Revisited*, 4–5. The reference is to Bernd Wannenwetsch, *Gottesdienst als Lebensform*, 127–29. O'Donovan makes reference also to John Milbank's *Theology and Social Theory*, 417, in support of the notion that antagonistic praxis has been superseded by the climax of salvation history, leading to the unifying order of the kingdom of God. The rejection of war is a distinctly evangelical rejection, not one flowing from natural law.

31. O'Donovan, *Just War Revisited*, 6, 14.

32. *Duellum* is the use of force for private ends by private individuals, or individual nations acting outside international law, as opposed to *bellum*, which is the use of force for public ends by public authorities responsible to defend those under their

assumed to wield the sword with worldly power, and Christians therefore cannot participate in war. Just-war proponents, however, assume that the sword can be wielded in just forms under the sovereignty of Christ over the nations, so that Christians may participate. As Arthur Holmes asserts, "Just war theory does not try to justify war. Rather it tries to bring war under the control of justice."[33]

This viewpoint has a deep history going back to Ambrose, Augustine (love-of-neighbor rationale), through Aquinas (justice rationale), and on to the Reformers. The initial qualifications for a just war involved the authority of a prince, a just cause, and a right intention for the war. This list has developed over the centuries.[34] Perhaps the most helpful is that listed and explained by John Stott, who states

1. that its *cause* must be *righteous*, that is, it must be defensive and not aggressive;

2. its *means* must be controlled, which means (a) it must be *proportionate*, as in the war should be the lesser of two evils, and the violence inflicted less than what would have been perpetrated by the aggression—another way to say this is that the gains should outweigh the losses, and (b) it must be discriminate, as in targets must be military ones and not civilians; and

3. its outcome must be predictable, as in there must be a reasonable expectation of success.[35]

In sum, the church can and should seek to influence the state with the peacemaking principles of the gospel. But when these break down, both just war and one form of pacifism allow for war as the best way to seek peace and minimize violence in this "now but not yet" state of kingdom existence.[36]

---

responsibility. *Bellum iustum* is just war. *Ius ad bellum* is justice toward war, or principles that justify war. *Ius in bello* governs conduct in war.

33. Holmes, *War: Four Christian Views*, 119.
34. Gushee and Stassen, *Kingdom Ethics*, 159–63.
35. Stott, *New Issues Facing Christians Today*, 100–101.
36. New Testament scholars such as N. T. Wright, Richard Bauckham, and Richard T. Hays lend support to the just war approach outlined here. Dietrich Bonhoeffer's work on this is also especially helpful.

Abortion

Abortion is not mentioned directly in the Bible, so theological deliberation on it requires looking at the broad contours of the biblical story, as well as at texts that infer principles that may be applied to it. Within the narrative of Scripture it may be discerned that human life in all its forms is sacred, and that the moment of death is the sovereign prerogative of God and is not to be caused by human action. Specific texts such as Ps 139 communicate at minimum that God considers life in the womb to be the subject of his special care and protection. They may not directly be metaphysical or ontological in their assertions, but conclusions of this may be drawn by inference.

Psalm 139:13–16 speaks of the action of God in human conception and of the crafting of the physicality and even the psychological expression of "persons" in the womb:

> For you created my inmost being;
> you knit me together in my mother's womb.
> I praise you because I am fearfully and wonderfully made;
> your works are wonderful,
> I know that full well.
> My frame was not hidden from you
> when I was made in the secret place,
> when I was woven together in the depths of the earth.
> Your eyes saw my unformed body;
> all the days ordained for me were written in your book
> before one of them came to be.

Notice three main ideas that may discerned in this text:

1. The fetus is the subject of God's creation ("For you created my inmost being; you knit me together in my mother's womb. I praise you because I am fearfully and wonderfully made").

2. There is continuity between the antenatal and the postnatal person. The psalmist surveys four stages of his life: before birth (v. 13, "You knit *me* together in my mother's womb"), after birth to the present (v. 1, "You have searched *me*"), the present moment (vv. 2–3, "You know when *I* sit and when *I* rise"), and the future (v. 10, "Your hand will guide *me*"). The psalmist sees no discontinuity between his personal identity in any of these phases.

3. Communion is what defines persons in a truly trinitarian way. The "I-You" and the "You-Me" covenant relationship between God and the psalmist, and the psalmist and God, is a key theme of this psalm. The "I-You" relationship is mentioned in almost every line (the pronouns "I," "me," "my" forty-six times, the pronouns "you" or "your" thirty-two times). The important issue for our purpose is that even the fetus has an "I-You" relationship with God: verse 13 says, "For *you* created *my* inmost being; *you* knit *me* together in my mother's womb."

Another text from which we may infer the nature of the fetus is that which describes the embryo of John the Baptist as having "leaped for joy" (Luke 1:44). By attributing an emotion to an embryo, the text seems to point to personhood, which is classically defined as having intellect, emotion, and will. Furthermore, in this paragraph, the word that is used for the prenatal "baby" (Greek *brephos*) is also used of a child already born (Luke 2:12; 18:15; Acts 7:19; 2 Tim 3:15). So the Bible in its contours and in the inferences that may be drawn from texts like this seems to be clear about what a human embryo is: it is a human person.

It is also important to add that while there is no specific mention of abortion in the Bible, we should not think that abortion was unheard of in biblical times. It was well known in the ancient world and was practiced in the Greco-Roman world. The Jews abhorred abortion because they understood the sixth commandment to be in opposition to it, and because they understood the positive aspect of the commandment was to procreate and bear children. They considered children to be a gift from God, and one of them might even be the Messiah. But the Jews were a bright spot in a dark world with respect to this issue. The fifth-century BC Hippocratic Oath did not succeed in restraining the practice in the Greco-Roman world, but it confirms that this was an issue even in the time period of the Old Testament: "I will apply dietetic measures for the benefit of the sick according to my ability and judgment; I will keep them from harm and injustice. I will neither give a deadly drug to anybody who asked for it, nor will I make a suggestion to this effect. Similarly I will not give to a woman an abortive remedy. In purity and holiness I will guard my life and my art."[37] When this oath was modernized to take ancient and obscure clauses out of it, this phrase was removed, and this

---

37. Edelstein, *Hippocratic Oath*.

was one factor in the liberalization of legal policies on abortion in most countries.[38]

Contemporary debates about abortion are complex in that it has medical, legal, theological, ethical, social, and personal aspects to it. This is for many people a highly emotional subject and can be a source of deep pain. I was once attending a service of a large charismatic church when the preacher stopped in the middle of his sermon and was prompted to pray for women in that congregation who had had abortions. The sheer number of women who raised their hands to be prayed for was overwhelming. When he prayed for forgiveness and emotional healing, there was audible wailing as they grieved and entered into some healing. The likelihood is high that all pastors have women in their congregation who long for absolution and healing. How you move into that will depend on the nature of your congregation and the circumstances, but it should be approached with wisdom and care, for silence is no resolution. In light of the millions of babies that have been sacrificed to abortion in the modern world, no Christian can opt out of having an opinion on it, seeking to influence the culture and the government on it, and offering forgiveness and hope to those who have experienced it. There is a profound intersection of the Christian doctrines of God and humanity that speaks to this issue with clarity, and specifically the sovereign right of God over human life in its conception and cessation. This is because of God's creational and providential activity in these matters, and therefore the sanctity of human life as created by that sovereign God.

There are some ethical complexities around abortion that require careful ethical deliberation in which the word of God, the Spirit of God, and the community of wisdom around us must speak. One of those is the situation when a mother's life is truly at stake. When both the lives of the unborn child and the mother are at serious risk, the mother's life is given preference because she could theoretically conceive again, and the lesser

---

38. The Declaration of Geneva (1948) modernized the oath to remove antiquated language, but also removed the abortion clause ("I will maintain the utmost respect for human life from the time of conception"). The modern version used in most medical schools, written in 1964 by Louis Lasagna, academic dean of the School of Medicine at Tufts University, is as follows: "I will respect the privacy of my patients, for their problems are not disclosed to me that the world may know. Most especially must I tread with care in matters of life and death. If it is given me to save a life, all thanks. But it may also be within my power to take a life; this awesome responsibility must be faced with great humbleness and awareness of my own frailty. Above all, I must not play at God."

of two evils would be abortion.[39] So-called therapeutic abortions may be valid in some cases, but advances in medical technology are such that this is very rarely an issue. The use of the term "therapeutic" has become the loophole for many inappropriate abortions.

Another complex situation I have encountered in pastoral ministry is where it is discovered that the embryo is anencephalic, that is, it does not have a brain. It may be possible to argue that a fetus without a brain is not truly alive, as it lacks a vital feature of what it means to be human, that is, to have intellect and emotion and will. But intervention should probably be avoided for two reasons: first, to allow for the sovereignty of God, and also for the emotional healing of the parents. These babies do not survive long after birth, and for the mother and father to hold them as they die can be helpful in the healing process.

In general, however, from the moment of conception (on one account) or from the moment of implantation when it becomes a viable human life (on another account), a fetus is a human person with a human life and must not be tampered with, even if the child will have some mental or physical defects. Personhood is an important aspect of this ethical stance. Personality is a psychological concept and can be formed by circumstances and relationships. Personhood, by contrast, is an ontological concept. It is the essence of human beings, uniquely created by God from the moment of fertilization, and is not able to be acquired gradually.

There have been three views of when a fetus becomes a human person, related to when the soul is deemed to be formed or given. Whereas the word "soul" in both Hebrew and Greek means the whole person, in this discussion "soul" means the inner aspect of the human person. The preexistence view of the origin of the soul was held by some of the church fathers, including Origen and Justin Martyr.[40] God creates souls from eternity, before the foundation of the world, and that soul becomes evident in the womb. On this view, the human is primarily thought of as a soul who has a body, and only the soul is immortal.

The second view that has been present in the history of the church is the creationist view. Again, God creates souls, but in this instance a soul is created and given to the fetus at conception, at animation, or at birth. Thomas Aquinas, following Aristotle's embryology, opted for the

---

39. As far back as Augustine, abortion was permitted when a mother's life was at stake. It was deemed "a necessary cruelty to kill the child in order to save the mother." Cited in Bockmuehl, *Christian Way of Living*, 97.

40. Schaff, *Nicene and Post-Nicene Christianity A.D. 311–600*, 490.

three-month point as that time when God imparted the soul to form a person.[41] Jerome was a strong patristic advocate for the creationist view, and in more modern times, Reformed theologian Charles Hodge also championed this view.[42]

The third view is the traducionist view. On this account, the body and soul develop together in the fetus from conception onward. Thus God creates, but he does so through the parents. An individual's soul, and not just the body, is therefore derived from the souls of that individual's parents. The assumption is that the only soul God created directly was that of Adam. This is considered to be the most orthodox view of the development of personhood in the womb. This is because it reflects a biblical and Christian view of human persons as body-soul entities, and a theological anthropology that affirms that the person is a body animated by the soul, and that the body and soul are inseparable. The first two views see the image of God as being present solely in the soul, whereas the traducionist view affirms the presence of the image in soul and body, and the immortality of both soul and body. Tertullian and Gregory of Nyssa were early proponents, with W. G. T. Shedd a notable advocate in modernity.[43] Augustine could not decide between the views, but did favor the traducionist view for its explanation of the transmission of original sin.[44]

The traducionist viewpoint leads to the view that abortion is always the taking of a human life from conception onward. The preexistence view has similar ramifications but is grounded in Greek philosophy rather than Christian theological anthropology. The creationist view speaks ambiguously to this issue depending on whether conception, three months, or birth is considered to be the point of the creation and impartation of the soul. This very language of bringing a soul to a body is Platonic in its origin. It is the official view of the Catholic Church that "the soul's creation coincides with its infusion into the human organism,"[45] and the

---

41. Aquinas, *Summae Theologiae*, question I, answer 2, ad 2.

42. Schaff, *History of the Christian Church*, 489; Charles Hodge, *Systematic Theology*, 65–72.

43. Schaff, *History of the Christian Church*, 3:489; Gregory of Nyssa, *De Hominis Opificio* 29, 44:233–34; Crisp, *American Augustinian*, 18.

44. Schaff, *History of the Christian Church*, 3:490. Writing to Jerome, Augustine says: "If that opinion of the creation of new souls is not opposed to this established article of faith [original sin] let it be also mine; if it is, let it not be thine." See Augustine, *Works of St. Augustine*, Epistle 166, n25.

45. Hall, "Ch. XIV. Q. 84. Traducianism and Creationism." For further study of

majority view specifies the moment of conception as that time when body begins and soul is created. This would thus be equally problematic for abortion at any stage. Creationists would argue that even if it is just the body from conception until the three-month point or the birth, the body is still sacred and should not be harmed.

In light of the church's understanding of abortion, how should it go about influencing the public square? It is an irony of our times that movies made about the Jewish Holocaust have, and I think rightly so, received great acclaim, yet the concept of a blockbuster movie about the holocaust of the unborn seems unthinkable. Francis Schaeffer and C. Everett Koop did not exaggerate this phenomenon when they described it in their book *Whatever Happened to the Human Race?* as "the slaughter of the innocents."[46] John Stott was on point when he said that "any society which can tolerate these things, let alone legislate for them, has ceased to be civilized."[47]

Abortion is a great test case for what it means for the church to have an influence evangelically in the public square that is pluralistic with respect to the metaphysical and moral foundations of ethical action. The church needs to face the grim reality that whatever we have done in Western countries has not worked to reduce the number of abortions. I remember going on a march on a cold wintry night to protest abortion in Kingston, Ontario, in the mid-1980s, when legislation was changing to allow abortion on demand in Canada. These protests are a thing of the past, and the church has largely gone to sleep on this issue. We need to start a movement of prayer for changes in legislation and for the protection of unborn babies and for the redemptive healing of mothers. We need at the private level also to offer forgiveness and healing for those who have undergone abortions. Through the atoning death of Jesus there is forgiveness for all sins, and through the resurrection there is hope of eternal life for both the mother and the infant who was taken in that untimely way.

---

this issue, see Francis Siegfried, "Creationism"; Clark, "Traducianism"; Crisp, "Pulling Traducianism Out of the Shedd"; Turretin, "Creationism or Traducianism?" For a creative alternative to the three historic positions, see also Farris, "Emergent Creationism," 321–39.

46. Schaeffer and Koop, *Whatever Happened to the Human Race?*, 29.

47. Stott, *Social and Sexual Relationships in the Modern World*, 191. Chapter 7 in this volume, "The Abortion Dilemma," 187–214, is still worth reading.

But we also need to be in the public square to continue to offer a *Christian alternative* for women with unwanted pregnancies, informing them of the choice of preserving the life that God has given and a means of support for the mother throughout the pregnancy, and support for the child that will be born, whether it is adopted or otherwise. I am grateful that crisis pregnancy centers offer that on behalf of the churches in our country. They are worthy of our support and involvement. In monasteries, "a revolving wooden chest used to be built into the wall so that poverty-stricken mothers could leave their children to the care of the nuns."[48] No doubt this continues, and there have also arisen adoption agencies with similar aims.

There is a strategy for the public square that is as yet undeveloped. Civil disobedience at abortion clinics has been tried and has its place.[49] However, when this devolves into violence, as it has by a minority of prolife advocates, it sends a contradictory message that has often driven people away from a prolife stance. Prolife movement leader Paul Swope has with regret commented that "for twenty-five years the pro-life movement has stood up to defend the most crucial principle in any civilized society, namely the sanctity and value of every human life. However, neither the profundity and scale of the cause, nor the integrity of those who work to support it, necessarily translates into effective action."[50] So what is the problem?

Swope believes that the movement has lacked discernment in the way it has made its moral appeal. The assumption has been that if only women "knew the moral status and nature of the fetus, they would never choose to abort."[51] Quite the opposite is true. It is reported that most women who go through with abortion are cognizant that they are taking a human life. When they weigh the options of unplanned motherhood, adoption, or abortion, the first "represents a threat so great to modern women that it is perceived as equivalent to a 'death to self.'"[52] Their perception is that their life is over, and that takes precedence over the life they cannot see. A moral appeal focused solely on the life of the fetus appears insensitive to the woman who feels she is trapped with no way out.

---

48. Bockmuehl, *Christian Way of Living*, 98.

49. See Piper's heartfelt plea in this regard in "Rescue Those Being Led Away to Death," in Rakestraw and Clark, *Readings in Christian Ethics*, 2:444–46.

50. Swope, "Abortion," 31.

51. Swope's argument as summed up in Hollinger, *Choosing the Good*, 270.

52. Swope, "Abortion," 32.

What is the solution? The moral appeal cannot compromise on the matter of the dignity and rights of the human life in the womb, but "public appeal . . . must make a connection with a woman's personal sense of well-being."[53] This is wise counsel for an evangelical approach in the public square. Beyond offering alternatives through crisis pregnancy centers, the church must in its speaking affirm the equality and dignity of women, find ways to communicate the dignity of childbearing, and do all it can to help women in that journey toward selflessness that does not detract from the true self.

The ultimate positive opposite of the negative of the sixth commandment is the story Jesus told of the good Samaritan. As that parable teaches us, it is not enough for us to deplore the crime; we must be ready to risk our own comfort and spend our money to bring healing to those in distress.

Prenatal and Preimplantation Genetic Testing

Discussion of the sanctity of human life in the fetus naturally leads to the ethics of compromising that life in the interest of harvesting fetal stem cells. To base our decisions on what good may arise from the use of these cells would be a utilitarian and spurious argument. We need to ask, What does the sanctity of human life have to say regarding *prenatal genetic testing*, which analyzes the genetic code of a fetus in utero, and *preimplantation genetic testing*, which is the assessment of embryos fertilized external to the womb through in vitro fertilization prior to implantation within the womb? On the basis of these technologies, parents may choose to terminate a pregnancy, select only nonabnormal embryos to implant, or select for a child of the sex that they may desire. Ethical deliberations on these issues can be complicated by the fact that genetic engineering can bring about the possibility of genetic therapy as a treatment of an abnormality or a disease. This factor aside, the pastor and Christian parents will increasingly face the ethical issues inherent to prenatal testing and preimplantation testing. What should guide us in these matters?[54]

A prime consideration must be the question of the sanctity of human life. Scott Rae has argued that promotion by public health officials

---

53. Swope's argument as summed up in Hollinger, *Choosing the Good*, 270.
54. I am indebted in this section to Ashleigh Brice and her research and essay "Prenatal and Preimplantation Genetic Testing," paper in Pastoral Ethics course at Regent College, April 13, 2018.

of genetic testing "for reducing the incidence of genetic diseases" can only be helpful if "the couples end their pregnancies," or if embryos are discarded.[55] Indeed, Ben Mitchell has argued that "decreasing numbers of children with disabilities are being brought to term, not because the disabilities have been cured, but because the screening test effectively paints a bullseye on their chest."[56] This "abortion assumption," as Rae terms it, is unacceptable given the sanctity of human life as implicit in the sixth commandment. There may be occasional exceptions in the case of pre-implantation, as for instance when genetic testing reveals the nonviability of a fertilized egg or zygote. As mentioned in the introduction, I encountered this situation in pastoral ministry, and it required intense prayer, listening to the word of God, and (most crucially for this case) receiving wisdom by consultation with a medical expert.

The questions of personhood and the emergence of the soul are crucial in the matter of the timing of genetic testing and actions that flow from it. As noted above, the majority voice in the tradition says that a human person exists from the moment of conception. Practically, it is difficult to ascertain when that moment occurs. Many Christian bioethicists would say that we can only know we have a viable fertilized zygote when it is implanted in the uterine wall, on approximately day eight or nine, while others think of the measurable beginning of life as the gastrulation on day fourteen, the moment when twinning can no longer occur. Other important markers have been suggested, such as the evidence of brain function, sentience, or the point of vitality.[57] This issue is important in the sense that if personhood exists from conception, then both abortions as a result of genetic testing and the discarding of embryos prior to implantation are problematic. If, however, the moment of implantation or gastrulation defines human personhood, discarding of zygotes may be permissible, and abortions of the fetus prior to these events is likewise permissible. While pointing to the majority opinion of the tradition that human life begins at conception, there is room for some disagreement, and any family or pastor will need to be convinced in their own mind. In my own opinion, implantation is the discernible place where we have a human person.

---

55. Rae, "Prenatal Genetic Testing, Abortion and Beyond," 138.

56. Mitchell, "Counting the Cost of Genetic Screening," 69.

57. Hui, *At the Beginning of Life*, 272–311. See also O'Donovan, *Begotten or Made?*, 51, for reflections on Jeremiah as a person in utero.

However, the bigger question in assessing the world of medical genetics is its view of the world. Joel Shuman has discerned well that medical ethics is embedded in a modern worldview in which progress and freedom from any limitation is the end goal. While not all modern aspirations are antithetical to Christian ones, medical genetics is ensconced within a "utopian project like modernity" and is therefore at odds with Christian thinking. Medical genetics has at its core "the unassailable belief that the proper goal of human life, and therefore the proper application of human knowledge, is the maximization of human freedom through an ever-increasing attainment of control over the effects of various kinds of freedom-robbing contingency." A Christian perspective is that the body in this fallen world is often "not what it ought to be," and while like modernity it looks forward to a "future state in which present perfections will no longer exist,"[58] the timing and means are very different.

There are two primary foci that distinguish Christian and modern ways of thinking about medical genetics. The first relates to anthropology, in particular whether humans are stewards or owners of creation. Whereas within a Christian worldview, "humans are charged with the responsible stewardship of creation,"[59] genetic testing may provide humans with the capacity to move beyond stewardship to playing God. Even within a Christian framework, it is not a trivial issue to decide when a human action or technology becomes a usurping of divine prerogative. This requires careful ethical reflection. Two realities are always in tension in medical practices. The first is that humans have been made as image bearers to be subcreators with God in his work in the world. The fact that humans have developed the ability to carry out sophisticated procedures such as genetic testing is a witness to the creativity of humans, and it reflects in some measure the creative wisdom and power of God. The second reality that must regulate the first is that we are not God, and our role is subservient and humble. Our role as faithful stewards informs us that whereas our capacity for human control of the generation of life may seem like the ultimate triumph of our existence as creative image bearers, we only do so in participation with God, in obedience to his commands, and in deference to the God-ness of God,

---

58. Shuman, "Desperately Seeking Perfection," 1010, 1012.
59. Shuman, "Desperately Seeking Perfection," 1013.

who has ownership of his creation and who sets limits with respect to life and death.

The second difference between a modern and a Christian understanding of medical genetics has to do with *eschatology*, and most particularly where we are in history, theologically speaking. This involves a place for a theology of suffering alongside a theology of healing.

Shuman points out that the nature of the calling of the Christian is to "wait patiently for the redemption of our bodies and to do the work of improving our lives only in ways that allow us to remain in proper relationship to God, to one another, and to the rest of creation."[60] The Christian orientation toward perfection in the present is that it awaits the fullness of the eschaton in the future. As Ashleigh Brice notes, "Such a teleological focus constrains the hope which Christians place on medical solutions to pain and suffering."[61] In light of the inbreaking of the kingdom of God now, research toward healing and wholeness is legitimate. Seeking to be redemptive in a broken world through medical care and research is a legitimate aim of medical doctors and researchers.

However, this does not have the utopic hope that suffering can be eradicated in this "now but not yet" era of history. The Christian worldview has a place for suffering within it. After all, Christian faith has at its center "a suffering, crucified God," a God who is with us as a "fellow sufferer."[62] The scandal of the cross of Jesus shows that the strength of God is in weakness and that the wisdom of God permits the vulnerability and suffering of his creatures, which may at times be refining, educative, and redemptive in their own journeys and in those of others. A life embedded in the incarnate and crucified Christ, rather than in modernity, acknowledges that "suffering is part of the human condition,"[63] and it does not seek to avoid death at all costs, for it has no ultimate fear of death. Not that suffering should be sought or romanticized, for masochism is not a Christian virtue. As Gilbert Meilaender has reminded us, "Suffering is not a good thing, not something one ought to seek for oneself or others." However, nor should we imagine "that suffering can be eliminated from human life," and "nor should we suppose that suffering must be eliminated by any means available to us."[64]

60. Shuman, "Desperately Seeking Perfection," 1013.
61. Brice, "Prenatal and Preimplantation Genetic Testing," 6.
62. Meilaender, *Bioethics*, 7; Swinton, "Body of Christ Has Down's Syndrome," 70.
63. Buttrey, "Toward a Moral Theology of Genetic Screening," 9.
64. Meilaender, *Bioethics*, 7–8.

Inherent with a theology of suffering is a theology of disability. In modernity, personhood has come to be measured on the basis of capacity. In terms of the image-of-God theology, this is to make the ontological or structural aspect of the *imago Dei* preeminent over the relational-belonging aspect, which is the core of the *imago*. The danger of measuring personhood or the image based on capacity is the utilitarian notion of "usefulness" gauged by markers such as "independence, productivity, intellectual prowess and social position."[65] As Michael Buttrey comments, we have reached the point of thinking that "having limitations is no longer part of the human condition but a deficient state."[66]

Into such a worldview, we must infuse a Christian theology of creation by a God who created every human being in love, a Christian theology of redemption revealed in its fullness in the cross of the Son, a Christian theology of sanctification that is accomplished by the Spirit through weaknesses made strong (2 Cor 12), and a Christian theology of the church as a body in which "the parts of the body that seem to be weaker are indispensable" (1 Cor 12:22). John Swinton reminds us of "dimensions of God" that are present in "the weakness and vulnerability of people with . . . disability" but that "have been hidden by our culture's preference for such things as power (and) strength."[67] A Christian way of being groans with the disabled in anticipation of the fullness of the new creation, but at the same time invites all into union with and dependence on the triune God of grace and comfort in all our trials.

Shuman puts together the present and the future with respect to being made perfect by reminding us that the "Christian expectation that we shall one day be made perfect is an expectation that requires us to accept the finally contingent nature of our lives and to acknowledge that we are dependent."[68] Thus, the role that suffering plays in the whole economy of God as well as the value that he places on those with disabilities adds up to a worldview that critiques the aims of genetic testing when associated with the assumption of abortion.

A factor that must also be given some consideration in weighing up the ethics of prenatal and preimplantation genetic testing is that of resources or cost. Research and usage of these technologies is costly and must be measured against the widening gap between the Global North

---

65. Buttrey, "Toward a Moral Theology of Genetic Screening," 9.
66. Buttrey, *Moral Theology of Genetic Screening*, 9. Swinton, "Body of Christ," 67.
67. Swinton, "Body of Christ," 67.
68. Shuman, "Desperately Seeking Perfection," 1015.

and South, or between Minority World and Majority World health challenges.[69] Spending what we do on gratifying our wishes for the kind of baby we want seems grossly immoral pictured against the site of malnourished babies in Somalia. Catering to privileged couples in this regard undervalues the problems of others in society, such as infertile couples, unwanted singleness, and so on.

In sum, while seeking to discern broad deliberative and prescriptive principles that guide the ethics of prenatal and preimplantation genetic testing (mostly negatively), it is important to say that there is a complexity to most individual situations that requires careful deliberation in wisdom by the power of the Holy Spirit. A pastor called on to give guidance on these situations should apply the strategy suggested throughout this book: seek to hear the word of God outside yourself, consult people around you with medical expertise and other pastors who have experience of the issues at hand, listen to the prompting of the Spirit from within, and offer answers humbly. When people make decisions contrary to your opinion, you are left with a choice. If the issues are unclear ethically speaking, and their action does not contradict clearly revealed biblical principles, the choice would naturally be to support them irrespective of what your advice was. If, however, the issues have been theologically clear and they have gone against them, then some form of church discipline may be required.

Euthanasia and Palliative Care

Another ramification of the sixth commandment is that life should be valued all the way to its end.

Categories of Euthanasia

Patient Will	Voluntary	Nonvoluntary	Involuntary
Method			
Passive (letting die)	Voluntary/ Passive	Nonvoluntary/ Passive	Involuntary/ Passive

---

69. See Maura Ryan, "Justice and Genetics: Whose Holy Grail?," 981.

| Active (intending death) | Voluntary/ Active (PAS) | Nonvoluntary/ Active (homicide) | Involuntary/ Active (homicide) |

There are three main kinds of euthanasia, which literally means "good death" or "mercy killings." The table above illustrates these kinds. The first may be categorized as to help in dying when a patient who is definitely terminal gives consent to their life being brought to a close, or it may involve the removal of life support when there is no reasonable sustainable life without the technology. This is passive in its action and not active, and so is voluntary euthanasia. There can also be situations where the patient's wishes cannot be known due to the fact that they are already not able to express a desire or decision. This is the nonvoluntary passive category. The involuntary passive category is the case of patients who are not able or competent to express a desire and whose relatives make the decision for them. Voluntary passive euthanasia is generally what occurs in palliative care or hospice wards. Pain medication is administered to ease or palliate pain to allow the patient to die by natural means in as comfortable manner as possible, but the medication is not the cause of death. It is normal for patients entering the final stages of their lives to sign a DNR—Do Not Resuscitate—form, which expresses the desire that if they should be in the moment of dying, no technologies or medical intervention should be employed to prevent them from dying. The hospice movement founded by Dame Cicley Saunders in the UK and was designed for this specialized end-of-life care, and from its inception was designed not to permit intervention of the kind that actively ends a life.

The second category of euthanasia is active and is defined as help toward dying. This most often occurs when the patient is not in the final stages of the dying process but sees no hope of recovery and asks for help to die more quickly than the normal process would take. This is the voluntary active euthanasia category (there is also nonvoluntary active and involuntary active, both of which would be considered to be homicide). This has become prevalent in the nation of Canada, for example, with the vigorous and strident imposition of medical assistance in dying.[70]

70. Moyse has written on despair and hope in relation to medical assistance in dying and modern anthropology in "Fodder for Despair, Masquerading as Hope." The bibliography in this article is a useful source for further study on this issue. See also Biggar, *Aiming to Kill*; Jason Goroncy, "Euthanasia: Some Theological Considerations for Living Responsibly," and his list of sources in "Euthanasia/Voluntary Assisted Dying: Some Theological and Pastoral Resources."

Physician-assisted suicide is another name for this phenomenon. This crosses the line from passive to active euthanasia and is clearly a contravention of the sixth commandment. The ethical challenge for nurses and doctors is considerable.[71] Roman Catholic hospices obviously do not permit medical assistance in dying and have attracted Christians from other traditions who wish to die in the safety of a palliative unit where lives are not being killed. The worldview that is embedded in the active euthanasia movement includes the same attitude toward perfection outlined above and a lack of appreciation of the value of suffering. It also is profoundly individualistic. The rights of the individual trump all else in modern society, including family, community, the moral law, and God.

The third category is the termination of a life not considered "worth living." This would be the involuntary active category. This also most definitely contravenes the sixth commandment—it is the usurpation of God's prerogative. The Nazis used categories such as "social usefulness" and planned to eradicate all special-needs people and epileptics on the grounds that they were "useless mouths." The truth is that no human is qualified to judge the value of a human life, and certainly no human being has the right to do so on the basis of "usefulness." It is our privilege to care for and profoundly value especially the helpless and the handicapped. In the act of caring for them, they often help us discover the true nature of love. We also, in caring for them, find ourselves caring for Christ (Matt 25).

Again, in the history of the world, there have, notably but not only in Nazi Germany, been many screams of silent victims whose injustices have filled the universe.

---

71. See for example an article by Ray Pennings of the Cardus think tank: "Why the Federal Rush to Amend Assisted Dying Legislation Is Risky." Pennings asks, "As it amends the legislation, how seriously is the government taking the urgent need to protect vulnerable patients from pressure to request MAID?" But then he adds: "It isn't just patients who are vulnerable. So are conscientious objectors to MAID. Conscience rights are Charter rights, yet health care workers who experience moral distress over MAID aren't adequately protected. Last year, the courts upheld a College of Physicians and Surgeons of Ontario regulation requiring doctors who object to assisted death as immoral to provide an effective referral to another doctor to carry out the procedure.

"This is problematic for at least three reasons. First, coercing doctors to provide a referral implicates them in subsequent actions their patients take. Second, it denies doctors the freedom to live according to deeply held personal beliefs, which no regulatory body has a right to dictate. And third, it can put them in the unenviable position of giving up careers in order to avoid moral distress. Yet the government has been ominously silent on conscience rights."

The matter of caring for dying persons and their families is an acutely sensitive one that comes under the subject of pastoral care rather than pastoral ethics. However, the pastor needs to be aware of these ethical realities.

Suicide

Suicide is a very painful and complex subject. On the one hand, to take one's own life is clearly a violation of the sixth commandment. On the other hand, it seems to be the case that most people who take their own lives are so ill emotionally with depression that their act is done in insanity, and I have to believe the Lord has mercy on them. There are those, however, who on intellectual grounds coldly commit suicide and boldly express the right to do so. This approach was evident going as far back as the Stoics in ancient times. It has recurred within the humanist movement in Europe, which has maintained the human "right" to kill oneself. Jean Améry's book *On Suicide: A Discourse on Voluntary Death*, even in his preferred use of the term "voluntary death" over "suicide," indicates a dedication to individual rights.[72] A reviewer makes the adroit comment that "he writes of suicide almost as if the act took place in an interpersonal vacuum."[73] Those who believe in this right have neglected the higher and sole right of God over human life.

Often a suicide is precipitated by an unbearable situation, or one that is perceived to be so. The Christian in her right mind believes that no situation is beyond the power of God to redeem and bring renewal. Christians have nevertheless committed suicide because in their depressive illness, this perspective escapes them. The threat of suicide, signaled by persistent suicidal ideation, should always be treated seriously, and the pastor or counselor must ensure that these parishioners or clients are directed to a medical doctor and held accountable to do so, or even better, taken directly there or to the local emergency department of a hospital.

Christians who refuse to take antidepressants when they have been diagnosed with professionally diagnosed clinical depression are turning down a means of grace for their well-being that God in his providence has given the medical profession. They are flirting with disrespect for the life God has given them. There is no doubt that antidepressants are

---

72. Améry, *On Suicide*.
73. Kirkus Reviews, "On Suicide."

overprescribed in our time and that counseling is necessary alongside pharmaceutical solutions. It is also a reality that the mechanism by which antidepressants work is not yet fully understood.[74] They are discovered empirically nevertheless and are valuable when taken responsibly and regularly. Christians who refuse to take them because they think of depression as a "spiritual" problem exhibit a gnostic tendency. Depression is complex, but it certainly involves the imbalance of compounds such as serotonin and norepinephrine. To say that one should not take antidepressants when one has depression is similar to saying that when one has diabetes one should not take insulin. There is a physical reality to depression, and it needs treatment. It may have a spiritual component, and it may lead to spiritual struggles such as the "dark night of the soul," as St. John of the Cross referred to it.

Pastors who refer people for professional medical and psychological help are still needed in the lives of depressed people. Their presence is very meaningful. The heart of pastoral care is presence. To be a listening presence is even more helpful, as are measured affirming comments about the love of the Father for these people. Pastors can also help to guide the person on the matter of where God is, and where they perceive God to be, in the midst of their painful journey. Good psychological, pharmaceutical, and pastoral care can prevent many a suicide.

THE REDEMPTION WITH REGARD TO THIS COMMANDMENT

The redemption that enables us to be forgiven of our failure to keep the negative statement of the commandment, and that empowers us to fulfil the positive expression of the commandment, is where I want to draw this reflection on the sixth commandment to a close. That redemption is at the cross.

Why did Jesus have to suffer and die? Why is penal substitution a valid and precious model of the atonement, among others (*Christus*

---

74. Depression certainly involves a biochemical reality, though this is complex rather than simple and still being researched. See Cowen and Browning, "What Has Serotonin to Do with Depression?" They write the following: "In an era of neural networks and systems level neuroscience, 'single' neurotransmitter theories of depression look increasingly implausible." They affirm that serotonin is still worth thinking about in relation to depression but that is a factor but one among others.

Victor, satisfaction, etc.)?[75] One reason was the justice deficit in the universe. It was because of the silent scream of infants murdered through abortion. It was because of the sometimes silent and repressed, and other times audible, screams of the victims of murder and genocide, and the rage of people against one another and against God. Jesus died to bring reconciliation to humanity in place of the alienation that sin caused. Our reconciliation was accomplished by God, the God whose justice demanded that a precious life, a holy life, be given as an atoning sacrifice for us. Instead of us paying the price for our rebellion and anger and alienation, one who became one with us by the incarnation paid that price. God in his righteous wrath against our sin could not sweep sin under the proverbial carpet. If he is going to justify his creation, that is, pronounce "right" over what went all wrong at the fall and since, he must do it justly. And it had to done by someone who had become a part of that creation, so that his life and death offering could authentically stand good for creation. That required a payment of the price for the precious lives forfeited, the payment of a life so precious that its being offered to God would justify the universe and make it righteous. That sacrifice of atonement, that propitiation, as Paul terms it in Rom 3:24, was the offering of the life of Christ on the cross.

There are two realities in the one event of the nailing of Jesus as our Savior, our representative, to the cross. The first is that expressed in the movie *The Passion of the Christ*, where Mel Gibson's hand on the hammer nailing Jesus's hands and feet to the cross is a fitting way to envisage that redemption. When it comes to direct causation of the kind that is sheer justice, our sins nailed him there. In an ultimate way, if these verses from Rom 3:24–26 mean anything, it was God himself who provided that very nailing.

The guilt for the nailing is ours, yet in the most amazingly redemptive way, our worst murder is God's best act of grace. Listen to Peter, just a simple fisherman, we say, state this most profound of all theological mysteries in his Acts 2 Pentecostal sermon: "This man was handed over to you by God's deliberate purpose and foreknowledge; and you, with the help of wicked men, put him to death by nailing him to the cross. But God raised him from the dead, freeing him from the agony of death, because it was impossible for death to keep its hold on him" (Acts 2:23–24).

---

75. For a defense of penal substitution as a model among others, with participation as the theory of atonement, see Hastings, *Total Atonement* (2019).

The second reality is that Christ's death was in God's foreordaining counsels. Note the care Scripture takes with wording here. It is wrong to say that God murdered his Son or nailed him to the cross. Humanity murdered him. The efficient cause of Jesus death was humanity. Yet in the sovereign will of God, he presented Christ as our atonement. By permitting his death, by permitting his being handed over to people, and actually by foreordaining the whole thing as Ultimate Cause, and through what was still a freely offered sacrifice on Christ's part—through our willful murder, Christ's willing sacrifice, and the Father's willed foreordination of the whole, the price was paid, God's justice was maintained, and our justification was achieved. His willingly offered life and blood alongside our greatest act of defiance and murder paid the price required to redeem and justify all our murders, murderous rages, thoughts, and all our abortions. We have been justly justified. We have been forgiven so much.

The social ethics of justice for lives taken remain. Alongside this, there are the personal ethics of the challenge of the journey toward forgiveness of those who have caused our deepest hurts, in light of the forgiveness we have received. It is at the cross where we find this resolution also.

9

Sexual Ethics (Commandment 7)

You shall not commit adultery.
EXODUS 20:14

If the sixth commandment was given to protect the sanctity of human life, the seventh protects the sanctity of marriage. Employing Calvin's synecdoche again, as with all the other commandments, it has a positive aspect. It assumes the existence of marriage, for one thing, because adultery has no meaning if there is no marriage. One positive fulfillment of this commandment, therefore, is the valuing and enrichment of marriage. The most effective strategy for the avoidance of adultery is the building of strong marriages in which each partners' needs are being met in a holistic way, spiritually, emotionally, and physically.

Second, this commandment assumes the reality of sexuality within humanity. It introduces the positive acceptance of the gift of sexuality, on the one hand, and it anticipates the appropriate and inappropriate expressions of sexuality in some sex acts, on the other hand. It must therefore be considered within its wider canonical context: the background concerning sexuality and marriage that precedes it in Genesis, where we discover the origin of sexuality and marriage; its exposition in the book of Exodus and in the rest of the books of the Law (Leviticus, Numbers, Deuteronomy); and its restatement and applications in the New Testament. There, the incarnation of Jesus and his resurrection from the dead reaffirm the goodness of the human body, including its sexed nature, and the apostles give moral and ethical instruction that reflects the importance of the body and sex over against Greek philosophy, which undervalued the body.

In this and the following chapter, this canonical interpretation will not be expressed linearly but will unfold in the course of discussion of the meaning of sex, the marital-covenantal context for the expression of the sex act, and universal human brokenness with respect to sex and its redemption. The important ethical topics of divorce and remarriage, homosexuality, and transgenderism will also be discussed. A final section will bring into focus the particular challenges that pastors encounter with respect to their own sexuality in the ministry.

THE MEANING OF SEX

All kinds of issues arise under the area code of this commandment. The most important are issues of identity and meaning. We are sexually differentiated persons made in the image of God, and although what sex we are may be secondary to our being, it is integral to who we are and how we relate. Our sexuality when created was pronounced by God to be "very good" (Gen 1:31), along with everything else about our originally created bodies. Our being made in the image of God (Gen 1:26–27) infers that there is something in God that corresponds to our sexedness (this term is preferable to "gender," which has come to mean a socially imposed *mental* construct that can be disconnected from the *body*). The image of God in its sexed aspect is embodied, and the resurrection of Jesus in a body reaffirms the goodness of sex and urges us not toward freedom *from* being sexual (repression) or freedom for whatever we like (license), but freedom *for* being sexual in ways that honor Christ and that serve what our embodied persons as a whole are called to (1 Cor 6:12–20). The embodied nature of sex must be primary in discovering sexual identity,[1] overriding desires that may come and go. God is mirrored when the distinctness of men and women is maintained *and* also when their equality and complementarity is honored.

---

1. Sexedness is an embodied reality that must be given priority over gender identity, though compassion must be extended toward people who for various reasons struggle with gender dysphoria (a state of dissatisfaction, anxiety, or restlessness around sexual identity). We must especially have compassion for those who are intersex, who are born chromosomally with the genotypes XXY, XXY, or XO and have phenotypes (physical features) of both sexes. Just as for other genetic abnormalities, we should assure people of the love and comfort of the Father and the hope of the "not yet," which is the eschatological nature of the image of God.

There is a distinction between sexuality as inherent to our *being* and the *act* of sex. Intercourse is not merely the exchange of bodily fluids but the interpenetration of persons, making intercourse outside marriage inappropriate. It is possible to embrace our sexual nature, on the one hand, and exercise self-discipline to avoid inappropriate acting out of our sexual desires in inappropriate sex acts, on the other. The identity marker of "married under a covenant made between a man and a woman" is God's designated criterion for the expression of sexual intercourse, for this has the possibility of procreation associated with it and prevents the proliferation of children outside the stability of a home. Or to say this another way, there are inappropriate acts of sex, which in both the Old Testament and the New include sexual intercourse outside the covenant of marriage between a man and a woman.

In navigating the maze of sexual issues, therefore, the most important questions that pastors must answer are questions of *meaning*. Peter Kreeft reflects this priority even though this question is frequently not asked in contemporary culture or even in the church's dialogues:

> We cannot know what X-in-Heaven is unless we know what X is. We cannot know what sex in Heaven is unless we know what sex is. We cannot know what in Heaven's name sex is unless we know what on earth sex is. But don't we know? Haven't we been thinking about almost nothing else for years and years? What else dominates our fantasies, waking and sleeping, twenty-four nose-to-the-grindstone hours a day? What else fills our TV shows, novels, plays, gossip columns, self-help books, and psychologies but sex? No, we do not think too much about sex; we think hardly at all about sex. Dreaming, fantasizing, feeling, experimenting—yes. But honest, look-it-in-the-face thinking?—hardly ever. There is no subject in the world about which there is more heat and less light.[2]

If these are not the questions people are asking, pastors must somehow prompt those questions. The question is not so much whether the Bible teaches that sexual intercourse is reserved for marriage only, and for marriage between and man and a woman only, but *why* it teaches that. Should two people who love each other not be able to have sex without being married? If not, why not? The most puzzling thing for our culture is how any restrictions on sex can possibly be loving, given that "love," as interpreted by the culture, is everything. The populist questions of our day are,

---

2. Kreeft, *Everything You Ever Wanted to Know about Heaven*, 117.

"how can it be wrong when it feels so right?" and "how can two people loving each other ever be wrong?" The answer in part is that love has no moral content in our culture, and that sexuality has lost its meaning. The most asked question ought not to be whether the Bible forbids premarital sex, for that is evident in a number of ways in various texts,[3] but *why* the Bible commands that.

The most pressing issue for most people who are Christians and who are honest about what Scripture teaches ought not to be whether same-sex sexual activity is biblically forbidden. Rather, it should be to ask what ontological and theological realities undergird biblical commands around sex. What goodness motivates these commands? Convincing contemporary culture, even the evangelical Christian culture, that someone with incurable same-sex desire must be celibate is a tough sell, principally because of a failure of the church to speak about *being*, or ontology, and specifically what in the triune Godhead our human sexuality mirrors. The greatest challenge that faces the faithful Christian church and its pastors is to communicate meaning, and in doing so to speak evangelically in this area.

Too often the church is known for what it is against and does not communicate the delight and wonder of what it means to be a sexual being whether single or married, and of the joy of sex within marriage. Stanley Hauerwas, while realistic about the nature of the challenge,[4] has made the point well that we need to convey sexual purity as even more of an adventure than sexual promiscuity:

> For example, when Christians discuss sex, it often sounds as if we are somehow "against sex." What we fail to make clear is that sexual passion (the good gifts of God's creation) is now subservient to the demanding business of maintaining a revolutionary

---

3. Genesis 2:24, where "the becoming of one flesh" is possible only after the public leaving of the parental home and the uniting in covenantal declaration; Deut 22:13–29 (esp. 14–15); Matt 1:18–24; Luke 1:26–38; 1 Cor 7:36–38. The Bible clearly forbids premarital sex, for example in Deut 22:28–29. There is an understanding from passages such as Deut 22:13–22 that stoning was mandated if a person was discovered not to be a virgin when married. Later, Joseph's reaction when he thought Mary had cheated on him is evidence of how seriously virginity was taken. When we have sex with someone outside marriage, we defraud that person's future spouse. Even if that person does become our spouse, we have violated God's will for sexual intercourse in the security of covenant commitment only.

4. Hauerwas states, "No ethic, not even the most conservative, should be judged by its ability to influence the behavior of teenagers in the back seat of a car." Hauerwas, *Community of Character*, 182.

community in a world that often uses sex as a means of momentarily anesthetizing or distracting people from the basic vacuity of their lives. When the only contemporary means of self-transcendence is orgasm, we Christians are going to have a tough time convincing people that it would be nicer if they were not promiscuous.[5]

The meaning of sex begins to unfold in the Genesis 1 statement, "So God created mankind in his own image, in the image of God he created them; male and female he created them" (1:27). Being male and female as humans is an integral part of being reflectors of the image of God. In light of the fuller revelation given to us in the New Testament of the content of the word "God," we may say that the attraction of male for female and vice versa, the sexual binary that runs throughout Scripture from Genesis to Revelation, is a picture (sacrament) of the relationship between God and humanity, Yahweh and Israel, Christ and the church, the eschatological wedding supper of the Lamb the union of the Bridegroom, Christ, and the Bride, the Church. In light of the fuller revelation of God in the New Testament we may say that maleness and femaleness of humanity is a sacramental reflection also of the differentiated union within the Trinity. The Trinity consists in completely interpenetrated, mutually internal persons in a union and communion in which each shares equally the same divine essence. It is also an echo of the differentiated union of the divine and human natures in the one person of Christ, the Son. The Trinity is the primal union in the cosmos, transcendent above, yet immanent to humanity, a union made up of coinherent persons who are irreducibly distinct. It is not surprising therefore that he has created human persons distinct with respect to their sexedness, designed for union with persons of the opposite sex. The Trinity is a communion of the attraction and communion that the persons of the Trinity have for each other. One person says of the other things like "I am in the Father, and . . . the Father is in me" (John 14:10), or "I and the Father are one" (John 10:30). The reality reflected in the sexedness of humans is that the persons of the Trinity are equal in that all three are God, but they are also persons who are distinct in their identity. A trinitarian anthropology suggests that our sexedness mirrors this one-yet-differentiated God, who reveals himself in Christ in this way because this is who he is in his eternal being.

---

5. Hauerwas and Willimon, *Resident Aliens*, 63.

The union of the Trinity is also echoed in the union between Christ and his church, which consists of both singles and male and female persons in the union of marriage, who reflect to Trinity in different ways, as we shall shortly see. Scripture thus not only knows only a sexual binary (male and female) in marriage and marital sex, but it "sees this binary as fundamental to the very picture of the relationship between God and his people."[6] It is acknowledged readily that the union of humans in their differentiated sexuality is not univocal. Divine persons are completely mutually internal to one another, whereas the relations between a man and a woman are an analogy of the Trinity. But analogy is what they are.

So, when we relate as persons to other persons in ways that are true to our differentiated sexedness, we are fulfilling our design as creatures made in the image of God. Honoring our distinctive sexedness profoundly honors the God who created us to commune as equals who celebrate their differentiation as distinct persons, including our distinct sexedness. In addition to this intratrinitarian anthropology is the divine triune romance toward humanity, which is the heart of the gospel that has pursued and found us. Human romance that is energized by sexual energy and culminates in sexual intercourse in marriage simply echoes the gospel. Pope John Paul II, in his *Theology of the Body*, has commented that the sexually differentiated nature of the bodies of married persons have *spousal* meaning. He states that "Let us not forget that the only key to understanding the sacramentality of marriage is the spousal love of Christ for the Church (cf. Eph 5:22–23)."[7] Our bodies actually speak the gospel in the way in which they are made for the other. This union of differentiated bodies is once again sacramentally significant indicating that our bodies are made ultimately for union with God. Our bodies are made for union. They are other-oriented.

In support of what we have insisted regarding the importance of ontology, John Paul II also points out that the Genesis 1 account of creation is both theological and that it contains a powerful metaphysic for viewing sexuality related to the Creator-created relation, and a "communion of persons, man in the image of God."[8] Commenting on Matthew 19 which has both Genesis accounts as context, and where Jesus says, "Have you not read that the Creator from the beginning made them male and female . . . ? (Matt. 19:4)," John Paul goes on to point out that Jesus

---

6. Bruce Hindmarsh, personal email communication, October, 5, 2024.
7. John Paul II, *Redemption of the Body and Sacramentality of Marriage*, 209.
8. John Paul II, *Theology of the Body*, 9–10, 24–25.

affirms the sexual binary in created humans, the nature of marriage as male-plus-female and marriage as intended to be permanent.[9] John Paul's resulting ethic is categoric: there must be faithfulness within marriage between a man and a woman, and celibacy outside of marriage. He insists that all Christians are called to chastity, and some to celibacy. He speaks also of how Christ outlines three explanations of conditions that call for celibacy: some are born that way (biological), some are made that way by men (social), and some choose this for the sake of the kingdom (a personally chosen calling).[10]

There can be no understanding of the meaning of sexuality, then, apart from its being grounded in the mystery of the God that we image, that is the mystery of trinitarian theology and the gospel. The goodness of seeing sexuality as a consequence of creation in the image of the triune God of grace is that it drives us out of ourselves and into relationship with others, but we do this with distinct personhood, of which our sexuality is a part. Our sexuality serves our personhood and draws us to love our neighbor in holiness. This is true of all persons, single or married. This is a reality that transcends genitalia, though it will govern and guide their functioning. James Houston states that "to know the Triune God is to act like Him, in self-giving, in inter-dependence, and in boundless love."[11] He also says that maleness and femaleness were essential for humanity to be the image of a triune, eternally intimate God. To be an artistic expression of God, we needed to be male and female, and this takes us beyond the biology and psychology of sex to its spirituality

God did not just create the sexual drive for procreation. Its purpose is to drive us to seek him, to seek community, to move outside self to the human other. It may be defined as energy that directs us to seek God and others. It is "the energy for relationships that compels us to seek connections with others."[12] Sexuality presses us toward the very core of Christian spirituality: to love God and to love neighbor. R. Paul Stevens expresses this well:

---

9. John Paul II, *Theology of the Body*, 9–10, .

10. John Paul II, *Theology of the Body*, 9–10, .

11. Houston, "Trinitarian Spirituality." See also Sarah Coakley, *God, Sexuality, and the Self*," for her call for a reconception of the relation between sexual desire and the desire for God, specifically using prayer as a means to discover how this relation has an intrinsic connection to trinitarian theology.

12. Clinical pastoral education training material cited in Bucher, "Personal Response to 'Betrayal of Trust.'"

> Therefore God-likeness is a social reality. True spirituality is interpersonal, relational. Relationships are pathways to God. So the purpose of human sexuality is not merely for procreation, or for the mutual blessing of covenant partners, though both are good in themselves. Sexuality was designed to be first and finally contemplative so that we would seek God Himself. Whether we marry and procreate, or remain as singles celebrating sexual diversity in a co-sexual community, sexuality is designed to turn us toward God, to make us prayerful, and to evoke our faith.[13]

Coming to terms with our identity as sexual beings in a healthy, God-honoring way is as much a challenge for married people as for singles. Disordered sexual desires are the common lot of all human persons. In fact, married people who are privileged to act out their sexuality in sex can often mask the fact that they are not healthy sexually. Good sex in marriage is sex in the context of respectful, mutual, and whole-personed intimacy, and it finds its proper place when marriage partners are satisfying their core longings in God.

Being in touch with legitimate sexual desires enables us to order our desires whether we are married or single. If married, the mutual pleasure of sexual intercourse is intended to be experienced within the relational intimacy between a man and a woman that covenant enables. The experience of relational intimacy within a marriage oscillates, and covenant is the house that holds the relationship together throughout the vicissitudes of turbulent seasons. However, agapē covenant love in turn inspires the pursuit of the intimacy and the eros that flows from it.

But what about being a single person with sexual desires? Must the single person forever be condemned to sexual frustration? On the one hand, Scripture does make clear that sexual intercourse is for marriage between a man and a woman. Pursuing the ordering of sexual desires as single people is the calling of every Christian disciple. Ordering them is not the same as repressing them. Resurrection life in Christ means neither repressing nor expressing our sexuality but *experiencing* ourselves as sexual beings and ordering our desires to what our persons are called to do. Christ incarnate reaffirms the goodness of our human bodies, including our sex hormones and organs. Christ as a single person also affirms that having sex is not necessary for being human. All of us are called to be aware, in touch with, our sexual desires, experiencing them in order to be able to choose what we will do with them. We order them toward God in

---

13. Stevens, *Disciplines of a Hungry Heart*, 68, 69.

worship and spiritual practices of all kinds. We order them toward loving our neighbor, which includes not causing them to miss what they are called to, not causing them to move beyond the boundaries a good God has placed on the expression of sex.

The Scriptures put covenantal bounds on sexual intercourse for good reasons. Sex unites persons, not just bodies. It is too powerful, too holistic an event to be treated casually, but it is countercultural for a person to believe in and practice biblical sexual boundaries in our time. My wife and I have recently been watching episodes of the sitcom *Friends* (1994–2004), which she did not see when they were shown originally. The casual sex between unmarried people in that show both reflects the culture of the time and no doubt influenced its generation too. In many contemporary movies and reality shows, people who are virgins are treated as unusual or deficient. The popular belief is that a person who does not have sex must be emotionally and physically frustrated. There is no "freedom" for such a person, it is imagined. What is the answer to this?

The Scripture that proscribes sex outside marriage also describes the creation of the human person in its totality, including its sexuality, to be "very good." Sexuality is good, and reflects the goodness of God in its expression and limitations. It is true that the fall has affected the whole human person, and perhaps this is most evident in the sexual aspect of our being that so closely corresponds to the nature of God. However, post-fall, sexuality is still celebrated in the biblical narrative, most notably in the Song of Songs. Old Testament scholar Iain Provan affirms its original intent to reveal the wonder of sexuality:

> Christians are called, therefore, to proclaim a resounding "yes" to sexual expression, *in the context of a resounding "yes" to God.* It is in this proclamation, rather than repression of humanness and in our preaching of negative rules, that the goodness of God will be seen by others. . . . We have presented God to the world . . . as a God of unreasonable prohibition (Gen 3:1) rather than as a God who blesses us with freedom.[14]

Elizabeth Gentry, in her reflections on singleness and sexuality in light of the celebration of sexuality in the Song, bemoans the repression of sexuality in her evangelical upbringing and the shame and fear associated with it: "The evangelical culture of *I Kissed Dating Goodbye* repression, in which sex is shame-producing, neglects the reality that we cannot

---

14. Provan, *Ecclesiastes, Song of Songs,* 252.

and should not deny our sexual being and experience it in union with Christ and by the power of the Holy Spirit."[15] Her answer was not to reject the biblical injunction to avoid sex before marriage. True freedom with respect to sexuality is not the freedom of license. It is the discovery of freedom in God's freedom. It is the cultivation of relationship with God and our fellow humanity that fulfills the purpose of sex. It is walking in the awareness that having sexual intercourse is not necessary for being human. It is looking to Jesus, the prime example of that, and walking in union with him, since he was the most fulfilled human person who ever lived, and that he was this without having sex. Gentry, responding to Provan's insight, describes this freedom:

> When we proclaim a resounding "yes" to sexual expression as single people, it must first and foremost be in the context of our original resounding "yes" to Jesus Christ and living into the life for which we were truly created. We let go of the fear and guilt and shame and embrace who we are as sexual human beings within the context of who God has created us to be. My fiancé and I are not abstaining from sex because some pastor told us to or because we're afraid it will someday ruin our marriage. We're abstaining from sex because we *love God* first and foremost and desire to experience the life God has for us! I would be lying if I told you neither of us ever struggle with shame. However, not a day goes by that I am not filled with an inexpressible joy and love for him as we pursue each other and God together and embrace our sexuality in godly ways.[16]

Why did God create within us this powerful drive? It is evidence of the goodness of God, who creates us in his image to be other-oriented persons, to be in relationship with himself in our spirituality and other humans in community.

In a similar vein, Ronald Rolheiser describes a godly pathway that embraces sexuality for which everyone—regardless of relationship status—can strive. He writes,

> Sexuality is a beautiful, good, extremely powerful, sacred energy, given us by God and experienced in every cell of our being as an irrepressible urge to overcome our incompleteness, to move towards unity and consummation with that which is beyond us.

---

15. Elizabeth Gentry, "My Resounding 'Yes' to God and Embracing My Sexuality." The reference is to Harris, *I Kissed Dating Goodbye*.

16. Gentry, "My Resounding 'Yes.'"

> It is also the pulse to celebrate, to give and to receive delight, to find our way back to the Garden of Eden where we can be naked, shameless, and without worry and work as we make love in the moonlight. . . . Sexuality is not simply about finding a lover or even finding a friend. It is about overcoming separateness by giving life and blessing it.[17]

Gentry gets to the heart of the path forward for Christian disciples and their sexual life:

> Embracing our sexuality while single is not about sexual conquest and denying the life God would have for us. Embracing sexuality while single is the ability to see where our lives and our world are incomplete and finding ways to give and receive life in the midst of the brokenness. Does this image Rolheiser presents take away the sting and pain of loneliness? No, not always. But slowly and surely God begins to open our imagination to see the transformation of our desires begin to take shape around what God has for us. So may we all learn how to embrace our sexuality by giving the best of ourselves to all relationships and all goodness in life. May our resounding "yes" to God ring out and show the world a godly sexuality in all its fullness—whatever form that may take.[18]

This helps us to understand how people (including those with same-sex desires) can be single and not sexually active but still sexually whole and fulfilled. Noted Christian leader John Stott, who was single all his life, commented that "sexual experience is not essential to human fulfillment. To be sure, it is a good gift of God. But it is not given to all, and it is not indispensable to humanness."[19] If marriage were required for sexual wholeness, Jesus would have been shortchanged. The single person's sexuality is expressed in his or her capacity to love and be loved. Loving does not need to be genital to be intimate. In the context of deeply caring, emotionally fulfilling, and healthy relationships, sexuality can be experienced without being expressed genitally.

In fact, Jesus's teaching that there will be no marriage in heaven relativizes the importance of sex in this life, and ameliorates the command of God that sex is preserved for marriage between a man and a woman

---

17. "A Mature Sexuality," Ron Rolheiser, OMI, May 28, 1998, cited in Gentry, "My Resounding 'Yes.'"

18. Gentry, "My Resounding 'Yes.'"

19. Stott, *Same-Sex Partnerships?*, 70.

in covenant. It is a cherished axiom of our age that all humans have the right to have sex, whether same sex or opposite sex, and that deprivation in this regard is unfair on God's part or even harmful to the single person. This Freudian assumption flies in the face of the good intentions of God for humanity.

Jesus's teaching suggests that sex as we experience it here is limited temporally and in terms of the fulfillment that we look to it to bring. I believe it also suggests that sex only points to the fulfillment of intimacy with God. The pleasure that will be ours in heaven must be so much greater than sex here that sex and its pleasure is small by comparison. All of this means that intimacy with God is the highest source of pleasure—higher than sex—and it is available to all humans, single or married.

Our sex drive, therefore, whether we are single or married, should drive us to seek intimacy with God. This will enable singles to handle their sexuality without sinning in the inappropriate acting out of sex, and it also helps married people not to put so much pressure on sex to satisfy desires that can only be satisfied by connecting relationally in emotional, intellectual, and spiritual ways, with God and with their spouses as well as with friends.

Our too-great obsession with sex is a sign that we thirst for something deeper. When we try to satisfy that deeper thirst for God in sex, sex becomes an addiction at worst, and an imposition in marriage at best. When we let our sex drive take us into ourselves instead of to God and others, it has lost its intended design—that of reaching out to the "other."

This points us also to the reason why sex is not ultimately for the self, why acts of sex that are self-focused cannot ultimately be the healthiest expressions of sex, and why even sex in marriage should not be carried out in a self-oriented way (1 Pet 3:7). Sexuality is other-orienting, or contemplative. In general, we *experience* sexuality to drive us out of ourselves toward others and God. It can be expressed as a consummation of covenant (two become one flesh), which involves a public act of leaving, a commitment to cleaving, and the pursuit of lifelong intimacy. Stanley Grenz points to the incongruity of premarital sex when he states, "Sex outside of marriage . . . involves two people in a life-uniting act who do not have a life-uniting intent."[20]

A common question that teenagers and unmarried people (and indeed married people) have about sex is, "Is masturbation wrong?" Since

---

20. Grenz and Bell, *Betrayal of Trust*, 83.

Scripture is silent on this, it is a diaphora issue, that is a gray area where each person or parent or community must make up their own mind. The only mistake that can be made by parents and pastors is not addressing it, in light of how much anxiety and guilt it may cause in teenagers who want to be godly.[21] Whilst it is difficult to say that masturbation is a sin, given it is never mentioned directly in Scripture,[22] it may be possible to say some things based on all that has been said about the meaning of sex in this chapter. On the one hand, we may say that the capacity to practice it is a product of having a body that was created good—a human body in fact that is pronounced as "very good" in all its aspects. It may be considered therefore to be a part of normal bodily and sexual development. On the other hand, one may also say that masturbation is not the ultimate good concerning sex. It is not an act that fulfills the intended orientation toward the other that sex is meant to have. Furthermore, we may also say that humans are fallen, including in their sexuality. In fact, especially in the area of sexuality, given its importance to reflecting the image of God (Gen 1:27). These factors urge us toward great care in the practice of masturbation lest it become addictive or compulsive,[23] or accompanied

---

21. Opinions range from the Catholic Church's, that it is "an intrinsically and seriously disordered act" and sin, to that of Charlie Shedd, who considers it to be "a gift from God" to avoid promiscuous sex, or a natural "safety valve" for teenagers while their growth in other areas (emotional and social) is synchronizing with their bodies. See Shedd, *Stork Is Dead*, 70–80. On the Catholic Church's position, see Lutzer, *Living with Your Passions*, 69–73. Parents should decide what they think about this issue and speak to their children about it. There is too much anxiety around this issue in teenagers for it not to be informatively and compassionately spoken about. As Richard Foster concludes, "Silence is no counsel, and repression is bad counsel." See Foster, *Money, Sex and Power*, 120.

22. Masturbation is not specifically mentioned in Scripture, though it may be implied in Lev 15:16, in which case there is an implication that it could have been allowed as an occasional release of sexual energy rather than a compulsive habit. That it is not mentioned in chapters such as Lev 18, which leaves no stone unturned in prohibiting inappropriate sex acts in a very graphic manner (the Bible is not prudish about sex, either in Leviticus, where it prohibits perversions, or in Song of Solomon, where it celebrates sex), or anywhere else in Scripture, surely must say something about its relative moral unimportance.

23. There are dangers to masturbation, however. It can be depersonalizing, and it can prevent reaching out in healthy relationships. It can also easily become obsessive and uncontrollable such that it dominates a person's life and keeps them in deep emotional and spiritual bondage. The very focus on overcoming it becomes an obsession, which is self-absorption. Such obsessiveness in practicing it and then seeking deliverance from it usually requires exploration of other under-the-surface issues such as unresolved anger, pain, and abuse. Masturbation should not become a substitute for relationships such that it becomes a "hell of self-love," as C. S. Lewis described it.

by pornography, which is an entirely immoral objectification of another human person. Richard Foster warns that "lust is an untamed, inordinate sexual passion to possess, and this is a very different thing from the usual erotic awareness experienced in sexual fantasy."[24]

The question as to whether sexual energy can be dissipated appropriately in masturbation without a person fantasizing inappropriately, as Foster is suggesting, is also a difficult one, but the reality of being created as sexual beings implies that having some level of generalized sexual fantasy is normal—it is the distortion of fantasy into lust that is prohibited. Lewis Smedes has articulated this distinction well: "When the sense of excitement conceives a plan to use a person, when attraction turns into a scheme, we have crossed beyond erotic excitement into spiritual adultery."[25]

The reportedly high percentage of persons who have engaged in masturbation[26] does not constitute an ethical principle. It may, however, point towards some plain bodily realities which it is impossible to ignore. Sexual maturation in a young person is part of the goodness of the body created by God. Encouraging total repression of created bodies is likely to be harmful, whereas failure to warn of the dangers of autosexuality in light of our fallen nature as human persons, is equally harmful. On the one hand, as Smedes has indicated, "masturbation aborts the interpersonal direction of sex," and on the other hand, he adds, "we must not . . . come down too hard on masturbation for its self-centredness," given that all people entering sexual unions look for self-fulfillment also. Using masturbation as a way of satisfying oneself would only be wrong, Smedes thinks, "if it were a lifelong substitute for interpersonal sex." He goes on to comment that for most young people, masturbation is a "passing phase of sexual release" on the way toward the "search for intimacy with another person," in that awkward phase of life when bodily development runs ahead of social or educational readiness for marriage. Smedes sums

24. Foster, *Money, Sex and Power*, 121.
25. Smedes, *Sex for Christians*, 210.
26. According to James McCary in *Human Sexuality*, 212, 95 percent of all men have masturbated at least once, and 50–90 percent of women also. Alfred Kinsey et al. reported 92 percent of men and 62 percent of women at least once in their lifetime in Kinsey et al., *Sexual Behavior in the Human Male*, 297–302. More recent studies suggest lower percentages. See Robbins et al., "Prevalence, Frequency, and Associations of Masturbation with Partnered Sexual Behaviors among US Adolescents." It is safe to say that the majority of males engage regularly in this practice as adolescents and that there is a marked difference in the statistics for females.

up his comments on masturbation by saying that "moral concern about masturbation must focus on its role in the youngster's total development toward a wholesome heterosexual life."[27] He advises parents to help their teenagers to see and accept masturbation as part of their growth as a human being, and show how it fits with their overall development.

Masturbation may therefore be considered as a provisional good for teenagers and single persons, thus preventing sexual promiscuity. That is, it may be a relative good when practiced with the kind of discipline that avoids pornography and intentional ideation of a particular person, when it is seen in the context of a temporary practice in the context of sexual maturation, and when it is limited in its frequency so that it brings sexual relief but does not master us (1 Cor 6:12–20). Such appropriate control is only possible if, as encouraged above, sexual energy is directed toward and dissipated through the emotional outlet of healthy friendships and practices that foster communion with God.

On the issue of how much physical contact is permissible before marriage, it should develop consensually in proportion to the level of commitment in the relationship, full sexual intimacy being reserved for marriage. This may seem profoundly out-of-date and counter-cultural in our time, but it is the way of shalom. Too much physical intimacy, too soon, can hinder the development of friendship and the emotional, intellectual, and spiritual aspects of a relationship.

THE GOODNESS OF THE MARRIAGE COVENANT

More detail is given about the origin of humanity and sexuality in the second chapter of Genesis. In particular, the expression of sexuality in the act of sexual intercourse is spoken of within the institution of covenant relationship, with procreation and the stability of the family unit in mind as the telos: "That is why a man leaves his father and mother and is united to his wife, and they become one flesh" (Gen 2:24).

This passage reflects three essential elements of marriage: (1) The concept of leaving is a public act of moving out from one's parental authority. (2) The word used for "be united" or "cleave" (KJV) is the Hebrew word dabaq, which means "to covenant" or to adjoin in a permanent way. It was the word used for the soldering of two pieces of metal. To be united in this way is to be superglued together. When wood that has been

---

27. Smedes, *Sex for Christians*, 139–40.

superglued is pried apart, it seldom breaks at the joint where it was glued. The splintering is evocative of what happens in divorce, and explains in part why divorce is so painful and requires great healing. (3) The third essential in marriage as God instituted it is that the two would become one flesh in their coming together sexually. This is highly evocative of the Trinity's oneness in plurality. More than one person mysteriously become one, with a communion that is an analogy of the oneness of the one true God.

So, if Gen 1 celebrates sexedness and calls us to embrace and experience ourselves in healthy ways as sexual beings, Genesis 2 celebrates sex when it is carried out within the covenant of marriage. But Genesis 2 also reveals the seriousness of sex in that it unites humans in a way that reflects the union of the persons in the triune Godhead. This is why God limits sex to those who, by means of the public declaration of a covenant, are in a permanent relationship that images in this life the permanency of the relationship that the persons of the Trinity have with each other. This is one reason why the Catholic faith calls marriage a sacrament—it is a sign of the Godhead, and Ephesians 5 indicates that it is also a sign of the union between Christ and his church! This is why sex is permitted only within the covenant—it brings people into profound and permanent union with each other.

Eight inferences for ethical reflection and ministry may be drawn from this text, which is repeated and reflected on in Matt 19:6 and Ephesians 5. The first is that sex is so meaningful that it *unites people*. Sexual intercourse creates a mysterious one-flesh bond. The most graphic evidence of this is given in 1 Cor 6:16. Paul states that when a Christian man has sex with a prostitute he becomes one body with her, and Paul uses Gen 2:24 to reinforce this. This reality is what undergirds the seventh commandment, which prohibits adultery for married people, but it is also what makes premarital sex and cohabitation so wrong for people who have not yet professed public covenant. Sexual intercourse, as Foster says, "involves something far more than just the physical, more than even the emotions and psyche. It touches deep into the spirit of each person and produces a profound union that the biblical writers call 'one flesh.'"[28] In the biblical way of viewing humans, we do not *have* a body, we *are* a body; we do not *have* a spirit, we *are* a spirit; and what touches the body touches the spirit. We are "bodypersons," as Smedes suggests.

---

28. Foster, *Money, Sex and Power*, 117.

Sexual intercourse is "a life-uniting act."[29] Derrick Bailey adds, "Sexual intercourse is an act of the whole self which affects the whole self; it is a personal encounter between man and woman in which each does something to the other, for good or ill, which can never be obliterated. This remains true even when they are ignorant of the radical character of their act."[30] Sex must therefore only be engaged in by those who have come into a level of commitment that is protected by covenant permanency. It should be remembered that God does not command singles in their sexedness to be contemplative and celibate because he is a killjoy. He just knows that the power of the sex act—it unites persons—is too great to be unleashed outside of covenantal marriage between a man and a woman. Nor does he command married couples to contemplation and to lifelong faithfulness to their spouses in order to be cruel but because this is the arena in which, over the long haul, character is built and true love is cultivated and in which children are reared in a stable context so that they may also take their place in society. Celibacy and marriage may thus be considered to be twin ascetic, sanctifying vocations.

The second inference from this text in canonical context is that *the practice of sex must reflect its meaning*, derived from the Trinity, creation, and the resurrection. This means that even sex in marriage should not be carried out in a way that is focused purely on the self. This is the sharp message of 1 Pet 3:7, where Peter tells Christian husbands that if they seek to fulfill their sex drive without honoring their wives as spiritual equals, and if they do so outside a context of relational and emotional nurturing of their wives, their prayers will bounce off the ceiling! Good sex in marriage is like other aspects of the life of Christian discipleship and the cross: it is as we seek the good of the other that we experience good for ourselves. The way "up" is "down." Give yourself away to the other in mutuality and reciprocity, as 1 Cor 7:4–5 encourages, and you will find yourself.

The third inference is that God's creation purpose for marriage has as a corollary intent: the purpose of *procreation*. The Song of Songs suggests that marital sex does involve legitimate and joyful recreation. Procreation is, however, one of the intended aims of marriage. One argument against same-sex marriage is that natural procreation is not a possibility for such a union. The telos of children being raised in families with a mother and father is not a possible outcome of such unions. There are other reasons

---

29. Smedes, *Sex for Christians*, 16–17, 35, 65, 128.
30. Bailey, *Mystery of Love and Marriage*, 53.

of a more ontological kind that explain why same-sex unions are prohibited by Scripture and Christian ethics that will be considered below.

A fourth corollary of marriage unions as instituted by God is that children were intended to be raised in *families* formed by them. The covenant of marriage plays out in faithful childrearing. However, the nuclear family cannot stand alone, and careful thought is required to express the fullness of the teaching of the Scripture and the kingdom of God on family. The creation of the nuclear family in Genesis 2 was preceded with the more general concept in Gen 1 of community without specific reference to marriage. The will of God and the givenness of creation is that *all* humans live in *community*, not as isolated individuals. Ray S. Anderson insists that from its inception as the penultimate contingent relation to God, family has to do with the fulfillment of the core social paradigm and therefore is a larger concept than the nuclear family.[31] He presents a compelling argument that where there has been breakdown in the nuclear family, there can still be the concept of family, which can house the nurture of children. He speaks of "familying," a verb expressing the universal need that all humans have for community in a home environment. Singles can avoid profound loneliness by being in missional community houses, by being "familied" by each other. Similarly, single parents can with their children know the blessing of being familied. Jesus's teaching on family also relativizes the concept of the human family so that we do not make idols of family, as is prevalent in North American culture. Under the new covenant, the family of God—the church—is the primary community of the Christian, though not to the exclusion of human families. It is best to speak of the family of the church, the family of grace, as that which includes and mutually nourishes and equips the natural biological family, the family of nature, as passages such as Eph 6:1–3 and Col 3:18–21 allow. Grace does not destroy nature but restores it. Churches must be sensitive to a variety of family situations and do all they can to support and nurture single parents, for example.

The fifth area for ethical and ministerial reflection is that of *marriage preparation* for couples. Given the depth of what is involved in marriage and its covenantal and sacramental dimensions, and given the rate of marital breakdown in our societies, it is a matter of ethical necessity to offer preparation for marriage. In fact, churches should develop policies and procedures around requests to conduct weddings that can

---

31. Anderson, *Something Old, Something New*, 168–70.

protect the pastors from taking the brunt of the fallout from decisions they make in this regard. Premarital counseling, carried out by the pastor or a trusted counselor or a couple that has been equipped by the pastor, ought to be mandatory. A policy that states the church's or denomination's stance on same-sex marriages is essential if the church is to avoid litigation. Guidelines for how to approach weddings between two non-Christians, between a Christian and a non-Christian, between couples who are already living together, and who may or may not have children, are also important. I use the term "guidelines" with intent. Whether a church does or does not allow same-sex marriage is a rule. The other situations are guidelines. This is an area of ethical deliberation that requires the approach I have proposed throughout this book: hear the word of God from outside yourself as clearly as you can; listen for the counsel of other wise scholars (old and new) and pastors and elders or deacons as you consult, consult, consult (with appropriate confidentiality); pray constantly and listen for the voice of the Holy Spirit within you, forming a conviction about what is the most principled and redemptive thing to do. What makes this ethical area difficult is that there will often be conflicting principles. Let me illustrate from my own experience as a pastor.

A woman made an appointment to see me about getting married to a man she had been living with for four years. She was a professed Christian, and he was not. She realized the untenable nature of this situation and so wanted to move beyond "living in sin." This was already complicated, but then came the further revelation that he had three kids from a previous marriage, who were now mothered by her, and they had one further child from their own union. They had started to come to church recently, and the husband was showing keen interest in the faith.

So, what should be done in a case like this? The first factor to bear in mind is that one does not need to give an answer right away. The first appointment should be about asking questions and offering a welcoming posture. This gives time for the hearing of the word of God, the consulting, and so on. The second appointment should involve both the woman and the man to ascertain their attitudes and affections. Any decision to marry them should, as with all couples, depend on how the premarital counseling goes. Beginning premarital counseling brings about the opportunity to know them and even to lead the unconverted to Christ. (In my years as a pastor, I led more people to Christ in premarital counseling than any other means, apart from preaching.)

At the end of the day, in the situation above, the desire to be married is an honorable one, expressing the wish of the Christian to repent and not to be cohabiting outside marriage any longer. Even though the woman in the example was not married, her attachments to the children and husband made her case comparable to the women Paul instructs in 1 Cor 7:12–14 to not leave their unbelieving spouses, given that they can be instrumental in sanctifying them. To refuse to marry them, even though it may be an "unequal yoke," would have been to ignore the bonds that had been formed in this home and perpetuated its unstable nature. In this case, the husband came to know Christ in the process of developing a relationship with me through premarital counseling, so there was no unequal yoke. There are deontological principles in play here; there are also missional or redemptive principles at play. Consequentialism can never be a primary argument, but when principles conflict it may be helpful, under the leading of the Holy Spirit and in keeping with the reconciling and redemptive purposes of the Son.

The sixth area of discussion precipitated by the concept of covenant and sacramental marriage is the ethics of *divorce and remarriage*. The entry into this complex area must be through the gate of what marriage is. A high view of marriage as covenant leads to a robust view of when divorce and remarriage are permissible. A low view of marriage leads to an easy divorce policy. Space does not permit a full discourse on divorce, which involves complex exegesis of a number of passages (Gen 2:24; Exod 21; Deut 22:13–21; 24:1–4; Matt 5:31–32; 19:4–6; 1 Cor 7:10–16; Eph 5:21–33, to name a few) and a multiplicity of views in the tradition.[32]

- The Catholic view allows no exceptions for divorce, but it does allow remarriage if an annulment is granted. The annulment is acknowledgment that the first marriage was not a sacramental marriage and that God was not part of the decision to marry. Divorce is not a sin that leads to excommunication. A divorced person can participate in the sacraments, unless that person remarries without an annulment given by Catholic diocesan tribunal.

- The majority patristic view considers that adultery is a legitimate cause for divorce, but remarriage is not permitted, based on the exegesis of Matt 19:9.[33]

---

32. See Cornes, *Divorce and Remarriage*; Hervey-Small, *Remarriage and God's Renewing Grace*; House, *Divorce and Remarriage*; Keener, *And Marries Another*.

33. A recent study of the New Testament and the ante-Nicene Fathers has sought to provide evidence for this view: Das, *Remarriage in Early Christianity*, 2024.

- The Erasmian-Reformed position[34] permits the adultery exception for both divorce and remarriage, based on an opposing view of the exegesis of Matt 19:9.
- The preteritive or Augustinian view suggests that Jesus avoided the issue in Matt 19 and upheld marriage as created by God.
- The betrothal view states that the word Jesus used for "adultery" (Greek porneia) meant "premarital sex" so that the only persons granted an exception are those who are espoused in engagement and whose spouse is unfaithful to them. Engagement, it is argued, was treated much more like a marriage in New Testament times.
- The consanguinity view defended by F. F. Bruce, for example, offers the opinion that the word used by Jesus for "adultery" was a technical term for incestuous relations (Acts 15:20), thus leaving no exceptions for divorce.
- The so-called "grace" view associated with Larry Richards looks beyond the issue of exception clauses and grounds for divorce, and urges the exercise of forgiveness, grace, and healing by the church. The wounds of divorce are great, for sure, and the church does what the church ought to do when it provides counseling toward healing so that people can genuinely move on. The example of Jesus offering forgiveness and life to the woman of Samaria who had had five husbands is our model in this regard.

The most important work done on this issue in recent times has been that of David Instone-Brewer, who suggests that adultery was not the only exception in the time of Jesus. Abuse and neglect were, on the basis of Exod 21, also an assumed basis for divorce in Jewish society.[35] This confirms what makes good intuitive sense when these phenomena are encountered. It is not that abuse or neglect or even adultery mean someone *should* get a divorce. Safety is of course paramount, and an abused spouse should separate immediately from the perpetrator for their own safety and those of their children. But every attempt should be made to make counseling available, and space should be given for the perpetrator to change before it is evident that this is not going to occur. In other words, the exceptions do not necessitate but they may legitimate divorce. If divorce does occur, it is apparent from the New Testament that it

---

34. Defended for example by Murray, *Divorce*.
35 Instone-Brewer, *Divorce and Remarriage in the Church*.

is not the "unforgiveable" sin, and the church should be a recovery ward where people repent and heal and move on.[36] A different approach and maybe even church discipline may be required for a person who moves through divorce in an unrepentant, arrogant manner with no regret, no self-awareness, and no ownership of the issues that led to divorce. Pastors who remarry such people do not do them any favors and damage the reputation of Christ's church.

Pastors will need to work through this issue to determine what their own considered opinion is on divorce and remarriage. They will also need to be aware of the policy of the denomination one joins or is a part of, for this will overrule personal opinions and necessarily guide what is to be done.

---

36. DivorceCare has been helpful in the churches I have served.

10

Sexual Ethics (2) Same-Sex Relations (Commandment 7)

The seventh area for ethical reflection arising from the divine institution of marriage relates to *same-sex relations*. Whereas persons who struggle with same-sex desires are to be welcomed into the church, same-sex sexual relations (and the institutionalizing of this act in same-sex marriage) violate the teaching of Gen 2:24 since the image of God in view there is differentiated persons in union, not undifferentiated entities in union. The exposition of this commandment later in the Pentateuch is clear: "If a man has sexual relations with a man as one does with a woman, both of them have done what is detestable. They are to be put to death; their blood will be on their own heads" (Lev 20:13). This is not a stray piece of ceremonial law, but moral law, and in this chapter on sexual offences it is the only one which is described as "detestable." There is also no trajectory as the biblical narrative progresses.[1] Whether or not the death penalty was actually carried out in the history of Israel is debatable, but the seriousness of this sin is certainly being emphasized at the time of its institution. As Tim Keller affirmed, "all the sex ethic of the Old Testament is re-stated throughout the New Testament (Matthew 5 v 27–30; 1 Corinthians 6 v 9–20; 1 Timothy 1 v 8–11). . ." and "if the New Testament

---

1. William Webb has pointed out that in comparison with slavery and the role of women there is a trajectory, this is not the case for same-sex relations. See Webb, *Slaves, Women and Homosexuals*.

has reaffirmed this commandment, then it is still in force for us today."[2] The New Testament prohibits same-sex sexual relations, first by inference in Jesus's reaffirmation of the adultery command, with all its ramifications, in Matt 5:27–30, and then specifically in 1 Cor 6:9–11, where Paul includes this in a list of sins from which converts have been delivered. If persons engage in them habitually and without repentance, they give clear evidence that they are not in the kingdom. In light of the plain sense of scripture in both testaments, this issue is therefore a gospel issue, not a secondary one. A matter concerning the authority of Scripture, not its interpretation.

These sentiments do not find concord with those expressed in the recently released book by Richard and Christopher Hays's in which Richard expresses his change of mind regarding same-sex marriage expressed in his *Moral Vision of the New Testament*, in the new book authored with his son Chris, in *The Widening of God's Mercy: Sexuality Within the Biblical Story*.[3] Given the gravity of the conclusions drawn by these respected scholars, this section will deal in some depth with their assertions. These authors choose not to contest the exegetical meanings of key texts, though they admit that they do prohibit same-sex sex acts. Rather, throughout the book they point to an overarching biblical narrative of changes of mind in God towards the inclusion of gentiles, eunuchs, "tax collectors and sinners," which in our age must include, they say, people who are same-sex married. A summation of the argument goes like this:

> The many biblical stories of God's widening mercy invite us to re-envision how God means us to think and act today with regard to human sexuality. The biblical narratives throughout the Old Testament and the New trace a trajectory of mercy that leads us to welcome sexual minorities no longer as "strangers and aliens" but as "fellow citizens with the saints and also members of the household of God" (Eph 2:19).[4]

Along with Preston Sprinkle in his review of this book, I affirm the love for LGBTQ people that the Hayses display in their writing and their concern for past dehumanization of persons in this community. They are, first and foremost, persons made in the image of God. Acceptance of people with same-sex desires is not to be equated, however, with the ethic

---

2. Keller, "Old Testament Law and the Charge of Inconsistency."
3. Hays and Hays, *Widening of God's Mercy*.
4. Hays and Hays, *Widening of God's Mercy*, 206.

of marriage between people of the same sex. Sprinkle states that he too advocates "for the full welcome and inclusion of people who experience different sexual orientations." The difference, says Sprinkle, is that he just disagrees "with the authors about what sexual ethic followers of Jesus are welcomed and included into, regardless of their sexual orientation."[5]

Whilst there are parts of the Hayses' book that demonstrate the acumen of these biblical scholars, it is the turn to apply their arguments to the inclusion of same-sex married persons as members of the body of Christ that is sudden and always puzzling. There are assertions one can agree with. For example, there is no question that same-sex attracted persons are formed in that way either by genetics or social factors and the possibility of change with respect to those desires is remote, short of divine intervention. However, Chris Hays[6] seems to think that God *creates* same-sexedness. In accordance with most doctrines of providence in the tradition, God permits rather than decrees brokenness, including the orientation of some persons to persons of the same sex. However, despite the prevailing narrative of our time, desires do not define a person. Just as heterosexual singles are commanded to be celibate, so also must those of same-sex attraction. The idea that one is disqualified from being in the spirit of the widening of God's mercy because one does not affirm same-sex sex or marriage is unfair. In the community where I work there have been a number of same-sex attracted persons through the years, and they have been loved and supported in the life of celibacy. All of us have sexual brokenness and all of us are on a journey towards wholeness and holiness.

There are also some serious theological and historical theological *faux pas* in the book. The characterization of Jonathan Edwards is a case in point. Edwards, especially in his maturity, became increasingly Trinitarian in his theology. "Heaven is a World of Love"[7] is the last chapter of Edward's classic work, *Charity and Its Fruits*, an exposition of 1 Corinthians 13, for example. One can agree that this scholastic Calvinist's particularistic view of election might have been tempered by, say, a more christological and communal view, such as that of Barth. However to say that he de-emphasized the love of God flies in the face especially of his view of the Holy Spirit as the mutual Love of the Father for the Son, and

5. Sprinkle, Review of *The Widening of God's Mercy* by Christopher B. Hays and Richard B. Hays.

6. Hays and Hays, *Widening of God's Mercy*, 36.

7. Edwards, "Heaven Is a World of Love."

his understanding that receiving the Spirit in regeneration led to an immediate (as opposed to mediate) appropriation of divine love. In fact, our entry into the life and love of the immanent Trinity, in turn leads us into the pathway of the ordering of our affections, the most crucial and seminal of which is love.

Another area is especially Chris's emphasis that God is always "changing his mind." He does mention an alternative to this viewpoint in the theology of John Calvin but does not give his theology of accommodation much space. Interpretation of Scripture is all important. One hermeneutical principle is that one must interpret obscure texts and concepts in the Bible in light of texts that are clear and perspicacious. There are many texts that clearly indicate the immutability of God, so the texts about God changing his mind must be seen as his gracious accommodation within his relationship with real humans. God is immutable, but he is not immobile. The reality of the relational mobility of God is to be acknowledged, but to contradict an attribute of God attested to in the text and the tradition is unfortunate. Paul indicates clearly that God "works out everything in conformity with the purpose of his will" (Eph 1:11). Human agency and divine response are somehow included within divine sovereignty and immutability of purpose. Karl Barth's doctrine of the concursus of divine and human agency is helpful in this regard. Supposed changes of mind in God cannot negate these clearly revealed divine attributes.

This evokes another challenge with the Hayses' book. Why must homosexuality be the thing that changes in God's mind? I kept thinking as I read the book, why not adultery? Will that be next? Why do the authors pick one issue that apparently God has changed his mind about? Why not murder? So from now on, we won't expect anybody to change their adulterous ways when they come to Christ, nor their abusive, murderous rage? Why is it that just homosexual acts are now legitimate? Is it possible that what has motivated this book is a deeply indiscriminate enculturation, a desire to accommodate the age? Offering reasons "why should God's mercy trump and override the Levitical laws about same-sex intercourse"[8] suggest a strange purpose. The authors' allusion to slavery as an example of liberation that finds analogy with same-sex practices is also slightly problematic since there are impulses in the New Testament that once fully realized could only lead to liberation in that regard. I am

---

8. Hays and Hays, *Widening of God's Mercy*, 211.

referring to Galatians where Paul asserts that within the kingdom, "there is ... neither slave nor free" (Gal 3:28) and the sentiments of the epistle of Philemon. There are no such hints regarding same-sex relations. There is no hint that God sees homosexual sex acts differently in the New Testament. He forgives all, but as in John 8, his message of "no condemnation" is accompanied by the command is to "leave your life of sin" (John 8:11).

One other major flaw in the book is the extrapolation of the theme of the inclusion of gentiles in the progression of the biblical narrative to the theme of the inclusion of same-sex-practicing people. The flaw is that the Old Testament flags the inclusion of all nations through Abraham as far back as the Abrahamic covenant, but there isn't a peep about the inclusion of same-sex attracted couples. Same-sex acts are immoral and unnatural in the Old Testament, and that is confirmed in the New. No change of mind.

A further challenge in the Hayses' book to historic orthodoxy, as this is grounded in the doctrine of the apostles, is the startling assertion on page 3 that divine revelation was not completed with the apostles. This flies in the face of how even the church fathers viewed themselves and their writings. They clearly reflect a belief in the finality of divine revelation of the foundational doctrines of the faith in the writings of the apostles, and their work as authoritative in only a secondary sense, and only as it faithfully echoed apostolic theology. Irenaeus is crystal clear that his ultimate authority lies in the finality of apostolic writings, which are both passed down in oral form, and then later through the writings. In Book III of *Against the Heresies*, he wrote that gospel was handed down by the apostles. He states, "We have learned from none others the plan of our salvation, than from those through whom the Gospel has come down to us, which they did at one time proclaim in public, and, at a later period, by the will of God, handed down to us in the Scriptures, to be the ground and pillar of our faith."[9] The essence of the apostolic faith was captured and passed down to the church by means of the rule of faith professed by converts at their baptism. Irenaeus's battle against the gnostics lay precisely in their rejection of both the written scriptures known in that day and the oral tradition passed on from the apostles to the bishops. The gnostics, says Irenaeus, used Scripture to "adopt and accommodate to their own baseless speculations."[10]

9. Irenaeus, *Against Heresies*, III.1.1.
10. Irenaeus, *Against Heresies*, I.1.3.

Furthermore, if what the Hayses mean by openness to new revelation such that the church might gain different perspectives on issues, their way of viewing this specific issue of same-sex relations is, as Sprinkle has said, "profoundly ethnocentric." He comments that

> The global church is growing exponentially in the Global South, Southeast Asia, China, the Middle East, and elsewhere in the majority world. Almost all of these churches believe that sex difference is an essential part of what marriage is and that all sexual relationships outside this covenant of marriage are sin. *The Widening of God's Mercy* implies that all these non-western Christians are not listening to the Holy Spirit, who is allegedly opening up fresh ways to read Scripture. The ethical viewpoint advocated for in *The Widening of God's Mercy* is held primarily by a relatively small number of (mostly white and affluent) modern Christians living in the West. Is the Holy Spirit really speaking much more clearly to western Christians than those in the majority world?[11]

I found many of the texts and examples used by the Hayses in the supposed "change of mind" narrative also most unconvincing, and indeed bordering on the misuse of Scripture. One case in point is the narrative of the daughters of Zelophahad.[12] On the one hand, this occurrence is indeed a great example of the ethical discernment required in making just and fair decisions for situations not previously encountered. But the leap from the case of these daughters to justifying same-sex activity is a long one indeed. The way in which so many of the case stories are suddenly invoked for the normalizing of same-sex relations is troubling. There really is no signalling of this move anywhere in either testament. There were too many theological challenges in this book for it to convince.[13] The so-called "narrative patterns" did not for this reader "disclose a deeper logic"[14] at all. Employing, for example, Paul's transformations of perception in his conversion story, as the authors do, seems almost ironic. This is the Paul who clearly condemns same-sex relations (Rom 1, 1 Cor 6). Yes, "the gospel of Grace can knock people off their high

---

11. Sprinkle, Review of *The Widening of God's Mercy*.
12. Hays and Hays, *Widening of God's Mercy*, 67, 70.
13. Employment of Kierkegaard's "theological suspension of the ethical" bears some scrutiny, for example (67, 70).
14. Hays and Hays, *Widening of God's Mercy*, 207.

horses and lead to surprising transformation"[15] but not off their consistent moral convictions based in the Old and New Testaments. One clue that the ethics of the New Testament with respect to sexual matters was in fact that of the Old Testament is the command given by Jewish apostles at the council of Jerusalem to gentile converts. They were to abstain from "sexual immorality" (Acts 15:29).

The Hayses' emphasis on Jesus's commitment to being with "sinners" throughout his ministry is commendable. It does represent a call to mission on our part, including showing love and friendship to same-sex attracted persons and making sure they are welcomed by the church in their search for God. The comment that these sessions with "sinners" were not necessarily directly evangelistic in their purpose is also noted. On the other hand it is clear that the holy presence and love of the Savior frequently draws people towards evangelical repentance and then to the receipt of forgiveness (e.g., Luke 7: 37–47). It repels a pharisaic spirit. His mission was to embody the wideness of God's mercy, but that implies that there is acknowledgement of the *need* for mercy.

The much-commented upon absence of reference by Jesus to homosexuality in his ministry[16] is no proof of an affirming position. The opposite is much more likely since he was a devout Jew who came to fulfill all righteousness. So much of what is said regarding Jesus and the Law in the book misses the point that consistently Jesus pointed back to the root of the commandment. He radicalized the commandment, not by being "radical" as in "cool." He was returning commandments to their original meaning in the Torah, which included their internal dimensions. He would have considered same-sex relations to be a sin. And of course, like all sins of all sinners these acts can be repented of and forgiven.

Sprinkle is correct in exposing the fact that the Hayses' book's "rather large lacuna" is that there is no offer of "a revised marriage and sexual ethic for their argument to succeed."[17] They frequently employ popular phrases in our time like "full inclusion,"[18] but, as Sprinkle states, "the current sexuality debate is not about (or shouldn't be about!) whether gay people are to be accepted. The debate is about which marriage and sexual ethic they are accepted *into*."[19] The Hayses' avoidance of debate on the six

15. Hays and Hays, *Widening of God's Mercy*, 167.
16. Hays and Hays, *Widening of God's Mercy*, 120.
17. Sprinkle, Review of *The Widening of God's Mercy*.
18. Hays and Hays, *Widening of God's Mercy*, 214.
19. Sprinkle, Review of *The Widening of God's Mercy*.

biblical passages that "disapprove" of same-sex relations because they are "superficial and boring"[20] leads Sprinkle to offer the following critique:

> I appreciate their reluctance to relegate this debate simply to six passages of Scripture. However, it seems a bit too convenient to wave a dismissive hand at the very passages that directly address the kinds of relationships the authors claim have been wrongly interpreted by the historic, global, and multiethnic church for nearly 2,000 years. More importantly, the authors ignore the very part of the debate that moves *beyond* these six passages: the way the whole witness of Scripture talks about marriage.[21]

Respectfully, I find even the book title and content of this book to be a red herring. How so? The mercy of God is already widened as far as it can go to include every person in the human race. The incarnate, obedient, crucified and risen Christ has already made provision for the forgiveness of all, in his person and by his own redeeming work. His desire is for all to be saved (1 Tim 2:4). What church that professes this cannot be a *welcoming* church for all people? A church community that is "welcoming but not affirming" can still be truly welcoming nevertheless. That is, such church communities welcome all sinners, with the understanding and hope that confession and repentance leads to real change for all. An essential part of the liturgy of any church is its words of confession and absolution. This immediately levels all and makes the community a community of grace. But just as persons who have committed heterosexual sin must repent and leave an adulterous relationship, so persons who are engaging in same-sex sex relations must also repent and leave this practice. Grace is not antinomianism. It leads to transformation. A "wider mercy" does not mean ignoring sin. Mercy, or the goodness of God, leads us to repentance (Rom 2:4). Welcoming all people is what a missional church is about, but there are no exceptions about the sinfulness of all and the need of all to repent and come to Christ. The church is a centred set, and the center is Jesus Christ its living Head, and the journey for all is one of evangelical repentance. This will indeed be a journey, but the goal is the same for all: likeness to Jesus Christ by the power of the Spirit.

In sum, the Hayses' approach is unconvincing for its neglect of *texts* or their acknowledged prohibitions of same-sex relations, and for its neglect of centuries of church theological *tradition,* which for all its early

---

20. Hays and Hays, *Widening of God's Mercy,* 206.
21. Sprinkle, Review of *The Widening of God's Mercy.*

foibles concerning sex is consistent in its condemnation of said relations. In place of these two foundational sources of knowledge in Christian theology and ethics, is a supposed Hayesian trajectory or narrative of the inclusion of various groups of people in the covenant community. This then leads the Hayses to make the leap to advocate the "full inclusion of believers with differing sexual orientations" today, full inclusion meaning all the way to leadership.[22] Sprinkle actually makes a convincing case that the New Testament has stricter sexual ethics than the Old Testament, so that there can be little ground for proposing a trajectory viewpoint.[23] I may suggest that we can at least assert that there is no change in the ethics of the two testaments, even with respect to the law's interiority.

In this author's opinion the blindspot in contemporary ethics, including that of the new Richard Hays, is *ontology*, meaning the nature of *being*, or what we are, in light of who God is. Hays's book shows an obsession with the horizontal narrative and complete neglect of ontology. Rather than merely question the plain sense of scripture in the Old and New Testaments that reveals that same-sex sex is disordered and consistently condemned, we ought also to ask *why* this might be, and, in turn, to look for how the text is informed by theology of this kind? Stated simply, if we do take the whole narrative of scripture seriously, we must ask what that narrative reveals about the triune God, and therefore about what it means to be human in his image. It is only sex between sexually differentiated and covenanted humans, that is, between a married man and a woman, and not between persons of the same sex, that images God in his differentiated oneness (Gen 2:24). The ontological question is expressed in Sprinkle's searching question to the Hayses, one they never answer: "Is sex difference an essential part of what marriage is?"[24] He goes on to say, "I'd say the most significant objection to their interpretation is that they offer a revision of the historically Christian view of marriage and sexual ethics without providing any argument for a revision of marriage and sexual ethics."[25]

Of course single persons in their maleness and femaleness together in society also constitute the image of God (Gen 1:27), but not with respect to sexual relations which are restricted to married people. The image of God has a number of facets as noted: relationality, intelligence

22. Hays and Hays, *Widening of God's Mercy*, 214.
23. Sprinkle, Review of *The Widening of God's Mercy*.
24. Sprinkle, Review of *The Widening of God's Mercy*.
25. Sprinkle, Review of *The Widening of God's Mercy*.

and functionality. Being a sexed person is part of that for everyone. However, for reasons that relate to the kind of stability within which a sexual relationship should function safely, and in turn for reasons that relate to procreation and the spawning of children, God has permitted the sexual intercourse aspect of relationality within marriage only. Single and married people reflect the image of God in different ways. The non-sexual relationships of single persons reflect the inclusiveness of the love of God in their friendships, whereas in marriage, his covenant faithfulness exclusively to his people is mirrored.[26] And for all, the phenomenon of sexuality drives us out of ourselves in contemplation of God and in community with spouse and friend and neighbor.

And who is this God? It turns out that he is the one God who is the triune God, who in his very integrated oneness of being is three differentiated persons of irreducible identity. These persons are one in essence, equal in dignity, mutually internal to one another by perichoresis, but they are at the same time, three differentiated persons, not amorphous beings. They are differentiated by their differing eternal origins. The Father eternally begets the Son and spirates the Spirit, the Son is begotten, and the Spirit proceeds from the Father through the Son. But these generations and processions also have a correspondence with the missions of the persons. In the economic Trinity, the Father elects, the Son is incarnate and reconciles, and the Spirit regenerates. This is a further evidence of differentiation within the Trinity.

This equality and unity with difference in God is what is mirrored in human sexuality. The nature of persons in the Godhead is not, of course, univocal with personhood in humanity. There is however an analogy between divine and human personhood as we have shown. This is one aspect of ontology that must guide us in our ethical thinking.

But there is another reality of being which guides the being and acting of human persons in the sexual realm. This is who Christ is in relation to what his church is. They are in one sense, one. Christ the Head of the church is one with his body, the church. However one may understand *totus Christus*, it is a concept reflected in the New Testament. Christ and his church in Christ, are one. However, they are in a differentiated union, not an amorphous or monistic one in which there is a confusion with respect to identity. Christ and his church are depicted as Bridegroom and Bride in Eph 5 as a means to motivate husbands and wives in their marriage

---

26. Grenz, *Sexual Ethics*, 252.

relationships. This analogy does not work for same-sex relationships. Other aspects of this theological ontology are referenced below.

Rather than interpreting texts within an understanding of this theological ontology, the Hays's seem to overturn what is the plain sense of scripture under the influence of modern, secular, societal assumptions. There are major lacunae in their book with respect to theological scholarship in this area of sexuality as well as the scholarship of the area of sexuality itself.[27] A sad consequence of the changing of opinions by respected scholars is that it makes life very difficult for the church in general, but particularly for godly persons with a lifelong same-sex attraction who have committed themselves to a life of pilgrimage in celibacy. In an article written in response to the initial review of the press on Amazon, Peter Valk has expressed this eloquently:[28]

> When I first saw the news, I was plunged into a now all-too-familiar cycle of emotions: fear, disappointment, betrayal, and hope. Over the past decade, various credible Protestant theologians have revealed that they've adopted a revisionist sexual ethic that God fully blesses same-sex marriages. Each time, gay Christians like me who are stewarding our sexualities according to historic sexual ethics are thrown for a loop. Many would consider us to be paying the greatest cost for continuing to believe in God's wisdom—namely, permanently giving up the prospect of romance or marriage or sex with the people to whom we're most attracted. Making sense of the news that another theological heavyweight has changed his mind only adds to our burden.[29]

Valk has obviously made it a point to study these issues deeply, understandably so, given they affect his own journey profoundly. His take on the 'newness' of the Hays's argument for a narrative in the Scriptures of increasing inclusion is that it is not new at all. "At least in the past," Valk has found "that the newest book about moving to revisionist sexual ethics has little new to say." He registers his disappointment, hoping he would "read something more convincing than the dozen books that came

---

27. As Sprinkle indicates, works by Robert Gagnon, Darrin Snyder Belousek, William Webb, or even key affirming works by James Brownson, Karen Keen, Robert Song, or Bill Loader, are neglected by the Hayses. See also Sprinkle's tempering of the "harm" language used by Chris Hays with respect to suicides of LGBTQ people, and further research on these matters. The proposal that *porneia* (Acts 15) did not include same-sex relations is also challenged by Sprinkle.

28. Valk, "When Heavyweights Change Their Minds."

29. Valk, "When Heavyweights Change Their Minds."

before." He goes on to say on the basis of the press blurb, "that *The Widening of God's Mercy: Sexuality Within the Biblical Story* will likely rest on the trajectory argument that Matthew Vines, Colby Martin, David P. Gushee, Julie Rodgers, Justin Lee, Sally Gary, and others have made in their own mind-changing volumes."[30] Valk suspects that the Hays approach will be to make the "core message of the Scriptures . . . a narrative of greater inclusion and liberty." He argues tellingly that this trajectory argument sets aside "the compelling evidence from passages that seem to directly address the immorality of same-sex sexual activity and the words of Jesus positively defining lifetime marriage between a man and a woman because the larger trajectory of the Bible suggests that God's ultimate ethic may be something different." His conclusion that "contemporary secular humanism has helped us discover what God's opinion really ought to be about gay marriage,"[31] is not far off the mark. Valk goes on to express that in his experience, many of his friends who turn from celibacy to same-sex practices, also defect from the faith altogether. By contrast, he references the work of Olya Zaporozhets and Mark Yarhouse, research psychologists, who in their work have "followed gay celibate Christians who have accepted the fact that their sexual orientation isn't going to change, yet continue to be convinced of the Bible's wisdom and are trying to make sense of their faith and sexuality, often in public." He indicates that "[t]heir research found that these gay celibate Christians scored in the normal range of mental health compared to the average American, and scored higher than average in overall life satisfaction."[32] My own experience in walking alongside gay celibate students at the college where I teach is not necessarily that the journey is easy, but that their faithfulness to Scripture, and the support of their small communities and counsellors sustains them.

The truth is that having two current scholars change their minds is actually insignificant compared to the witness of the scholarship of the church for two thousand years. Stephen McAlpine in his blog regarding the Hays's volume states rather caustically that "Perhaps there's a genuine change of mind after some serious exegesis that orthodox Christianity over the past two thousand years hasn't picked up on."[33] Robert Gagnon has already written an almost 1,500-word thread on X countering Hays's

30. Valk, "When Heavyweights Change Their Minds."
31. Valk, "When Heavyweights Change Their Minds."
32. Valk, "When Heavyweights Change Their Minds."
33. McAlpine, "Blurred Vision of Richard B Hays."

new book. He states, "God hasn't changed his mind. Hays and son have changed their minds. They are now swimming in the sea of heresy, rejecting the clear and overwhelming witness of Scripture . . . ."[34] Similarly, McAlpine bemoans the fact that Richard Hays, having created a robust ethical ecosystem for Christian ethics in his first book, *Moral Vision*, has now disturbed that ecosystem with disastrous effect. He comments that "[o]nce again we have major scholars—erstwhile evangelicals—who cannot see the irony in the fact that the secular culture that is decidedly post-christian—and doesn't simply hate grace, but as Rhys Laverty reminds us, hates nature as well, leading Christians by the nose."[35] This comment on nature is significant in the debate and urges the church to listen well to voices outside of the so-called liberated West, such as the African church, as well as the indigenous church even in North America. These Christians who often live more closely to nature cannot even get their minds around the news they hear that Christians in the West affirm same-sex sex and/or marriage. The comment on nature also beckons theologians and biblical scholars to pay attention to at least some forms of natural law which speak loudly to the disordered nature of same-sex relations.

But of course, some form of natural law justified by Oliver O'Donovan, for example, must come under and be validated by the witness of Scripture. Reacting to the new volume by Hays, McAlpine states, "It's just a 'few relevant New Testament passages' after all, isn't it? Not much in the scheme of things. But that's not true, is it? The whole of the New Testament presupposes the moral and ethical framework of the Old Testament both in terms of natural law and creation, and of covenant promise."[36] Old Testament passages such as Lev 20 cannot be placed on the scrapheap of "law." It is clear that Jesus upheld the moral law, as we have shown. And in fact, as already noted, the sentiments of the Old Testament regarding same-sex sex are reinforced, not minimized in the New. There is both grace and judgment there, and expectation of transformation away from such culturally prevalent practices, for converts to Christ. McAlpine puts it well: "the New Testament itself states in no uncertain terms that the widening of God's mercy is accompanied by the deepening of his wrath for all those who refuse it. I mean, the whole widening of mercy trope, in which revelation around sexuality being far broader in

---

34. Merritt, *Conservative Christians*.
35. McAlpine, "Blurred Vision of Richard B Hays."
36. McAlpine, "Blurred Vision of Richard B Hays."

application than the early documents could fathom, is not borne out by the balancing effect of judgement."[37]

Having clearly stated the ethical stance on same-sex sex and marriage which I believe to be in accordance with normal biblical interpretation—that is grammatical, rhetorical, historical, contextual, analogy of faith (all of Scripture interprets every text) interpretation that emphasizes perspicuity and the plain sense of scripture, and in particular, the role that theology has in hermeneutics—it is important to also emphasize that we are always talking about human persons who must be treated with dignity and love. Church-going youth who identify as LGBTQ+ are statistically more prone to suicide and self-harm than the general population. These realities cannot be ignored. Church pastors must speak to this issue, on the one hand expressing the view that same-sex attraction is not itself a sin, and on the other hand, offering emotional support and pointing towards role models of persons who have found peace in the celibate life.

For people with these struggles within the church and those who come to the church seeking help, the church must be welcoming. "*Welcoming* but not affirming" begins rightly with welcoming. Jonathan Merritt, himself a celibate same-sex attracted person writes, "[i]n contrast to the bad and ugly that both a revisionist sexual ethic and pray-the-gay-away theology lead to, these gay Christians are experiencing spiritual and psychological health by stewarding their sexualities according to historic sexual ethics. Thanks to the Holy Spirit, some have seemingly miraculously carved out a path of good and beautiful lives."[38] He proposes that these gay celibate Christians, welcomed into the life of the church, might embody wisdom for LGBT+ people. "Perhaps for the first time," he suggests, "Christians have all of the ingredients we need to compassionately embody historic sexual ethics.... We could discover how gloriously good and beautiful a Church filled with LGBT+ Christians thriving according to God's wisdom can actually be."[39] This vision for the church would involve kids who are constantly bombarded with these matters growing up "hearing and seeing the testimonies of Christians publicly navigating same-sex attractions, committed to historic sexual ethics, and experiencing just as much connection and community as their opposite-sex attracted brothers and sisters in Christ." His approach, which is both pastoral

37. McAlpine, "Blurred Vision of Richard B Hays."
38. Merritt, "Conservative Christians."
39. Merritt, "Conservative Christians."

and true to scripture, involves "believers of various sexual orientations linking arms, spurring one another on toward love and good deeds, and the whole body of Christ flourishing according to God's wisdom." It also envisions "believers living out vocational singleness and others living out marriage with someone of the opposite sex, but all would find deep belonging as they daily depend on the Holy Spirit to resist lesser loves."[40] Such a welcoming but non-affirming church would be one "where kids, having noticed how God's wisdom has led to the good and beautiful in the lives of LGBT+ people, are sad but not scared if they notice broken sexuality in their own lives, because they're confident they can share with their parents and find lifelong support from their local churches to thrive according to God's wisdom."[41]

An example of a minister of the gospel and apologist who is same-sex attracted but faithful to the historic Christian ethic is Sam Allberry. His book *Is God Anti-Gay?: And Other Questions About Jesus, the Bible, and Same-Sex Sexuality*[42] is a sensitive but orthodox treatment of these issues, grounded in Trinitarian perspectives, that offers celibacy as a viable pathway from same-sex attracted persons. His updated edition especially corrects the popular cultural assumption that having sex is the right of every human person.

The truth is that the line of sexual brokenness actually runs right through the heart of every human person. The extent to which we are all broken and sinful in the area of our sexuality is highlighted by how Jesus repeats and internalizes this commandment in his Sermon on the Mount: "You have heard it was said, 'You shall not commit adultery.' But I tell you that anyone who looks at a woman lustfully has already committed adultery with her in his heart" (Matt 5:27–28). Jesus does not abrogate the commandment. He reflects its internal nature even as the Old Testament does, and in so doing points us to the need of forgiveness. For Paul, we all need righteousness that surpasses mere avoidance of sinful sexual behavior. This includes a righteousness imputed to us as justified people in Christ and also a growing wholeness with respect to sexuality, in union with Christ in his death and resurrection, by the Spirit practicing the mortification and vivification that define our sanctification.

The principal way sin distorts our sexuality is that it redirects our sexuality inward instead of outward to God and others. Distortions arise

40. Merritt, "Conservative Christians."
41. Merritt, "Conservative Christians."
42. Alberry, *Is God Anti-Gay?*

when we use sexuality outside its contemplative, relational context. The roots of inappropriate sexual behavior or thinking usually stem from brokenness in relationships with parents and from relational isolation. If not used to stimulate relationship with God and people, the sex drive becomes one of Jeremiah's broken cisterns: "My people have committed two sins: They have forsaken me, the spring of living water, and have dug their own cisterns, broken cisterns that cannot hold water" (Jer 2:13). Addictions arise because no sexual experience can deliver the pleasure real intimacy brings.

Evidence of the battle with human sexuality is everywhere: pornography, insensitivity of men to female sexuality and misunderstanding of male sexuality by women, homophobia, the prevalence of premarital sex, the practice of same-sex sex and the belief that those with same-sex attractions have the right to be married, gender confusion, and insistence on the right of even children to choose their "gender," as if gender were something disembodied. Sexedness is an embodied reality that must be given priority over gender identity, though compassion must be extended toward people who for various reasons struggle with gender dysphoria (a state of dissatisfaction, anxiety, or restlessness around sexual identity), especially those who are intersex.[43] With the exception of intersex where the wrong sex may have been chosen by doctors or parents, transgenderism should be discouraged.[44]

Speaking specifically to the issue of same-sex attraction, this, as with all sexual brokenness, is a result of the fall, and it usually persists in this already-not yet era of the kingdom. As Allberry reminds us, being same-sex attracted does not disqualify a person from Christian service. He has found that some same-sex attracted people "have spoken of feeling like damaged goods, as though they were beyond repair and forever displeasing to God."[45] They can feel "doubly ashamed" when they are tempted

---

43. True gonadal intersex, in which persons are born chromosomally with the genotypes XXY, XXY, or XO and have phenotypes (physical features) of both sexes.

44. Research shows that the psychological angst that accompanies gender dysphoria is not greatly relieved by sex-change surgery. See the work of former Johns Hopkins chief psychiatrist Paul McHugh and the findings of the US National Transgender Discrimination Survey, referenced by Rick Thomas, Christian Medical Fellowship (UK), "Gender Dysphoria," and references therein. See also Yarhouse, *Understanding Gender Dysphoria*. Irrespective of how troubled persons are and what persons do to relieve this, the church must remain committed to caring for and discipling them, and helping them to heal in community.

45. Allberry, *Is God Anti-Gay?* 44.

towards a form of sexual expression that is wrong. Thus it is "not just that they are tempted by a wrong thing but a wrong kind of wrong thing."[46] Allberry is correct to suggest that whilst this condition is not how it is meant to be, this actually points to the reality of the gospel, to the fact that none of us has inherent merit, that our acceptance before God is on the basis of the vicarious life and death of Jesus for us, that temptation itself is not sin, but acquiescence to it. For the further encouragement of same-sex attracted persons, Allberry addresses the tendency to believe that their feelings "represent the sum total" of their identity.[47] Contrary to prevailing narratives of the culture which equate sexuality with core identity, which equate feelings with identity, the biblical understanding is that our biological sexedness is an important part of our identity, but not everything about us. Our sexual feelings certainly do not define us or our lives. Allberry speaks of the tendency of same-sex attracted persons to allow this attraction to "become the lens through which the whole of our Christian life is viewed,"[48] just as other areas of moral challenge can be an obsession for any of us, rather than our identity in Christ. Paul indicates in 1 Cor 6:11 that people once characterized by same-sex relationships now had entered into a radical change of identity in Christ. This does not mean that temptation was removed, but it did imply that the power of the risen Christ could be accessed to resist temptation to act on it. Allberry speaks also to the fact that desires can change especially for teens going through puberty. In these turbulent years, some teens go through periods of same-sex attraction "only to discover that their desires eventually reverted to attractions to the other sex."[49] It can revert in the other direction also. Conclusions about one's attraction, and decisions about sex changes, are certainly inadvisable during these teen years, and especially for children.

This generates the question, can the direction of our sexual desire be changed if in fact it becomes apparent that this is our permanent orientation? In the sovereignty of God, we may clearly say, yes, it can be changed. God is able. This is different to the question, will it be changed? In this now but not yet phase of the kingdom, many who have prayed for change intensely, and been prayed for, intensely, have not had this happen. A "complete change of sexual desires in this life is never promised

46. Allberry, *Is God Anti-Gay?* 44.
47. Allberry, *Is God Anti-Gay?* 44–45.
48. Allberry, *Is God Anti-Gay?* 45.
49. Allberry, *Is God Anti-Gay?* 45.

in the Bible,"⁵⁰ Allberry observes. Indeed the removal of sexual desires is not promised for anyone. It is vital that churches provide opportunities for emotional support, accountability and prayer for persons who have ongoing struggles and addictions, whether of same-sex or other-sex attraction.

Same-sex attraction is not in itself sinful, but persons with same-sex desires are not permitted by God to act out their desires in the same-sex sex act. Human desires are not reliable guides for morality (whether one is same-sex or other-sex attracted),⁵¹ and the sex act between two persons of the same sex is disordered. Arguments that it is not feel disordered for persons who have same-sex attraction fail to take into account that this is issue is much bigger than the desires of individual persons. This is precisely where evangelicals fail with respect to *ontology* as already emphasized.

First, we recall that the being of God must be the starting place with respect to the creation of humans in his image. Their maleness and femaleness together reflect the image of a relational God. The image is seriously distorted when two people of the same-sex have sex, and same-sex "marriage" does not change that. Basic theological anthropology is at stake here. Sex in created humans is something ontological, something basic to what it means to be human. But anthropology is grounded in theology Proper, that is the revelation of who God is as the One who chooses to image himself in humanity. In light of the full revelation of who God is in the whole biblical narrative, it is evident that he is the triune God.⁵² So it's not just that Scripture in both the Old and New Testaments condemns same-sex sex. It is abundantly clear that there is no trajectory, for example, of an improvement in how God views the same-sex act in the movement from the Old Testament to the New.⁵³ But

---

50. Allberry, *Is God Anti-Gay?* 47.

51. Just as the desires of pedophiles for sex with children do not justify their sex acts of adults with children.

52. Mark MacDonald, Indigenous bishop of the Anglican Church of Canada, attributes the "widespread ambivalence and reluctance among Indigenous Anglicans to change the marriage canon to allow same-sex marriage" to their faith in the authority of Scripture and their strong doctrine of creation, in which marriage is viewed as "a unique communal ceremony, designed and practiced to express a worldview where the difference between man and woman is an embodied portrayal of an essential aspect of how Creation works." See MacDonald, "On the Marriage Canon," 5.

53. Space does not permit a long section with detailed exegetical content. So-called traditional moral teaching on sex and marriage is based on interpreting the Bible using grammatical, historical, rhetorical, and canonical interpretation, or the plain sense of

the deeper question is why? This has to do with the very being of God. Specifically his own differentiation within unity, as already noted. That God is "one" is the creed of the Old Testament (Deut 6:4). However, the Hebrew word for "one" (*ehad*) is not a statement of a mathematical kind. Unicity, that there is one God rather than four or forty, is implied. But the main idea in this word has to do with God's nature, that he is a unity. This is not contradicted by either Old Testament hints of the triune nature of God, or its full revelation in the New Testament in the Son and by the Spirit. God's unity is a differentiated unity. God's oneness is not sameness. Significantly, this same word *ehad* is used when God introduces marriage in Gen 2:24, asserting that the two human persons differentiated by their sex, "male and female," shall by their sexual union "become one flesh." This act of sex with two persons of opposite sex signals something about God, the triune God, who is one in essence, but differentiated with respect to personhood. The partners in sex acts within covenantal marriage can only reflect its purpose when they are not the same as each other. Marriage is, in a word, sacramental, in that very profound way.

In Gen 2, which focuses on humanity in God's creation, God is described seeking to remedy the aloneness of the man. As Sam Allberry has written, "there is something which the creation of Eve brings to Adam—leading to the first marriage—the creation of further men would not have achieved. The interplay between men and women, regarded as vital in corporate leadership, is no less significant in the most intimate human setting." He concludes that "What matters in the boardroom matters even more in the bedroom."[54] He goes on to say that the "issue is not the feelings of commitment or faithfulness that two people may have for one another," virtuous though they may be. The crucial issue rather is "the kind of union that God gives to a man and a woman when they become physically one."[55] Complementarity of a kind that mirrors the being of God and that is expressed as essential to the image of God, is what determines the ethic.

Scripture that is perspicuous for the people of God. Attempts to derail the fruit of this interpretation, which is built on more than twenty centuries of tradition, may be called revisionist. See Gagnon, *Bible and Homosexual Practice*; Gagnon, "Leviticus and the Times"; Gagnon, "No, God Isn't Transgender." See also the helpful work of Provan, *Seeking What Is Right*; Guroian, "Ethic of Marriage and Family," 322–30, esp. 324. See Boulton et al., *From Christ to the World*, 319, for a summary of biblical perspectives.

54. Alberry, *Is God Anti-Gay?* 30–31.
55. Alberry, *Is God Anti-Gay?* 31.

A further crucial ontological matter that must ground our thinking about same-sex sex is the nature or being of Jesus himself. If Jesus is who he claimed to be, that is the Son of God, then what he taught about sexuality must be listened to. The fact is that Jesus upheld the teaching of Genesis regarding marriage which we just considered (Matt 19:4–6). This is what you might expect of a devout Jewish person committed to fulfilling the moral law. In addition he taught clearly that all sex outside of marriage between a man and a woman is sinful. In Mark 7:20–23, Jesus describes a list of sins that characterize fallen humans. There the includes the term translated as "sexual immorality, " which is a translation of the Greek word, *porneia*. It includes all sexual activity outside of heterosexual marriage, and as Allberry observes, "none of Jesus hearers would have doubted that this included same-sex relationships."[56] Allberry describes his experience when he became a Christian: "I came to a sobering realization: given what Jesus says about sexuality, it would not be right for me to explore my same-sex attraction." This conviction was founded on his coming to the awareness that although Jesus did not specifically mention same-sex relations, "his teaching does not leave room for them. Following Jesus would mean my having to say no to those sexual desires."[57] But his teaching is not just any old teaching. As Allberry points out, these are the teachings of our Creator, "the one who not only made me, but came up with the idea of me in the first place. He thought me up! He knows far, far better than I do how I should live."[58] He is the one who loved us "enough to code himself into human DNA, live in this broken world, and face, the worst of human suffering and pain. I'd be a fool, not to follow him, even in this area of life . . . "[59] What then are same-sex attracted persons to do? In another passage in the authoritative teaching of Jesus, he makes it clear that the only alternative to marriage between a man and a woman is celibacy (Matt 19:10–12). Celibacy is not an easy life, but then, it is not just for same-sex attracted persons, but for all persons outside of marriage. And as stated above, celibacy and marriage twin ascetic vocations. The task of the church is to acknowledge and speak openly about the reality of same-sex attraction, whilst at the same time offering discipleship in the life of celibacy. Some helpful guidelines for Christians

---

56. Allberry, *Is God Anti-Gay?* 35.
57. Allberry, *Is God Anti-Gay?* 33.
58. Allberry, *Is God Anti-Gay?* 33.
59. Allberry, *Is God Anti-Gay?* 33.

who live with same-sex attraction have been offered by Allberry in *Is God Anti-Gay?*[60]

But recall another ontological reality, one that has echoes in the human sex act and marriage. This is the being of Christ and his church together, "the Christ," Christ in his union with his church. In the Eastern Orthodox tradition of the church, the differentiated union of the Trinity, the union between Christ and his church, and the union of two persons in marriage are all closely related. The church is an icon of the Trinity, and marriage is an icon of the church. Sexual intercourse is spoken of as *synousia*, a term which means consubstantiality, and as such an echo of the differentiated persons of the Trinity. The husband and the wife are considered to be an "ecclesial entity," reflecting Christ and his church as in Eph 5. The first good of Christian marriage is therefore the *union* of persons, differentiated by their sexedness, "who in freedom and sexual love and through their relationship to Christ image the triune life of the Godhead and express the great mystery of salvation in Christ's relationship to the church."[61] These realities of being, or ontology, rule out the possibility of same-sex marriage being sacramental.

SHOULD CHRISTIANS ATTEND GAY WEDDINGS?

A number of high profile cases have recently arisen in which pastors or Christian leaders who are orthodox with respect to faith and ethics, have given qualified approval for parishioners who have asked if they should attend weddings of gay relatives or involving transsexual person or persons. Before passing judgment in these cases, it is vital for critics to ascertain the ethical level of this discussion. This ethical area is not referenced directly in scripture. It is therefore what is termed an adiaphora matter. That is, Christians have freedom within the bounds of what is revealed, to decide one way or another. Romans 14 is a case in point in the New Testament. Some believers felt free to eat meat offered to idols, and some did not. The "strong" were those who decided that it was just meat. The "weak" would not eat it because of its associations. Mutual grace offered between the strong and the weak, and not condemnation, was encouraged. In the case of attending the gay wedding of relatives, or weddings involving a person who has had a sex-change, is in this territory, and

60. Allberry, *Is God Anti-Gay?* 41–56.
61. Guroian, "Ethic of Marriage and Family," 324.

media wars are inappropriate, bringing dishonor to the Lord, and divisions based not on the essentials of the faith, but on minor issues.

This does not mean there are no principles to guide us. Often there are conflicting principles and weighing which principles should prevail is the challenge. Here are some guidelines gleaned from higher order ethical principles. The first is witness to the gospel, which includes ethics. Does the person asking for advice understand what is clearly revealed in scripture about same-sex relations, and crucially, have they made it known to the relatives or friends being married that they are believers and in no way approve of the marriage. The questions posed by Alistair Begg are a model of truth spoken in love to a grandmother wondering if she should attend her grandson's transgender wedding. They were, "Does your grandson understand your belief in Jesus?" followed up by, "Does your grandson understand that your belief in Jesus makes it such that you can't countenance in any affirming way the choices that he has made in life?"[62] We must indeed be careful not to give the appearance that we are endorsing what we consider to be sin, by simply appearing at such a wedding as if all is just fine. The second guideline is intertwined with the first. Does the action of the person seeking advice maintain the relationship with the person being married, or will it destroy it? The central command of Christian ethics, as we have noticed, is to love the Lord, and to love our neighbor. Certainly Jesus demonstrated what it was like to be a "friend of sinners," to be in the presence of both prostitutes and tax-gatherers, as well as those of the pharisaic kind who couldn't see their own sins. As Sam Allberry says, "it is good to be the kind of person someone would want at their wedding,"[63] that is, a person who truly and defiantly loves their loved ones. It is important to note that Jesus's presence with "sinners" in these occasions was always redemptive. He was not just there to have a good time like everybody else. He was there both to show love and then to administer forgiveness to repentant people. The ongoing presence of a devout and prayerful relative in the lives of those who have taken broken pathways may be valuable for their conversion in the longterm. If the position of non-affirmation has been made sufficiently clear, attendance at these weddings can be redemptive. It communicates that friendship with this person matters. If this is not the case, or in cases where a Christian's conscience does not allow it, some Christians should

---

62. Jackson, "Alistair Begg Takes Heat for Advising Grandmother To Attend Grandchild's Transgender Wedding."

63. Allberry, *Is God Anti-Gay?* 89.

choose not to attend, and trust that their absence will speak. Relationships may survive, and that is always best, giving the opportunity for redemptive presence in the life of the loved one, something often not possible until crisis hits. A third criterion relates to whether the persons being married are Christians or non-Christians. Paul is clear in 1 Cor 5:9–11 that we are not called to separate ourselves from immoral people who are Christians, since if we did, we would have no context for witness. Distance from people is appropriate in cases of the church discipline of believers. This can be applied to attendance at non-Christian same-sex marriages, though the first guideline still applies—not without expressed concern about the gospel ethic in play. For Christians who persist in carrying out a covenantal and sacramental act in this inappropriate way, the decision is much more difficult. As Allberry, flatly states, "this would be a compelling argument, not to attend a same sex wedding that involves a professing believer."[64] This would certainly be the case for someone who has arrived at the conclusion that the same-sex marriage ethical issue is not a mere matter of hermeneutics, but of biblical authority.

HOSPITALITY TO SAME-SEX ATTRACTED PERSONS

What about those who have same-sex desires?[65] Is the same-sex attraction itself a sin? The attraction itself is not a sin. The giving way to lustful thoughts and actions, as in the case of opposite-sex attracted persons, is sin. Same-sex attracted Christians are to remain celibate, as is the case for heterosexual singles. Oliver O'Donovan comments that those who want to live the life of imitating Christ are all "called to bear his cross, to 'mortify' those aspects of their own nature which are inclined to compromise 'upon the earth' (Col 3:5 KJV). They are called to accept exclusion from the created good as the necessary price of a true and unqualified witness to it."[66] This applies to the Christian disciple with same-sex desires who chooses to refrain from same-sex sex, and in so doing is excluded from the created good of having sex as the necessary price of bearing witness

---

64. Allberry, *Is God Anti-Gay?* 91.

65. The terms "heterosexual" or "homosexual" are a product of the nineteenth century and have particular social agendas behind them. See Hannon, "Against Heterosexuality." The Scripture knows nothing of orientation, but only behavior.

66. O'Donovan, *Resurrection and Moral Order*, 95–96.

to what that created good is: an act between a man and a woman within the covenant of marriage.

Christians of non-affirming conviction who profess to be "welcoming" can often be guilty of failing to love the same-sex attracted. We need to be showing concrete signs that we love people whose struggle with sexual brokenness is a same-sex and not an opposite-sex one. If we were as passionate about loving the same-sex-attracted person as we are about hating sin, we might be more credible as the community of Christ. We need to be offering forgiveness, redemption, and healing to strugglers in this area who are genuinely seeking to overcome, in the same way that we are to those in our community who are strugglers in the heterosexual arena.

An important part of that journey toward holiness for a same-sex attracted person is the hospitality of the church.[67] Hospitality in a gospel and trinitarian sense invites people, irrespective of orientation, to the *center*, that is, to Jesus and discipleship, which includes celibacy. It portrays unconditional love, but not unconditioned love. That is, it can only ultimately embrace into its membership those who wish to follow Jesus and the command of God, which he reiterated and reaffirmed (Matt 5) in his ministry and through his apostles (Rom 1; 1 Cor 6). The church is both a *centered* set, which invites all people to the center, Jesus, and a *bounded* set, made up of true disciples of Jesus who are committed to the word of God in its ethical fullness. This latter aspect means that appropriate boundaries may be placed within the church's life for the protection of the flock, and especially its younger members.

The truth is that all sexual sins and perversions are a result of misdirected contemplation. Sexual wholeness is not guaranteed by marriage, and it is as important to be a sexually whole married person as it is to be a sexually whole single person. No one is perfect, none of us is immune to failure. Therefore, we all need forgiveness and healing to recover greater sexual wholeness.

---

67. For an excellent discussion of true Christian hospitality, see Bretherton, *Hospitality as Holiness*.

UNIVERSAL HUMAN BROKENNESS WITH RESPECT TO SEX AND ITS REDEMPTION

The following are four disciplines from three passages that reflect the viewpoint of Jesus on the road to recovery and holiness in this area. Holiness usually depends on wholeness, yet holiness may need to be pursued in a behavioral sense even when wholeness is not yet there. The journey toward both is a trinitarian, christological, pneumatological pathway toward sexual recovery, which is a lifelong journey for all of us.

To the woman caught in adultery in John 8, Jesus reveals the *first discipline, which is experiencing forgiveness—again and again*. At the beginning of this passage, Jesus is in a tough legal dilemma. If he commands to spare the woman, he appears to violate the Mosaic law. But if he commands her to be killed, he violates Roman law, avoids the issue of the missing man in the story (thereby colluding with flagrant sexism), and will take Israel back into the era when those laws of the infant theocracy applied. But if he avoids the issue, he will be guilty of exonerating sin. So what does he do? He writes in the sand, perhaps to indicate that the further revelation of God's mind on this issue is being given. Then he speaks these great words, "Let any one of you who is without sin be the first to throw a stone at her" (John 8:7).

After the crowd has slunk away, he, the only one who could have cast the stone, does not. He forgives her: "Then neither do I condemn you" (John 8:11). In light of the teaching of the whole New Testament, all sinners who come in faith and repentance to Jesus and become one with him are assured of forgiveness of the permanent judicial kind (Eph 1:7), which may be referred to as justification in Christ (Rom 3:24–25). But people in union with Christ are not merely justified; they are being sanctified by the power of the Holy Spirit. In the time before they are perfected, though, justified sinners will sin, and they will need confession for their relational restoration to the Father (1 John 1:9).

The church is to be a community where we confess sin and receive absolution (John 20:19–23). Pastors must facilitate confession and must administer absolution on the grounds of said confession. Liturgies must include confession, even if this is not necessarily where they should begin. They must begin with God and with the gospel, just as the Lord's Prayer does not begin with confession but with worship and surrender to the kingdom. Pastors must also embrace the fact that a significant part of their priestly ministry is hearing confession and administering absolution. Reformation churches have often thrown the baby out with the bathwater amid a justified reaction to medieval confession and indulgences. James 5 exhorts believers to confess their sins to one another, and whom they confess to will be determined largely by whom they trust. Such confession will open up the possibilities for seeking healing and wholeness through pastoral counseling and accountability.

The beauty of Christ is, however, that he also upholds the ethic of sexuality in his interaction with this victimized woman: "Go now and leave your life of sin" (John 8:11). Even in his forgiveness he upholds the ethic. Forgiveness does not abolish the commandment but its transgression. The forgiving Christ calls sin what it is: sin. The Mosaic commandment remains intact. *This is the second* discipline for pursuing wholeness and holiness in all areas, including our sex lives: *the call to pursue obedience again and again*—empowered by our forgiveness in Christ, our identity in Christ, and our solidarity with Christ.

Forgiveness moves us back into the pursuit of what is right. The commandment returns to us after forgiveness, as a gift to guide us. Forgiveness, if it is real, moves us back into the journey of seeking obedience to the commandment, not into license. To the person whose marriage has broken down and divorce has happened, Jesus would say, "You are forgiven, but go and deal with the issues that contributed to the demise of your marriage, seek counsel and healing. If you are remarried, go and build your new marriage and seek grace so that you can avoid it happening again."

The basis for the forgiveness again and again, and the power for pursuit of obedience again and again, is our union with Christ. It is our union with Christ, as those who have come unto it by faith, that gives us justification (Rom 3–5). But our union with Christ also brings us into the sanctification journey of living out our pursuit of mortification of sinful tendencies and vivification of graces. We do this in union with his death and his resurrection (Rom 6) by the power of the Spirit (Rom 8:4, 9). This makes the journey evangelical, not legal. We have amazing resources to use and depend on. Thus, the *third discipline is communion with the triune God*. With him we connect powerfully and have fulfilling intimacy that satisfies us and empowers us for mastery and wholeness. It is the principle of dependent contemplation of God and intimacy with God—again and again.

Jesus spoke of this to the woman in John 4, who struggled deeply with relational and sexual brokenness, as evidenced by her five marriages.

The reason for our sexual brokenness is our spiritual thirst, which we try to quench through sex, food, or possessions. Christ offered her the living water of his own person and love. Then her sexual appetites would be restored to normality. When Jesus cried, "I thirst," on the cross, he was probably reflecting the thirst of humanity for God. As thoughtful counselor Larry Crabb has said, our experience of intimacy with Christ "expels the controlling and compulsive power of lesser affections."[68] There is an untapped and untested depth of joy and satisfaction for our deepest thirst to be explored in experiencing communion with the Father, the Son, and the Spirit.

Our first response to our thirst is often to turn to the broken cisterns that hold no real water. Christ's cry on the cross calls us to drink deeply of him and walk intimately in union with him by the Spirit's fullness. Our task is to satisfy our core thirst in him. This happens through communal and spiritual practices such as reading, meditation, prayer, and contemplation. It also happens through other believers, including counselors and pastors, in whom we encounter Christ. When we connect deeply with other new-covenant people, we connect deeply with Christ. This moderates our sexual desires, keeps them in perspective, and enables us either to abstain from the acts of sex that are illegitimate or, if married, to fulfill our spouse and ourselves in unpressured and holistic ways. The ultimate key to wholeness lies in *connecting* deeply with God and with people. We are empowered to connect with God by connecting with people, and vice versa. As Crabb has said,

> When two people *connect*, when their beings intersect as closely as two bodies during intercourse, something is poured out of one and into the other that has the power to heal the soul of its deepest wounds and restore its health. The one who receives experiences the joy of being healed. The one who gives knows the even greater joy of being used to heal. Something good is in the heart of each of God's children that is more powerful than everything bad. It's there, waiting to be released, to work its magic. But it rarely happens.[69]

Pastors must return to their primary calling, which is contemplation and communion with God, in this way bringing others into the life of the triune God.

---

68. Crabb, "Traits of a Sexually Healthy Pastor," 38.
69. Crabb, *Connecting*, xi.

But there is a *fourth discipline, which is that of determined action—in mortification and vivification—again and again.* We do not pursue wholeness and holiness passively. We are dependent, but not passive. We pursue wholeness in union and communion with Christ by the Spirit such that his reality becomes ours. But still, there is effort. Action done in dependence becomes his action through us, and as we do it, he does it. It is asymmetric action in that God is the initiator and prime doer: "Continue to work out your salvation with fear and trembling, *for it is God who works in you.*" But it requires us to be active in our pursuit: "work out your own salvation" (Phil 2:12–13).

Paul says elsewhere that he strikes a blow to his body and make it his slave (1 Cor 9:27). Jesus is just as radical as he addresses the problem of lustful looking: "If your right eye causes you to stumble, gouge it out and throw it away. It is better for you to lose one part of your body than for your whole body to be thrown into hell. And if your right hand causes you to stumble, cut it off and throw it away. It is better for you to lose one part of your body than for your whole body to go into hell" (Matt 5:29–30). Just as Jesus internalized the seventh commandment, he spiritualizes its penalty of death. His intent is to say, "Put your sinful distortions to death, seriously and radically." This is similar to what Paul expounds in Rom 6 and 8 and in his other epistles, where mortification of the flesh and vivification of the graces, in union and communion with Christ in his death and resurrection, is the primary paradigm for sanctification. These are not passive pursuits but require stringent discipline, empowered by the Spirit.

One of those areas of action may be pursuit of healing with our fathers and mothers, sometimes through in-depth counseling. But the ultimate goal will not be blame of our parents. Rather, it will be to move on into deep connection with our heavenly Father, who is the father to the fatherless and the one whose approval and affirmation we all deeply need. In Christ, it is there! The affirmation he received from the Father at his baptism is ours vicariously in him. Perhaps there is no greater source of sexual healing than in this relationship. We can become increasingly Father-affirmed, Son-conjoined, Spirit-filled men and women moving toward greater wholeness and anticipating the full satisfaction of our thirst for God in heaven. This is the true conversion therapy we all need.[70]

70. The matter of conversion therapy for people with same-sex desires is beyond the scope of our discussion here. Even if sexual orientation is permanent and has genetic

PUBLIC SQUARE CONSIDERATIONS

In considering the question of same-sex marriage, the question of how to operate in the public square arises. The orthodox Christian conviction on this matter is not popular in the secular West. It is not popular within the liberal wing of the church, and even some evangelical denominations are capitulating to the prevailing culture at the expense of centuries of tradition and orthodox theology. For the church to interact with the state on this matter is important, usually through denominational heads or through representative bodies such as the Evangelical Fellowship of Canada, the Evangelical Alliance in the UK, the National Association of Evangelicals in the United States, or equivalent bodies in other countries. One approach in a secular, post-Christian democracy is to endorse same-sex marriages as civil unions granted by the state while the church maintains that sacramental marriage is only valid for heterosexual marriage. The church would then abandon its role as a broker of civil marriages, offering only sacramental marriages. Theologian John Milbank demonstrated an interesting public-square interaction of this in the midst of parliamentary debate on this issue in 2013. Milbank observed that, as the British Parliament grappled with same-sex marriage, it had "gradually become apparent that the proposal itself is impossible. For legislators have recognized that it would be intolerable to define gay marriage in terms equivalent to 'consummation,' or to permit 'adultery' as legitimate ground for gay divorce." In fact, Milbank said "that the intended circumscription of gay marriage is so diluted as to render it indistinguishable from gay civil partnership."[71] In other words, it is impossible for the rights of married people to be the same for heterosexual and homosexual marriages.

Milbank expressed the fear that, despite these differences, secular thought would "not so readily let go of the demand for absolutely equal rights based on identical definitions." This would generate the dire prospect that "not only would 'marriage' have been redefined so as to include gay marriage, it would inevitably be redefined even for heterosexual people in *homosexual terms*. Thus 'consummation' and 'adultery' would cease to be seen as having any relevance to the binding and loosing of straight unions." It would have further consequences, since "the joining together and harmonization of the asymmetrical perspectives of the two

---

and physiological roots, conversion of the heart toward God and the lifestyle of the kind depicted in the New Testament is still relevant.

71. Milbank, "Impossibility of Gay Marriage."

sexes are crucial both to kinship relations over time and to social peace. Where the reality of sexual difference is denied, then it gets reinvented in perverse ways—just as the over-sexualization of women and the confinement of men to a marginalized machismo." It would also "end the public legal recognition of a social reality defined in terms of the natural link between sex and procreation," possibly leading to the requirement that children of naturally married parents be legally adopted by them. This loss of the grammar of families originated by male and female married parents "would thus imply a society no longer primarily constituted by extended kinship, but rather by state control and merely monetary exchange and reproduction."[72]

Milbank then offered opinions on matters such as surrogate motherhood and sperm donation, which "should be rejected" in light of "the biopolitical rupture which they invite," including the fact that children produced by artificial insemination "are rightly demanding to know who their natural parents are, for they know that, in part, we indeed *are* our biology." This is usually unacceptable "for donors who gave their sperm or wombs on the understanding that this was an anonymous donation for public benefit." Citing the "psychological confusion, family division and social conflict involved here," Milbank suggests "we have sleep-walked into the legalization of practices whose logic and implications have never been seriously debated." He further insisted that "we should not *re-define birth* as essentially artificial and disconnected from the sexual act—which by no means implies that each and every sexual act must be open to the possibility of procreation, only that the link in general should not be severed." The cost for this separation is, he says, "surely the commodification of birth by the market, the quasi-eugenic control of reproduction by the state, and the corruption of the parent-child relation to one of a narcissistic self-projection." The refusal of these practices would then make it clear "that a gay relationship cannot qualify as a marriage in terms of its orientation to having children, because the link between an interpersonal and a natural act is entirely crucial to the definition and character of marriage." He clarified also that even though not all heterosexual marriages can fulfill these conditions, "they still fulfil through ideal intention this linkage, besides sustaining the union of sexual difference which is the other aspect of marriage's inherently heterosexual character."[73]

---

72. Milbank, "Impossibility of Gay Marriage."
73. Milbank, "Impossibility of Gay Marriage."

The positive aspects of this interaction are that state and church are kept distinct, with a realism about the state. Yet Milbank does not in any way capitulate to the secular viewpoint. He skillfully deconstructs it while at the same time remaining true to the gospel and trinitarian nature of marriage. I believe he fulfills the commitments to the vision of the church as a community of the gospel called to spill over into society with a purifying influence as salt and light, influencing without seeking to control. He lets the state be the state, perhaps recognizing that same-sex civil unions are a "provisional good" in society in that they may curb promiscuous same-sex sex. The clarion call for the church to be the church is also evident in that the church is urged to continue its biblical and theologically grounded insistence that marriage is only marriage when it is asymmetrical, heterosexual marriage. It might be argued that the church might not wish to leave the state as it is in this matter and speak evangelically toward what is the good for all humanity in this regard.

Why do we have these distortions in the human experience and working out of sexuality if God gave us sexuality as a gift and as a reflection of his triune being? The answer lies not in Gen 2, that is, in creation, but in Gen 3 and the fall. As a result of the entrance of sin into the universe, sexuality became prone to distortion and corruption.

PASTORS AND THEIR SEXUALITY

This final section focuses on the particular challenges that pastors face with respect to their own sexuality. Every pastor and every elder ought to be aware of the particular sexual challenges they face in ministry. There is no better text for understanding the vulnerabilities of pastors for sexual malfeasance, for urging and guiding policies for churches to seek to avoid this and for when it happens, and for healing for all who are involved in this process than the book by the pastor Roy Bell and the theologian/ethicist Stanley Grenz, *Betrayal of Trust: Confronting and Preventing Clergy Sexual Misconduct*.[74]

Just a few comments will hopefully inspire further reading on this area. Pastors are often unaware that they are in a position of power, ethically speaking. They are thus also unaware that having a sexual encounter with a congregant is always an abuse of power and could lead to

---

74. Grenz, *Betrayal of Trust*. The following article has greater sensitivity to women in ministry: Lind, "What Makes Good Ministry Good?" 65–88.

litigation. Pastors who fall in this area are in one of three categories: the predator, the lover, and the wanderer. The predator moves from church to church, somehow undetected, often through a failure of accountability or the refusal of male leaders to hear the claims of female victims of clergy misconduct. The lover is the person who is prone to infatuation and imagines that parishioners are often in love with them. The wanderer is the one-time offender who repents and seeks healing and wholeness. An area of emotional woundedness is often the root cause a of pastor's fall into sexual malfeasance. Persons in the first category should not be in the ministry, and those in the second need healing and emotional awareness if they are to continue in the ministry. All pastors have a vulnerability in this area, given that they are trusted with deep level of intimacy as they counsel and pray for people of the opposite sex. Pastors are often unaware of the transference and countertransference that occurs in a long-term relationship with persons of the opposite sex. When pastors move into the forbidden zone, they are always compounding and not healing the brokenness of the other person.

Ethics for this area should involve the writing of clear policies regarding when and how a pastor should visit or counsel or pray with a person of the opposite sex, what should occur if there is an accusation against a pastor in this regard, and what should be said and done for the victim, the victim's spouse if they have one, the spouse of the pastor, the families of both perpetrator and victim, and for the whole church. Silence is not an option. The church and denomination will also need to work out policies for pastors who fail in this and other areas. The question of whether and when a pastor may be reinstated must be considered. The general guideline "Swift to restore and slow to reinstate" is a good one.[75]

---

75. Stuart Briscoe, personal conversation.

11

Ethics of Work (Commandment 8)

You shall not steal.
EXODUS 20:15

This commandment's intent seems obvious: do not steal anybody else's property, money, spouse, dignity, and so on. But there are more and less obvious ways to steal. In the pastoral realm, pastors have been dismissed not just for reasons of sexual malfeasance, but because they have stolen the church's finances, while others have been deemed to have a poor work ethic and therefore to have "stolen" the church's money in that way. Other pastors have felt so badly about taking money from the church that they have become workaholics and so stolen time from their spouses and children.

THE COMMANDMENT IN THE NEGATIVE

When applied in church, negative application of this commandment could focus on less obvious ways in which people can steal: they can steal time from their employers by showing up late or by cheating with their time cards, pilfering office supplies, and pretending illness and receiving sick pay, or they can cheat the government by making inappropriate claims about tax deductions or by not declaring items purchased at customs. The prophecy of Malachi makes it clear that failure to tithe is to rob God, whereas generosity invokes the blessing of God in this life and the life to come (Mal 3:8–12). Too great an absorption in work can also rob children of childhood and emotional stability. Saying yes to something always means saying no to something else. We can rob our spouses of dignity when we do not respect them and love them sacrificially, and especially when we publicly put them down or ridicule them. We also rob the poor of their dignity as human persons made in the image of God when we fail to take care of them. The example of Jesus motivates us: "For you know the grace of our Lord Jesus Christ, that though he was rich, yet for your sake he became poor, so that you through his poverty might become rich" (2 Cor 8:9).

The principle of making restitution is an ethic that arises from this commandment, as is evident in Exod 22:1–14; 2 Sam 12; and Luke 19, sometimes five- and sometimes fourfold. In the case of Zacchaeus when he encountered Jesus, he said, "Look, Lord! Here and now I give half of my possessions to the poor, and if I have cheated anybody out of anything, I will pay back four times the amount" (Luke 19:8). In addition to the principle of restitution, this story demonstrates the connection between spiritual and moral transformation. There is no such thing as one without the other. The evidence of true inner-heart repentance is moral restoration and actions that prove it. This story and Zacchaeus's comment also gives a hint about the positive meaning of this commandment as involving generosity.

THE COMMANDMENT IN THE AFFIRMATIVE: HOW WE WORK

When we begin to consider the positive restatement of this commandment, it takes on a surprising depth, width, and attractiveness. The opposite of stealing, as Eph 4:28 reveals, is honest work that leads to provision for one's family and generosity toward the church and the poor: "Anyone who has been stealing must steal no longer, but must work, doing something useful with their own hands, that they may have something to share with those in need." The fourth commandment invokes the theology and ethics of work, but the eighth can equally well do so. C. S. Lewis's famous remark, "I believe in Christianity as I believe that the Sun has risen, not only because I see it, but because by it I see everything else,"[1] is well illustrated by how we may consider work. Work is sadly thought of even

---

1. Lewis, *Weight of Glory*, 140.

by Christians as an area of independence of God or of trite invocation of God when crises occur in work and family life.

Ephesians 4:28 brings the positive and negative version of this commandment together in a profoundly evangelical or gospel manner. In the context of the whole epistle to the Ephesians, this section illustrates the importance of moral formation for the Christian. Chapters 1–3 are the most brilliant description of the identity of the believer in Christ in the New Testament. But understanding that we are seated in the heavenlies must lead to walking (five times in Eph 4–6) on the earth lies with heavenly perspective. Paul gets very specific about this in this text. This is down-to-earth spirituality. The mind-to-heart appropriation of who Christ is and who we are in Christ will show itself in moral formation where the rubber hits the road around issues of work and theft. Remember that Christ as incarnate represents heaven on earth. Our spirituality is not otherworldly, but is incarnational in the secondary sense that Christ is in us as we live out our lives here on earth. We are connected with Christ in the heavenlies, but we are also grounded, living out Christ in the earthy and earthly realm.

With respect to this, Klaus Bockmuehl calls this passage in Ephesians a "brilliant application of ethics." This is moral formation in its very essence, the "transformation from parasite to provider." There is a "threefold sequence of reform." The thief must "desist from thieving," adopt the "positive alternative," which is "to work," and the positive outcome is the ultimate opposite that is included in this commandment. He is to "give to the poor." That is, generosity is the opposite of stealing. Thus, says Bockmuehl, "So the New Testament replaces theft with thrift and greed with giving. Instead of covetousness, charity."[2] In sum, the positive obedience to this commandment is that of honest work and of giving generously. By the grace of God and life in the incarnate Christ, the calling of the Christian is to be an honest worker and a generous giver—to our nation, state, and community through our taxes, to the church through our tithes, and to the poor through our offerings.

The Christian virtue of sharing and generosity was integrated into the early church, as is evident in Acts 2:44–45: "All the believers were together and had everything in common. They sold property and possession to give to anyone who had need" (see also Acts 4:32–35). Concern for the poor was paramount at the first council of the church in Jerusalem

---

2. Bockmuehl, *Christian Way of Living*, 114.

(Gal 2:10). The early church also cared for distant as well as near neighbors, even engaging in transcontinental sharing (2 Cor 8–9). There is also evidence of the concept of economic equality in a passage such as 2 Cor 8:13–15: "Our desire is not that others might be relieved while you are hard pressed, but *that there might be equality.* At the present time your plenty will supply what they need, so that in turn their plenty will supply what you need. The goal is equality, as it is written: 'The one who gathered much did not have too much, and the one who gathered little did not have too little.'" This is deep Christian community rather than primitive communism, since in the New Testament all giving was voluntary and in accordance with the ability to give and according to the need of the beneficiary.

The scope of generosity is described in Matt 25, which speaks of six works of mercy. It includes feeding the hungry, quenching the thirsty, giving hospitality to the stranger, clothing the naked, healing the sick, and visiting the prisoner. The force of this passage is that Christ comes to us sacramentally in the people in each category. Doing what we do for them is to do these acts unto Christ. Isaiah 58 depicts also six acts that are all about sustaining the life in need. If this is what is required of the personal Christian, it should be also that which defines the mission of the church.

A commandment such as this hints that the church's commission is not just the Great Commission, involving evangelism and discipleship. This important task can and should only be carried out within the wider callings of the biblical narrative to obey the Great Commandment (made up of the ten commandments) and the cultural mandate. The former concerns generosity and justice for the poor, and the latter outlines what it means to be fully human, which includes work and caring for creation in doing so. An important ethic surrounding work must be how that work affects God's good creation. This commandment in fact provides an area code for consideration of environmental ethics. A full account of that is not possible here, but suffice it to say that caring stewardship is avoiding the rape and plunder of creation, negatively speaking, and positively acting toward the creation in ways that bestow goodness and generosity and cause it to flourish.[3]

---

3. See Wilkinson, *Caring for Creation*, for an introduction to ways of caring for creation as persons and churches. See also the blogs of Katharine Hayhoe on climate change and what we can do about this, as well as a book coauthored with her husband, Farley, *Climate for Change*. Other helpful works that reflect a healthy ecotheology are as

The context of this commandment is most often that of the marketplace or work, and it has significant value in teaching a theology and an ethics of work. Some ways in which the commandment was applied in the Old Testament that still have application in marketplace ethics are the payment of fair wages, as addressed in Deut 24:14–15; refraining from the exploitation of widows, orphans, and the poor, which is a recurring and even dominant theme (Isa 10:1–3 is one example); and avoiding the "evil machinations" that are present in the business world (Amos 8:4–6) and demonstrating the biblical and moral alternative in that realm (Lev 25:14; Prov 11:26; 20:17).[4]

Importantly, however, this commandment is not an encouragement to withdrawal, but rather engagement in the marketplace, in the created realm. It is an encouragement to engage in morally upright ways that honor this commandment. It is an exhortation to live with creational and kingdom perspectives in the realm of business. Working to bring justice and equity in society is first and foremost a Christian enterprise. An attempt at such engagement was made by Martin Luther in a pamphlet called *On Trade and Usury* (1524), which addresses the issue of what "just price" is.[5] He offers a Christian alternative to the law of supply and demand. In light if this, Bockmuehl recommends that all Christians, and not just pastors, think of themselves as "salaried employees of the Lord."[6] This is true to the doctrine of creation, which acknowledges that the earth is the Lord's, not ours, and all God's people are its priests, its stewards, its tenants, keeping the land and administering it for him.

This commandment thus overcomes a dualism often present in the perspective of evangelical Christians regarding work. The idea that all work is important to God, and not just work in the church, overcomes the dichotomized view that church work is more sacred than work in the world. Further, *how* we do our work matters to God. Our holy priesthood as worshipers in the church matters no more than our royal priesthood in which we carry over our worship into our work in the world. The idea that the pastor does the really important work while the rest of the people of God work so the pastor's salary can be paid is a travesty. The roots of this go back a long way to the monastic movement. While it had validity for its

---

follows: Brunner et al., *Introducing Evangelical Ecotheology*; Brueggemann, *Sabbath as Resistance*; and Berry, *Art of the Commonplace*.

4. Bockmuehl, *Christian Way of Living*, 112.
5. Luther, "On Trade and Usury" (1524), 4:8–26.
6. Bockmuehl, *Christian Way of Living*, 115.

time and produced some remarkable goods, it led to "the false assumption that there is a special calling, a vocation, to which superior Christians are invited to observe the counsels of perfection while ordinary Christians fulfill only the commands; but there simply is no special religious vocation since the call of God comes to each at the common tasks."[7]

It does not matter what our particular work may be. Our work matters to God, it will matter on judgment day, and it will matter in the new creation. This lengthy quote from William Tyndale, English Reformer, reflects these insights about work well, even if in quaint language, from our perspective:

> Moreover, put no difference between works; but whatsoever cometh into thy hands that do, as time, place, and occasion giveth, and as God hath put thee in degree, high or low. *For as touching to please God, there is no work better than another*. . . . Let every man therefore wait on the office wherein Christ hath put him, and therein serve his brethren. If he be of low degree, let him patiently therein abide, till God promote him, and exalt him higher. Let kings and head officers seek Christ in their offices, and minister peace and quietness unto the brethren. . . . Let every man, of whatsoever craft or occupation he be of, whether brewer, baker, tailor, victualler, merchant, or husbandman, refer his craft and occupation unto the common wealth, and serve his brethren as he would do Christ himself. Let him buy and sell truly, and not set dice on his brethren; and so sheweth he mercy, and his occupation pleaseth God.[8]

Tyndale is expressing the Reformation value placed on the work of the whole people of God and the priesthood of all believers. But he is in this passage also exhorting pastors, or prophets and apostles, as he calls them to, to take their work seriously. All that this commandment implies, and all that Paul and Peter in the New Testament write about the importance of work, applies also to pastoral work. This includes diligence, the rhythms of work and rest, and above all an orientation toward the Lord and not human approval.

The greatest challenge of the pastor's work is that most of it is not seen by people. Hours of prayer and exegesis in preparation for exposition of the word and in preparation for appointments for spiritual counsel will not be seen. Results are also not seen. On the one hand, the pastor

---

7. Bainton, *Here I Stand: A Life of Martin Luther*, 156.
8. Tyndale, *Parable of the Wicked Mammon* (1527), (emphasis added).

hopes that the people of God will heed Paul's instruction when he urges them "to acknowledge those who work hard among you, who care for you in the Lord and who admonish you" (1 Thess 5:12). But ultimately what motivates the servant of God is the reward of the Lord, sometimes sensed now, but mostly to come. It is Christ's generosity that must keep the generosity of pastors flowing, for most often they will not be remunerated in a way that is comparable to other vocations.

The most important perspective to be gained about this commandment about integrity and generosity is the moral and spiritual formation that undergirds it. In the prophecy of Hosea, theft is linked to a lack of faithfulness, love, and knowledge of God:

> Hear the word of the LORD, you Israelites,
>   because the LORD has a charge to bring
>   against you who live in the land:
> "*There is no faithfulness, no love,*
>   *no acknowledgment of God in the land.*
> There is only cursing, lying and murder,
>   *stealing* and adultery;
>   they break all bounds,
>   and bloodshed follows bloodshed.
> Because of this the land dries up,
>   and all who live in it waste away;
>   the beasts of the field, the birds in the sky
>   and the fish of the sea are swept away." (Hos 4:1–3)

What we do matters, and what we do at work matters, but whether we have integrity and how we work is an indicator of something deeper—our moral formation, which in turn is an indispensable aspect of our spiritual formation. This, according to Hos 4, is our faithfulness of character, our love as a disposition toward God and neighbor, and our God-consciousness, or, one might say, our practiced sense of the presence of God. What do morality and ethics have to do with Christ and Christian formation and identity? The commandments, such as the eighth, seem so outdated, and a call to obey them so lacking in what many perceive to be the *gestalt* or form of the gospel. The connection between morals and a life in God in Hos 4 gives evidence that they are integrally related. The law not only convicts us of sin so that we recognize our need of the grace of the gospel; it returns to us as Christians and by the Spirit guides the formation of virtue and the pursuit of just behavior. Ethics and dogmatics belong together. Obedience is the consequence of true saving faith. Paul tells us that the coming of Christ and his being crucified in the likeness of sinful flesh was so that "the righteous requirement of the law might be fully met in us" (Rom 8:4) who live according to the Spirit. Faith results in love, and the life of love is the life lived according to the Ten Commandments.

I fear that our culture thinks that law and freedom are opposites. Those who declare that the Decalogue is out of date or that Christians should not worry about obeying the commandments—they just need to "flow in the Spirit," not be bound by laws—are reasoning on the basis of a house of cards. What does freedom to steal look like? What about freedom to gossip? Does adultery ever produce freedom for the deceived spouse, the spouse who has been cheated on, and does it lead to greater relational and emotional freedom for all the parties concerned? Paul declares that love fulfills the law. The Bible indicates that obedience to the moral law is an outflow of regeneration, and that justification defines freedom, and that sanctification, which follows justification, is the freedom from theft and the freedom for honorable work and generosity. Character matters, and behavior matters as much as character. I fear we have a spirituality divorced from physicality. I fear we have a theology divorced from ethics. I fear we have a spirituality that leaves out parts of life—divorced from what we do with our money. The essence of the task of the pastor is to pull those things together into an integrated whole.

A CASE STUDY IN INTEGRITY IN THE WORKPLACE

An excellent study for the cultivation of moral character and action for the workplace is the life of Joseph in the book of Genesis. Joseph is defined by trustworthiness working under the Egyptian ruler Potiphar: "Potiphar put him in charge of his household, and he entrusted to his care everything he owned.... *So Potiphar left everything he had in Joseph's care; with Joseph in charge, he did not concern himself with anything* except the food he ate" (Gen 39:4, 6). Even in prison after the false accusation of Potiphar's wife, Joseph again shows his integrity working under the prison warden: "But while Joseph was there in the prison, the Lord was with him; he showed him kindness and granted him favor in the eyes of the prison warden. So the warden put Joseph in charge of all those held in the prison, and he was made responsible for all that was done there. *The warden paid no attention to anything under Joseph's care, because the Lord was with Joseph and gave him success in whatever he did*" (Gen 39:20–23). Then, when Joseph is vindicated, in prosperity as in affliction, working under Pharaoh, we read the same sentiments: "Then Pharaoh said to Joseph, 'Since God has made all this known to you, there is no one so discerning and wise as you. *You shall be in charge of my palace, and all my people are to submit to your orders.* Only with respect to the throne will I be greater than you'" (Gen 41:39–40).

In sum, Joseph engaged and did not withdraw from the business world of his day. He was astute and "successful" as a businessperson. He managed losses and successes with integrity and serenity. He was the same whether in the palace or the prison. I am fascinated not just by his example of integrity but by the dynamics and disciplines that brought this about.

Acid Tests of Integrity

Joseph illustrates first what it means to pass the *ultimate tests of integrity*, the first of which is *what we do when no one's looking*. His response to Potiphar's wife reveals what motivated his integrity: "How then could I do such a wicked thing and sin against God?" (Gen 39:9). My late father-in-law, Robert M. Rae, used to say, "Joseph lost his coat but he kept his character."

Another test of integrity is *how we handle ourselves when false accusations come our way*. When you are wrongly assessed or impugned with motives that you did not have, are you serene or anxious? Joseph's attitude throughout his unjust imprisonment is remarkable—his serenity, the absence of bitterness, the willingness to help fellow prisoners, the continuance of his service even though he had been wrongly judged. He does not panic because "the Lord was with Joseph and gave him success in whatever he did." His trustworthiness continues. He does not become embittered and twisted into rebellion or cynicism about bosses. He serves as graciously and with as much integrity in the prison as he had done in the palace. His sense of identity holds up through this false accusation and adversity. He did not need everybody to like him, or even think well of him.

I will never forget the question I was once asked by R. Paul Stevens when I was a student at Regent College and he was a professor. I asked him about a church that I had received a call to, a church he knew well.

He is the kind of spiritual mentor who does not say much but who asks pithy questions that can unravel you. He simply asked me, "Ross, do you need everybody to like you?" The implication was that if I was going to accept the call to that church, I better be sure I did not need everyone's approval. Joseph managed to come through a season of accusation and aspersions by means of a deep trust in the word of God. Psalm 105 affirms this: "till the word of the Lord proved him true" (Ps 105:19). Joseph was able to function, avoid bitterness and insecurity, and still behave ethically and be utterly trustworthy both in palace and in prison.

Temptations abound in both scenarios. Theft and fraud sometimes happen when people are in poverty or when there has been a downturn or major loss in business. Sometimes it happens in the palace context—when things are going well and we have executive privilege, it easily drifts over into inappropriate privilege, the abuse of expense accounts and the fudging of figures for self-gain. Joseph handles himself with integrity in the palace of Potiphar the military chief of Egypt, as well as in the prison where he sat for years under a cloud of suspicion, and again in the ultimate pinnacle of his success as the prime minister under Pharaoh.

Perhaps the greatest test of integrity is *when success comes our way*. How do you handle success? Does it fill you with pride, or do you recognize who really gave you that success? Joseph, the immigrant, is certainly attributed success. Many people who have been successful as self-made businesspeople really do believe that. They sometimes believe that strongly enough that they become very pragmatic about morals and ethics. "The law is a rough guide, but I am over it" is the attitude. There is none of this in Joseph even as prime minister; Joseph is a great example for people in public office in our day of frequent scandals of the fiscal kind. Popularity, fame, and public office corrupt many, but not Joseph. He remained steady and humble, and was viewed with great credibility all through his career as the prime minister. How Joseph stayed humble in success was likely due to his awareness of the source of that success: "'I cannot do it,' Joseph replied to Pharaoh, 'but God will give Pharaoh the answer he desires'" (Gen 41:16).

Dynamics of Moral Formation toward Integrity

How might we learn from Joseph's moral formation? There were some dynamics at work in him that account for his moral fortitude and consistency, his utter trustworthiness. These were both a consequence of what God had done and things that he did, the disciplines that cultivated formation. Although our practices and God's work in us are inseparable, what God does comes first. We should be far more interested in what God is doing for and in us than the business of moral formation by our efforts. We are wise to be wary of human-centered methods and techniques for quick-fix transformation that avoid pain, adversity, and ambiguities, and that have little bearing on the trenches and trials of the workplace, including the pastorate, and in relationships.

The case of Joseph illustrates that divine working and human working are inseparable, even though divine working is logically first. There is evidence of a cultivation in his consciousness of God, born of divine revelation. God-consciousness was what determined *who he was and what he did when no one was looking* (Gen 39:8). His biggest concern was not his violation of Potiphar's trust; it was his God. This was only because God had revealed himself to Joseph in his youth through dreams and through hearing the narrative of the history of Yahweh with his people through his father. God-consciousness was what sustained *his sense of identity and serenity in the midst of false accusation* in the pit and in prison. Joseph cultivated the presence of God. Genesis 39:21 indicates that when he was in prison, "The Lord was with him; he showed him kindness." This means that God was in fact with him.

Cultivation of the Lord's presence is the great goal of Christian life, and therefore of the life of the pastor. Our capacity to experience it goes up and down, and there are times when the Lord may withhold a sense of his presence, but we can be assured he is always there. The practice of the divine presence is assisted by practicing the presence of God communally in church, in the Lord's Supper, in the preaching of the word. In private, it can be encouraged by reading and meditating on the word of God prayerfully and so moving into contemplation. Jesus said, "You have your heads in your Bibles constantly because you think you'll find eternal life there. But you miss the forest for the trees. These Scriptures are all about me! And here I am, standing right before you, and you aren't willing to receive from me the life you say you want" (John 5:39–40, The Message). Joseph's practice of the presence was what kept him from bitterness and caused him to rise above his rejectedness, his injustices, his false accusations. There was no chip on his shoulder because there was God in his vision. This is the power of contemplation, the power of God in human consciousness.

This is revealed later when Joseph makes himself known to his brothers. In Genesis 45, in Joseph's urging them not to be angry with themselves, his divine orientation comes out: "Because it was to save lives that *God sent me ahead of you.... God sent me ahead of you* to preserve for you a remnant on earth and to save your lives by a great deliverance" (Gen 45:5, 7). In chapter 50, he reassures his brothers again with his awareness of God's sovereignty. God had provided for his covenant people through his hardships, even bringing good out of the evil they had done:

> His brothers then came and threw themselves down before him. "We are your slaves," they said.
> But Joseph said to them, "Don't be afraid. Am I in the place of God? *You intended to harm me, but God intended it for good to accomplish what is now being done, the saving of many lives.* So then, don't be afraid. I will provide for you and your children." And he reassured them and spoke kindly to them. (Gen 50:18–21)

When things get tough in the pastorate and the temptation arises to compromise integrity, steal dignity from others, or just coast rather than work with diligence, a sense of the sovereignty of God will sustain us. He is the Lord, and not brothers and sisters who may sometimes harm us. Having an orientation toward him, living as unto the Lord, is a product of his revelation of himself and of our contemplation of him in the word and in prayer.

A cultivated sense of God-consciousness is also what kept Joseph from pride in his successes. He makes no bones about the fact that God enabled him to do what he did. Joseph makes this plain when his jailer expresses confidence that he can interpret a dream: "'I cannot do it,' Joseph replied to Pharaoh, 'but God will give Pharaoh the answer he desires'" (Gen 41:16). He tells his brothers, "God has made me lord of all Egypt" (Gen 45:9).

Joseph had a cultivated consciousness that God was the source of his ability to interpret dreams and that it was God who was empowering him all along. God did this, first, by giving to Joseph a profound consciousness of himself that was transforming. But second, God crafted him into the image of Christ. Christlikeness is the goal of God in the formation of his people, and Joseph is an Old Testament picture of that. Christlikeness is moral formation that flows out of relational formation and intimacy with Christ. Joseph is as Christlike as any character in the Old

Testament. He is a son beloved of his father, is hated and rejected by his own brothers, "dies" and "rises again" (at least from Jacob's perspective), is the means thereby of the salvation of his people, saves the whole world from destruction (from famine), and has all his people bowing down to him (just as his dreams had predicted).

Philippians 2:6–11 describes who Christ is. This passage is prefaced by the exhortation to "have the same mindset as Christ Jesus," and it is followed by an expression that reveals that this is what we are to do, because it is what God is doing in us: "Continue to work out your salvation with fear and trembling, for it is God who works in you to will and to act in order to fulfill his good purpose" (2:12–13). God's work in us does not make our work superfluous. It is what motivates and makes meaningful our attempts to work out our salvation. The same cycle of humility before exaltation that characterized the history of Christ (v. 12) is exhorted for us. But what is that "good purpose" of God? Philippians 3:10 reveals that it is to be like Christ in his death and resurrection, and 2 Cor 3:18 reveals that it is to be formed into the image of Christ. God does this, but we do have a role: contemplation. In turn, contemplation transforms only because God by the Spirit is doing it in us.

It is fascinating that this Old Testament character models the christification journey of the people of God for all time. It is also fascinating that he is spoken of as a man "in whom is the Spirit of God" (Gen 41:38). One could say that trinitarian sanctification was at work in Joseph. He was God-conscious and Christ-fashioned, and filled and transformed by the Spirit of God. What precisely was Joseph's "working out" role?

First, he stayed open and responsive to receiving the revelations of God to him. That is why he could survive the rejection of his family, the false accusations of Potiphar and his wife, and the forgetfulness of the baker. What God thought of him mattered much more than what any human being thought. When we live in receipt of revelation, we are morally formed. It was also why he was not afraid to give both good news to the baker and bad news to the butler. This man had a sense of identity and security rooted in God that was rock-solid.

Moral formation is about staying open to God's revelations in all their forms: his written word, his preached word, his Spirit's promptings, dreams and visions, words and prophecies of others in the body of Christ. Above all, we need to be readers of Scripture in order to know God and be transformed (Ps 119:9; Heb 4:12, 13). We read to encounter the living Word, and spend good time thinking and growing in our understanding of

> Who Christ is—which means contemplation.
>
> Who Christ is for us—which brings rest of spirit.
>
> Who Christ is in us—which is appropriation and embracing of who Christ is for us.
>
> Then, and only then, we meditate on who we are in Christ.

Scottish pastor Robert Murray McCheyne (1813-1843) once said, "For every look at self—take ten looks at Christ."

Second, as I have noted, Joseph cultivated a sense of the presence of God. He practiced the presence of God with him. Moral formation is inevitable when we live in the consciousness of the presence of God. His presence has to form us morally. Things incompatible with his presence stand out and are repulsive.

Third, Joseph remained dependent on the power of God in him. Power for our moral formation as well as power for giftings comes from God. The power of his resurrection transforms us—so depend on it. Express that dependence constantly. Galatians 5 describes the essence of moral formation. In verse 16, Paul says, "So I say, live by the Spirit, and you will not gratify the desires of the flesh." Life in the Spirit crafts the fruit of the Spirit within us (vv. 22-23). Then Paul emphasizes the relational nature of life in the Spirit: "Since we live by the Spirit, let us keep in step with the Spirit" (v. 25). Moral formation flows as the power of the Spirit transforms us. The means by which he does this is contemplation of the Christ, whom the Spirit loves to draw attention to. This is expressed in 2 Cor 3:17: "Now the Lord is the Spirit, and where the Spirit of the Lord is, there is freedom." Our role is then to "contemplate the Lord's glory" and to be "transformed into his likeness with ever-increasing glory, which comes from the Lord, who is the Spirit."

Moral formation for the workplace is about developing rhythms that reflect the history of Christ such that his history becomes our soul history: dying to ways of falsehood, living into the work he gives us. Death, burial, and resurrection disciplines must characterize us, enacted in the realms of family, work, and church.

I close this chapter with some practical considerations related to the ethics of work in the pastorate. I hope one result of this is that readers will start to think about policies and procedures in various areas of pastoral life. I hinted at one in the previous chapter with respect to sexual boundaries and policies should failures occur. Below there will be some guidelines for how teams should function in the pastorate.

WORK ETHICS IN THE PASTORATE

Understanding ministry in light of Jesus and the triune God we serve makes us see ourselves as collaborators, complementary to each other rather than competitors. Jesus transforms our relationships in every realm, including in teams where synergistic function is the goal. This is an echo of the divine team, in which Jesus says and does only what he sees the Father doing, and says and does these things in the power of the Spirit. This applies to kingdom ministry in mission, where Jesus always sent out teams. The apostles also followed this pattern. In fact, plural leadership is the nature of leadership in New Testament church life. There is a growing consensus among churches in many places in the world that the one-pastor model needs to be replaced with a team model. The Sri Lankan pastor Ajith Fernando has contended, for example, that the common one-pastor model should be replaced by team ministry, which he states "was the standard model of ministry in the New Testament."[9]

Another author, George Cladis, wrote *Leading the Team-Based Church* after seeking to find a biblical-theological model, which led him to establish strong teams in his church. The model he found was the perichoretic image of the Trinity, in which "the three persons in God are in constant movement in a circle that implies intimacy, equality, unity yet distinction, and love."[10] He presents perichoresis as the goal for which Christian leaders should strive in the ministry of the church.

It sounds idealistic to assume human leaders can act in a way that even echoes the communion of the Trinity. Divine and human personhood is not univocal. We cannot be mutually internal to one another, for example, though we can practice interdependence. Unlike the Trinity, teams of *mere* humans, and teams of *sinful* mere humans, have to work much harder to function as synergistic teams. For one thing, it requires commitment on behalf of leaders to an other-orientation toward their fellow leaders, which in turn requires in each person a strong sense of self-worth and humility. They need to be comfortable in their own skin.

---

9. Fernando, *Jesus Driven Ministry*, 131.
10. Cladis, *Leading the Team-Based Church*, 4.

There is both a particularity and a mutuality about team leadership. This is worked out in a life of prayer for each other. Paul Fiddes, in *Participating in God*, writes, "In intercession we meet others in the perichoresis, the divine dance of Father, Son and Spirit. . . . We enter into the life of prayer already going on within the communion of God's being."[11] When we intercede for others we are not so much praying *to* Jesus on their behalf as we are praying *with* Jesus for them. As we dwell in him and he dwells in us, we become co-laborers, partners with Christ in his work of intercession. Knowing this frees us from seeing intercession as a burden, making it a delight.

Within the Trinity there are functions that do involve authority/submission, which are best spoken of not as subordination but the submission of equals. Catherine LaCugna indicates that the triune persons "experience one fluid motion of encircling, encompassing, permeating, enveloping, outstretching." She insists that "there are neither leaders nor followers in the divine dance, only an internal movement of reciprocal giving and receiving, giving again and receiving again. The divine dance is fully personal and interpersonal, expressing the essence and unity of God."[12] I affirm much of this, but I differ with respect to leadership. There is leadership within the Trinity; the Father is described as an initiator continually in the New Testament (John 5; Eph 1:3–14, 15–23; 3:14–19). By analogy, leadership in the church must be team leadership, and leadership within teams is best thought of as a "first among equals" kind. Different people in a leadership team will lead in different areas, and all will lead in a manner that reflects mutual submission to the other.

It may be helpful to make this commitment to team leadership explicit at your church. For example, the following document was crafted as a result of a team exercise about ethical operating principles in the pastoral team I served:

- We will hold and protect those matters that are confidential
- We will listen for God's direction on all issues
- We will reach decisions by consensus recognizing that the Senior Pastor is ultimately responsible
- Silence will be assumed as agreement
- We will handle conflict in accordance with biblical principles

11. Fiddes, *Participating in God*, 72.
12. LaCugna, *God for Us*, 272.

- We will value and respect each other's time
- We will not bring an issue to the team prior to processing it with the applicable person responsible
- We will function as a team; we commit to a common purpose to act and serve as a member of the group not as an individual
- We will celebrate what God has done in our lives and in the lives of our congregation members
- We will not speak/represent a fellow staff member in a negative manner
- Our team environment will be safe, with the understanding that it is normal and healthy to voice contrary opinions. We will attack the issue, not the person
- We will commit to be fully engaged in meetings and follow through on responsibilities assigned
- We will value humor and make time for fun together.[13]

These operating principles are not expressed here because they are perfect. Not all of them are even directly ethical in nature, though most have underlying ethical principles. They can be improved on and appropriated for any particular church. The point is that making explicit principles that are implicit can be a helpful practice for a team.

Another ethical area for pastors and boards to consider is employment standards and evaluation. Clear job descriptions are essential. Annual evaluations are essential for pastors, as they are for any employee of any company. The unethical firing of pastors causes more disturbance in congregations than anything I know. Unethical dismissals are those that happen without proper evaluations measured against explicit job descriptions and without clear warnings. Even dismissals where proper procedures have been followed cause ripples within congregational life because of the sense of loyalty groups of people have. Leaders involved in issuing these dismissals sometimes have to be confidential about the reasons for dismissal for the protection of the pastor and to avoid libelous slander (I am not referring to grave moral sin, which must be exposed, according to 1 Tim 5:20). Respect for a dismissed pastor can naturally create questions within the congregation. Ethical issues easily become legal issues in our litigious times, and legal counsel should be sought

13. Peace Portal Alliance Church, March 1999, under the facilitation of consultant Bruce Gordon.

before proceeding with any public statements. Legal proceedings from those who are dismissed should be anticipated and prepared for with proper records of the dismissal procedure. On the other hand, failure to hold pastors accountable to moral and doctrinal rectitude leads to a loss of respect for leadership. Maintaining standards and evaluations is an important part of the hard work of discipleship on behalf of the church.

The way in which pastors are hired also invites careful ethical thought. Recruiting pastors from a church nearby, for example, perpetuates a sense of competition between churches rather than collaboration. It is a flagrant denial of the unity of the church and must grieve the Holy Spirit. Even recruiting a pastor from a church that is reasonably distant from your own should be done with sensitivity to and in communication with the senior leadership there. A pastor of a large church who shall remain nameless was famous in my own area for trying to recruit pastors away from their churches, near or far away, with an opening question: "How much are you making right now in your church?"

In sum, the eighth commandment offers great insight into an important aspect of human life, that of vocation and work. The meaning of work inspires integrity and ethics in the workplace. Work is continuance and participation in God's work, and its purpose is to glorify him, supply the needs of our families and the church and the poor in society, and bring an appropriate sense of self-fulfillment. Removing the dualism between the work of the pastor and that of the people makes all of this applicable to the whole people of God.

12

Ethics of Speech (Commandment 9)

You shall not give false testimony against your neighbor.
EXODUS 20:16

This commandment suggests that the dynamics of moral formation includes oral formation. What we say, as well as what we do, matters to God. Although ethics flows from being—the being of God and our participation in his relational being—it rightly concerns our doing and our *speaking*.

Here we follow the Lord Jesus, who displayed this characteristic of the expected Messiah: "You are the most excellent of men and your lips have been anointed with grace, since God has blessed you forever" (Ps 45:2). The source of that speech was a well-attuned ear, an instructed tongue, as Isaiah informs us: "The Sovereign Lord has given me a well-instructed tongue, to know the word that sustains the weary. He wakens me morning by morning, wakens my ear to listen like one being instructed" (Isa 50:4). Jesus in his high-priestly prayer to his Father makes it clear that the source of his words was always the words of the Father: "Now they know that everything you have given me comes from you. For I gave them the words you gave me and they accepted them" (John 17:7–8). His life-giving words came from a deep perichoretic communion with the Father. The wonder of God's grace is seen in that when Jesus sends his disciples out on a ministry trip, they are promised that the Father will do the same for them: "For it will not be you speaking, but the Spirit of your Father speaking through you" (Matt 10:20).

By the Spirit of the Father and the Son, we too can speak words that are the words of the Father. This no doubt refers primarily to witness and preaching, but in our everyday conversation or preaching or counseling, our communion with Christ can empower us. People "were amazed at the gracious words that came from [Jesus'] lips" (Luke 4:22), but Paul makes this the expectation and the possibility for all of us: "Let your speech always be with grace, seasoned with salt, that you may know how you ought to answer each one" (Col 4:6 NKJV).

For pastors, who use their mouths as instruments in ministry, sanctification of the tongue is all-important. James stresses this, making the use of the tongue the acid test of the sanctification of our whole being and the measure of the integrity of our ministry: "Not many of you should become teachers, my fellow believers, because you know that we who teach will be judged more strictly. We all stumble in many ways. Anyone who is never at fault in what they say is perfect, able to keep their whole body in check" (Jas 3:1–2).

Doing and saying good things, and avoiding doing and saying bad things, does not justify us. However, our actions and words do tell the truth about whether we are really persons in union with Christ and indwelled by the Spirit. They provide a window into whether the character of Christ is being formed in us. This chapter will explore the meaning and dynamics for obedience to this commandment in both its negative and positive statements, and then offer reflection on two primary areas where speaking is the primary means for ministry: the ethics of confidentiality and the ethics of preaching.

THE MEANING AND DYNAMICS OF THE COMMANDMENT

The Commandment in the Negative

The commandment as it is stated in the negative means we are to avoid speaking untruths about our neighbor, whether in the law court or in casual conversation. The positive affirms we are to speak truth to and about our neighbor in a way that builds community rather than dividing it. In one sense, this commandment is a specific case of theft probably worse than any: stealing a person's reputation with false testimony. A piece of

Jewish rabbinic wisdom literature makes this interesting observation: "Nasty talk and slander kills all three people involved. The person one talks about, the speaker, and the eager listener."[1] The real gravity of the commandment lies in its relation to the third commandment, which has to do with the majesty of the divine name and not misusing it. The ninth commandment urges us not to misuse and misrepresent the name and reputation of those made in the image of God, our neighbors. We should not tarnish the name and character of God, and we should also not damage the name of our human neighbor, who is made in the image of God. Examining the ninth commandment, including how it is expounded in Scripture in both its negative and its positive form, reveals that of all the areas of moral formation, our use of our tongues is the most demanding. Perhaps there is no greater gauge of moral formation than oral formation.

The motivation for this commandment is therefore a profound God-consciousness that derives from the covenant relationship the Decalogue implies, and from living out the first table of the Decalogue. The code of holiness in Leviticus makes this very connection: "Do not go about spreading slander among your people . . . but love your neighbor as yourself. I am the Lord" (Lev 19:16, 18). The gravity of the use of the tongue relates to the remarkable gift of communication between human beings and God that speech permits. It is given to communicate love to one's neighbor, to build community and not tear it down.

Of the seven sins listed in Prov 6:16–19, this commandment shows up three times: "There are six things the Lord hates, seven that are detestable to him: haughty eyes, *a lying tongue*, hands that shed innocent blood, a heart that devises wicked schemes, feet that are quick to rush into evil, a *false witness* who pours out lies, and a man who *stirs up conflict in the community*." Notice the connection between use of the tongue and community reflected here. If consciousness of God and his glory is the first dynamic in the transformation of our speech, the goal of community wholeness is the second.

Why does what we say about other people matter so much? It is such a horrendous distortion of a gift we have been given as those made in the image of God: the gift of being able to communicate to build community. When God made humanity, he gave us a capacity he himself possesses. He has been communing within the Trinity with perfect love and harmony and beauty for all eternity, and he is revelational with his

---

1. Bockmuehl, *Christian Way of Living*, 118. See also Palatnik and Burg, "Gossip: The Triple Murder Threat."

creatures. So when he creates humanity, he does so that they might commune with him and each other. This is essential to our being and belonging as persons in communion with God and neighbor. We are communal creatures made in the image of a God who is communion itself and who communes. That we have the capacity to self-reveal and communicate is not surprising given we are made in the image of such a God. It behooves us to use our tongues to speak truth in love that builds community, and the distortion of this is serious. When we slander others, we grievously distort the purpose for which we were given the capacity to communicate: "Slander leads to the breakdown of every community."[2]

The Commandment in the Positive

The positive aspect of this most searching of commandments is well expressed by Paul in Eph 4, where it is clear that the opposite is to use the means of communication God has given us to speak truth that reflects and builds community:

> Therefore each of you must put off falsehood and speak truthfully to your neighbor, *for we are all members of one body.* "In your anger do not sin": Do not let the sun go down while you are still angry, and do not give the devil a foothold. . . . Do not let any unwholesome talk come out of your mouths, but only what is helpful for *building others up according to their needs*, that it may *benefit those who listen.* And do not *grieve the Holy Spirit of God*, with whom you were sealed for the day of redemption. Get rid of all bitterness, rage and anger, brawling and slander, along with every form of malice. Be kind and compassionate to one another, forgiving each other, just as in Christ God forgave you. *Follow God's example*, therefore, as dearly loved children and walk in the way of love, *just as Christ loved us and gave himself up for us as a fragrant offering and sacrifice to God.* But among you there must not be even a hint of sexual immorality, or of any kind of impurity, or of greed, because these are improper for God's holy people. Nor should there be obscenity, foolish talk or coarse joking, which are out of place, but rather thanksgiving. (Eph 4:25–27, 29–32; 5:1–4)

The motivational dynamics in this text are in italics. There is a consciousness of God here that is trinitarian: imitation of God, imitation of Christ

---

2. Bockmuehl, *Christian Way of Living*, 118.

in loving and sacrificial giving, sensitivity to the Spirit, who is grieved by unwholesome talk. There is also a profound consciousness of community, for we are all members of one body. The goal of our speech is "building others up according to their needs, that it may benefit those who listen." When we fail the ethic, as all of us do, forgiveness is needed: "forgiving each other, just as in Christ God forgave you." We must only speak what is truthful, what is praiseworthy, what is thankful, what is helpful, and what is merciful.

This area of moral formation is especially challenging for pastors, who multiply words upon words, using their tongues all the time in counsel, in councils, and in the pulpit. This sends us all the more urgently to seek to find some answers about how moral formation, including oral formation, happens. As already observed, exhortations concerning this ninth commandment are often in the New Testament at the very heart of how moral transformation happens. No moral issue is more closely linked with the matter of how Christians grow in moral formation by transformation in union with Christ than the use of the tongue to speak truth in love. This builds community and avoids speaking lies, slander, and gossip that destroy community. The essence of this moral growth is consciousness of the example of God, contemplation of his person and work, and participation by the Spirit in our identity in Christ. The art of looking away from ourselves to who Christ is *for us* paradoxically changes who we are. Sitting at Jesus's feet and contemplating his earthly and high-priestly glory and all his graces, including how he spoke and how he speaks, is a road less traveled. This is the art of cultivating worshipful, awestruck, and fresh descriptions of who Christ is rather than who we are. The key to transformed speech is a contemplative heart toward Christ and all his amazing attributes and actions on our behalf.

Here is the essence of a life with God that can transform your common speech, your counseling, and your preaching. Give yourself to the life of God-centered contemplation and intimacy, to discerning his work in the daily circumstances of your life in which he is at work in resurrection formation of you. Journal daily in retrospect how he has been at work in your life each day as you scan it back over. Cultivate the habit of exposing yourself frequently to his revelation—his written word in the work of Scripture reading. Sit at his feet and hear his word. Worship him in response with liturgies and good worship songs. Cultivate the habit of dying daily to sin and self. Submit yourself to the Spirit so that you are filled and in communion by the Spirit with Christ moment by moment, so that he can continue to craft in you the fruit of the Spirit. Avoid saying things that grieve the Spirit. Speak only as prompted by the Spirit. And go frequently to the Lord and to people you have offended for forgiveness. It will keep you humble in the way that is reflected in these words of Martin Luther:

> The first thing I ask is that people should not make use of my name, and should not call themselves Lutherans but Christians. What is Luther? The teaching is not mine. Nor was I crucified for anyone.... How did I, poor stinking bag of maggots that I am, come to the point where people call the children of Christ by my evil name? ... I simply taught, preached, wrote God's Word; otherwise I did nothing. And while I slept, or drank Wittenberg beer with my friends Philip and Amsdorf, the Word so greatly weakened the papacy that no prince or emperor ever inflicted such losses upon it. I did nothing; the Word did everything.[3]

AN ETHICS OF PREACHING

The use of words is crucial in the pastor's vocation. Naturally, the life and actions of the pastor must be consistent with what is preached. James makes the connection that use of the tongue in ordinary life should be consistent with its use in our worship (and therefore preaching): "With the tongue we praise our Lord and Father, and with it we curse human beings, who have been made in God's likeness" (Jas 3:9). Perfection is not possible with regard to this commandment for any pastor, but the life of confession and integrity in the pursuit of holiness is possible. Pastors hold so much information, and speak so much in private and public, that it is easy to lapse into a betrayal of confidentiality. This can be done in order to look important, or to engage in manipulative speaking to champion their own agendas, or just in speaking carelessly. Parishioners are generally brilliant at assessing whether a pastor is a safe person in whom they can confide. Integrity of general speaking will then serve the credibility of the pastor well in preaching.

The use of words in preaching is our primary concern in this section, however. There are some obvious ethical aspects of preaching. Avoiding plagiarism is one. Failure to acknowledge the source of quotes and illustrations, or outlines if they have been borrowed from someone else, is unethical and even illegal. I would hope that, for a pastor who is

---

3. Ebeling, *Luther: An Introduction to His Thought*, 31.

serious about expository preaching, borrowing somebody else's big idea or outline would be never be necessary anyway. A pastor who reads and studies the word of God as a first priority cannot fail to have material to preach. It was said of the English preacher G. Campbell Morgan (1863–1945) that when he retired after sixty-seven years of faithful preaching, he had enough material from his study of the Bible to preach for another fifty years. When asked about his approach to preaching, he said, "Two things are vital. First, personal first-hand work on the text; and then, all scholarly works available."[4]

Another ethical matter is avoiding the use of illustrations about your spouse or children unless you have asked for their permission. Be wary of too many personal illustrations. Being vulnerable is good, but too many stories about yourself and your family can sound self-attracting. Timing is everything, also. Your congregation does not need to know that you and your wife had a conflict on the way to church. This lands in their hearts, and they do not know what to do about it. It is unacceptable to use the pulpit for your own agenda when you and your board are deliberating on an issue of nonessential importance. Be careful also how you refer to public figures when you preach. I once slammed a politician for a stance he had taken on an ethical issue. His nephew was in the audience and was "choked" that I had referred to his uncle on one issue without knowing how fine a person he was.

However, the *most* crucial matter in developing an ethic of preaching revolves around the question of what preaching is. Once that is decided, we can set the criteria as to whether preachers are using their tongue appropriately. True preaching, according to the New Testament and the tradition, is *theo-participatory*, and it is that only as it is *expository*. Preaching is a participational act such that when the preacher speaks the very words of God are spoken, as 1 Pet 4:11 says: "If anyone speaks, they should do so as one who speaks the very words of God." Paul says something similar in 1 Cor 2:13: "This is what we speak, not in words taught us by human wisdom but in words taught by the Spirit, explaining spiritual realities with Spirit-taught words." This idea is not intended to give preachers license to think they speak from the throne room of God every time they preach. What it does say is that their primary task is serious, humble, diligent exegesis of the text so that what they say is thoroughly grounded in what God, by the Spirit, has said and is saying.

---

4. Smith, "Preaching Ministry of G. Campbell Morgan."

When their exposition, given in dependence on the power of the Spirit, is a product of serious exegesis and canonical interpretation, they can take it by faith that God is speaking as they are speaking, and that as they speak God is speaking. Most importantly, because the living Word, Christ, is the substance and speaker in the written word, when we listen to the written word we encounter the living Word, and when we preach the written word the Living Word speaks! I am with Darrell Johnson in his conviction that every text is ultimately about Christ, that Christ speaks through every text, and that therefore expository preaching is not merely explaining a text; it is encountering a person who then encounters the persons we are preaching among.[5]

This notion of preaching is a treasured tradition of the Reformed faith. The Second Helvetic Confession of the Protestant Reformation says, "The preaching of the Word of God is the Word of God." This may sound arrogant and even blasphemous. Yet it is in fact a truly humble statement, for implicit in this confession is the notion that we ourselves have nothing of importance to say comparable with what God has said. As Bryan Chapell says, "When we speak, therefore, we design our messages to express the truths of the eternal Word so that the church may be the 'mouth house' of God that Martin Luther described."[6]

Karl Barth expressed this theo-participatory and Christocentric view of preaching most eloquently. Barth's concept of preaching is a practical application of his theology of revelation. His view of the nature of the biblical text may not satisfy the verbal and plenary aspects of an evangelical view of Scripture, yet Barth's seriousness about the nature of preaching as expository shames the pulpits of many preachers who profess a "higher" view of Scripture. Barth actually challenged the liberal ideology of his day by demonstrating the action of God in the human event of preaching. In its proclamation, the word of God is given a human channel in the mouth and life of a preacher who is expository in approach, such that it maintains the quality of being the word of God. Thus John McConnachie writes, "Barth defines preaching as the declaring of the Word of God."[7] Barth emphasized that the expository approach is crucial to the theo-participatory assumption. He introduced his lectures on homiletics with these words: "Preaching must conform to revelation."[8]

5. This is the essence of Johnson, *Glory of Preaching*.
6. Chapell, *Christ-Centered Preaching*, 32.
7. McConnachie, *Significance of Karl Barth*, 169.
8. Barth, *Homiletics*, 47.

Thus, only when preaching "conforms" to the revelation of God is it really preaching and can it really have power. This means that preaching must conform not just to the intent of a text but to its genre.

Barth went on to say that, in light of what preaching is, it could in fact be considered to be the Protestant sacrament: "It is very clear that the Reformation wished to see something better substituted for the Mass it abolished, and that it expected that that better thing would be—our preaching of the Word. The *verbum visible*, the objective clarified preaching of the Word, is the only sacrament left to us. The Reformers sternly took from us everything but the Bible."[9] If we have a high view of Scripture, we ought to see preaching as an audible sacrament. The real presence of Christ is what makes a speech into a sermon, and a sermon into the gospel, as P. T. Forsyth expressed it.[10] This Reformed understanding of preaching is well summed up by Bernard Manning, who says that preaching is "a manifestation of the incarnate Word, from the written Word, by the spoken Word."[11] What does this have to do with the ethics of preaching?

When preachers place technique above the text, they begin to be unethical in the sense that the expectation of the church is to hear the word of God preached. Some attention to communication and rhetoric is not wrong. It is impossible not to use rhetoric while preaching. But when this becomes our primary focus, or the color of the tie we are wearing, or the gestures we are using, we are on the way to a breach of ethics. The warning of William Willimon with regard to general pastoral praxis should be heeded also for preaching: "That many ministers base their ministry on models of leadership uncritically borrowed from the latest fads in business leadership or therapeutic processes is yet another testimony to our failure to believe that God raised Jesus Christ from the dead, thus radically changing the world."[12] James Stewart spoke to the issue of theo-participatory preaching when he said,

> Beware of any course on "How to Preach: By One Who Knows." The creature is an imposter! No man knows how to preach. You will have to reckon with this significant, disconcerting fact, that the greatest preachers who have ever lived have considered themselves poor bunglers to the end, groping after an ideal which has eluded them forever.... It is one thing to learn the

---

9. Barth, *Word of God and the Word of Man*, 114.
10. Forsyth, *Positive Preaching and the Modern Mind*, 80.
11. Manning, *Layman in the Ministry*, 138.
12. Willimon, *Pastor*, 96.

mechanics and technique of preaching: it is quite another to preach a sermon which will draw back the veil and make the barriers fall that hide the face of God.[13]

What is needed desperately in our time is the preaching of the Bible In order to renarrate the lives of the people of God in light of the biblical story. What is needed, in other words, is to help people reimagine the world in light of the overall narrative of the Word of God that is told week by week, and in light of the individual texts that are expounded. When instead the people are offered trinkets, stories strung together without reference to the text, manipulative mood sermons and unbaptized psychology, the people of God are cheated and the beginnings of ethical issues evolve.

The challenge is that many pastors in the West have sold out to administrivia and leadership technique, as Eugene Peterson said.[14] It is as if we have forgotten the lesson that the apostles learned in their busyness in Acts 6. Referring to this, G. Campbell Morgan brings this challenge to pastors that is still relevant in our time: "Nothing is more needed among preachers today than that we should have the courage to shake ourselves free from the thousand and one trivialities in which we are asked to waste our time and strength, and resolutely return to the apostolic ideal which made necessary the office of the diaconate. [We must resolve that] 'we will continue steadfastly in prayer, and in the ministry of the Word.'"[15] Failing to feed the sheep is a moral issue, and it becomes an ethical one when the shepherd has been hired to do this.

AN ETHICS OF CONFIDENTIALITY

A further aspect of pastoral life that involves truthful speaking is that of confidentiality. This sounds like a cut-and-dried matter. Congregants have the right to expect that what they share with their pastor will be held confidential. Pastors build a reputation with respect to whether they are in fact confidential in character. However, there are some complications that may require a breach of confidentiality, and some that may need discernment in this regard. In this sense, confidentiality is more challenging for pastors than it is for either counseling psychologists or medical

13. Stewart, *Heralds of God*, 89–90.
14. See, for example, Peterson, *Working the Angles* and *Under the Unpredictable Plant*.
15. Smith, "Preaching Ministry of G. Campbell Morgan."

doctors. The reason for this is that pastors wear more than one hat when they give pastoral counsel. They have a responsibility to the person being given counsel, but they also have a responsibility to the church and its governing body, and a responsibility to the state. Counselors, doctors, and pastors all have a duty to the state and are required to report child abuse of any form to the appropriate body.[16] Some congregants who bring a case of abuse in their family to the pastor may naively assume that the issue can be resolved in-house. This is especially the case for traditions that are antinomian in tendency. This is a mistake, as child abuse is not just a sin; it is a crime and requires reporting to the state. The pastor and counselors may help to bring healing to the abused person and the perpetrator, but they cannot help the perpetrator avoid the demands of the law.

Failure of a pastor to report a crime can lead to legal suits and charges, though this depends somewhat on the law and the denomination. Roman Catholic priests are forbidden by church canon law to make any disclosure of what their parishioners confess. This arrangement is supported by the law in many countries, but is in conflict with civil law in some jurisdictions. The need for clergy to consult with a lawyer when situations of this nature arise is important. Pastors need to be aware of the rules in their own country and state.[17] The following paragraph makes the important distinction between the *duty of confidentiality* and *clergy privilege*:

> Privilege simply means the information cannot be shared in court. The duty of confidentiality applies in all contexts and is an ethical matter every minister must navigate carefully. A minister's duty of confidentiality is breached when they disclose confidences to anyone, anywhere. However, there may be times when it is appropriate to share confidential information, under extreme circumstances where people may be killed or severely injured.[18]

The complexity of this issue in many countries makes it imperative that pastors discover the laws and precedents in their own country and that

---

16. In British Columbia, Canada, where I reside, under the Child, Family and Community Services Act, abuse or neglect of anyone under nineteen years of age must be reported to the police if the child is in danger, and otherwise to a phone number of the Child Services department (1-800-663-9122 at any time of the day or night). See https://www2.gov.bc.ca/gov/content/safety/public-safety/protecting-children/reporting-child-abuse.

17. For rules with regard to confidentiality privileging in the US, see, for example "Church Liability: Clergy Privilege."

18. "Church Liability: Clergy Privilege."

they consult with legal experts when they encounter challenging situations of this nature.

There is a second set of situations that may require a breach of confidentiality for a pastor. These are sins, rather than crimes, that are confessed to the pastor that require church discipline, or that compromise the relationship between children and parents. An example of the first kind might be when an elder comes to the pastor to confess that he is having an affair with the wife of another elder. Unlike a counselor, who can keep this confidential, a pastor will need, by means of a carefully thought-out process, to inform the elder's wife (or get him to inform her, or do so in the pastor's presence), as well as the husband of the woman he is having the affair with. The pastor will then need to inform the whole team of elders, who in turn will need to make an announcement to the whole church that explains why the elder is stepping down from eldership.

An example of the second kind might be when a sixteen-year-old girl informs the pastor that she is pregnant and with her doctor's consent has arranged to have an abortion (in Canada, sixteen is the age at which parental consent is not required for abortion). Whereas a doctor does not need to report this to the parents, and indeed is duty bound to maintain confidentiality, the pastor is not bound in that way. The pastor has to weigh his allegiance to the girl against an allegiance to the parents, and indeed to the church. If it is discovered after the fact that he knew but did not tell the parents, he will have a significant challenge in his relationship with them. Knowing exactly what to do in these complex situations draws out the need for the essential aspects of ethical discernment I have presented throughout the book: hearing the word of God, praying, especially seeking consultation from someone removed from the situation, as well as from local doctors and counselors and even lawyers when necessary, and thinking about the effect on the church community.

Policies and procedures regarding confidentiality should be worked out by every church and become part of the bylaws of the church.[19] Being

---

19. Some examples of resources that can help guide churches in this process are Audette, "Confidentiality in the Church"; Griffith and Young, "Clergy Counselors and Confidentiality"; Hutchinson, "Analysis"; Diocese of Toronto, "Confidentiality"; Evangelical Church Alliance International, "ECA Policy on Clergy-Penitent Privilege"; Morgan, "Burdens of Disclosure"; Diocese of London, "Confidentiality." The last resource reflects the fact that priest–penitent privilege does not apply in English law, and privileged communication is valid only when legal advice has been sought. Don Hutchinson is the vice president and general legal counsel with the Evangelical Fellowship of Canada, a body that should always be consulted by Canadian churches on this topic.

a pastor is a tough calling in many ways, but especially when it comes to confidentiality because of multiple allegiances. You cannot have a sign outside your door saying, "I can promise confidentiality as long as you don't report this or that"! The best a pastor can do is to show trustworthiness of character and affect, and care with speech in general, and people *will* come to be counseled and prayed for despite these limitations. When these difficult situations arise, the pastor needs to say, "I am very sorry, but I have a duty to report this." If the pastor is challenged by an irate parishioner, the pastor can point to the policy written on this.

Once again, the width and depth of the commandments has been shown in consideration of this ninth commandment. The capacity for speech and language is at least one evidence of the image of God in humans. It can be used for lofty things such as worship and preaching and encouragement. It is perhaps for these reasons that sin and Satan work toward our speech being careless and corrupted. The very same instrument we use for praising God is used to become blasphemous, corrosive, and destructive of community. It is perhaps the commandment that more than all the others drives us almost in despair to Christ so that by his Spirit's work in us we may speak always what is pleasing to the Father and what is edifying in our communities. This anticipates also the subject of the last commandment, that which addresses the desires behind our speech and action.

13

Ethics and Ordering Desires (Commandment 10)

You shall not covet your neighbor's house. You shall not covet your neighbor's wife, or his male or female servant, his ox or donkey, or anything that belongs to your neighbor.

EXODUS 20:17

The searching depth and gravity of this commandment reemphasizes for us the radically internal nature of the moral law. It is repeated in the New Testament on a number of occasions, illustrating again the transcovenantal relevance of the Decalogue. The shorter length of this chapter is by no means a reflection of its importance. It cuts to the heart of personal formation, character, and holiness. It undergirds all of the other commandments. It provides the etiology of sin. It illustrates the spirituality of the Torah. It speaks to the ordering of our desires as the root issue in Christian moral formation and ethics. I hope that the brevity itself will provide an impetus toward personal application of its message in each reader.

Jesus has this commandment in mind when, in Luke 12:15, correcting the obsession with material riches, he says, "Watch out! Be on your guard against all kinds of greed; life does not consist in an abundance of possessions." Jesus then tells the parable of the rich fool, whose perpetual expansive business ventures failed to take into account that an account would be required of him. Jesus ends with this saying: "This is how it will be with whoever stores up things for themselves but is not rich toward God" (Luke 12:21).

One of the tasks of the pastor in our age of consumerism and materialism is to preach the message of the tenth commandment. But first, the pastor will have to search inwardly to ensure that the same desires are not present in his or her soul. It is not just the rich who are guilty of covetousness. It is easy for pastors to slip into envy and covetousness when they compare their salaries and what they can afford for their kids with the affluence of others in the congregation.

Paul quotes this commandment in Rom 13:9, making it, along with all the others, applicable for the new-covenant era. But he also emphasizes its internal nature and its convicting use: "What shall we say, then? Is the law sinful? Certainly not! Nevertheless, I would not have known what sin was had it not been for the law. For I would not have known what coveting really was if the law had not said, 'You shall not covet.' But sin, seizing the opportunity afforded by the commandment, produced in me every kind of coveting" (Rom 7:7–8). In Eph 5:3–5, Paul reveals its gravity by coupling covetousness with sexual immorality, the former being the internal desire that creates the external action. He also equates covetousness with idolatry:

> But sexual immorality and all impurity or covetousness must not even be named among you, as is proper among saints. Let there be no filthiness nor foolish talk nor crude joking, which are out of place, but instead let there be thanksgiving. For you may be sure of this, that everyone who is sexually immoral or impure, or who is covetous (that is, an idolater), has no inheritance in the kingdom of Christ and God. (ESV)

All of us are deeply challenged by this most directly internal commandment of the Decalogue. What does this mean for the pastor? How can it then be taught for the people of God?

What is so stretching is that this commandment deals with our desires, not just our deeds. Sexual failures and material obsessions come from within. Ethics is not just about actions. They are rooted in motives and desires that are in turn rooted in our character and personhood. The greatest challenge of Christian sanctification is the ordering of our desires, which can be disordered for a long time before moral failure transpires. It is possible that a life, including that of a pastor, can be lived with the best of behavior, in a way that pleases the people and adheres to the mores of the community we are in, yet all the while with great distortion of desire and affection.

From my own experience and what I have seen in others, pastors are commonly tempted to covet success more than faithfulness. They covet larger churches more than health in their own; they covet the approval of people more than the delight of God; they covet popularity and refrain from showing tough love or saying the prophetic kinds of things a pastor sometimes needs to say; they covet praise and struggle when they hear other preachers being praised in their presence; they covet money to keep up with other families in their churches rather than being contented with how God has provided for them; they covet fame to bolster their sense of self rather than finding a sense of worth in the Father who has created them, the Son who has been united with and has redeemed them, and the Spirit, the Giving Gift, who indwells and has gifted them uniquely.

How does the ordering of desires happen in us, and how do we encourage others in this way? Desires are ordered by practices. The heart and the body are linked inseparably. The reordering of our desires has to begin with the chief of our affections, which is love. This covet commandment is in some ways an *inclusio* or bookend, answering to the first three commandments, which are about the turn from idolatry to loving the one true God with our whole beings. Paul's searing exposé of the value of ministry without love in 1 Corinthians 13 is worthy of frequent reading and rereading, but we must always remember that love is not self-generated. It is responsive. It is cultivated by meditation on the love of God, who first loved us and gave himself in Christ as a propitiation for us (1 John 4:10). It is a fruit of practiced intimacy with the Holy Spirit, who is the mutual love of the Father for the Son, who is poured into our hearts (Rom 5:5). Long before we encounter people in our daily routine, we need to encounter and receive the love of God in reading and prayer, where affections are shaped. When we are operating in the love of God, the covetous temptations of the ministry can be tempered and overcome.

In addition to daily reading and prayer, the Lord's Supper is a crucial practice for forming our desires. It is a physical and visceral way of gazing on Christ and feeding on Christ. The week-by-week practice of communion—the contemplation and consumption of Christ, of participating afresh in his crucifixion and his catching up of our beings in his ascension to the Father's right hand—weans our desires from all that is really a mirage and directs them to the one whose glory surpasses all.

The practice of solitude also cures us of the desire for approval of people and focuses that desire on the approbation of the Father. The practice of silence cures us of too grandiose an opinion of our ability to speak, causing us to be like those who are wakened morning by morning to hear the instruction from the Father, those who are taught before they dare to teach (Isa 50:4).

It can also be helpful to read literature that unveils the importance of the affections. Perhaps the two most helpful books in this regard are Augustine's *Confessions* and Jonathan Edwards's *The Religious Affections*. For Edwards, the affections run much deeper than shallow desires. They are the strongest urges and motivations of our hearts, and they awaken us and ignite our purest actions. Above all, they are wrapped up in the affection of love.

But Edwards was really following in the train of Augustine (354–430). What we are is our desires, and principally the love in our hearts defines us and determines our behavior. In his *Confessions*, Augustine states:

> My weight is my love, and by it I am carried wheresoever I am carried. My weight is my love; by it am I borne wherever I am borne. By Your Gift we are inflamed, and are borne upwards; we wax hot inwardly, and go forwards. We ascend Your ways that be in our heart, and sing a song of degrees; we glow inwardly with Your fire, with Your good fire, and we go, because we go upwards to the peace of Jerusalem; for glad was I when they said to me, Let us go into the house of the Lord. There has Your good pleasure placed us, that we may desire no other thing than to dwell there forever.[1]

Augustine's trinitarian underpinnings shaped his convictions about anthropology. If God is love, and if humans are his embodied likeness, then we too, when we live as regenerate children of God, are governed and led principally by love. Augustine described an unholy or disordered love as *cupiditas* (the carnal). But he also spoke of a godly, ordered love, which he labeled *caritas* (the spiritual love).[2] If the Holy Spirit is, in the tradition, the *vinculum caritatis* (bond of love),[3] the love that binds the Trinity, it is logical that our practices of communion in the triune communion will shape an ordered love in us. If this is true of pastors, it is true for every child of God.

---

1. Augustine, *Confessions* 13.9.
2. Augustine, *Confessions* 2.2.
3. Augustine, "On the Trinity," 131.

Conclusion: Ethics as Freedom

A friend who is a pastor recently told me that he was having more and more conversations with believers who are uncomfortable asserting any kind of moral or ethical explanation on another person—and wonder whether the church should as well. He also noted the polar opposite was prevalent in opinionated Christians who are making judgments on everyone and everything. Both of these positions are unfortunate. The latter is moralism, law imposed outside the gospel: unevangelical ethics. We may interpret the former stance as a capitulation to modernity, and specifically to the very core of Enlightenment dogma that fact and values must be separated, that faith is private, and fact or science is public. It is also sometimes associated with antinomianism of a particular kind that neglects the legitimate use of the moral law in a civic setting, and neglects the moral order given to humanity by creation and reaffirmed by the resurrection. There is, as I have noted, also a third viewpoint in some especially Anabaptist settings, which seeks to reserve moral formation and ethical reflection for the church.

This is the kind of ecclesial formation and reflection that I have encouraged throughout this book, but with a view to an outward missional influence on the world. This influence depends on ethics being ensconced within the gospel—ethics that are evangelical, not legal. The church's ethical pronouncements must be presented as flowing from the love of God, for the good of humanity, with a view to redemption and not condemnation, with the telos of justice and human flourishing in mind. This ethics is presented in the power of the Spirit, trusting in the Spirit's power to have its redemptive, cleansing effect.

In brief, the kind of pastoral ethics I have been arguing for throughout goes like this: Pastors do moral formation and ethics *from above*, that is, from God. As *persons*-in-relation, they cultivate moral formation, make ethical decisions, and speak ethically in the public square in union with Christ and in communion with the triune God. The triune God is love and holiness, and as such is the good, the true, and the beautiful. Christian ethics is participation in his life and love and holiness. Personhood and community will both be vital concepts in defining the ethos and the telos of Christian ethics. Consciousness of the triune God will mean awareness of his goodness and the goodness of his laws, which bring shalom and human flourishing to humanity, not drudgery.

HOW PASTORS PURSUE THE ETHICAL LIFE

Pastors and those they lead should live the ethical life *from gospel reality*, from justification, ensconced in the Son and empowered by the Spirit. Ethics is therefore *evangelical*, not legal. God is not a policeman but a lover, who woos us with a love that has moral content. Ethics outside the gospel is bad news; ethics operating within the gospel is part of the good news.

Pastors are informed by the word of God *from outside themselves*, and this is summed up in the two great commands of God. The first is the Great Commandment to love God and our neighbor. This tells us what it means to be human—to bear God's image. It invokes all of the Ten Commandments, which we have considered as area codes for all ethical areas. The second is the Great Commission, which is to make disciples of all nations, teaching them all of the commands included under the Great Commandment. In obeying these commands, Scripture is our final authority, as properly interpreted. Pastors will have an open ear to what the word of God says and what it means, again and again, as they encounter new ethical challenges in every age. This means discernment is crucial to interpreting ethical issues and how Scripture speaks to them. We must discern both the culture in which Scripture was written and the culture now. Culture includes positive elements that reflect the image of God in humans, but it also has sinister elements that are the product of our fallenness. Pastors will responsibly contextualize the gospel with discernment while avoiding indiscriminate enculturation.

Pastors are formed morally and guided in ethical decisions by the ministry of the Holy Spirit, who is *inside us*. This moves pastors to live the life of prayer in order to be able to hear the voice of the Spirit. Cultivating internal character will occur as we devote ourselves to following Christ, and this will have a significant influence on behavior. However, the need we have as persons for the existential work of the Holy Spirit in ethical decision-making remains. Even if we are persons of godly character, our character is not enough. We need Jesus, we need his Spirit, every hour!

Pastors seek counsel from the community of wisdom *around themselves*—they consult before making decisions, if there is time, and there usually is. Building a team of physicians, nurses, counselors, psychiatrists, lawyers, and scientists with whom we can consult is vital.

FORGIVENESS AND FREEDOM

Two important words accompany the pursuit of the ethical life: forgiveness and freedom. No one I know makes perfect ethical decisions all the time. No pastor I know gets it right 100 percent of the time. Whenever a congregation gathers on Sunday, every person present needs to be able to confess their imperfections and sins of omission and commission, and to hear words of absolution. The practice of lifestyle repentance needs to be encouraged for every believer, as well as the confession to each other that James encourages. The need for confession and forgiveness includes the pastor, of course. A pastor's ethical breach requires both discipline and forgiveness. The church will be swift to restore, but slow to reinstate a fallen pastor back into ministry.

The final word is freedom! Two verses in Ps 119 emphasize the simplicity and the joy of the vocation of the believer, seen simply as obedience to the commands of God enabled by his transforming of our minds, hearts, and behavior. In verse 32, the psalmist says, "I run in the path of your commands, for you have set my heart free" (web). In verse 35, he adds, "Direct me in the path of your commands, for there I find delight." Ethics is not about bondage to rules. It wasn't in the Old Testament, and it isn't in the New. It is freedom *in* Christ to pursue the good, the true, and the beautiful. It is freedom *from* the things that God precludes because he knows they are not shalom inducing. It is freedom *for* a life in God that brings joy even when it involves suffering, a freedom for enjoyment of every spiritual blessing in Christ, a freedom that will be full when the not-yet of the kingdom will come, but one that can already be experienced now.

Bibliography

Abraham, William. *The Bible: Beyond The Impasse*. Dallas: Highland Loch, 2012.
Adams, Robert Merrihew. *Finite and Infinite Goods*. Oxford: Oxford University Press, 2002.
———. *The Virtue of Faith*. New York: Oxford University Press, 1987.
Alberry, Sam. *Is God Anti-Gay?* Epsom: The Good Book Company, 2013.
Allender, Dan, and Tremper Longman III. *Bold Love*. Colorado Springs: NavPress, 1992.
Améry, Jean. *On Suicide: A Discourse on Voluntary Death*. Translated by John D. Barlow. Bloomingtom: Indiana University Press, 1999.
Anderson, Ray, and Dennis B. Guernsey. *On Being Family: A Social Theology of the Family*. Eugene, OR: Wipf & Stock,1985.
———. *The Shape of Practical Theology: Empowering Ministry with Theological Praxis*. Downers Grove, IL: InterVarsity Academic, 2001.
———. *Something Old, Something New: Marriage and Family Ministry in a Postmodern World*. Eugene, OR: Wipf & Stock, 2007.
Aquinas, Thomas. *Summae Theologiae*. Green Bay, WI: Aquinas Institute, 2023.
Aristotle. *Nichomachean Ethics*. Translated by J. A. K. Thomson. London: Penguin Classics, 2004.
Atkinson, David, ed. *New Dictionary of Christian Ethics and Pastoral Theology*. Downers Grove, IL: InterVarsity, 1995.
Audette, Elizabeth. "Confidentiality in the Church: What the Pastor Knows and Tells," *Religion Online*, 2010. https://www.religion-online.org/article/confidentiality-in-the-church-what-the-pastor-knows-and-tells/.
Augustine. *Confessions*. In *Nicene and Post-Nicene Fathers*. Philip Schaff and J. G. Pilkington. Buffalo: Christian Literature, 1987.
———. "On the Trinity." In *St. Augustine: On the Holy Trinity, Doctrinal Treatises, Moral Treatises*, translated by Arthur West Haddan and edited by Philip Schaff, 3:6–131. Buffalo, NY: Christian Literature, 2009.
———. *Works of St. Augustine: A Translation for the Twenty-First Century*. New York: New City, 1990.
Avioz, Michael. "On the Religious Significance of Shedding Blood." Bar-Ilan University's Parashat Hashavua Study Center, Parashat Mattot-Masei 5767, July 14, 2007. https://www.biu.ac.il/JH/Parasha/eng/massey/avi.html.
Baker, David L. *The Decalogue: Living as the People of God*. Downers Grove, IL: InterVarsity Academic, 2017.
Bailey, D. S. *The Mystery of Love and Marriage*. New York: Harper, 1952.

Bainton, Roland H. *Here I Stand: A Life of Martin Luther*. New York: Penguin, 1977.
Barth, Karl. *Church Dogmatics*. 4 vols. Edinburgh: T. & T. Clark, 1956–1975.
———. *Ethics*. Eugene, OR: Wipf & Stock, 2013.
———. *Homiletics*. Translated by Geoffrey W. Bromiley and Donald E. Daniels. Louisville, KY: Westminster John Knox, 1991.
———. *The Word of God and the Word of Man*. Translated by D. Horton. New York: Harper and Row, 1961.
Bell, Roy, and Stanley Grenz. *Betrayal of Trust: Confronting and Preventing Clergy Sexual Misconduct*. Grand Rapids: Baker, 2001.
Benner, David G. *The Gift of Being Yourself: The Sacred Call to Self-Discovery*. Downers Grove, IL: InterVarsity, 2015.
Berry, Wendell. *The Art of the Commonplace: The Agrarian Essays of Wendell Berry*. Berkeley: Counterpoint, 2002.
Bevans, Stephen B., and Roger Schroeder. *Constants in Context: A Theology of Mission for Today*. Maryknoll, NY: Orbis, 2004.
Biggar, Nigel. *Aiming to Kill: The Ethics of Suicide and Euthanasia*. Cleveland: Pilgrim, 2004.
Bockmuehl, Klaus. *The Christian Way of Living: An Ethics of the Ten Commandments*. Vancouver: Regent College, 1994.
Bonhoeffer, Dietrich. *Ethics*. New York: Touchstone, 1995.
———. *Life Together*. Translated by John W. Doberstein. Grand Rapids: HarperOne, 2009.
Bretherton, Luke. *Hospitality as Holiness: Christian Witness amid Moral Diversity*. New York: Routledge, 2016.
Bretherton, Luke, and Andrew Walker. *Remembering Our Future: Explorations in Deep Church*. Eugene, OR: Wipf & Stock, 2013.
Brice, Ashleigh. "Prenatal and Preimplantation Genetic Testing." Research paper in Pastoral Ethics course, Regent College, April 13, 2018.
Bromberg, Howard. "Pope John Paul II, Vatican II, and Capital Punishment." University of Michigan Law School Scholarship Repository, 2007. https://repository.law.umich.edu/articles/949.
Bromiley, Geoffrey W. "Ethics and Dogmatics." In *International Standard Biblical Encyclopedia*, edited by James Orr et al., 2:186–90. San Francisco: Harper and Row, 1987.
Brown, Jeannine K. "Commentary on Luke 14:25–33." *Working Preacher*. https://www.workingpreacher.org/preaching.aspx?commentary_id=667.
Browning, R. S. *Christian Ethics and the Moral Psychologies*. Grand Rapids: Eerdmans Books for Young Readers, 2006.
Brueggemann, Walter. *Sabbath as Resistance: Saying No in the Culture of Now*. Louisville, KY: Westminster John Knox, 2016.
Brugger, Eugene Christian. *Capital Punishment and Roman Catholic Moral Tradition*. 2nd ed. Notre Dame: University of Notre Dame, 2014.
Bucher, Bonnie. "Personal Response to 'Betrayal of Trust.'" Paper for Pastoral Ethics course, Regent College, 2008.
Burgess, John P. "Reformed Explication of the Ten Commandments." In *The Ten Commandments: The Reciprocity of Faithfulness*, edited by William P. Brown, 78–99. Louisville, KY: Westminster John Knox, 2004.
Burns, Bob, et al. *Resilient Ministry: What Pastors Told Us About Surviving and Thriving*. Downers Grove, IL: InterVarsity, 2013.

Buttrey, Michael. "Toward a Moral Theology of Genetic Screening." *Crux* 46 (2010) 2–14.
Calvin, John. *Institutes of the Christian Religion*. 2 vols. Edited by John T. McNeil. Translated by Ford L. Battles. The Library of Christian Classics. Louisville, KY: Westminster John Knox, 2001.
———. *Commentary on Ephesians*. Translated by William Pringle. https://biblehub.com/commentaries/calvin/ephesians/6.htm.
Chapell, Bryan. *Christ-Centered Preaching: Redeeming the Expository Sermon*. 2nd ed. Grand Rapids: Baker, 2005.
Chesterton, G. K. *The Everlasting Man: The Christian Theology Classic*. Glasgow: Moncreiffe, 2023.
"Christians and Capital Punishment." A Report of the Christian Life Commission of the Baptist General Convention of Texas, January 10, 2003. http://texasmoratorium.org/rgraphics/baptist_fulltext.pdf.
"Church Liability: Clergy Privilege, Confidentiality, and Reporting: Insurance, Risk Management." AG Financial. https://www.agfinancial.org/blog/bid103391church-liability-clergy-privilege-confidentiality-and-reporting/.
Cladis, George. *Leading the Team-Based Church: How Pastors and Church Staffs Can Grow Together into a Powerful Fellowship of Leaders*. San Francisco: Jossey-Bass, 1999.
Clark, Gordon H. "Traducianism," Trinity Foundation, July/August 1982. http://www.trinityfoundation.org/journal.php?id=56.
Clark, Kelly James, and Anne Poortenga. *The Story of Ethics: Fulfilling Our Human Nature*. London: Pearson, 2002.
Coakley, Sarah. *God, Sexuality, and the Self*. Cambridge: Cambridge University Press, 2013.
Cochrane, Arthur C., ed. *The Church's Confessions Under Hitler*. Philadelphia: Westminster, 1952.
———. *Reformed Confessions of the Sixteenth Century*. Louisville, KY: Westminster John Knox, 2003.
Cornes, Andrew. *Divorce and Remarriage: Biblical Principles and Pastoral Practice*. Grand Rapids: Eerdmans, 1993.
Cowen, Philip J., and Michael Browning. "What Has Serotonin to Do with Depression?," *World Psychiatry* 14 (2015) 158–60.
Crabb, Larry. *Connecting: Healing Ourselves and Our Relationships*. Nashville: Thomas Nelson, 1997.
———. "Traits of a Sexually Healthy Pastor." *Leadership* 16 (1995) 38.
Crisp, Oliver. *An American Augustinian: Sin and Salvation in the Dogmatic Theology of William G. T. Shedd*. Eugene, OR: Wipf & Stock, 2007.
———. "Pulling Traducianism Out of the Shedd." *Ars Disputandi* 6 (2006) 265–87.
Danaher, William J. *The Trinitarian Ethics of Jonathan Edwards*. Louisville, KY: Westminster John Knox, 2004.
Das, A. Andrew. *Remarriage in Early Christianity*. Grand Rapids: Eerdmans, 2024.
Danby, Herbert, trans. *The Mishnah*. London: Oxford University Press, 1933.
Dates, Charlie. Why We Can't Wait for Christ-Exalting Diversity. In *Letters To A Birmingham Jail: A Response to the Words and Dreams of Dr. Martin Luther King Jr.* Edited by Bryan Loritts. Chicago: Moody, 2014.
Dawn, Marva. *A Royal "Waste" of Time: The Splendor of Worshipping God and Beimng Church for the World*. Grand Rapids: Eerdmans, 1999.

Dennison, William D. "Review of VanDrunen's Natural Law." *Westminster Theological Journal* 75 (2013) 349–70.

Diocese of London. "Confidentiality." https://www.london.anglican.org/kb/confidentiality/.

Diocese of Toronto. "Confidentiality." *Liturgical Standards and Resources (2010) of the Anglican Church of Canada.* https://www.toronto.anglican.ca/clergy-resources/liturgical-standards/.

Ebeling, Gerhardt. *Luther: An Introduction to His Thought.* Translated by R. A. Wilson. Philadelphia: Fortress, 1970.

Edwards, Jonathan. "Heaven Is a World of Love." In *Charity and Its Fruits*, 178–88. Wheaton, IL: Crossway, 2020.

———. *Religious Affections.* In *The Works of Jonathan Edwards*, Volume 2. Edited by John E. Smith. New Haven, CT: Yale University Press, 2009.

Ellul, Jacques. *To Will and to Do: An Introduction to Christian Ethics.* Eugene, OR: Cascade, 2020.

Enns, Peter. *Exodus.* NIV Application Commentary. Grand Rapids: Zondervan, 2000.

Estes, James. "The Role of Godly Magistrates in the Church: Melanchthon as Luther's Interpreter and Collaborator." *Church History* 67 (1998) 463–83.

Evangelical Church Alliance International. "ECA Policy on Clergy-Penitent Privilege." https://www.ecainternational.org/policies-of-the-eca.

Farris, Joshua R. "Emergent Creationism: Another Option in the Origin of the Soul Debate." *Journal of Religious Studies* 50 (2014) 321–39.

Fernando, Ajith. *Jesus Driven Ministry.* Wheaton, IL: Crossway, 2002.

Flynn, Casey. *The Theological Ethics of Jacques Ellul.* MA thesis, Regent College, 2009.

Ford, David F. *Self and Salvation: Being Transformed.* Cambridge: Cambridge University Press, 1999.

Forsyth, P. T. *Positive Preaching and the Modern Mind.* 2nd ed. Eugene, OR: Wipf & Stock, 2007.

Foster, Richard. *Celebration of Discipline: The Path To Spiritual Growth.* New York: HarperCollins, 1988.

———. *Money, Sex and Power: The Challenge of the Disciplined Life.* New York: HarperCollins, 1987.

Frame, John. *The Escondido Theology: A Reformed Response to Two Kingdom Theology.* Lakeland: Whitefield Media, 2011.

Gagnon, Robert. *The Bible and Homosexual Practice: Texts and Hermeneutics.* Nashville: Abingdon, 2001.

———. "Leviticus and the Times." *First Things*, August 1, 2018. https://www.firstthings.com/web-exclusives/2018/08/leviticus-and-the-times.

———. "No, God Isn't Transgender." *First Things*, August 15, 2016. https://www.firstthings.com/blogs/firstthoughts/2016/08/no-god-isnt-transgender.

Geisler, Norman. *Christian Ethics: Contemporary Issues and Options.* Grand Rapids: Baker, 2012.

Gentry, Elizabeth. "My Resounding 'Yes' to God and Embracing My Sexuality: Singleness and the Song of Songs." *Priscilla Papers*, January 30, 2018. https://www.cbeinternational.org/resource/article/priscilla-papers-academic-journal/my-resounding-yes-god-and-embracing-my-sexuality.

Goroncy, Jason. "Euthanasia: Some Theological Considerations for Living Responsibly." *Pacifica Australasian Theological Studies* 29 (2017) 221–43.

———. "Euthanasia/Voluntary Assisted Dying: Some Theological and Pastoral Resources." July 9, 2017. https://jasongoroncy.com/2019/07/09/euthanasia-voluntary-assisted-dying-some-theological-and-pastoral-resources/.

Gregory of Nyssa. *De Hominis Opificio 29*. In *Gregory of Nyssa: Patrologia Graeca*, edited by Jacques-Paul Migne, 44:233–34. Paris: n.d, 1863.

Grenz, Stanley. *The Moral Quest: Foundations of Christian Ethics*. Downers Grove, IL: InterVarsity Academic, 1997.

———. *Renewing the Center*. 2nd ed. Grand Rapids: Baker Academic, 2006.

———. *The Social God and the Relational Self: A Trinitarian Theology of the Imago Dei*. Louisville, KY: Westminster John Knox, 2001.

———. *Sexual Ethics: An Evangelical Perspective*. Louisville, KY: Westminster John Knox, 1990.

Grenz, Stanley, and Roy Bell. *Betrayal of Trust: Confronting and Preventing Clergy Sexual Misconduct*. 2nd ed. Grand Rapids: Baker, 2004.

Griffith, E. E. and J. L. Young. "Clergy Counselors and Confidentiality." *Journal of the American Academy of Psychiatry Law* 32 (2004) 43–50

Guroian, Vigen. *Ethics After Christendom: Toward an Ecclesial Christian Ethic*. Eugene, OR: Wipf & Stock, 2004.

Gushee, David, and Glen Stassen. *Kingdom Ethics: Following Jesus in Contemporary Context*. Grand Rapids: Eerdmans, 2016.

Habets, Myk. "In Him We Live and Move and Have our Being." In *Third Article Theology: A Pneumatological Dogmatics*, 395–417. Minneapolis: Fortress, 2016.

Hall, Francis J. "Ch. XIV. Q. 84. Traducianism and Creationism." Theological Outlines, August 12, 2005. http://disseminary.org/hoopoe/dogma/2005/08/ch_xiv_q_84_tra_1.html.

Hannon, Michael. "Against Heterosexuality." *First Things*, March 1, 2014. https://firstthings.com/against-heterosexuality/.

Hansen, David. *The Art of Pastoring: Ministry Without All the Answers*. Downers Grove, IL: InterVarsity, 2012.

Harris, Joshua. *I Kissed Dating Goodbye*. Colorado Springs: Multnomah, 2003.

Hart, Darryl G. *A Secular Faith: Why Christianity Favors the Separation of Church and State*. Chicago: Ivan R. Dee, 2006.

Hart, Trevor. *Regarding Karl Barth: Toward a Reading of His Theology*. Milton Keynes, UK: Paternoster, 1999.

Hastings, W. Ross. "Divine and Created Agency in Asymmetric Concursus: A Barthian Option." In *Divine Action and Providence*, edited by Oliver Crisp and Fred Sanders, 115–36. Grand Rapids: Zondervan, 2019.

———. *Jonathan Edwards and the Life of God: Toward an Evangelical Theology of Participation*. Minneapolis: Fortress, 2015.

———. *Theological Ethics: The Church's Integrity in Contemporary Context*. Grand Rapids: Zondervan Academic, 2021.

———. *Total Atonement: Trinitarian Participation in the Reconciliation of Humanity and Creation*. Minneapolis: Lexington/Fortress Academic, 2019.

Hauerwas, Stanley. *A Community of Character: Toward a Constructive Christian Social Ethic*. Indiana: University of Notre Dame Press, 1981.

———. *The Hauerwas Reader*. Edited by John Berkman and Michael Cartwright. 2nd ed. Durham, NC: Duke University Press, 2001.

———. "Punishing Christians: A Pacificist Approach to the Issue of Capital Punishment." In *Religion and the Death Penalty: A Call for Reckoning*, edited by Erik C. Owens et al., 57–72. Grand Rapids: Eerdmans, 2004.

———. *With the Grain of the Universe: The Church's Witness and Natural Theology*. Grand Rapids: Baker Academic, 2013.

Hauerwas, Stanley, and William Willimon. *Resident Aliens: Life in the Christian Colony*. Nashville: Abingdon, 2014.

Hayhoe, Katharine, and Andrew Farley. *A Climate for Change: Global Warming Facts for Faith-Based Decisions*. New York: FaithWords, 2011.

Hays, Christopher, and Richard Hays. *The Widening of God's Mercy*. New Haven, CT: Yale University Press, 2024.

Hays, Richard. *The Moral Vision of the New Testament*. New York: HarperOne, 1996.

Hendricks, Howard. "The Process of Failure." Moody Bible Conference, January 1, 1984.

Henry, Carl. *Christian Personal Ethics*. Grand Rapids: Baker, 1977.

Hervey-Small, Dwight. *Remarriage and God's Renewing Grace: A Positive Biblical Ethic for Divorced Christians*. Grand Rapids: Baker, 1986.

Heschel, Abraham Joshua. *The Sabbath: Its Meaning for Modern Man*. New York: Farrar, Straus, and Giroux, 1951.

Hinlicky Wilson, Sarah. "Martin Luther, Pacifist?" *Plough*, October 18, 2017. https://www.plough.com/en/topics/justice/nonviolence/martin-luther-pacifist.

Hodge, Charles. *Systematic Theology*. 3 vols. Grand Rapids: Eerdmans, 1940.

Hollinger, Dennis P. *Choosing The Good: Christian Ethics In A Complex World*. Grand Rapids: Baker Academic, 2002.

———. *The Meaning of Sex: Christian Ethics and the Moral Life*. Grand Rapids: Baker Academic, 2009.

Holmes, Arthur F. "Just War." In *War: Four Christian Views*, edited by Robert G. Clouse, 115–35. Downers Grove, IL: InterVarsity, 1991.

Horton, Michael. "Calvin and Law-Gospel Hermeneutic." *Pro Ecclesia* 6 (1997) 27–42.

House, Wayne. *Divorce and Remarriage*. Downers Grove, IL: InterVarsity, 1990.

House, Wayne, and John Howard Yoder. *The Death Penalty Debate: Two Opposing Views of Capital Punishment*. Dallas: Word, 1991.

Houston, James. "Trinitarian Spirituality." Lecture, Regent College, 1992.

Howatch, Susan. *Glittering Images*. New York: Fawcett, 1988.

Hui, Edwin C. *At the Beginning of Life: Dilemmas in Theological Bioethics*. Downers Grove, IL: InterVarsity, 2002.

Hutchinson, Don. "Analysis: The State of Clergy-Parishioner Privilege in Canada." *National Post*, July 25, 2011. https://nationalpost.com/holy-post/analysis-the-state-of-clergy-parishioner-privilege-in-canada.

Instone-Brewer, David. *Divorce and Remarriage in the Church: Biblical Solutions for Pastoral Realities*. Bletchley, UK: Paternoster, 2003.

Irenaeus. *Against Heresies*. Edited by A. Roberts and J. Donaldson. Peabody, MA: Hendrickson, 1995. https://www.ccel.org/ccel/irenaeus/against_heresies_iii.html.

Jackson, Jesse T. "Alistair Begg Takes Heat for Advising Grandmother To Attend Grandchild's Transgender Wedding." Church Leaders, January 19, 2024. https://churchleaders.com/news/466629-alistair-begg-takes-heat-for-advising-grandmother-to-attend-grandchilds-transgender-wedding.html.

Jenson, Robert. *America's Theologian: A Recommendation of Jonathan Edwards*. New York: Oxford University Press, 1988.

———. "God's Time, Our Time: An Interview with Robert W. Jenson." *Christian Century* 123 (May 2, 2006) 33.
Johnson, Darrell W. *The Glory of Preaching: Participating in God's Transformation of the World*. Downers Grove, IL: InterVarsity Academic, 2009.
John Paul II, Pope. *The Encyclicals of Pope John Paul II*. Edited by J. Michael Miller. Huntingdon: Our Sunday Visitor, 2001.
———. *The Redemption of the Body and Sacramentality of Marriage (Theology of the Body)*. From the Weekly Audiences of His Holiness September 5, 1979—November 28, 1984. https://stmarys-waco.org/documents/2016/9/theology_of_the_body.pdf.
Jones, L. Gregory. *Transformed Judgment: Toward a Trinitarian Account of the Moral Life*. Eugene, OR: Wipf & Stock, 2008.
Keener, Craig S. *And Marries Another: Divorce and Remarriage in the Teaching of the New Testament*. Peabody, MA: Hendrickson, 1991.
Keil, Carl Friedrich, *Exodus*. Translated by James Martin. Peabody, MA: Hendrickson, 2006.
Keller, Timothy. "Old Testament Law and the Charge of Inconsistency." https://timothykeller.com/blog/2012/6/12/old-testament-law-and-the-charge-of-inconsistency.
Kelsay, John. "Prayer and Ethics: Reflections on Calvin and Barth." *Harvard Theological Review* 82 (1989) 169–184.
Kerr, Fergus. "The Doctrine of God and Theological Ethics according to Thomas Aquinas." In *The Doctrine of God and Theological Ethics*, edited by Alan J. Torrance and Michael Banner, 71–84. London: T. & T. Clark, 2006.
Kierkegaard, Sören. *Works Of Love*. New York: Harper Perennial 1964.
Kirkus Reviews. "On Suicide: A Discourse on Voluntary Death." *Kirkus Reviews*, 1999. https://www.kirkusreviews.com/book-reviews/jean-amery/on-suicide/.
Kreeft, Peter. *Everything You Ever Wanted to Know about Heaven . . . But Never Dreamed of Asking*. San Franscisco: Ignatius, 1990.
Lahdenperä, Mirkka, et al. "Fitness Benefits of Prolonged Post-reproductive Lifespan in Women." *Nature* 428 (2004) 178–81.
Lewis, C. S. *God in the Dock: Essays on Theology and Ethics*. Edited by Walter Hooper. Grand Rapids: Eerdmans, 1970.
———. *Mere Christianity*. London: Geoffrey Bles, 1952.
———. *The Weight of Glory and Other Addresses*. New York: HarperOne, 2001.
Lind, Christopher. "What Makes Good Ministry Good? Women In Ministry" in *Theology & Sexuality*, 11, No. 3 (2005), 65–88.
Liptak, Adam. "Does Death Penalty Save Lives? A New Debate." *New York Times*, November 18, 2007. https://www.nytimes.com/2007/11/18/us/18deter.html.
Livingstone, J. Kevin. *A Missiology of the Road: Early Perspectives in David Bosch's Theology of Mission and Evangelism*. Eugene, OR: Wipf & Stock, 2013.
Long, Edward L. *A Survey of Christian Ethics*. New York: Oxford University Press,1967.
———. *A Survey of Recent Christian Ethics*. New York: Oxford University Press, 1982.
Luther, Martin. *Luther's Works*. Edited by J. Pelikan and H. Lehmann. Philadelphia: Fortress, 1962.
———. "On Trade and Usury" (1524). In *The Works of Martin Luther*, 4:8–26. Albany, NY: Book for the Ages, 1997. https://media.sabda.org/alkitab-8/LIBRARY/LUT_WRK4.PDF.
Luther King, Martin, Jr. *Why We Can't Wait*. San Francisco: Harper and Row, 1964.
Lutzer, Erwin. *Living with Your Passions*. Grand Rapids: Victor, 1983.

MacDonald, Mark. "On the Marriage Canon." *Anglican Journal* 145 (2019) 5.

MacIntyre, Alasdair. *After Virtue: A Study In Moral Theory.* 3rd ed. Notre Dame: University of Notre Dame, 2007.

MacPherson, Ryan. "The Magdeburg Interpretation of Romans 13: A Lutheran Justification for Political Resistance." Hausvater Project, July 2016. https://www.hausvater.org/articles/336-the-magdeburg-interpretation-of-romans-13-a-lutheran-justification-for-political-resistance.html.

"Major Depression." National Institute of Mental Health, July 2023. https://www.nimh.nih.gov/health/statistics/major-depression.shtml.

Manning, Bernard. *A Layman in the Ministry.* London: Independent, 1942.

Maurice, F. D. *Reconstructing Christian Ethics: Selected Writings.* Edited by Ellen K. Wondra. Louisville, KY: Westminster John Know, 1995.

McAlpine, Stephen. "The Blurred Vision of Richard B Hays." April 10, 2024. https://stephenmcalpine.com/the-blurred-vision-of-richard-b-hays/.

McConnachie, John. *The Significance of Karl Barth.* London: Hodder and Stoughton, 1931.

McDermott, Gerald R. Review of Wilson H. Kimnach, Kenneth P. Minkema, and Douglas A. Sweeney, eds., *The Sermons of Jonathan Edwards: A Reader.* American Religious Experience, December 1999. http://are.as.wvu.edu/mcderm.htm.

McIllhenny, Ryan C. *Kingdoms Apart: Engaging the Two Kingdoms Perspective.* Phillipsburg: Presbyterian and Reformed, 2012.

Meilaender, Gilbert. *Bioethics: A Primer for Christians.* Grand Rapids: Eerdmans, 1996.

———. *Faith and Faithfulness: Basic Themes in Christian Ethics.* Notre Dame: Notre Dame Press, 1992.

———. *The Limits of Love: Some Theological Explorations.* University Park/London: Pennsylvania State University Press, 1987.

Meilaender, Gilbert, and Werpehowski, William, eds. *The Oxford Handbook of Theological Ethics.* Oxford: Oxford University Press, 2005.

Melancthon, Philip. *Melancthon on Christian Doctrine: Loci Communes, 1955.* Grand Rapids: Baker, 1982.

Merritt, Jonathan. "Conservative Christians Just Lost Their Scholarly Trump Card On Same-Sex Relationships." April 16, 2024. https://www.jonathanmerritt.com/article/2024/4/16/conservative-christians-just-lost-their-scholarly-trump-card-on-same-sex-relationships.

Michaud, Derek. "Stanley Hauerwas (1940-)." *Boston Collaborative Encyclopaedia of Western Theology.* http://people.bu.edu/wwildman/bce/hauerwas.htm.

Milbank, John. "The Impossibility of Gay Marriage and the Threat of Biopolitical Control." *ABC Religion and Ethics*, April 23, 2013. https://www.abc.net.au/religion/the-impossibility-of-gay-marriage-and-the-threat-of-biopolitical/10099888.

———. "The Second Difference: For A Trinitarianism without Reserve," *Modern Theology* 2 (1986) 213–34.

———. *Theology and Social Theory.* Oxford: Blackwell, 1990.

Mitchell, Ben C. "Counting the Cost of Genetic Screening." *Ethics and Medicine* 28 (2012) 69.

Moore, George F. *Judaism in the First Century of the Christian Era: The Age of the Tannaim.* New York: Schocken, 1971.

Morgan, "Burdens of Disclosure: A Pastoral Theology of Confidentiality." PhD diss., University of Denver/Iliff School of Theology, June 2010.

Moyse, Ashley. "Fodder for Despair, Masquerading as Hope." *Religions* 10 (2019) 651.

Muller, Richard A. *Post-Reformation Reformed Dogmatics: The Rise and Development of Reformed Orthodoxy, ca. 1520 to ca. 1725*. Second Revised Edition. Grand Rapids: Baker Academic, 2010.

Murray, John. *Divorce*. Phillipsburg: Presbyterian and Reformed, 1961.

Newbigin, Lesslie. *Foolishness to the Greeks: The Gospel and Western Culture*. Grand Rapids: Eerdmans, 1988.

Nugent, John, C., ed. "Noah's Covenant and the Purpose of Punishment." In *The End of Sacrifice: The Capital Punishment Writings of John Howard Yoder*, 90–106. Harrisonburg: Herald, 2011.

O'Donovan, Oliver. *Begotten or Made?: Human Procreation and Medical Techniques*. New York: Oxford University Press, 1984.

———. "The Death Penalty in *Evangelium Vitae*." In *Ecumenical Ventures in Ethics: Protestants Engage Pope John Paul II's Moral Encyclicals*, edited by Reinhart Hütter and Theodore Dieter, 220–23. Grand Rapids: Eerdmans,

———. *The Just War Revisited*. Cambridge: Cambridge University Press, 2003.

———. *Resurrection and Moral Order: An Outline for Evangelical Ethics*. 2nd ed. Grand Rapids: Eerdmans, 1994.

Ogden, Greg. *The New Reformation: Returning the Ministry to the People of God*. Grand Rapids: Zondervan, 1990.

Owens, Erik C., et al., eds. *Religion and the Death Penalty: A Call for Reckoning*. Grand Rapids: Eerdmans, 2004.

Palatnik, Lori, and Bob Burg. "Gossip: The Triple Murder Threat." *Aish HaTorah*, print article 71. https://www.aish.com/jl/i/s/48949916.html.

Pastoral Care. "Statistics in the Ministry." 2025. http://www.pastoralcareinc.com/statistics/.

Pauw, Amy Plantinga. *The Supreme Harmony of All: The Trinitarian Theology of Jonathan Edwards*. Grand Rapids: Eerdmans, 2002.

Pennings, Ray. "Why the Federal Rush to Amend Assisted Dying Legislation Is Risky." Canadian Broadcasting Corporation Opinion, January 30, 2020. https://www.cbc.ca/news/opinion/opinion-assisted-dying-legislation-maid-1.5437433.

Peterson, Eugene H. *Working the Angles: The Shape of Pastoral Integrity*. Grand Rapids: Eerdmans, 1987.

Picard, André. "Role of Grandmothers Crucial for Tree of Life." *The Globe and Mail*, March 11, 2004. https://www.theglobeandmail.com/life/role-of-grandmothers-crucial-for-tree-of-life/article4087958/.

Piper, John. "Rescue Those Being Led Away to Death." In *Readings in Christian Ethics*, edited by Robert Rakestraw and David Clark, 2:444–46. Grand Rapids: Baker, 2008.

Provan, Iain. *Ecclesiastes, Song of Songs*. NIV Application Commentary. Grand Rapids: Zondervan, 2001.

———. *Seeking What Is Right: The Old Testament and the Good Life*. Waco, TX: Baylor University Press, 2020.

Purves, Andrew. *The Crucifixion of Ministry: Surrendering Our Ambitions to the Service of Christ*. Downers Grove, IL: InterVarsity, 2007.

———. *Reconstructing Pastoral Theology: A Christological Foundation*. Louisville: Westminster John Knox, 2004.

———. *The Resurrection of Ministry: Serving in the Hope of the Risen Lord*. Downers Grove, IL: InterVarsity, 2010.

Powell, John. *Why I Am Afraid to Tell You Who I Am*. Grand Rapids: Zondervan, 2012.
Quinn, Philip L. *Divine Commands and Moral Requirements*. Oxford: Oxford University Press, 1978.
Rae, Scott B. "Prenatal Genetic Testing, Abortion and Beyond." In *Genetic Ethics: Do the Ends Justify the Genes?*, edited by John F. Kilner et al., 136–45. Grand Rapids: Eerdmans, 1997.
"Revenge Begins to Seem Less Sweet: Capital Punishment in America." *The Economist*, August 30, 2007. https://www.economist.com/briefing/2007/08/30/revenge-begins-to-seem-less-sweet.
Robbins, Cynthia L., et al. "Prevalence, Frequency, and Associations of Masturbation with Partnered Sexual Behaviors among US Adolescents." *Journal of the American Medical Association, Pediatrics* (December 2011). https://jamanetwork.com/journals/jamapediatrics/fullarticle/1107656#.
Ryan, Maura A. "Justice and Genetics: Whose Holy Grail?" In *On Moral Medicine: Theological Perspectives on Medical Ethics*, edited by M. Therese Lysaught et al., 973–90. Grand Rapids: Eerdmans, 2012.
Salzman, *Deontology and Teleology: An Investigation of the Normative Debate in Roman Catholic Moral Theology (Bibliotheca Ephemeridum Theologicarum Lovaniensium)*. Leuven: Peeters, 1995.
Schaff, Philip. *History of the Christian Church: Nicene and Post-Nicene Christianity A.D. 311–600*. Broken Arrow, OK: Vision for Maximum Impact, 2017.
Schaeffer, Francis, and C. Everett Koop. *Whatever Happened to the Human Race?* Wheaton, IL: Crossway, 1983.
Schleiermacher, Friedrich. *The Christian Faith in Outline*. Edinburgh: W.F. Henderson, 1922.
Schulweis, Harold M. "The Uniqueness of Judaism, Lecture 1, The Image of God." 1998. http://www.vbs.org/page.cfm?p=706.
Scots Confession (1560). In *Reformed Confessions of the Sixteenth Century*, edited by Arthur C. Cochrane, 159–84. Louisville, KY: Westminster John Knox, 2003.
Shedd, Charlie. *The Stork Is Dead: Straight Answers to Young Peoples' Questions*. Rev. ed. Waco, TX: Word, 1983.
Shuman, Joel. "Desperately Seeking Perfection: Christian Discipleship and Medical Genetics." In *On Moral Medicine*, edited by M. Therese Lysaught et al., 1010–13. Grand Rapids: Eerdmans, 2012.
Siegfried, Francis. "Creationism." In *The Catholic Encyclopedia*. New York: Robert Appleton Company, 1908. http://www.newadvent.org/cathen/04475a.htm.
Smail, Tom. *The Giving Gift: The Holy Spirit in Person*. Eugene, OR: Wipf & Stock, 2004.
Smedes, Lewis B. *Sex for Christians: The Limits and Liberties of Sexual Living*. Grand Rapids: Eerdmans, 1994.
Smith, Andrew. "The Preaching Ministry of G. Campbell Morgan." May 21, 2019, https://www.pastorandrewsmith.com/news/2019/5/21/the-preaching-ministry-of-g-campbell-morgan.
Sprinkle, Preston. "Review of The Widening of God's Mercy by Christopher B. Hays and Richard B. Hays." The Center for Faith, Sexuality and Gender. https://www.centerforfaith.com/blog/review-of-the-widening-of-god-s-mercy-by-christopher-b-hays-and-richard-b-hays.
Stevens, R. Paul. *Disciplines of a Hungry Heart: Christian Living Seven Days a Week*. Wheaton, IL: Harold Shaw, 1993.

———. *Doing God's Business: Meaning and Motivation for the Marketplace*. Grand Rapids: Eerdmans, 2006.
———. *The Other Six Days: Vocation, Work, and Ministry in Biblical Perspective*. Vancouver: Regent, 1999.
Stewart, James S. *Heralds of God: A Practical Book on Preaching*. Vancouver: Regent College, 1987.
Stott, John R. W. *Issues Facing Christians Today*. Rev. ed. Grand Rapids: Zondervan, 1999.
———. *Same-Sex Partnerships? A Christian Perspective*. Grand Rapids: Revell, 1998.
Strobel, Kyle C. *Jonathan Edwards's Theology: A Reinterpretation*. London: Bloomsbury/T. & T. Clark, 2013.
Dan Strange, "Not Ashamed! The Sufficiency of Scripture for Public Theology," *Themelios* 36 (2011). https://www.thegospelcoalition.org/themelios/article/not-ashamed-the-sufficiency-of-scripture-for-public-theology/.
Strong, Augustus Hopkins. *Systematic Theology*. Edited by Anthony Vyl. Woodstock, ON: Devoted, 2017.
Swinton, John. "The Body of Christ Has Down's [sic] Syndrome: Theological Reflections on Vulnerability, Disability, and Graceful Communities." *Journal of Pastoral Theology* 13 (2003) 66–78.
Swoboda, A. J., et al. *Introducing Evangelical Ecotheology: Foundations in Scripture, Theology, History, and Praxis*. Grand Rapids: Baker Academic, 2014.
Swope, Paul. "Abortion: A Failure to Communicate." *First Things* 82 (1998) 31–35.
Teresa of Ávila. *The Complete Works*. Edited and Translated by E. Allison Peers. London: Burns and Oates, 2002.
Theology of Work. "Vocation in Historical-Theological Perspective." https://www.theologyofwork.org/resources/vocation-in-historical-theological-perspective/.
Thielicke, Helmut. *Theological Ethics: Foundations* Minneapolis: Fortress, 1981.
Thomas, Rick, and Peter Saunders. "Gender Dysphoria." Christian Medical Fellowship, 2016. https://admin.cmf.org.uk/pdf/cmffiles/59_gender_dysphoria.pdf.
Torrance, Alan J. "On Deriving 'Ought' from 'Is.'" In *The Doctrine of God and Theological Ethics*, edited by Alan J. Torrance and Michael Banner, 167–90. London: T. & T. Clark, 2006.
Trull, Joe, and James Carter. *Ministerial Ethics: Moral Formation for Church Leaders*. Downers Grove, IL: Baker Academic, 2009.
Turretin, Frances. "Creationism or Traducianism?" A Puritan's Mind. https://www.apuritansmind.com/puritan-favorites/francis-turretin/creationism-or-traducianism/.
Tyndale, William. *A Parable of the Wicked Mammon*. 1527. https://www.adventbeliefs.com/assets/BBR/23/Parable-of-the-Wicked-Mammon-The-William-Tyndale-16th-Cen.pdf.
Valk, Pieter. "When Heavyweights Change their Minds: Richard B. Hays and Human Sexuality" *Firebrand*, April 16, 2024. https://firebrandmag.com/articles/when-heavyweights-change-their-minds-richard-b-hays-and-human-sexuality.
VanDrunen, David. *Living in God's Two Kingdoms*. Wheaton, IL: Crossway, 2010.
———. *Natural Law and the Two Kingdoms*. Grand Rapids: Eerdmans, 2009.
Vanhoozer, Kevin. *First Theology: God, Scripture And Hermeneutics*. Leicester, UK: Apollos, 2002.
———. "Holy Scripture." In *Christian Dogmatics: Reformed Theology for the Church Catholic*, edited by Michael Allen and Scott R. Swain, 30–56. Grand Rapids: Baker Academic, 2016.

———. *The Pastor as Public Theologian: Reclaiming a Lost Vision*. Grand Rapids: Baker Academic, 2015.
Vickers, Jason. *Invocation and Assent: The Making and Remaking of Trinitarian Theology*. Grand Rapids: Eerdmans, 2008.
Wagner, Peter. *New Apostolic Leadership: Rediscovering the New Testament Model of Leadership and Why it is God's Desire for the Church Today*. Ventura: Gospel Light and Regal, 1998.
Weaver, Darlene Fozard. *Self-Love and Christian Ethics*. Cambridge: Cambridge University Press, 2002.
Webb, William. *Slaves, Women and Homosexuals*. Downers Grove, IL: InterVarsity, 2001.
Webster, John. *Barth's Ethics of Reconciliation*. Cambridge: Cambridge University Press, 1995.
———. *Barth's Moral Theology*. Grand Rapids: Eerdmans, 1998.
Weeks, David L. *Evangelicals in the Public Square: Four Formative Voices on Political Thought and Action*. Grand Rapids: Baker Academic, 2006.
Welker, Michael. "Travail and Mission: Theology Reformed." In *Toward the Future of Reformed Theology*, edited by David Willis and Michael Welker, 136–52. Grand Rapids: Eerdmans, 1999.
Westermann, Claus. *Genesis 1–11: A Continental Commentary*. Minneapolis: Augsburg Fortress, 1984.
"Westminster Confession of Faith." In *The Creeds of Christendom*, vol. 3, edited by Philip Schaff, Christian Classics Ethereal Library. https://www.ccel.org/ccel/schaff/creeds3.iv.xvii.ii.html.
Whitford, David Mark. *Tyranny and Resistance: The Magdeburg Confession and the Lutheran Tradition*. St. Louis: Concordia, 2001.
Wilkinson, Loren, and Mary Ruth. *Caring for Creation in Your Own Backyard*. Vancouver: Regent College, 2001.
Willard, Dallas. *The Spirit of the Disciplines*. San Francisco: HarperOne, 1999.
Willimon, William. *Pastor: The Theology and Practice of Ordained Ministry*. Nashville: Abingdon, 2002.
Wilson, Jonathan R. *Gospel Virtues: Practicing Faith, Hope, and Love in Uncertain Times*. Eugene, OR: Wipf & Stock, 2004.
Witvliet, John. "The Doctrine of the Trinity And the Theology and Practice of Christian Worship in the Reformed Tradition." PhD diss., University of Notre Dame, 1997.
Wollebius, Johannes. *Compendium Theologiae Christianae*, 1626. https://onlinebooks.library.upenn.edu/webbin/book/lookupid?key=uma96805.
Wright, N. T. *The New Testament and the People of God: Christian Origins and the Question of God*. Minneapolis: Fortress, 1992.
Yoder, John Howard. *The Christian and Capital Punishment*. Institute of Mennonite Studies 1. Newton: Faith and Life, 1961.
———. "Noah's Covenant and the Purpose of Punishment." In *Readings in Christian Ethics*, edited by Robert Rakestraw and David Clark, 471–81. Grand Rapids: Baker, 2008.
Zimmermann, Jens. *Incarnational Humanism: A Philosophy of Culture for the Church in the World*. Downers Grove, IL: InterVarsity Academic, 2012.

Subject & Author Index

abortion, xi, 151–52, 154–55, 168–80, 186, 270
Abraham, William, 37
abuse
    of children xvi, 87, 130, 132, 138, 140, 141, 149, 199, 269
    of creation, 23
    of finances, 250
    of power, xii, 85, 119, 123, 142, 144, 239
    of spouse, 207
Adams, Robert Merrihew, 25
adultery, 25, 31, 56–58, 138, 157–58, 187, 202, 206–7, 210, 212–13, 223, 233, 237, 247–48
affirmations, 101
Akiba (Rabbi), 158–59
Akiva (Rabbi), 153
alcohol use, 80
Allberry, Sam, 223–31
Allender, Dan, 141
ambition, 85, 87, 89, 116
Ambrose, St, 167
Améry, Jean, 183
Anabaptist, 146, 148, 166–67, 276
analogia entis, 24, 41–42
analogia fide, 24
analogia relationis, 42
Anderson, Ray, 10, 51, 204
anencephalic embryo, 171
Anselm, St, 31
antidepressants, 183–84
antinomianism, xiv, 105–6, 126, 149, 216, 269, 276

anxiety disorders, 83
applied ethics, 1–2, 24, 40
Aquinas, Thomas, St, 26, 41, 159, 167, 171
Aristotle, 26–27, 31, 171
artificial insemination, 238
asymmetric concursus, 12, 21, 47, 212
atonement, theories of, 184–86
Audette, Elizabeth, 270
Augustine of Hippo, St, 20, 24, 44, 47, 76, 148, 159, 167, 171–72, 275
authority, 81, 118, 127–50, 153, 167, 201, 256
    of Scripture 35–36, 38–39, 43, 52, 210, 213, 226, 231, 277
autosexuality, 200
Avioz, Michael, 154
Azariah, Eliezar ben (Rabbi), 158

Bailey, Derrick, 203
Bainton, Roland H., 246
Baker, David L., 152
Barmen, Theological Declaration of, 147
Barth, Karl, xiv, 5–8, 20–21, 24–25, 36, 40, 44–45, 47, 55–56, 110, 147, 211–12, 266–67
Bauckham, Richard, 189
Baxter, Richard, 43
beauty, 23, 33–34
Begg, Alistair, 230
behaviorism, 60
Bell, Roy, xii, 123, 198, 239
Belousek, Darrin Snyder, 219
Benner, David, 100–101

Berry, Wendell, 245
Bevans, Stephen B., 50 9
Bible study or Bible reading. *See* reading Scripture
bioethics, 176, 178
Bockmuehl, Klaus, 43, 56–59, 80, 82, 86, 95, 106–8, 113–14, 125, 129, 145, 148, 171, 174, 243, 245, 261–62
Bonhoeffer, Dietrich, xv, 3, 24, 31, 84, 147, 167
Boom, Corrie ten, 25
Bosch, David, 51
Bretherton, Luke, 232
Brice, Ashleigh, 175, 178
Bromiley, Geoffrey, 15
Brown, Jeannine K., 139
Brownson, James, 219
Bruce, F. F., 207
Brueggemann, Walter, 245
Brunner, Daniel L., 245
Burgess, John P., 74, 78, 82, 84
burnout (pastoral), 84, 103, 105, 119
Butler, Jennifer L., 245
Buttrey, Michael, 178–79

Calvin, John, 11, 20–21, 25, 43, 47, 58, 74–75, 78–79, 82, 95, 100, 112, 128, 132, 136, 145–47, 187, 212
capital punishment, 151–52, 156–58
Carter, James, 32
casuistry, xvii, 1, 43, 58–59, 61, 106
categorical imperative, 6
Catholic (Roman Catholic), xiii, xvii, 11, 24–25, 60, 100, 145–46, 159, 161, 172, 182, 199, 202, 206, 269
celibacy, 190, 193, 203, 211, 219–20, 222–23, 228, 231–32
Chapell, Bryan, 266
chastity, 193
character ethics. *See* ethics: virtue
character formation, 71–74
Chesterton, G. K., 23
child abuse. *See* abuse: of children
Christian reconstructionist. *See* theonomist movement
Christocentric, 23, 74, 266

christological, 9, 21, 28, 78, 111, 126, 211, 233
church and state, 141, 145–50, 156–61, 163, 165, 239
church discipline. *See* discipline, church
civil disobedience, 145, 149, 174
Cladis, George, 255
Coakley, Sarah, 193
coinherence, 36, 66, 102, 116, 126, 191
common grace, 5, 81
Communion. *See* Eucharist
conception of life, 168–76
confession, practice of, 47–48, 61, 101, 122, 150, 216, 233–34, 264, 278
confessions of faith, historic, 36–38, 43, 74, 145, 146, 266
confidentiality, 149, 268–71
conscience, 48, 67, 80, 105, 182, 230
consequentialism, 26, 206
consultation, xvi–vii, 29, 34–35, 59–61, 150, 176, 180, 205, 269–70, 278
contemplation, 20, 61, 64, 66–67, 74, 77, 83–84, 88, 94, 109, 125, 198, 203, 218, 224, 232, 234–35, 251–54, 263, 274
counseling, 83, 87, 98, 108, 123, 136, 156, 184, 205, 207, 220, 236, 240, 269–70
pastoral 83, 260, 263, 269, 271
covetousness, 138, 243, 272–74
Crabb, Larry, 235
creation care, 23, 124, 126, 244
crisis pregnancy centers, 174–75
critical realism, 29–30

Dawn, Marva, 105
death penalty. *See* capital punishment
decision-making, xi–xvi, 1, 17, 18, 28–29, 32, 41, 43–47, 60–61, 63, 144, 162, 175, 180–81, 205, 214, 225, 231, 256, 277–78
depression, 83, 89, 103–5, 155, 183–84
differentiation, 76, 139, 191, 209, 218, 227, 229
  sexual, 188, 191–92, 209, 217, 218, 227, 229
discipline
  of children, 132–33

SUBJECT & AUTHOR INDEX 293

of the church, xvi, 122, 149, 169,
    180, 208, 231, 240, 270
disciplines. *See* spiritual disciplines
divorce, 188, 201–2, 206–8, 234
DNR (Do Not Resuscitate), 181
doctrine of appropriations of roles, 66
doctrine of the concursus of divine and
    human agency, 212
doctrine of creation, 106, 126, 226, 245
doctrine of depravity, 140
doctrine of God, 36, 100
doctrine of Scripture, 36–38
doctrine of the Trinity. *See* Trinity:
    doctrine of
doctrine of two kingdoms. *See* two-
    kingdom theology
doctrine of vocation, 118
dogmatics, xiv, 5, 7–8, 21, 36, 247
Downs, Frederick, xv–xvi
drinking. *See* alcohol use
dual-role relationships, xv
duellum, 166–67

Eastern Orthodox, 11, 160, 229
ecotheology, 244
Edwards, Jonathan, 20–21, 33, 44,
    211–12, 275
Ellul, Jacques, 3–4
Enlightenment, 6, 8, 276
epistemology, xiii, 6, 29, 37, 60
eschatology, 22, 113, 115, 129, 135, 178,
    188, 191
ethical discernment, xvii, 1, 19, 24, 29,
    31, 34, 47, 64–65, 69, 214, 270,
    277
ethical egoism, 26
ethics
    biblical, 17, 33–35, 38–42, 51, 52
    Christian, ix, 3, 5–6, 8, 14–15,
        17–18, 22, 25, 33–35, 38–41,
        43–46, 51–53, 56, 58–59, 75, 80,
        82, 204, 221, 230, 277
    of creation, 55, 80, 124, 244
    deliberative, theological deliberative
        41–46, 52–54, 59, 74
    deontological, 2, 15, 25, 27, 31, 35,
        61, 157, 164, 206
    ecclesial, 17, 33–34

    environmental, 23, 244
    evangelical, 33, 42, 46–49, 51, 60,
        80, 162, 277
    of the Father, 80
    of the kingdom, 55–56, 80
    of participation, 7, 61
    pastoral, ix, xii–xiii, xvii, 1, 2–3,
        56, 60–61, 66, 105, 123, 149,
        183, 277
    of preaching, 67–69, 143, 260,
        264–68
    prescriptive, 52–53, 59, 79
    of race, 50, 124
    Reformed, 79
    relational. *See* situational ethics
    salvation, 80
    sexual, 24, 39, 48, 59, 102, 123, 138,
        144, 187–208, 209–40
    situational, 2, 41, 43–46, 52–53, 59
    social, 178, 186
    of the Son, 80
    of speech, 259–71
    of the Spirit, 80
    theological, 1–3, 21, 33, 45, 60–62, 74
    theonomic trinitarian, 34
    trinitarian (theological) 2, 4, 8, 14,
        15, 20, 22, 24, 25, 27–29, 31–35,
        38–39, 46–47, 49, 51, 60–61, 71,
        80, 135, 161–62, 193, 211
    utilitarian 2, 15, 26–27, 35, 157,
        161, 175, 179
    virtue ethics, 2, 10, 15, 25–28,
        31–33, 35, 49
    of work, 241–58
Eucharist, 48, 90, 112, 136, 251, 274
euthanasia, 59, 151–52, 180–83
Evangelium Vitae, 160–61

faith seeking understanding, xiii, 31
fasting, 48, 85, 108
Fernando, Ajith, 255
fertilization, xi, xiii, 35, 171, 175
Fiddes, Paul, 256
forgiveness, 24, 48, 65, 122–23, 140–41,
    147–48, 155–57, 163, 165–66,
    170, 173, 184, 186, 207–8, 213,
    215–16, 223, 230, 232–34,
    262–64, 278

Forsyth, P. T., 267
Foster, Richard, 133–34, 199–200, 202
Frame, John, 148
freedom, 4, 54, 64–66, 133, 136, 177, 188, 195, 229, 248, 254, 276–77
    in ministry, 63
    of submission, 133
fruit of the Spirit, 28, 54, 254, 264

Gagnon, Robert, 219–21, 227
Gamaliel, Simeon ben, 159
Gary, Sally, 220
gay, 209–40
gay marriage. *See* same-sex marriage.
Geisler, Norman, 25
gender, xiii, 59, 124, 134, 188, 224, 227, 230
gender dysphoria, xviii, 188, 224
gender identity, 188, 224
genetic engineering, 175
genetic testing, 175–76, 179
Geneva, Declaration of, 170
Gentry, Elizabeth, 195–97
gospel, xiii–xiv, 3–13, 15, 16, 18, 26, 27, 32–33, 35, 41–43, 46–49, 53, 55, 69, 73–79, 113, 122, 124, 132, 136–37, 145–46, 149, 160–61, 192–93, 213–14, 230–32, 239, 247, 267, 276
gossip, 248, 261, 263
Gnosticism, xiv, 60, 80, 105, 125, 184, 213
Goroncy, Jason, 181
gratitude, 90, 97, 102
Great Commandment, 5, 17, 33, 49, 77–78, 126, 165, 244, 277
Great Commission, 124, 126, 244, 277
Gregory of Nyssa, 172
Grenz, Stanley, xii, 34, 51, 123, 134–35, 198, 218, 239
Griffith, E. E., 270
Gunton, Colin, 8
Guroian, Vigen, 227, 229
Gushee, David, 164–65, 220
Gustafson, 41

Hannah, John, 85
Hansen, David, 83
Harnack, Adolf von, 41
Hart, Darryl, 148
Hart, Trevor, 7
Hauerwas, Stanley, ix, 6–7, 161–62, 190–91
Hayhoe, Katharine, 244
Hays, Christopher, 210–21
Hays, Richard, 164, 167, 210–21
hell, 154, 199, 236
Henricks, Howard, 64
Henry, Carl, 22, 43
Heschel, Abraham Joshua, 107
Hippocratic Oath, 169–70
Hitler, Adolf, 26
Hodge, Charles, 172
Hollinger, Dennis, 15, 16, 18, 43–45, 175
Holmes, Arthur, 167
homophobia, 224
homosexuality, 157, 188, 215, 231, 237
Horton, Michael, 148
hospice, 181–82
Houston, James, 193
Howatch, Susan 85
Hui, Edwin, 176
Hutchinson, Don, 270

idolatry, 47–48, 80, 82–83, 85–86, 91, 100, 140, 204, 229, 273–74
imago Dei, 10, 17, 22–23, 33, 60, 115, 125, 134, 144, 153–54, 158–59, 161, 172, 176, 179, 188, 191–93, 199, 209–210, 217–18, 226–27, 242, 261–62, 271, 277
immoralism, 4
immutability of God, 212
Instone-Brewer, David, 207
intercourse (sexual), 189–96, 201–3, 212, 218, 229, 235
intersex, 188, 224
in vitro fertilization. *See* fertilization
Irenaeus, 24, 213

Jenson, Robert, 8, 33
Jerome, 172
John of the Cross, St, 184
John Paul II (Pope), 160, 192–93
Johnson, Darrell, 97, 266

justification, 11, 16, 19–21, 47, 54–55, 60, 63, 73, 124, 154, 161, 163, 186, 223, 233–34, 248, 277
just war, 152, 163–67

Kant, Immanuel, 6, 21, 25, 157
Keen, Karen, 219
Keller, Tim, 209–10
Kelsay, John, 136
Kierkegaard, Søren, 2, 214
King Jr., Martin Luther, 50
Koop, C. Everett, 173
Kreeft, Peter, 189
Kuyper, Abraham, 147

LaCugna, Catherine, 256
Laverty, Rhys, 221
leadership (pastoral, church), 69, 85, 94, 118–19, 127, 141–43, 217, 227, 255–56, 258, 267–68
lectio divina, 88, 90
Lee, Justin, 220
Lewis, C. S., 41, 99–100, 199, 242
LGTBQ+, 210, 219, 222–23
Loader, Bill, 219
logical positivism, 30
Long, Edward L., 41, 44
Longman III, Tremper, 141
Lord's Prayer, 95, 233
Lord's Supper. *See* Eucharist
love, 248, 274–75, 277
    defined culturally, 189–90
    for enemy, 133
    for God, 17, 28, 30, 44, 46, 54–55, 57, 60, 75–78, 81–82, 86, 97, 104, 124, 139, 193, 196, 230, 247–48, 277
    of God, xiv, 4, 15–17, 22, 32, 35–36, 40, 48, 50–51, 60, 71–76, 86–94, 98–99, 101, 104, 111, 135–36, 139, 179, 184, 188, 192, 211–12, 215, 218, 228, 232, 235, 247, 253–54, 274–77
    for neighbor or one another, 17, 28, 30, 43, 49, 54–55, 58–60, 72, 74–78, 86, 99, 104, 111
    for oneself, self-love, 99–100, 134, 199

    as ordered affections, 20–21, 69, 90, 211–12, 235, 273–75
    as part of God's nature, 10, 17, 20, 30, 33, 36, 40, 46, 86, 118, 122, 124, 135–37, 142, 148, 165, 167, 182, 193–97, 203, 215, 223, 230, 232, 242, 247–48, 261–63, 274–75, 277
    as a virtue, 26–28, 72
Luther, Martin, 11, 20, 25, 44, 117–18, 145–49, 245, 264, 266

MacDonald, Mark, 226
MacIntyre, Alasdair, 26
MAID. *See* euthanasia
Malfeasance. *See* sexual misconduct by clergy
Manning, Bernard, 267
marriage, 23, 130, 133, 138, 140, 155, 187–240
    gay or same-sex, xiii, 209–40
    for pastors, 87
    as sacrament, 191–92, 202, 204, 206, 227, 229, 237
marriage preparation and counseling. *See* premarital counseling
Martin, Colby, 220
Martyr, Justin, 171
masturbation, 198–201
Maurice, F.D., 82
McAlpine, Stephen, 220–22
McCheyne, Robert Murray, 254
McConnachie, John, 266
McGrath, Alister, 29
McHugh, Paul, 224
medical assistance in dying. *See* euthanasia
medical ethics, 177
Meilaender, Gilbert, 135, 178
Melanchthon, Philip, 57
Merrit, Jonathan, 222–23
metaethics, 1
Milbank, John 73, 166, 237–39
Mishnah, 158
Mitchell, Ben, 176
Moltmann, Jürgen, 8
moral failure, xiixiii, 19, 84, 273

moral formation, xiii–xiv, xvi–xvii, 1–2, 11, 13, 18, 19, 22, 40, 43, 58, 60–61, 65, 66, 70, 71–72, 74, 79–81, 103, 105, 107, 127, 129, 131, 133, 135, 137, 139, 141, 143, 145, 147, 149, 243, 247, 250–254, 259, 261, 263, 272, 276–77
   communal, 13
moralism, 4, 32, 276
moral law, 29, 43, 54–56, 61, 64–65, 73–75, 80–81, 106, 130–31, 145, 158, 182, 209, 221, 228, 248, 272, 276
moral philosophy, 41
Morgan, G. Campbell, 265, 268
Morgan, Virginia R., 270
mortification, 48, 79, 81, 223, 231, 234, 236
Mouw, Richard, 43
Muller, Richard, 36
murder, 26, 31, 56–57, 59, 138–39, 150–64, 185–86, 212, 247, 261

narrative ethics. *See* ethics: virtue
natural law, 25, 31, 41–42, 44–45, 48, 80, 145, 147–48, 165–66, 221
natural theology, 6–7
Newbigin, Lesslie, 36
nihilism, 30
norma normans, 39
norma normata, 39
nuclear weapons, 35, 163

obedience, xvi, 3, 12, 16, 33, 43, 45, 53–54, 56, 61, 64, 71–75, 77–78, 80–81, 86, 105, 111, 124–25, 130–31, 136, 138, 144–45, 149–50, 177, 234, 243, 247–48, 260, 278
O'Donovan, Oliver, ix, 5, 46, 55–56, 75–77, 161, 164–66, 176, 221, 231
ontology, xiii, 7, 19–21, 23, 31, 37, 60, 76, 80, 127, 134–35, 141, 144, 164, 166, 168, 171, 179, 190, 192, 204, 217–19, 226, 228–29
Origen, 171

pacificism, 118, 161, 163–64, 166–67
Palagianism, 12
palliative care, 180–83
Pannenberg, Wolfhart, 8
parenting, 127, 132–141
pastoral decision-making. *See* decision-making
pastoral ethics. *See* ethics: pastoral
pastor as ethicist, 2
pastor-theologian, 2
penal substitution, 184–85
Pennings, Ray, 182
perichoresis, 40, 51, 118, 135, 218, 255–56, 259
persecution, 68, 80, 93, 148–49
personhood, 18, 27, 29, 31–34, 60, 73, 122, 169, 171–72, 176, 179, 193, 218, 227, 255, 273, 277
persons-in-relation, 10, 12, 17–19, 28, 33–34, 42, 60–61, 100, 101, 135, 277
Peterson, Eugene, 83, 268
physician-assisted suicide. *See* euthanasia
Pliny, 115
politics, 85, 98, 127–28, 146–47, 150, 162, 166
pornography, 200–201, 224
Powell, John, 100
praise, 75, 95–97, 116, 168, 264, 274
prayer, xv, 12, 48, 50, 63, 70, 83, 85, 88–90, 94–95, 97–98, 101, 103, 109, 112, 114, 133, 142, 145, 170, 173, 176, 193–94, 203, 205, 226, 233, 235, 240, 246, 251–252, 256, 259, 268, 270–71, 274, 278
preimplantation genetic testing, 175–76, 179
premarital counseling, 204–6, 235
premarital sex, 190, 207, 224
prenatal genetic testing, 175–76, 179
proportionalism, 26
prosperity, 85, 92
Provan, Iain, 195–96, 227
Purves, Andrew, 63, 120

Rae, Scott 175

reading Scripture as spiritual practice, xv, 83, 87, 90, 93, 136, 235, 251, 253-54, 263, 274
regeneration, 11, 18-19, 23, 27, 55, 58, 65, 69, 73, 80, 81, 99, 212, 218, 248, 275
relational participation. *See* trinitarian participation
relationis, 24
remarriage, 188, 206-8, 234
retribution. *See* revenge
Reformed theology, 3, 5, 8, 11, 37, 82, 146
revenge, 156-57, 161, 166
Richards, Larry, 207
Rodgers, Julie, 220
Rolheiser, Ronald, 196-97

Sabbath, 59, 90, 102-26, 131, 137, 157, 245
Sabbatical, ix, 104, 114, 122
sacrament, 1, 13, 27, 60, 69, 84, 90, 191-92, 202, 204, 206, 227, 231, 229, 237, 244, 267
salaries, 85, 121-22, 142, 245
same-sex relations, marriage, 59, 203-5, 209-40
sanctification, 11, 19-21, 24, 47, 57-58, 73, 78-79, 179, 223, 233-34, 236, 248, 253, 260, 273
  of the tongue, 260
sanctity of human life, 152-54, 170, 174-76, 187
sanctity of marriage, 187
Satan, 22, 85-86, 155, 271
Saunders, Dame Sicley, 181
Schaffer, Francis, 147, 173
Schleiermacher, Friedrich, 8, 21
Scripture. *See* word of God
self-defense, 160-61
self-hatred, 99
Sermon on the Mount, 16, 44, 57, 65, 73, 80, 109, 145, 148, 156, 164-65, 223
sexedness, 188, 191-92, 202-3, 214, 217-18, 224-25, 229
sex trafficking, 144
sexual identity, 188

sexual immorality, 24, 262, 273
sexual misconduct of clergy, xiii, 123, 235-236, 239-41
sex outside marriage, 189-90, 195, 198, 228
Shedd, Charlie, 199
Shedd, W. G. T., 172
Shuman, Joel, 177-79
silence (as spiritual practice), 48, 90, 170, 275
sin, xiv, xvii, 3, 18, 21-22, 23, 24, 37, 42, 47-48, 54, 57, 63-65, 68, 91, 96, 97, 99-102, 122-23, 129, 146, 153-55, 158, 162-63, 172-73, 185, 198-99, 205-6, 208-10, 213, 214-17, 222-28, 230-34, 236, 239, 247-49, 255, 257, 261-63, 269-73, 278
singleness, 23, 180, 190, 192-98, 203-4, 211, 217-18, 223, 231-32
Smail, Tom, 73
Smedes, Lewis, 200-203
Smith, Adam, 26
sola Scripture, 39
solitude (as spiritual practice), 48, 90, 275
Song, Robert, 219
sovereignty (of God), 68, 82, 154, 167, 171, 212, 225, 252
special revelation, 6
sperm donation, 238
spiritual counsel. *See* spiritual guidance
spiritual disciplines, 12-13, 47-48, 60, 63-64, 72, 88, 90, 114, 195, 235
spiritual formation, 1, 22, 65, 69, 81, 247
spiritual guidance, xv, 83-84, 180
spiritual practices. *See* spiritual disciplines.
Sprinkle, Preston, 210-11, 214-17, 219
Stassen, Glen, 164-65, 167
stem cells, 35
Stevens, R. Paul, 118, 125, 193-94, 249-50
Stewart, James, 267-68
Stott, John, 116, 121, 124, 167, 173, 197
Strachan, Owen 2
Strong, Augustus H., 17, 40

submission, 49, 127, 133–35, 138, 141–45, 256
  in church, 141–44
  in the state, 145–50
  in the workplace, 144
suicide, 151, 182–84, 219, 222
suffering, 68, 120, 144, 163, 165, 178–79, 182, 228, 278
surrogate motherhood, 238
Swinton, John, 179
Swoboda, A. J., 245
Swope, John, 174–75
Systematic Theology, xiv, 5

Tarfon (Rabi), 158–59
Taylor, Charles, 7
Ten Commandments
  First Commandment, 71–102, 76, 81, 82, 85–86, 123
  Second Commandment, 71–102, 76, 91, 94, 124
  Third Commandment, 58, 71–102, 94–95, 97–98, 101–2, 261
  Fourth Commandment, 71, 102, 103–26, 105, 125, 242
  Fifth Commandment, 57, 127–50, 128, 139, 140
  Sixth Commandment, 26, 57–59, 138, 150, 151–186, 166, 169, 175–76, 180, 182–84, 187
  Seventh Commandment, 58–59, 123, 187–208, 202, 209–240, 236
  Eighth Commandment, 57, 138, 241–58, 242, 247, 258
  Ninth Commandment, 26, 57, 150, 259–71, 261, 263, 271
  Tenth Commandment, 57, 138, 272–75, 273
temptations, 86, 147, 225, 250, 252, 272
  of the pastorate, xv, 83, 85
Teresa of Ávila, 77
Tertullian, 172
theft and stealing, 31, 116, 138, 241–43, 247–48, 250, 252, 260
theological anthropology, 10, 172, 176, 191–92, 226, 275

theology
  of disability, 179
  of suffering, 178–79
  of vocation. *See* theology of work
  of work, 115–26
theonomist movement, 147
theosis, 11
tithing, 92, 94, 241, 243
Torrance, Alan, ix, 4, 5, 8, 46, 49
Torrance, James, 51
Torrance, T. F., 8, 29
totus Christus, 218
traducionist view, 172–73
transgender, 59, 188, 224, 227, 230
transhumanism, xii–xiii, 59
transsexual, xiii, 229
trinitarian, 8–15, 18, 20, 30, 40, 46, 51–52, 59–60, 62, 66, 71, 73–75, 80, 100, 102, 115–16, 125, 135, 161–62, 169, 191–92, 223, 232–33, 239, 253, 262, 27
  anthropology, 10, 191–92
  ethics. *See* ethics: trinitarian
  hermeneutic, 30–31
  heuristic, 80
  participation, xv, 1, 3–8, 11–12, 16–17, 20–27, 32–36, 47, 51, 60, 63, 72, 75, 90, 116, 120, 133
  theology, 2, 42, 115–16, 193
Trinity, 8–11, 13, 15, 17, 20, 22, 33, 36, 40, 46, 49–50, 66, 72–74, 76–77, 80, 94, 96–98, 125–26, 134–135, 191–92, 202–3, 212, 218, 229, 255–56, 261, 275
  doctrine of, 8–9, 13, 80, 100
Trull, Joe, 32
two-kingdom theology, 145–48
Tyndale, William, 246

union with Christ, 11–12, 19, 20, 22, 28, 32, 54–55, 59–61, 64–65, 71–72, 78–79, 136, 155, 192, 196, 223, 229, 233–34, 236, 260, 263, 277

Valk, Peter, 219–20
Vanhoozer, Kevin, 2, 37–38
Van-Drunen, David, 148

Van Til, Cornelius, 147
Vatican II, 160
vice, 25, 28, 79
Vickers, Jason, 13
Vines, Matthew 220
virtue, 5, 10, 11, 26–28, 33, 59–60, 65, 71–75, 90, 99, 146, 243, 247
virtue ethics. *See* ethics: virtue
vision, 84
vitro. *See* fertilization.
vivification, 28, 81, 223, 234, 236

Wagner, Peter, 119
Wannenwetsch, Bernd, 166
war, 118, 145, 151–152, 160, 163–67
Weaver, Darlen Fozard, 99
Webb, William, 209, 219
Wesley, John, 47
Westerman, Claus, 158
Wilkinson, Loren, 244
Willard, Dallas, xiv, 48

Willimon, William, 267
word of God, 27, 29, 52–71, 60, 69–70, 79, 83, 90, 112, 136, 143, 147, 162, 170, 176, 205, 251–53, 267–68, 270, 277
work. *See* theology of work
works of mercy, 244
worship (musical and liturgical), xii, 12–13, 48, 50, 59, 63, 75, 77, 86, 89–91, 93–95, 97, 106, 109, 111, 113–15, 125, 143, 195, 233, 245, 263–64, 271
Wright, N. T., 29–30, 167

Yarhouse, Mark, 220, 224
Yoder, John Howard, 43, 157–58, 161–63
Young, J. L., 270

Zaporozhets, Olya, 220

Scripture Index

To simplify, some scripture references have been listed within a larger section of text. For example, references to Ephesians 1:2–3 may be listed within Ephesians 1:1–6.

OLD TESTAMENT

Genesis

1	23, 116, 192, 202, 204
1:26–30	23, 115, 188
1:27	23, 191, 199, 217
1:31	188
2	23, 80, 111, 116, 202, 204, 239
2:7	153
2:24	130, 190, 201–2, 206, 209, 217
3	xiv–xv, 3, 23, 48, 239
3:1	195
9:5–7	153, 155, 158
29:30–31	139
39:4, 6	248
39:8	251
39:9	249
39:20–23	248–49, 251
41:16	250, 252
41:38	253
41:39–40	249
45:5,7	252
45:9	252
50:18–21	252

Exodus

	53, 71
14:31	128
20	71, 77, 80–82, 130–31
20:1–2	17, 53, 75, 77
20:4–6	91
20:7	94–102
20:8–11	103
20:8	105
20:10	109
20:11	109, 115
20:12	127
20:13	151
20:14	187
20:15	241
20:16	259
20:17	272
21	206–7
21:12–14	152
21:15, 17	128
22:1–14	242
23:12	107
31:14–15	113, 157
31:18	3
33–34	94
33:11	94
35:2–3	113

Leviticus

11:44, 45	17, 78
15:16	199
18	199
19:2	17
19:3	128
19:12	95
19:16	261
19:18	57, 261
20	221
20:9	128, 130
20:10	157
20:13	157, 209
20:27	157
22:19	157
24:10–16	95
24:17, 21	152
25:14	245

Numbers

15:32–36	113
25:15–28	152
27	214
35:6–15	152
35:33–34	163

Deuteronomy

4:24	83
5:12–15	110
9:15	158
12	91
12:4	91
12:18–21	128
19:1–13	152
21:15–17	139
22:13–29	190, 206
24:14–15,	245
35:31–33	152

Joshua

4:14	128
20	152

2 Samuel

12	242

1 Kings

	137

2 Kings

	137

Job

	158

Psalms

	158
8	81
8:1	95
23	1
27:10	129
40:8	135
45:2	259
104:29	154
105:19	250
119:9	253
119:32	278
119:35	278
139:13–16	168

Proverbs

	131, 158
3:7	128
6:16–19	261
10:1	131
11:26	245
19:13	131
19:26	128
20:17	245
20:20	128, 130
27:19	31
119:32	136

Ecclesiastes

	158

Song of Songs

	195, 199, 203

Isaiah

1:13–14	113
10:1–3	245
50:4	259, 275
58	113, 244
58:13–14	108, 113

Jeremiah

2:13	224
7:23	65, 78
17:21–23	123
31:33–34	65

Ezekiel

36:26–27	65

Hosea

4:1–3	247

Joel

2:32	97

Amos

8:4–6	113, 245

Micah

6:8	32

Malachi

	91–92
1:2	92
1:6—2:9	92
3:6	91–92, 135
3:8–12	92, 241–42

APOCRYPHA

Judith

8:6	108

NEW TESTAMENT

Matthew

1:18–24	190
3	87
3:1–6	110
3:16–17	98
4	85–86
5	138, 154, 232
5–7	57, 73
5:8	31
5:13–16	49
5:27–30	209–10, 223, 236
5:31–32	206
5:39	134
5:44	133
5:48	16
6:9	95
10:20	260
10:23	149
10:37	139
10:39	101
11:28	111
11:29–30	114
12	110
12:31–32	95
12:48–50	139
15:3–9	57, 129–30
15:19	57
19	57, 192
19:4–6	202, 228
19:9	206–7
19:10–12	228
19:16–17	3
22	55
22:34–35	75
23:9	141
25	182, 244
25:24–25	92
26:52	158
28	87
28:18–20	97

Mark

2	110
2:27	106, 110

Mark (continued)

3:4	155
7:10	129
7:20–23	31, 228
10	93
10:29–30	140
14:36	98

Luke

1:26–38	190
1:44	169
2:12	169
2:49	139
2:51	139
4:22	260
7:37–47	215
10:4	121
10:25–37	175
12:15	272
12:21	273
14:26–27	139
13:10–17	110
18:15	1169
19	242

John

1:12	97
2:3–4	139
3:34	63
4	234–35
4:24	94
5	256
5:18	95
5:39–40	251
8	233–34
8:11	213
8:29	135
10:30	191
13	73, 99, 134
14	72–73, 91
14:10	191
14:13	102
14:15	86
15	73–74
15:10	86
17	98

17:1	101–2
17:7–8	259
19:26–27	139
19:28	235
20:19–23	233

Acts

	66
2:23–24	185
2:44–45	243
4:12	97
4:32–35	243
5:19	139
5:29	145
6	268
7:19	169
14:14	119
15	219
15:20	207
15:29	215
17:2	112
17:25–28	154
20:7	112
20:34–35	121

Romans

	54–55
1	214, 232
1:20	42, 55, 96
1:30	129
2:4	216
2:14–15	42, 55, 81
3–5	234
3:24–26	185, 233
4:25	55
5	91
5:5	274
6	81, 234, 236
6:11–14	47
7:7–8	273
7:12	54, 65
7:14	54
8	54, 236
8:1–8	28, 54
8:4, 9	234, 248
8:13	81

8:15–16	93, 98	4	67
8:19–21	116	4:1, 16	61, 67
10:13	97	4:3–6	68
12	118	4:4	23
13	145, 165	4:7–11	68
13:1–7	42	4:10	68
13:4	152	4:13–15	68
13:8–10	75, 248	8–9	244
13:9	57, 273	8:9	242
13:19	57	8:13–15	244
14	80, 229	9:7	94
14:5	105	12	179
16:7	119	12:14	129
		12:22	179

1 Corinthians

2:11	265	## Galatians	
3:9	120		54–55
5:7	110	2:10	244
5:9–11	231	2:20	13, 54
5:11	122	3:13–14	75
6	24, 214, 232	3:14	54
6:9–20	97, 209–10, 225	3:24	54
6:12–20	188, 201, 202	3:28	144, 213
7:3–4	138	4:5–7	54, 97
7:4–5	203	4:19	21
7:10–16	206	5	118
7:36–38	190	5:1	54
9:1–12a	121	5:13–14	54–55
9:27	236	5:16	254
12–14	118	5:18	54
13	211, 274	5:22–23	54, 91, 254
14:3	119	5:14–23	28
14:29–33	119		
15	55	## Ephesians	
16:2	112		
16:15	141		243
		1:3–14	256
## 2 Corinthians		1:3	77
		1:5	98
	61–69	1:7	233
3:1–4:18	61	1:11	212
3:3, 6	62	1:15–23	256
3:4	62	1:17	19
3:5–6	62, 64	2:5	55
3:12	66	2:19	210
3:16–18	20, 23, 64, 66, 73, 95, 253, 254	3:2, 8	120
		3:14–17	256

Ephesians (continued)

3:15	134
4:11–16	118, 143
4:25–32	154–55, 262–63
4:28	116, 242–43
5	202, 229
5:1–5	262, 273
5:18	133
5:19–6:9	133
5:20	97
5:21–33	206
5:24	142
6:1–4	129–32, 138, 204
6:5–9	144

Colossians

1:15	23
1:27	19
2:3	19
3	81
3:5	231
3:18–21	204
3:22–25	144
3:23	116, 120
4:6	260

Philippians

2	134
2:5–13	12, 21, 47, 236, 253
3:10	253
4:10	121
4:11–13	121

1 Thessalonians

2:14	16–17
4:11–12	115–16
5:12–13	142, 247

2 Thessalonians

3	120
3:6–10	117

1 Timothy

1:8–11	57, 129, 209
2:4	216
2:8–11	42
3	141
3:4	133
5	117
5:8	129
5:17–21	120–22, 142, 257

2 Timothy

2:3	129
3:15	169

Titus

1	141
1:6–7	133

Philemon

	144

Hebrews

	111–12, 162–63
1	111
1:3	111
2	81, 111
2:10	111
2:11–13	98
3–4	105
4	111
4:4	111
4:9–10	112
4:11	112
4:12–13	112, 253
4:14–16	112
5:13–14	2, 80
8	58
8:1	111
9:15	18, 73
10:5–10	135
10:12	111
10:12–13	163
10:14	163
10:19–21	112
12:2	111
12:19	83
13:17	142

James

1:5	19, 29
3:1–2	260
3:9	264
5:16	123, 234

1 Peter

1:6–9	93
1:16	17
2:9	50
2:18–26	144
3:7	138, 198, 203
4:11	265
4:13	120
5	119
5:1–4	141–42
5:4	120
5:5	142

2 Peter

1:3–8	71, 90

1 John

1:9	122, 233
4:8	17, 40
4:10	17, 76, 274
4:12	86
4:19	55
4:20	76

Jude

1:3	38

Revelation

2:4	90

www.ingramcontent.com/pod-product-compliance
Lightning Source LLC
Chambersburg PA
CBHW021344300426
44114CB00012B/1067